INFORMAL LOGIC

Possible Worlds and Imagination

INFORMAL LOGIC

Possible Worlds and Imagination

John Eric Nolt
The University of Tennessee

McGraw-Hill Book Company

New York   St. Louis   San Francisco   Auckland   Bogotá   Hamburg
Johannesburg   London   Madrid   Mexico   Montreal   New Delhi   Panama
Paris   São Paulo   Singapore   Sydney   Tokyo   Toronto

INFORMAL LOGIC: Possible Worlds and Imagination

1 2 3 4 5 6 7 8 9 0 HALHAL 8 9 8 7 6 5 4 3

ISBN 0-07-046861-3

Library of Congress Cataloging in Publication Data

Nolt, John Eric.
  Informal logic.

  Bibliography: p.
  Includes index.
  1. Logic. I. Title.
BC61.N64 1984   160   83-12107
ISBN 0-07-046861-3

This book was set in Trump Medieval by J.M. Post Graphics, Corp.
The editors were Kaye Pace, Anne Murphy,
and James R. Belser;
the designer was Joan E. O'Connor;
the production supervisor was Marietta Breitwieser.
The cover was illustrated by Karen Bailey Nolt.
Halliday Lithograph Corporation was printer and binder.

To my parents,
Herbert J. Nolt and Jane E. Nolt

Contents

vii

Contents

x

Preface

Interest in informal logic has increased rapidly over the last decade or so. This seems to be due to a coincidence of two factors: (1) the realization that even the sophisticated formalisms of the twentieth century are of limited utility in practical reasoning and (2) a growing demand for a logic which does work efficiently in practice. The inadequacies of formal logic have long been evident to many; they formed a central theme of the ordinary-language school of philosophy which flourished in the 1950s and 1960s. But it was only in the late 1960s and early 1970s, with the wave of strident calls for a curriculum "relevant to life," that many logicians began to look anew at the problem of application.

An early pioneer in this direction was Monroe Beardsley, whose *Practical Logic* (1950) introduced the argument-diagraming technique now used in many informal logic texts. But Beardsley's technique did not achieve widespread attention until after the appearance of Steven N. Thomas' groundbreaking book *Practical Reasoning in Natural Language* (1973). Thomas revised and expanded Beardsley's method and deftly demonstrated its flexibility and breadth, showing that informal logic met an unmistakable need. Thomas' book is now a classic; had it not been unavailable for a brief period between editions, I might not have been motivated to begin this one. My debt to Thomas will be obvious to anyone familiar with his work.

A new text can be justified only if it offers substantial innovations. The present work offers several. Most fundamental is the introduction of the apparatus of possible worlds as a comprehensive framework for organizing and clarifying major logical concepts. This provides unity and rigor beyond the standard customary in informal logic. It also gives the reader early familiarity with ideas now indispensable in advanced logic and analytic philosophy. New techniques for argument evaluation, less haphazard and subjective than the usual informal methods, emerge smoothly from this conceptual framework (see Chapter 3).

A second innovation, too often neglected in introductory texts, is a discussion of argument construction (Chapter 9). Skill in formulating rationally persuasive arguments is no less important than skill in argument analysis and evaluation, and an introduction to logic should neglect neither.

Finally, in recognition of the fact that informal logic is not an isolated discipline, but complements and merges with more formal studies, I have included a chapter on formal logic (Chapter 10). For readers who wish to advance into the formal realm, Chapter 10 should ease the transition.

On the negative side, I have omitted much that is standard in traditional introductions to logic. There is, for example, no extensive discussion of categorical syllogisms. The main reason, of course, is that syllogistic logic is formal, not informal. But even in the chapter on formal logic, categorical syllogisms receive only cursory treatment. This is because for nearly a century now we have had something far more comprehensive and efficient— the predicate calculus. Continuing to teach logic by syllogisms is like continuing to teach arithmetic by Roman numerals.

Though I discuss correlations and causes extensively (Sections 6.7 and 6.8), there is no explicit discussion of Mill's methods. Instead, causes and correlations are dealt with as they occur in actual arguments. I believe that this approach is more readily applicable than Mill's rather artificial techniques.

Definitions of major concepts used in this book are frankly stipulative and sometimes at variance with tradition. I define a fallacy, for example, as an argument such that even if its premises were true, its conclusion, based on these premises, would not be probable, and I stick to this definition very strictly. The traditional concept is a hodgepodge under which are included some valid arguments (e.g., begging the question), some rhetorical tricks (e.g., complex questions), some arguments with false premises (e.g., false dilemmas), and some genuine faulty reasoning. Lumping these diverse errors into a single category blunts understanding of their differences and, in my experience, creates endless confusion. Where I have thus departed from tradition, my aim has always been to fashion a conceptual system which is maximally clear, coherent, and useful.

Logical possibility, perhaps the most central concept in this system, is defined as coherent conceivability or imaginability, abstracting from the mental limitations of particular individuals. This provides the reader a natural passage into logical thought from ground which is already intimately familiar—his or her own imagination. Indeed, the role of imagination in logic is this book's leading theme, as its subtitle indicates.

Logically sophisticated readers will notice many points at which fine details, ambiguities, and nuances are passed over without comment. Though undoubtedly my own shortsightedness is often at fault, in many cases the omissions are deliberate. This is an introductory work, designed for readers with no previous acquaintance with logic, and too much detail rapidly overburdens a novice's understanding and capacity for interest. Thus, though I have always striven for accuracy, I have sometimes sacrificed thoroughness to more pressing pedagogical needs.

The progression of ideas is generally linear, later chapters presupposing earlier ones. But there is more material here than can easily be covered in a quarter or, probably, even in a semester, so that for classroom use some omission or rearrangement of topics will often be desirable. The following table indicates the extent to which this is possible:

Chapter	Presupposes Sections
2	1.1–1.6
3	1.1–2.8
4	1.1–3.7
5	1.1–4.2
6	1.1–4.2, 5.1–5.2, 5.5 (first part)
7	1.1–3.7, 4.1–4.2, 6.1–6.3
8	1.1–3.7, 4.1–4.2
9	1.1–3.6
10	1.1–3.7, 4.1–4.2, 5.1–5.2, 5.5 (first part)

Thanks are due to a number of people who made important contributions to this book—Robert F. Barnes, Lehigh University; James Greene, Northern Michigan University; Lawrence Hinman, University of San Diego; Philip A. Pecorino, City University of New York; William J. Rapaport, State University of New York, Fredonia; and Ben Starr, Modesto Junior College.

Thanks for important contributions are also due to Kristine Whitnable, Leslie Shapard, Roger Jones, Pete Lazarra, Charles Hornbeck, Barbara Moser, Jeri Stinson, Dolores Scates, Becky McKenzie, Roy McClean, Ann Pearce, Catherine McCue, and Jerry Brown—and to all the students of my Philosophy 2510 classes on whom rough drafts were inflicted. Karen Bailey Nolt contributed not only ideas, but also her inexhaustible strength, energy, and love. Much of the life in this book is hers.

John Eric Nolt

1

The Nature of Argument

Logic is the study of arguments. This is not to say that logicians study heated emotional confrontations—the kind that result in red faces, clenched fists, raised voices, and occasionally combat. That isn't what the word "argument" means in logic, though it's what it usually means in daily life. In logic, an argument is a process of giving evidence—a process which, fortunately, is best pursued in a calmer state of mind.

1.1 ARGUMENT STRUCTURE

Suppose someone asserts to you that during certain periods of history sorcerers and witches have wielded genuinely supernatural power. Your first inclination, unless you've already made up your mind on the subject, may be to say something like, "Really? What makes you think so?" This reply is a request for evidence—that is, a request for an argument. Perhaps the response would be something like this: "Because a number of historical documents say so, and these documents are accurate." Just how good is this evidence? Should you believe this person or not? That's the sort of question logic tries to answer.

Let's look more closely at this argument. We see at once that it is composed of two parts: (1) the conclusion, "Sorcerers and witches have wielded genuinely supernatural power," and (2) two sentences expressing the evidence for this conclusion, "A number of historical documents say so," and "These documents are accurate." Each of these sentences is declarative in form. The argument is not composed of questions, commands, exclamations, or the like, but only of sentences which make statements. This is characteristic of arguments. An **argument,** in fact, may be defined as a sequence of declarative sentences, one of which, called the **conclusion,** is intended to be evidentially supported by the others, called **premises.** An argument may have any number of premises, from one on up; but as the definition indicates, it has only one conclusion. In ordinary conversation or writing, the conclusion may occur anywhere in the sequence—at the beginning, in the middle, or at the end. But to avoid confusion it is often convenient to write arguments in a **standard form.** We'll adopt the convention of writing premises first and the conclusion last. Thus, the standard form of the argument we're discussing is this:

A number of historical documents say that sorcerers and witches have wielded genuinely supernatural power.

These documents are accurate.

∴ Sorcerers and witches have wielded genuinely supernatural power.

The three dots in front of the conclusion mean "therefore." It's customary to put them there.

Note the presence of the phrase "is intended to be" in the definition of "argument." It's there because not all arguments really do evidentially support their conclusions. The purpose of logic is to determine which ones do and which ones don't. To make this determination, we need to answer two questions: (1) Are the premises true? (2) How strong is the reasoning; that is, how likely would the conclusion be if the premises were true? Logic, as we'll see in Chapter 3, deals mainly with the second of these; but we'll begin with the first, using the argument about sorcerers and witches as an illustration.

You've probably already noticed that this argument is not likely to change anyone's mind on the subject. This is because anyone who doubts the conclusion is also likely to doubt the second premise. The first premise, of course, is undeniably true. Such documents exist. There are, for example, extensive records of witch trials in Europe and America; there are even whole books on the subject—such as *Malleus Maleficarum*, written at the end of the fifteenth century by James Sprenger and Heinrich Kramer. But the accuracy of such sources is surely subject to doubt. Does this mean that they are true for the people who think they're true and false for those who don't? Of course not! There *is* a fact of the matter, regardless of what people think. Believing something does not make it so. You can believe as strongly as you like that you can sprout wings and fly to the moon, but you won't be able to do it. (If you doubt this, experiment! You won't succeed even if you resort to such extravagant means as chanting mantras or frying your brain with hallucinogens. You might feel like you're doing it, but you're not—as anyone watching you could see.) It is worth recalling that at the time *Malleus Maleficarum* was written, nearly everyone believed that the earth was stationary and flat. The earth, however, ignored them. It just rolled on majestically through the heavens in its own self-contained, roughly spherical fashion. In the same way, there are (or were) facts which determine the truth or falsity of *Malleus* itself and similar historical documents, regardless of what anyone believes.

But how can we ascertain these facts? The rational way is to seek further evidence. We might begin by asking the argument's author for his or her reasons for believing the second premise. Once again, our query is a request for an argument. Now suppose the author replies, "I can tell that these documents are accurate because they are remarkably detailed." This is a new argument, which has as its conclusion the second premise of the original argument:

> The documents in question are remarkably detailed.
> ∴ These documents are accurate.

This new argument links with the first to form a **complex argument,** a chain of reasoning in which some premises are supported by others. The simple arguments which make up the links of this chain are called **inferences.** An inference may contain any number of premises, from one on up; but each inference has only one conclusion, and each inference is simple, in the sense that it is not composed of further inferences. Our current example, which now consists of two inferences, can be written in standard form as follows:

> The documents in question are remarkably detailed.
> ∴ These documents are accurate.
> These documents say that sorcerers and witches have wielded genuinely supernatural power.
> ∴ Sorcers and witches have wielded genuinely supernatural power.

The first two statements make up the first inference, and the last three constitute the second. The second statement is a part of both inferences, being the conclusion of the first and a premise of the second. Notice that to keep each inference together as a unit, I switched the order of the premises in the second inference. This is harmless, since the order of premises within a given inference is irrelevant; and it gives a clearer indication of the argument's structure.

Though the second statement is the conclusion of the first inference, from the point of view of the argument as a whole it is merely a premise. An argument, you should recall, has only one ultimate conclusion, and the conclusion of this one is "Sorcerers and witches have wielded genuinely supernatural power." Statements like the first and third, which have no additional premises supporting them, are called **basic premises** or **assumptions.** Statements like the second, which function as a conclusion of one inference and a premise of the next, are called **nonbasic premises** or **intermediate conclusions.** Nonbasic premises are the points at which the inferences constituting a complex argument link together.

1.2   ARGUMENT STRENGTH

Now that we've surveyed the structure of our argument, let's return to the question of how good it is. This question, as I noted earlier, breaks into two components: (1) Are the premises true? (2) How good is the reasoning? I've already talked a bit about question (1), but now I need to be more precise. The premises relevant to answering question (1) are just the basic ones. As we'll see shortly, if the basic premises are true and the reasoning is fairly strong, then we'll have good evidence for the conclusion. So in answering question (1) we are concerned only with basic premises. The basic premises are:

The documents in question are remarkably detailed.

and

These documents say that sorcerers and witches have wielded genuinely supernatural power.

Both are true. Thus there are no grounds for objection with respect to question (1).

So let's turn to the second question, How strong is the reasoning? In other words, how likely is the conclusion, given the truth of the basic premises? The answer to this question will not be a simple yes or no. Strength of reasoning is a matter of degree, as the following examples illustrate:

All elves drink stout.

Olaf is an elf.

∴ Olaf drinks stout.

95 percent of elves drink stout.

Olaf is an elf.

∴ Olaf drinks stout.

A few elves drink stout.

Olaf is an elf.

∴ Olaf drinks stout.

In the first case, the truth of the premises guarantees the truth of the conclusion. If Olaf is an elf and all elves drink stout, then it *has to be* that Olaf drinks stout. There's no getting around it. In other words, it's impossible for the argument's basic premises to be true and its conclusion false. Such an argument is called a **valid argument** or **deductive argument** (the two terms may be used interchangeably).[1]

The second argument is an **invalid argument**; that is, it is possible for its basic premises to be true and its conclusion false. Even if it's true that Olaf is an elf and 95 percent of elves drink stout, Olaf might still be among the 5 percent who don't. But though the basic premises, if true, do not guarantee the truth of the conclusion, they nevertheless make it probable. The reasoning here is still strong, though not as strong as in the first example. We'll call this sort of argument an **inductive argument**.[2] "Probable" in this

[1]Though most logicians agree on the definition of "valid," some define a deductive argument as any argument whose conclusion is *intended to be* certain, given the truth of the basic premises. But in informal reasoning it is usually both pointless and impossible to tell whether this is the intention. So we'll avoid unnecessary complication by using these terms synonymously.

[2]Sometimes inductive arguments are defined as arguments whose conclusions are *intended to be* merely probable, given the truth of their basic premises. Arguments whose conclusions really would be probable if their basic premises were true (i.e., those which are inductive by the definition I gave) are then termed "inductively correct," "inductively strong," or even "inductively valid." But this distinction, like the corresponding one for deduction (see footnote 1, above) creates more problems than it solves in informal reasoning. Therefore, although we'll recognize degrees of inductive strength (a set of premises which makes a conclusion 97 percent probable constitutes stronger reasoning than one that makes a conclusion only 60 percent probable), we'll ignore the generally unfruitful question of how strong the reasoning is *intended to be*. We're interested, rather, in how strong it really is.

Some readers may be familiar with other, still older, sets of definitions. Arguments used to be considered inductive if they moved from specific premises to general conclusions and deductive if they moved from general premises to specific conclusions. But this definition is now widely rejected. If you are already familiar with one of these other conceptions, note now that it is quite different from the one used in this book. Here we'll stick strictly to the definition I gave above.

context means "more likely than not," or more precisely, "having a probability greater than 50 percent." Thus an inductive argument is an argument such that if its basic premises were true, the probability of its conclusion, based on those premises, would be between 50 and 100 percent.

We'll use the term **rational argument** to designate any argument which is either inductive or deductive. A rational argument whose basic premises are true provides good evidence for its conclusion. If you bet on the conclusion, then on the basis of the information contained in the premises, you are more likely to win than to lose.

The third of our three arguments is not rational. That is, it is neither inductive nor deductive. We'll call such an argument a **fallacy** and describe it as a **fallacious argument** or an **irrational argument**.[3] In a fallacious argument, even if the basic premises were true, there would still be no more than a 50 percent chance, based on these premises, that the conclusion was true. Thus the probability of the conclusion, given the basic premises, lies somewhere in the interval from 0 to 50 percent. The most extreme sort of fallacy is an argument in which the premises make the conclusion absolutely impossible, as in this rather odd example:

No elves drink stout.
Olaf is an elf.
∴ Olaf drinks stout.

Here the probability of the conclusion, given the premises, is 0 percent.

Every argument is either deductive, inductive, or fallacious, for in every argument the probability of the conclusion, given the truth of the basic premises, is either 100 percent, between 50 percent and 100 percent, or 50 percent or less. There are no other alternatives.[4] These three concepts, then, provide a complete classification of arguments according to the strength of their reasoning. In deductive arguments, the reasoning is maximally strong, in inductive ones it is good but could be better, and in fallacies it is poor to worthless. The following chart summarizes the relations among the terms we've just discussed:

---

[3]This definition is narrower and more precise than the traditional one. Traditionally, a fallacy is defined as any argument which should not persuade a reasonable person. That includes even rational arguments with false premises. On the narrower definition presented here no rational argument is ever fallacious, though some do have false premises.

[4]It should be noted, however, that for most nondeductive arguments it is impossible to state the probability of the conclusion, given the premises, as a precise percentage, so that at best we can only make a rough estimate. A method for making such estimates will be introduced in Section 3.3. Sometimes this probability may be radically indeterminate (see the Appendix), so that a nondeductive argument may be neither clearly inductive nor clearly fallacious. Our threefold classification of arguments is therefore an idealization.

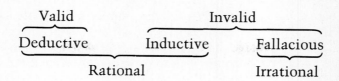

These terms all describe the strength of the reasoning from premises to conclusions. They apply, therefore, only to inferences or whole arguments, never to individual statements. It is important not to confuse any of them with the terms "true" and "false," which apply only to individual statements. In logic it is nonsense to speak, for example, of a "valid premise" or a "false argument." Don't be guilty of such nonsense!

Another mistake to avoid is to be misled by the negative connotations of the term "invalid" into thinking that all invalid arguments are worthless. Arguments which are invalid in the logical sense range from those whose conclusions would certainly be false if their basic premises were true (0 percent probability) to those whose conclusions would almost certainly be true (near 100 percent probability). Some of them, therefore, are very good arguments.

Armed now with this new terminology, let's return to our original argument. How strong is its reasoning? We noted before that this argument consists of two inferences. We'll examine each separately and then try to decide about the argument as a whole. The second inference, once again, is this:

> These documents are accurate.
> These documents say that sorcerers and witches have wielded genuinely supernatural power.
> ∴ Sorcerers and witches have wielded genuinely supernatural power.

It shouldn't take you long to see that this inference is deductive, that is, that it's impossible for its premises to be true and its conclusion false. There is a link of certainty between premises and conclusion. However, the first inference:

> The documents in question are remarkably detailed.
> ∴ These documents are accurate.

is surely fallacious. Detail alone is not even a probable indicator of accuracy or truth. Consider the detail in complex novels, the alibis of clever criminals, or the paranoid delusions of the insane. The inference is therefore irrational.

Now we have one inference which is deductive and one which is fallacious. What can we say about the argument as a whole? Well, a chain of inferences, like a physical chain, is generally no stronger than its weakest link. (There are a few exceptions to this principle, as we'll see in Chapter 3, but this is not one of them.) In this argument the weakest link is a fallacy. So the argument as a whole is fallacious as well. It proves nothing.

Should we conclude, then, that there have not been sorcerers or witches with supernatural powers? Definitely not. We have shown nothing of the sort. All we have shown is that one argument attempting to show that there have been some is faulty. Though this particular argument does not provide evidence strong enough to establish its conclusion, perhaps another one does. We might, for example, try to modify the argument by replacing the fallacious inference with a better line of reasoning. Or perhaps there is a good argument to show that there are no supernatural powers. These possibilities remain untouched by our criticism. It is a common but serious mistake to suppose that because you have refuted an argument you have thereby shown its conclusion to be false. Don't make this mistake!

To settle the issue with certainty, we'd have to construct a sound argument either for or against the claim that there have been sorcerers and witches with genuinely supernatural powers. A **sound argument** is an argument which meets two requirements: (1) its basic premises are all true and (2) it is deductive. A deductive argument, as we saw, is an argument such that if its basic premises were true, its conclusion would have to be true. Hence if an argument is deductive and all of its basic premises are true, its conclusion has to be true. Soundness, in other words, guarantees the truth of the conclusion. A sound argument is a proof. Soundness is the logical ideal.

Could we construct a sound argument for or against the claim at hand? Maybe. However, I suspect that to find appropriate premises we'd have to learn a lot of history, sociology, physics, and perhaps even psychology. It wouldn't be easy, and even a great effort might not produce a satisfactory solution. Yet logical effort succeeds often enough that in combination with careful observation and solid common sense, it has enabled humanity to resolve many questions with certainty or near certainty. I hope the extent of this achievement will become clear to you as you work your way through this book. And I hope, too, that your own logical skill will improve, so that if you care about such issues, you will be better able to resolve them yourself.

At this point it might be useful to summarize what has been said so far about the relations between basic premises and conclusions in the three kinds of arguments. Since by definition a deductive argument is an argument such that it is impossible for its basic premises to be true and its conclusion false, there is no such thing as a deductive argument with all true premises and a false conclusion. But any other combination of truth and falsity is possible. Here are some examples ("T" means true and "F" means false):

If you are reading this argument, then you can see it.	T
You are reading it.	T
∴ You can see it.	T

All logicians are knaves.	F
All knaves study logic.	F
∴ All logicians study logic.	T

Nothing at all exists.	F
∴ The Easter Bunny does not exist.	T

All insects are either magenta or chartreuse.	F
Socrates was an insect.	F
Socrates was not magenta.	T
∴ Socrates was chartreuse.	F

$2 + 2 = 3$ and $2 + 2 = 5$	F
∴ $3 = 5$	F

All these arguments are deductive. Think carefully about each and see if you can recognize the connection of certainty between the premises and conclusion. (Ability to recognize this connection develops with practice. If you're having trouble now, don't be overly concerned; just keep at it. You'll get better as you go along.) Note especially that valid reasoning can lead from false premises to true conclusions, as in the second and third examples. Notice also that some deductive reasoning is downright weird, as in the last example. So don't assume that an argument is invalid just because it sounds silly.

Any combination of truth and falsity is possible in inductive and fallacious arguments, including true premises and a false conclusion. Here's an example:

Large, well-built ocean liners rarely sink on their maiden voyages.

The *Titanic* was a large, well-built ocean liner.

∴ The *Titanic* did not sink on her maiden voyage.

This argument is inductive. If its premises are true (which they are), then its conclusion is probable. But as we all know, the improbable sometimes happens. So sometimes we get an inductive argument with true premises and a false conclusion. This does not happen very often, however. Inductive arguments with true premises tend to have true conclusions.

One common misconception is that any argument with all true premises and a true conclusion is deductive. To see that this is wrong, consider the following argument:

Bertrand Russell read some books.   T

∴ Bertrand Russell read *Alice in
Wonderland.*   T

(Bertrand Russell was a twentieth-century British philosopher and logician and an acquaintance of Lewis Carroll, author of the Alice books. Carroll himself, by the way, wrote a number of entertaining books and articles on logic.) Now both the premise and conclusion of this argument are true. The reasoning, however, is fallacious. The fact that the premise is true does not make it even probable that Russell read *Alice in Wonderland.* So the argument is certainly not deductive. In a deductive argument, if the premises are true, the conclusion *must* be true. But there is no "must" here. In fact, there is virtually no connection whatever between the premise and conclusion.

Exercise 1.2   For each of the following descriptions, make up an original argument consisting of a single inference which satisfies the description. Put your argument in standard form, and label each statement with a "T" or an "F" to indicate whether it is true or false. If you are doing this as an assignment, make sure you use statements whose truth or falsity will be obvious to the reader—not fictional statements or statements whose truth is known to you alone.

1 Deductive with all false premises and a false conclusion.
2 Deductive with all false premises and a true conclusion.
3 Deductive with a mixture of true and false premises and a true conclusion.
4 Deductive with a mixture of true and false premises and a false conclusion.
5 Sound.
6 Inductive with all false premises and a false conclusion.
7 Inductive with all false premises and a true conclusion.
8 Inductive with all true premises and a true conclusion.
9 Inductive with all true premises and a false conclusion.
10 Fallacious with all false premises and a false conclusion.
11 Fallacious with all false premises and a true conclusion.
12 Fallacious with all true premises and a true conclusion.
13 Fallacious with all true premises and a false conclusion.

1.3   RECOGNIZING ARGUMENTS

Now that you know what an argument is and what kinds of arguments there are, the next thing you need to do is to become proficient at recognizing one when you see it. Recall the definition of an argument: an argument is a sequence of declarative sentences, one of which is intended to be evidentially supported by the others. A couple of things follow immediately from this definition. First, as we noted earlier, passages of writing or speech containing exclamations, questions, or commands are not arguments. They sometimes function as arguments, but technically they are not. So if we want to consider them as arguments, we'll have to rewrite them as declarative sentences. Here's an example:

> What kind of fool do you think I am? I wouldn't go out with that scroungeface.

This isn't an argument, since it contains a question. But it's intended to work like one. The speaker is trying to persuade us that he or she wouldn't go out with a certain apparently unattractive person. That's a conclusion. And the question suggests a premise, "I'm no fool." Thus we can consider the whole thing as an argument, like this:

> I'm no fool.
>
> ∴   I wouldn't go out with that scroungeface.

We'll often run into cases like this, where an argument is suggested by a passage of writing containing nondeclarative sentences. The way to handle these cases is, just as we did here, to rewrite the nondeclarative sentences in declarative form.

The second thing that follows from the definition of an argument is that an argument expresses an intention; its conclusion is *intended to be* evidentially supported by its premises. How, exactly, is this intention expressed? The answer is that it is usually embodied in **inference-indicator expressions.** Consider the following argument:

> The Soviets have made a number of overtures toward disarmament in recent months. (Therefore) it is crucial that we prepare some constructive response. (For) it is our responsibility never to let an opportunity for disarmament pass without positive action.

I've circled the words "therefore" and "for," because they are words which suggest evidential links between statements. They are inference-indicator expressions. Each, however, has a different function. "Therefore" at the beginning of a statement indicates that the statement is intended as a conclusion from previously mentioned premises. "For" at the beginning of a statement indicates that the statement is a premise. From this information we can infer the argument's structure. "Therefore" indicates that the second statement, "It is crucial that we prepare some constructive response," is a conclusion from a previously stated premise. But only one statement, "The Soviets have made a number of overtures toward disarmament in recent months," was made previously. So it must be a premise for this conclusion. Moreover, since the last statement is prefixed by the premise indicator "for," it must be a premise too. This suggests that the argument is a single inference, consisting of two premises and a conclusion, like this:

> The Soviets have made a number of overtures toward disarmament in recent months.
>
> It is our responsibility never to let an opportunity for disarmament pass without positive action.
>
> ∴ It is crucial that we prepare some constructive response.

All inference indicators function either like "therefore" or like "for"; that is, all of them are either conclusion indicators or premise indicators. A list of some of the most common inference indicators is given below:

Conclusion Indicators	*Premise Indicators*
(These are prefixed to conclusions to indicate that they follow from previously stated premises.)	(These are prefixed to premises and often link these premises to the conclusions they support.)
Therefore	For
Thus	Since
Hence	Because
So	Assuming that
Then	Seeing that
Accordingly	Granted that
Consequently	Here's why
That's why	This is true because
This being so	The reason is that
It follows that	In view of the fact that
Which implies that	As is implied by the fact that
This entails that	As is shown by the fact that

Conclusion Indicators (cont.)	*Premise Indicators (cont.)*
This proves that	Given the fact that
Which means that	Inasmuch as
From which we can deduce that	
As a result, we may infer that	

This is only a sample. There are almost endlessly many ways of elaborating premise and conclusion indicators in English. Fortunately, most of them are just variants of others, and with a little practice it's fairly easy to spot them all.

Unfortunately, however, many of these expressions have several uses, so they don't always function as inference indicators. The word "since," for example, functions as a premise indicator in this sentence:

It's likely to rain, since the barometer is falling.

but not in this one:

She's been a little monster ever since she was born.

The first sentence, which is composed of two subordinate statements, is an argument. It cites the fact that the barometer is falling as evidence for the conclusion that it is likely to rain. But the second one is not an argument at all. It's just a description of an ill-behaved brat. "Since" is used in this description, not to indicate an inference, but to indicate the passage of time. Accordingly (note that I'm using a conclusion indicator here; you may infer that an argument is passing under your nose this very second), when you see one of these expressions, you should not automatically assume that it is an inference indicator. To decide, you have to consider whether it is intended to indicate that one statement is evidence for another. If so, it's an inference indicator. If not, it's something else. Once you've decided that it is an indicator, though, you'll know whether what follows is a premise or a conclusion. Premise indicators are always followed by premises. Conclusion indicators are always followed by conclusions. (These may be either intermediate or final conclusions.)

Indicator expressions are one of the main clues for recognizing an argument and understanding its structure. Skillful argumentative writers use them frequently to make clear exactly what is supposed to follow from what. In a complex piece of reasoning containing several inferences, their presence is often crucial for understanding. Consider this example:

Cocaine is plainly and simply illegal. (So) people who use it should be punished, (because) we can't simply let them break the law as they please. (Therefore), (since) your friend uses it, she certainly does deserve to be punished.

Again, I've circled the indicator expressions. This argument is a bit more complicated than those we've discussed before, and only close attention to the indicators will enable us to determine its structure. Note first of all that "so" is a conclusion indicator, so that the statement which follows it is a conclusion. Moreover, the statement immediately preceding it, the first statement, is a premise supporting this conclusion, because conclusion indicators prefixed to statements indicate that they follow from previously asserted premises, and the first statement is the only thing asserted prior to "so." But is it the only premise supporting that conclusion? Notice that the third statement begins with the premise indicator "because." It is therefore a premise. Furthermore, this "because" obviously draws a connection between the second and third statements, which makes it pretty clear that the third statement, too, is functioning as a premise for the second. This suggests that the first part of the argument is structured as follows:

Cocaine is plainly and simply illegal.
We can't simply let people who use it break the law as they please.
∴ People who use it should be punished.

Now what about the last part? Here we have something peculiar—a conclusion indicator ("therefore") shoved right up next to a premise indicator ("since"), followed by two statements separated by a comma. This sort of construction is actually rather common. It always works like this: the premise indicator goes with the first statement, and the conclusion indicator goes with the second. (Don't ask me why, but that's the way it works.) So the fourth statement, "Your friend uses it," is a premise, and the fifth, "She certainly deserves to be punished," is a conclusion. Furthermore, as I mentioned above, conclusion indicators, of which "therefore" is one, generally prefix conclusions which are supposed to follow from previously asserted premises. So the fifth statement, which is the conclusion prefixed by "therefore," is supposed to follow, not simply from the fourth, but from the fourth together with something that was said earlier. What could this be? Well, the thing that makes most sense in combination with the fourth statement as evidence for the last is the second statement, which is the conclusion of the first inference. (Check for yourself to see that this is true.) Putting the second statement together with the fourth, we get the inference:

People who use cocaine should be punished.

Your friend uses it.

∴ She certainly does deserve to be punished.

And putting the two inferences together, we see that the argument is structured as follows:

Cocaine is plainly and simply illegal.

We can't simply let people who use it break the law.

∴ People who use it should be punished.

Your friend uses it.

∴ She certainly does deserve to be punished.

If you can't see that this is the structure of the argument, go back and read this explanation again. Recognizing argument structure is another skill you'll need to develop; and like estimating the strengths of inferences, it is a skill which improves with practice.

The point of this convoluted and messy example was to show you how important those seemingly insignificant indicator expressions are. Without them, it would be nearly impossible to figure out the argument's structure. Here's what happens if we take them out:

Cocaine is plainly and simply illegal. People who use it should be punished. We can't simply let them break the law as they please. Your friend uses it. She certainly does deserve to be punished.

If you can make sense of this now, you're a better reader than I am. (Incidentally, did you notice as you read this explanation how many inference-indicator expressions it contains? Be alert. Arguments are everywhere!)

Exercise 1.3 Some of the following passages are arguments. Some are not. Write those which are in standard form and identify their basic premises, nonbasic premises, and conclusion.

1 Hemlock is poison, so you shouldn't drink it.

2 There have always been wars ever since history began.

3 All even numbers are divisible by two. And all prime numbers are divisible only by themselves and one. Therefore, two is the only even prime.

4   Olaf doesn't like mushrooms, and so he seldom eats them. Therefore, since Ophelia, his wife, puts mushrooms in everything she
eats, they seldom eat the same thing.

5   Oil reserves are finite. Accordingly, since consumption is continuing at a rapid rate, eventually the world will run out of oil.

6   Adult nerve cells cannot divide mitotically and cannot, therefore,
replace any that happen to be destroyed. (Ernest Gardner, *Principles
of Neurology*)

7   It is arguable that all communication is based on selective information, because two people in communication must employ a common language. It is therefore implied that the art of communication
consists merely in passing to each other selected words out of the
previously agreed dictionary. (D. A. Bell, *Intelligent Machines*)

8   The patient went into a sort of trance after struggling with the cube
for about four hours. Thus he remained, unable or unwilling to
communicate with the outside world, for a period of several days.

9   An oily face begins deep within your pores. So that's where your
cleanser should reach for your face to be really clean. That's why
you need pHisoDerm Skin Cleanser. (pHisoDerm ad, *Mademoiselle*, April 1980)

10 If ever, oh ever a Wiz there was,
The Wizard of Oz is one becoz, becoz, becoz, becoz, becoz, becoz,
Becoz of the wonderful things he does. (E. Y. Harburg and Harold
Arlen, "We're Off to See the Wizard (The Wonderful Wizard of
Oz)")

1.4   SMALL INTERJECTORY SERMON

As you read through the discussion of the last example in the previous
section, probably one of two things happened: (1) you eventually got tired
of looking back and forth from the original argument to the words you were
reading, and you got slightly annoyed at me for not managing to make the
discussion simpler to understand, or (2) you didn't look back at all, and so
sometimes it wasn't clear what I was referring to. If the first is what happened, I apologize for being long-winded, thank you for your patience, and
encourage you to keep it up. You're a good reader. If the second is what
happened, then either you just don't care or you've never really learned to
read well. If you don't care, skip this sermon. It won't help. But if you care
and it just never occurred to you to flip back, read on; you need to change
your reading style.

Students in elementary school are taught to read in a linear fashion—
that is, smoothly and without breaks. At first this is done by reading aloud.

Sometimes teachers even discourage students who pause too often to consider or ask questions. Later on, this process is internalized; students learn to say the words silently to themselves as they pass their eyes across the page. But still the emphasis is on speed and continuity. Many people never pass beyond this stage. But reading can and should be much more than just listening to yourself broadcasting words from a printed page on your internal audio system. The best readers are those who engage the author in a dialogue, who stop and ask, "What does this mean?" or "Why is this said in this way?" and who pause frequently to compare what is being said with what was said before. Such readers refuse to move on until they have understood a point thoroughly. When a text refers to something said previously, they look back and check it out. They are active, questioning, aware. If you don't read in this nonlinear way, you'll miss a lot of what this book has to say. And when you read good books of any sort, you'll probably miss much that is crucial.

It was only a short time ago, historically speaking, that reading became commonplace. Before that, people who could read were often regarded with awe—and for good reason. Reading at its best is an activity of great power, a power which enables you to enter into another person's experience and benefit from it as if it were your own. Yet today we take reading for granted— partly because now nearly everyone can read, but mostly, I think, because we seldom experience it at full power. But this can be changed. What is needed is to slow down, engage in a dialogue with the author, and read nonlinearly.

1.5 ARGUMENTS WITHOUT INDICATOR EXPRESSIONS

Not all arguments contain indicator expressions. Lack of indicators may make a passage practically impossible to decipher, as we saw in Section 1.3. Sometimes, though, context will make the argument structure clear even in the absence of indicators. Here's a simple example of this second type:

Alice isn't going to the dance. I heard her say so.

Here the second statement is probably given as evidence for the first. Though no inference indicator is present, we could easily supply one. We don't change the speaker's intention if we say, for example, "Alice isn't going to the dance, for I heard her say so" or "I heard Alice say she isn't going to the dance. Therefore, she's not going." These are different ways of saying the same thing. When you are not sure whether to regard a passage without indicators as an argument, supply the indicators in your imagination. If this does not change the author's intention, then you're doing fine.

Notice, too, that in this case it wouldn't make much sense to read the argument the other way, with the first statement as premise and the second

18

as conclusion. No one would say "Alice isn't going to the dance. Therefore, I heard her say so." The first statement is just not the sort of thing that would be used as evidence for the second. So our first interpretation is probably right.

There's nothing mysterious about interpreting the structure of an argument without indicators. As this example shows, it's primarily a matter of common sense. And of course, you must always keep in mind that premises have to function as evidence. If a statement is not intended as evidence, then it's not a premise.

> **Exercise 1.5** Some of the following passages are arguments. Others are not. Write those which are in standard form.
>
> 1 You'll get wet if you go out. It's raining.
> 2 We went camping last weekend. The weather was great.
> 3 You never pay any attention to me. Every time I say something, you change the subject.
> 4 I left the tickets right here on the desk in plain sight. Nobody would have carried them off by accident. They must have been stolen.
> 5 When an engine is burning a lot of oil, the problem is usually worn valves or rings. In either case, repair is usually expensive.
> 6 It doesn't look like cheese. It doesn't smell like cheese. And it doesn't taste like cheese. How could it be cheese?
> 7 It's not time to go back to work yet. We've still got ten minutes of break time left.
> 8 It was clear that the villagers had left quickly. They took few belongings, and meals were left half eaten or cooking on untended stoves.
> 9 The predominant by-product of the frustrating, civilizing process is negative feelings. On the basis of these feelings the little person early concludes, "I'm not OK." We call this comprehensive self-estimate the NOT OK, or the NOT OK Child. (*I'm OK—You're OK*, Thomas A. Harris, M.D.)
> 10 . . . buying compliance has its obvious drawbacks. It can often be too expensive, and it can be seen as illegitimate. (*Power in Management*, John P. Kotter)

1.6 EXPLANATIONS AND CAUSAL DESCRIPTIONS

Probably the main sources of confusion in recognizing arguments are explanations and descriptions of cause and effect. These often look like arguments; but if they merely explain or describe rather than give evidence, they are not. Here's an example of an explanation which you read in Section 1.3 (just after the first occurrence of the disarmament argument):

> I've circled the words "therefore" and "for," because they are words which suggest evidential links between statements.

If your eye is captured by the word "because," you might be tempted to interpret this as an argument:

> The words "therefore" and "for" suggest evidential links between statements.
>
> ∴ I've circled them.

But this is totally wrong. I did not intend to give evidence that I had circled these words. No evidence was needed. You could see that I circled them. So what I was doing does not fit the definition of "argument." I was merely explaining why the words were circled.

Descriptions of cause and effect are also sometimes confused with arguments. Here's an example:

> Mothers were taught correct methods of sanitation and prenatal care, and as a result infant deaths declined dramatically.

This passage describes a causal process. It tells us that one series of events led to another. But it would be easy to mistake the phrase "as a result" for a conclusion indicator and thus to misinterpret this passage as an argument. It is not an argument, as you can see by noting that neither of the component statements is offered as evidence for the other. The passage simply describes what happened.

Intention to give evidence is always the criterion by which we distinguish arguments from nonarguments. Sometimes knowledge of the context of what was said is necessary to determine whether there was intention to give evidence. But often the intention is fairly clear, even apart from context. Here are some further examples of explanations and causal descriptions which are not arguments. Consider each carefully until you can see that no intention to give evidence is present.

> She left him because he drank too much.

> The spring thaw came quickly, which caused a series of huge avalanches on the mountain's southern flank.

> Since you didn't help me with the dishes, I won't go shopping with you.

> You left the butter out in the hot sun. That's why it melted, you fool.

Arguments and explanations are not mutually exclusive. That is, some utterances function as both. Here's a typical case:

You won't find any blueberries now because they're out of season.

The second statement is intended both to give evidence for and to explain the first. Thus this is both an argument and an explanation. Don't make the mistake of thinking that something is not an argument simply because it is an explanation.

Arguments which double as explanations can be treated exactly like those which do not. What you have to watch out for are explanations or causal descriptions which are not arguments. Recognizing them is important for two reasons. First, they sometimes function as premises of an argument; and as we'll see in Section 2.1, when they do, treating them as inferences or component arguments results in substantial misinterpretation of the argument's structure. Second, explanations and causal descriptions which are not arguments should not be judged by the same criteria we apply to arguments. It would be both misleading and unfair, for example, to charge that the person who said "She left him because he drank too much" committed a fallacy because the conclusion "She left him" is not even made probable by the premise "He drank too much." It is true that the first statement is not made probable by the second. But this is irrelevant. There was no attempt to prove the first statement, only an effort to explain why it is true. By treating this explanation as an argument, we have seriously misunderstood it.

Explanations and causal descriptions are not the only forms of discourse that get confused with arguments, but they are the most common. You should keep in mind, however, that there are countless other modes of communication as well. Though arguments may crop up just about anywhere, only a fraction of what you read or hear is argumentative. Only where there is intention to give evidence is there argument.

Exercise 1.6 Some of the following passages are arguments. Others are not. Determine the basic premises, nonbasic premises, and conclusion of those which are, and briefly explain why those that aren't aren't.

1 He loves her because of her brown eyes.
2 The reason why I don't like you is that you think you're so damn superior.
3 I'd like you to meet my sister, since you two have a lot in common.
4 Since my sister will be at the party, you'll have a chance to meet her.
5 I want to know what time it is so I can see how soon I have to leave.

6   In phantasy, the self can be anyone, anywhere, do anything, have everything. It is thus omnipotent and completely free—but only in phantasy. (R. D. Laing, *The Divided Self*)

7   If I am told a number and merely think about it, I am likely to forget it or transpose some of the digits. If I repeat the numbers out loud or write them down, then I can remember them quite well. This surely means that there is a part of our brain which remembers sounds and images, but not thoughts. (Carl Sagan, *The Dragons of Eden*)

8   I went to the woods because I wished to live deliberately, to front only the essential facts of life, and see if I could not learn what it had to teach, and not, when I came to die, discover that I had not lived. (Henry David Thoreau, *Walden*)

9   From the moment of its birth surrealism was an international phenomenon—the spontaneous generation of an international and fraternal *organism* in total contrast to the artificial manufacture of a collective *organization* such as the League of Nations. It would therefore be contrary to the nature of the movement to disengage, as some have suggested, a specifically English version of 'surréalisme'. (Herbert Read, *The Philosophy of Modern Art*)

10   Half-way down a by-street of one of our New England towns stands a rusty wooden house, with seven acutely peaked gables, facing towards various points of the compass, and a huge, clustered chimney in the midst. The street is Pyncheon Street; the house is the old Pyncheon House; and an elm-tree, of wide circumference, rooted before the door, is familiar to every town-born child by the title of the Pyncheon Elm. (Nathaniel Hawthorne, *The House of the Seven Gables*)

11   The things confession is concerned with belong to the very heart of personality, to its freedom and responsibility. The danger of psycho-analysis is that it will deal with these same things from the point of view of natural occurrences and that it will constantly direct the attention of the patient to himself and his temporal existence. Thus the soul's center of gravity may be transferred from the center—from the point of personal responsibility in the presence of the Unconditioned—to the impersonal, unconscious, purely natural sphere. (Paul Tillich, *The Religious Situation*)

12   On Saturday, May 22, 1971, I went to Sonora, Mexico, to see don Juan Matus, a Yaqui Indian sorcerer, with whom I had been associated since 1961. I thought that my visit on that day was going to be in no way different from the scores of times I had gone to see him in the ten years I had been his apprentice. The events that took place on that day and on the following days, however, were

momentous to me. On that occasion my apprenticeship came to an end. (Carlos Castaneda, *Journey to Ixtlan*)

13   . . . we know that there is no greatest prime number. But of all the prime numbers that we shall have ever thought of, there certainly is a greatest. Hence there are prime numbers greater than any we shall have ever thought of. (Bertrand Russell, "On the Nature of Acquaintance")

2

Diagraming Arguments

As the arguments we encounter become increasingly complex, it will become increasingly important to represent their structure clearly. But writing complex arguments in standard form can be tedious, confusing, or even impossible. Often, for example, conclusions are supported by branching chains of reasoning, and these cannot be clearly represented in standard form. There are two possible solutions to this problem. One is to elaborate arguments in standard form with various annotative devices. This relieves the confusion, but not the tedium. The other, the more satisfactory of the two, is to represent the argument's structure in a flow chart, or diagram. We'll discuss both solutions in this chapter, but the emphasis will be on constructing flow charts.

2.1   BRACKETING AND DIAGRAMING ARGUMENTS

The following example provides an illustration of the shortcomings of standard form:

We will not have any daylight left (because) it will be past midnight when we leave. Moreover, (since) the moon is new, there will be no moonlight either. Obviously, (therefore), we will have to travel in darkness.

I've circled the inference indicators for emphasis. (Check to see that each does express an intention to give evidence.) From them we will infer the argument's structure. The premise indicator "because" indicates that the statement "It will be past midnight when we leave" is evidence for the conclusion "We won't have any daylight left." Similarly, the premise indicator "since" shows that the premise "The moon is new" is evidence for the conclusion "There will be no moonlight either." Finally, the conclusion indicator "therefore" shows that "We'll have to travel in darkness" is a conclusion. Moreover, a moment's thought reveals that this is the final conclusion and that it is intended to follow from the two previous conclusions, "We won't have any daylight left" and "There will be no moonlight either." The argument's final inference is therefore:

> We won't have any daylight left.
> There will be no moonlight either.
> ∴ We'll have to travel in darkness.

But because each of the premises of this final inference has additional support, we cannot represent the entire argument unambiguously in standard form. Suppose, for example, we try this:

> It will be past midnight when we leave.
> ∴ We won't have any daylight left.
> The moon is new.
> ∴ There will be no moonlight either.
> ∴ We'll have to travel in darkness.

This makes it seem that the final conclusion follows just from the statement "There will be no moonlight either," rather than from this statement in combination with "We won't have any daylight left." Any other arrangement is equally unsatisfactory, as you can check for yourself.

One solution to this problem is to number each statement and then after each intermediate and final conclusion write the numbers of the premises from which it is inferred. This makes the structure of the argument unambiguously clear:

> 1   It will be past midnight when we leave.
> ∴ 2   We won't have any daylight left.   1

   3   The moon is new.

∴ 4   There will be no moonlight either.   3

∴ 5   We'll have to travel in darkness.   2,4

Now the order of the statements is less important, because the structure is indicated by the numbering of the statements, not by their order. This method of writing arguments is called **annotated standard form.** It is less ambiguous and more flexible than ordinary standard form and is especially useful when you are rewriting complex arguments (as we'll see in Section 4.3) or constructing your own (Chapter 9).

In argument analysis, however, it is often more convenient simply to number the statements as they stand in the original passage and then use the numbers as labels to construct a flow chart of the evidential connections between these statements. There are three steps to this procedure:

(i)   Circle all indicator expressions.

(ii) Bracket and number each statement.

(iii) Diagram the argument, using the numbers to represent corresponding statements, plus signs and lines to join premises used in a single inference, and arrows to represent intended evidential support.

I'll perform the first two steps on the argument we just examined:

   ①[We won't have any daylight left]   (because)   ②[it will be past midnight when we leave.] Moreover, (since)   ③[the moon is new,] ④[there will be no moonlight either.] Obviously, (therefore) , ⑤[we'll have to travel in darkness.]

Circling the indicators makes them stand out clearly, and the square brackets and numbers provide a clear labeling system. To prevent confusion, let's adopt the convention of always writing numbers at the beginnings of statements and always numbering the statements in the order in which they occur in the original passage. (Note that this produces a numbering different from the one we used when we wrote the argument in annotated standard form.)

Now we're ready for the third step, which probably sounded like hieroglyphic mumbo jumbo to you when you first read it. But it's easy to understand with a concrete example. To begin the diagram, let's confine our attention to the final inference. We saw earlier that this inference consists of the premises ① and ④ and the conclusion ⑤ . (These numbers refer to the corresponding bracketed statements. Notice how they conveniently enable us to refer to these statements without constantly repeating them.) To indicate that ① and ④ work together as premises of the same inference, we join them with a plus sign and underline them as follows:

$$\underline{① \ + \ ④}$$

Then to show that they support the conclusion ⑤, we draw an arrow leading to ⑤, like this:

This is the diagram of the argument's final inference. Now to show that ② is a premise for ① and ③ is a premise for ④, we add these numbers to the diagram and draw arrows as follows:

$$
\begin{array}{cc}
② & ③ \\
\downarrow & \downarrow \\
\underline{① \ + \ ④} & \\
\downarrow & \\
⑤ &
\end{array}
$$

There is no need to underline ② or ③, since the function of the line is simply to provide a base for drawing arrows from premises linked by plus signs. This, then, is the completed argument diagram. Compare it with the argument as stated in annotated standard form. The diagram graphically represents each feature of the argument. Each arrow means "is intended as evidence for," and each represents an inference. The plus signs and lines signify the joining together of premises in an inference. We can read them as meaning "together with." The whole diagram, then, is read as follows: Statement ② is intended as evidence for ①, ③ is intended as evidence for ④, and ① together with ④ is intended as evidence for ⑤. Numbers without arrows pointing toward them represent basic premises. Those with arrows pointing both toward and away from them represent nonbasic premises (intermediate conclusions). And the one with no arrow pointing away from it designates the final conclusion. It is standard practice to make all the arrows point downward, so that the final conclusion always comes at the bottom of the diagram.

There are a couple of other important points to notice about this example. The first is that from a grammatical point of view this passage is composed of only three sentences. In bracketing it off, however, I wound up with five. This is because the first and second sentences are both compound, each consisting of two subordinate sentences. It is generally best to break up such grammatical compounds in order to reveal as much of the argument's logical structure as possible. But there are several important classes of exceptions to this rule, as we'll see shortly. It is always best to break up a compound, however, if the component sentences are linked by an inference indicator. Inference indicators reveal the presence of an inference from one of the component sentences to the other, and that's just what we're trying to diagram.

If a compound is formed by a premise indicator which occurs between the two subordinate statements, then the second statement is a premise supporting the first. This is the case in the sentence composed of statements ① and ②. If the premise indicator occurs at the beginning of the compound, as "since" does in the sentence consisting of statements ③ and ④, then the first statement is a premise supporting the second. Either way, the premise indicator is always prefixed directly to the premise, which is the way premise indicators standardly behave. Conclusion indicators, too, exhibit their normal behavior of being prefixed directly to conclusions when they link two sentences into a compound. When a compound is formed by a conclusion indicator which occurs between two subordinate statements, the second statement is a conclusion from the first. There are no compounds formed solely by conclusion indicators occurring at the beginnings of sentences.

Though the rules stated in the previous paragraph hold in almost all cases, I don't recommend that you memorize them. Memorization leads to mechanical, unthinking application. Rather, you should rely on and strive to develop your intuitive understanding of the argument indicators. Logic is concerned with meanings, not with grammatical appearances. If you occupy yourself too much with rules, your understanding will be focused only on the outward form of arguments, and you will fail to grasp their inner meanings. Then when you encounter complications or exceptions you will feel lost and confused, and you won't know why. So don't clutter your mind with a bunch of complicated rules. Learn to rely on your intuitions. If at some point you get really stuck, then come back and review these rules—but only as a last resort!

Another thing to notice about our recent example is that the words "moreover" and "obviously" were neither circled nor included in the brackets. You might have thought that this was a mistake and that one or both of them should have been circled as inference indicators. But it was no mistake. Though these words may look like inference indicators, they are not, since they can occur before premises and conclusions alike. They belong to a broad class of words and phrases called **transitional expressions,** which are used stylistically to achieve smooth connections between sentences. Inference indicators, too, are members of this class, but most transitional expressions are not inference indicators. Here are some examples:

TRANSITIONAL EXPRESSIONS WHICH ARE NOT
INFERENCE INDICATORS

But	Still	It is obvious that
And	Yet	We can see that
However	Although	Likewise
Moreover	Even though	Similarly
Furthermore	Clearly	In addition
Nevertheless	It is clear that	Also
On the contrary	Obviously	Too
Besides	Of course	Now
In fact	Certainly	Finally

This list, of course, is by no means complete. The most convenient way to tell whether a particular transitional expression is an inference indicator is to ask yourself whether it could occur prefixed to both basic premises and final conclusions. If so, then it is neither a premise indicator nor a conclusion indicator and hence not an inference indicator at all. All the expressions listed above may occur with both basic premises and final conclusions.

Transitional expressions which are not inference indicators should not be circled. If they come at the beginning or end of a bracketed statement, we'll just leave them out of the brackets. Compound sentences formed by them should usually be broken into their components. It is sometimes desirable not to break up compounds formed by "and" and some of the others, but we needn't worry about this until Chapter 5. For now we'll split them, unless there is some compelling reason not to. Incidentally, when "and" occurs between two premises, it is often an indication that they should be joined with a plus sign.

Another kind of transitional device is the semicolon. Sentences joined by semicolons, like sentences joined by transitional expressions, should usually be broken into their components.

There are several kinds of compound sentences, however, which should not be broken up. Among these are explanations and causal descriptions of the sort discussed in Section 1.6. To see why, consider the following argument:

①[There has been a resurgence of German measles lately, because parents have become more lax about having their children vaccinated.]

(Therefore), ②[the incidence of measles can be reduced by making sure that children get their vaccinations.]

This argument is bracketed and numbered correctly, and its diagram is simply this:

Thus interpreted, it makes good clear sense. If a decrease in vaccinations is causing an increase in measles, then it is reasonable to conclude that ensuring vaccinations will help. But if we didn't realize that statement ① was a description of cause and effect, we might mistake it for an inference and bracket the passage this way:

①[There has been a resurgence of German measles lately]   (because)
②[parents have become more lax about having their children vaccinated.]   (Therefore), ③[the incidence of measles can be reduced by making sure that children get their vaccinations.]

This is incorrect, because we have wrongly interpreted "because" as a premise indicator and broken up the compound sentence which it forms. This makes it appear that ② is supposed to be evidence for ① and thus yields the following diagram:

This interpretation makes very little sense. Statement ② is not intended as evidence for ①, and it wouldn't be good evidence even if it were. The fact that *parents* are becoming lax does not even make it probable that that there has been a resurgence of measles. (Perhaps someone else is responsible for the vaccinations or maybe the virus has been wiped out.) Moreover, ③ certainly does not follow from ①. Given only that there has been a resurgence of German measles, we can conclude nothing about what will stop it. The reasoning here appears gappy and fallacious, not because it is, but because we have misinterpreted its structure. Our crucial mistake was to misidentify the first sentence, a causal description, as an inference by breaking it into its components. To avoid this sort of mistake, we must be careful not to break up causal descriptions and explanations.

Another class of compound sentences which should not be broken up under any circumstances are **conditional statements.** Conditional statements are statements of the form "If _____then _____" where the blanks are filled in by subordinate sentences. Sometimes the "then" is omitted. Here are some examples:

If the moon is made of green cheese, then it's edible.

If you tickle Olaf, he bellows.

If a layer of warm air is trapped beneath a layer of cold, then thunderstorms are likely to result.

People often mistake conditionals for inferences and break them up, like this:

If ①[the moon is made of green cheese,] (then) ②[it's edible.]

But this is wrong. What tempts us to see things this way is that "then" looks like a conclusion indicator. In fact, it is a conclusion indicator in some contexts, but never in the context of a conditional statement. So when it occurs in a conditional, it should not be circled. Moreover, a conditional should never be broken into its components, because in uttering a conditional we do not assert its components but only consider them hypothetically.

In a genuine inference, the premise(s) and conclusion are actually asserted. That is, they all are claimed to be true. If, for example, I make the inference:

The moon is made of green cheese.

∴ It's edible.

I am saying both that the moon is made of green cheese and that it's edible; furthermore, I intend the first statement to be taken as evidence for the second. However, in uttering the conditional:

If the moon is made of green cheese, then it's edible.

I am not saying either that the moon is made of green cheese or that it's edible, and I'm not concerned with evidence. I am only saying what would be the case if, hypothetically speaking, the moon were a big green cheese ball. If you break up the conditional and treat it as an inference, you make it appear as though I were asserting both these statements, and thus you misunderstand me. If my statement were part of an argument, this misunderstanding could create significant errors in evaluation. So remember, *never break up a conditional.* This rule, so far as I know, has no exceptions.

There are several other common expressions which always form unbreakable compounds. Chief among these are "or" and "unless." If I say, for example, "Either cutworms ate my tomato plants or else slugs did," I am not asserting that cutworms ate my tomato plants, nor am I asserting that slugs did. I'm only saying that it was one or the other. As with conditionals, if we break this statement into its components, we make it appear that I am saying both these things, which is clearly wrong. "Unless" functions similarly, as you can check by formulating your own examples. Though conditionals and compounds formed by "or" and "unless" are the most common compounds whose components are not asserted, there are others as well. As a general rule, you should never break up any sentence unless both its components are asserted.

2.2   SPLIT-SUPPORT ARGUMENTS

In some arguments there are two or more independent lines of reasoning leading to the same conclusion. We will call these **split-support arguments.** Their diagrams are characterized by the presence of two or more arrows pointing to the same number. Here is an example:

①[There is absolutely no demand for an appliance that converts earthworms into ice cream.] Besides, ②[it would be so costly to produce that no one could afford it anyway.] So ③[such a device will never be marketable.]

Here we have two premises, statements ① and ②, and a conclusion, statement ③. But in contrast to previous examples, each of these premises functions by itself as a reason for ③. They work independently; neither needs to be completed by the other. The author indicates this independence by the use of the word "besides," which signals that the second premise is not necessary to complete the evidence contained in the first, but stands by itself as a separate line of reasoning. Accordingly, instead of linking the two premises together, as we did in previous examples, it is more accurate to treat them as constituting two separate inferences, like this:

Notice that this diagram exhibits the characteristic mark of split-support arguments—two or more arrows pointing to the same number.

We'll use the term **normal argument** to designate all those arguments which do not embody split support. Prior to the last example, we had considered only normal arguments. We can identify split-support arguments by asking whether the premises are supposed to work separately, each by itself being presumed to imply the conclusion, or whether they are to be taken as a single complex of evidence. In the first case the argument is split support; in the second, it is normal.

Split-support arguments are relatively rare. If you are in doubt about a particular case, you are less likely to go wrong if you link the premises and treat it as normal. Here's a case which could go either way:

①[The existence of haunting phenomena is well supported by eye-witness accounts.] ②[There is, for example, the famous case of Borley Rectory in England, scene of numerous haunting phenomena witnessed over a period of centuries by many impartial observers.] ③[Equally well documented are the apparitions regularly encountered in the Tower of London.]

Here we have a general conclusion, statement ①, and two examples supporting it, statements ② and ③. Examples often function as premises, and that is what they're doing here. But are they working in conjunction, or is each a separate line of reasoning? It's not easy to tell. Each premise could function alone, since each speaks of many different instances in which haunting phenomena were observed. Thus each, if true, would by itself be good evidence for the conclusion. However, joining the two together produces a single inference which is somewhat stronger than either of the two inferences obtained by keeping them separate, for accumulation of similar observations makes a stronger case. Hence the author, assuming that he or she was trying to make the strongest case possible for the conclusion, probably intended the two premises to be taken as a single unit of evidence. The best diagram, therefore, is the normal one:

In borderline cases like this, the argument is often strongest if regarded as normal. Since it is reasonable to assume that an author intends his or her argument in the way in which it is strongest, we have still further justification for the policy of treating doubtful arguments as normal.

About most cases, however, there should be little doubt. To help you keep the contrast between normal and split-support arguments firmly in mind, consider the following example of an unmistakably normal argument:

①[Either Ophelia is very sick or else she's faking.] But ②[she's not capable of faking.] (So)   ③[she must be very sick.]

The correct diagram for this argument is:

$$\frac{① \; + \; ②}{↓}$$
$$③$$

Compare this argument and its diagram with the split-support argument about the earthworms-to-ice-cream transmuter with which we began this section. In the split-support case, each premise stood alone as a reason for the conclusion. But that can't be true here. Neither ① nor ② can function by itself as evidence for ③. It's only when we put them together that we can see how ③ follows. So this argument is clearly normal. (Notice, too, that in this example I did not break up the compound sentence ①, because ① is a compound joined by "or," and as I said in Section 2.1, these compounds must be treated as units. You'd get unintelligible garbage here if you broke ① up.)

Sometimes the premises of a split-support argument are themselves supported by further premises, so that we get two or more converging chains of reasoning. The following argument is an example:

①[Mr. A. would not have cheated on his income taxes,] (because) ②[he is an honest citizen,] (as is amply demonstrated by the fact that) ③[he is in a position of great responsibility in the community.] Moreover, ④[he had no motive to cheat,] (since)   ⑤[his annual income reaches six digits]and ⑥[he is not in debt.]

The final conclusion here is that Mr. A. would not cheat, and it is supported by two separate lines of reasoning. One of these lines deals with his character, arguing that he would not cheat because he is honest. The other deals with his lack of motive. Statements ② and ③ belong to the first line, statements ④, ⑤, and ⑥ to the second. Using the premise indicators "as is amply demonstrated by the fact that" and "since," we can see that ③ supports ②, and ⑤ and ⑥ together support ④. (Note that ⑤ and ⑥ are not split support for ④; they are intended to be taken together, though even together they constitute very weak evidence.) Assembling these observations into a diagram, we have:

Again, this is clearly the diagram of a split-support argument, since two arrows point directly to ①.

It is important not to confuse split-support arguments with complex normal ones. To repeat: In a split-support argument, at least one statement is supported by two or more inferences, while in a normal one each statement is supported by at most one inference. Thus each number in the diagram of a normal argument has at most one arrow pointing to it, while in the diagram of a split-support argument, there is at least one number with two or more arrows pointing to it. Here are some typical diagrams of normal arguments:

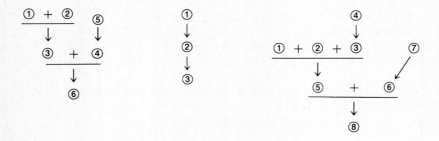

And here are some typical diagrams of split-support arguments:

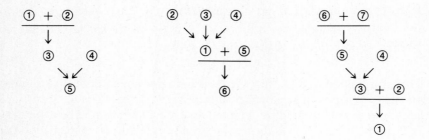

Make sure you can recognize the difference. The distinction between split-support and normal arguments will become useful in Chapter 3, when we begin to look carefully at techniques of evaluation. We'll see there that split-support arguments must be evaluated differently from normal ones.

2.3 REPEATED STATEMENTS

Occasionally statements will be repeated in an argument, often with some slight rewording. Our policy in these cases is to bracket the repeated statement as usual but give it the same number as the original. Here's an example:

It is obvious that ①[anything capable of causing effects must exist.] Now ②[the unconscious is not only capable of producing neuroses;] ③[it is in fact one of the prime sources of human motivation.] ②[It can clearly produce neuroses,] (since) ④[the unconscious roots of neurosis are revealed in psychoanalysis.] And ③[it is responsible for many of our motivations as well,] (for) ⑤[often we act on impulses we cannot fathom.] (This surely proves that) ⑥[an unconscious mental life exists.]

Here we have two repeated statements, ② and ③. Each is reworded in its second occurrence. In accordance with the policy stated above, I've given the same number to each occurrence of the same statement. We'll see as we construct the flow chart that statements ② and ③ are each used in only one inference, so that if we gave each two different numbers we wouldn't know what to do with the second number. Our policy prevents this problem, and if the same statement does happen to crop up in more than one inference, we can just list it more than once in the diagram.

To construct the diagram we must, as always, look to the indicators. The premise indicator "since" shows that ④ supports ②. Similarly, the premise indicator "for" shows that ⑤ supports ③. Statement ⑥ is prefixed by the conclusion indicator "this surely proves that" and is evidently the argument's final conclusion. It remains to determine the role of ①. Statements ② and ③ are each about effects produced by the unconscious, and ① tells us that whatever produces effects exists; so together ①, ②, and ③ imply that the unconscious exists, which is just the final conclusion, ⑥. This makes it pretty clear that the diagram should be as follows:

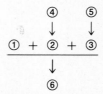

Notice that statements ② and ③ each occur only once in this diagram.

It is also possible in this case to regard statements ② and ③ as each constituting a separate reason, together with ①, for the conclusion, ⑥. This interpretation produces a split-support diagram, as follows:

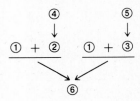

Neither diagram has any outstanding advantages over the other, and both might well be considered correct. It is fairly common in working with arguments to see two or more equally reasonable ways to produce the diagram. In such cases it makes little difference which diagram we choose, though it is good to be aware of all the possibilities. Here I would be inclined to choose the first diagram, simply because it is normal, and it's our policy to regard doubtful cases as normal.

As you have no doubt noticed, we have not been worrying at all about how good our sample arguments are. At this stage, we're only concerned with how to diagram them. If you're interested, you can try to test them yourself by asking the two questions mentioned earlier: (1) Are the basic premises true? (2) How strong is the reasoning? But there is no need to do this just yet. The important thing for now is to develop a very clear perception of argument structure.

2.4   NESTED AND INCOMPLETE STATEMENTS

Let's now take a look at a longer and more complex argument which illustrates a variety of complications involved in bracketing and diagraming:

①[Many of the major foreign-policy problems faced by our nation in the recent past have been the direct result of our support of ruthless and oppressive dictators.] ②[Castro rose to power in Cuba as a result of a popular revolt against the U.S.-backed dictator Batista.] ③[American support of a series of corrupt and autocratic regimes in Saigon culminated in the Vietnam war.] ④[We are continually in trouble in South America and Africa for our support of dictatorships on those continents.] And ⑤[our support of the shah of Iran, an extremely cruel and bloody tyrant, precipitated the Islamic revolution and the consequent taking of American hostages.] (Therefore), ⑥[those who argue that such dictators are valuable allies for America are wrong,] not only (because) of ⑦[the dangerous problems to which support of dictatorial regimes eventually gives rise,] but also (because) ⑧[no nation founded on the principles of freedom and equality, as ⑨[America is,] can ever count dictators as its allies.] (For) ⑩[allies are persons or nations which share fundamental principles,] but ⑪[the principles of freedom and equality are utterly opposed to those of tyranny.]

There are several novelties here. For one thing, two of our bracketed expressions, ⑦ and ⑨, are not complete declarative sentences. Clearly, however, both can be expanded into complete sentences without changing the author's intention, as follows:

⑦   Support of dictatorial regimes eventually gives rise to dangerous problems.

⑨   America is founded on the principles of freedom and equality.

Thus there's no harm in bracketing them off and regarding them as parts of the argument.

Statement ⑨ is also a bit unusual in that it occurs nested inside statement ⑧. This presents no special problems, though, since our brackets clearly show where each statement begins and ends.

The main problem in dealing with an argument like this is just its complexity. Your mind is apt to boggle at first, but take it a bit at a time and you'll see that it all makes sense. Notice first that statement ① makes a claim which is supported by four examples, statements ②–⑤. We noted earlier that examples often function as premises, and that is certainly the case here. Statements ②–⑤ constitute the evidence for ①. The only question now is whether they should be linked or treated as four separate inferences. The answer is contained in statement ① itself, which asserts that *many* foreign-policy problems have been the result of our support of dictators. Now none of these examples by itself could show that *many* problems were so caused. Only a number of examples taken together could establish this. So it is most reasonable to link ②–⑤ as follows:

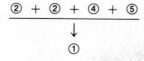

This takes care of a big chunk of the flow chart. Now notice that the next statement, ⑥, is prefixed by the conclusion indicator "therefore." It is obviously a conclusion from what went before. Note, however, that it is followed by two occurrences of the premise indicator "because," one before statement ⑦ and the other before statement ⑧. This suggests that there may be two separate lines of reasoning leading to ⑥ (i.e., that we have a split-support argument). A rereading of the argument confirms this suggestion; there are indeed two lines of reasoning, the first concerned with problems created by support of dictators and the second dealing with some abstract considerations about the nature of allies. The "therefore" preceding ⑥ shows that it is a conclusion from the first of these two lines. But is ⑥ inferred directly from ①—that is, from the part of the argument we have already diagramed—or is it drawn indirectly from ① via ⑦ or ⑧? Well, ⑧ has no connection with ①, so we can rule it out. But ⑦ refers to "dangerous problems," which are also the subject matter of ①. In fact, it's pretty clear that ⑦ is supposed to follow from ①, especially when you rewrite ⑦ as we did above. Statement ⑦, in turn, will lead to ⑥, as is indicated by the "because" preceding ⑦. This completes the first of the two chains of reasoning leading to ⑥:

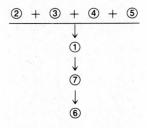

There is another way of diagraming this chain that I would regard as reasonable, too. Statement ⑦ is so similar to statement ① that we might give it the same number. In that case, ⑦ and ① would be collapsed into a single circle, and the diagram would look like this:

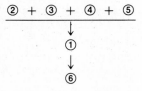

Either way is acceptable. We'll stick with the first, though, since there is some difference between ① and ⑦. Statement ① asserts that support of dictators *has caused* many of our recent foreign-policy problems, while ⑦ seems to go a bit further and claim that *as a general rule* support of dictatorial regimes eventually gives rise to such problems.

Now what about the second chain of reasoning? The "because" in front of ⑧ indicates that ⑧ supports ⑥, and pretty clearly it does so in conjunction with statement ⑨, which is nested inside of it. So we have:

The "for" in front of ⑩ shows that it is a premise supporting ⑧, and the "but" joining ⑪ to ⑩ suggests that ⑩ is to be linked with ⑪ in a single inference. Putting this information together, we can construct the final flow chart of the argument as follows:

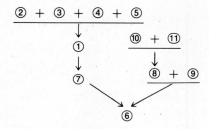

Check over this flow chart, comparing it with the original argument, and reading each arrow as "is intended as evidence for" to see that it is correct.

2.5   IRRELEVANT STATEMENTS

Sometimes argumentative writing is interspersed with statements which make no logical contribution. We may bracket and number such statements, but in constructing the diagram, we'll leave them out. Here's a typical example:

①[American military strength is the only way to end the violence and terrorism which plague underdeveloped nations.] ②[We may hope that education will make people more civilized.] ③[We may hope that eradication of poverty will make them less desperate.] But ④[so long as we remain weak, terrorists will perceive an opportunity,] and ⑤[they will grasp at any opportunity available to kill and maim for their fanatical causes.]

Statements ② and ③ mention hopes of dealing with terrorist violence apart from military strength. But these are simply mentioned and dismissed; no conclusions are drawn from them. Their role is rhetorical rather than logical. They serve as a foil for the real premises of the argument, statements ④ and ⑤. We should therefore leave them out and draw the diagram as follows:

Compare this diagram with the argument to see that we have accurately characterized what is essential in the author's reasoning. Whenever you find statements in an argument which are not essential to the reasoning, feel free to leave them out, as I did here.

2.6   PREMISES USED IN MORE THAN ONE INFERENCE

Another peculiar twist which you will see occasionally is the use of a single premise in more than one inference. This is not the same thing as repeating a premise in stating the argument, which we discussed in Section 2.3. Though premises ② and ③ of the example in Section 2.3 were mentioned more than once, each was used in only one inference. In the sorts of cases we're now discussing, a premise may be mentioned only once in the argument but it functions in more than one inference. This occurred with premise ① in the split-support version of the argument of Section 2.3. Here is perhaps a clearer example:

(Because)   ①[the UFO was seen straight overhead at Morristown and simultaneously at 45° above the horizon in Jonesville 50 miles away,] (we can deduce that)   ②[its altitude was approximately 50 miles.] (So)   ③[it was not an aircraft,]   (for)   ④[no aircraft can reach such altitudes.] Moreover, ⑤[it was not a cloud,]   (since)   ⑥[the atmosphere at 50 miles is too thin to support cloud formation.] Finally, ⑦[it could not have been a satellite, planet, or star,]   (because)   ⑧[all such objects are more distant than 50 miles.] But ⑨[if it was not any of these things, then what, besides an extraterrestrial vehicle, could it have been?]   (We can only conclude that)   ⑩[it was indeed a vehicle piloted by alien visitors.]

Before we diagram this argument, we should note that ⑨ is a question and hence technically not a part of the argument. Nevertheless, it does suggest the following conditional statement:

If it was not any of these things, then it was an extraterrestrial vehicle.

This statement makes good sense in the context of the argument and does not seem to violate the author's intention, so we will treat ⑨ as if this were what it said.

The trick in diagraming the argument is to see that statement ②, a nonbasic premise, is used in conjunction with each of ④, ⑥, and ⑧ to infer the conclusions ③, ⑤, and ⑦, respectively. Each time ② occurs, we must reproduce the argument leading to it, so that ①, which supports ②, will also occur three times. The diagram is:

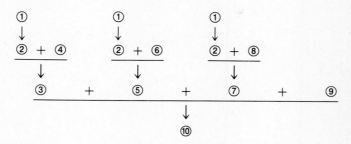

Once again, you should compare this diagram with the argument to see that it is correct.

2.7   MULTIPLE CONCLUSIONS

Another diagraming problem which arises from time to time involves passages of reasoning with more than one final conclusion. Such passages cannot be regarded as single arguments, since an argument by definition has only one final conclusion. That leaves only two options: either we merge the multiple conclusions into a single statement, or we keep them distinct and treat the passage as consisting of two or more arguments. If the passage is short, the latter strategy is probably easiest. Here's an example:

①[The suspect must have been at the bowling alley at the time of the robbery,]   (since)   ②[several witnesses saw him there.]   (So)   ③[he certainly was not at the liquor store.] And ④[he couldn't have been at home, either.]

Probably the simplest way to deal with this passage is to regard it as two separate arguments, as follows:

The thing to avoid is to treat the passage as a single argument with a multiple conclusion, like this:

or perhaps like this:

Both diagrams above are wrong. An arrow should never point to a plus sign, nor should two arrows ever emerge from the same number. Not only does this violate the definition of "argument," but also, if we allowed such diagrams, the evaluation procedures to be introduced in Chapter 3 would have to be extensively complicated to allow for them. Banning them now prevents unnecessary trouble later on.

There is, as I suggested, another way to deal with multiple conclusions; we can combine them into a single statement. We could regard statements ③ and ④, for example, as the single statement:

③ He was neither in the liquor store nor at home.

The diagram would then be simply:

This requires some rewriting, but it does not seriously alter the intended meaning. Also, since it results in an acceptable diagram, there is no good reason to regard it as wrong. Ultimately, then, it makes little difference whether we combine multiple conclusions into a single statement or split the passages in which they occur into several arguments. But we should avoid regarding them as single arguments with multiple conclusions.

2.8 OBSCURE ARGUMENTS

Arguments in real life are seldom as simple as examples in logic texts. Typically, real-life arguments contain one or more of the sources of confusion we have discussed already, and others as well. Don't get discouraged if you can't run out right now, buy a newspaper, and diagram the day's editorial. Accurate diagraming takes practice and perseverance. It is, in fact, nothing less than mind reading—that is, figuring out the structure of another person's thought. Of course, nothing psychic is involved. We simply use the evidence present on a printed page or in the spoken word to infer what someone had in mind. But it is not a simple mechanical process either. It requires creativity and intelligence.

Before leaving the topic of diagraming, let's take a look at a difficult and obscure argument. It is from the book *Being and Nothingness* by the French existentialist philosopher Jean-Paul Sartre:

①[. . . the lover can not be satisfied with that superior form of freedom which is a free and voluntary engagement.] ②[Who would be content with a love given as pure loyalty to a sworn oath?] ③[Who would be satisfied with the words, "I love you because I have freely engaged myself to love you and because I do not wish to go back on my word."]

(Thus) ④[the lover demands a pledge,] yet ⑤[is irritated by a pledge.] ⑥[He wants to be loved by a freedom] but ⑦[demands that this freedom as freedom should no longer be free.] ⑧[He wishes that the Other's freedom should determine itself to become love—and this not only at the beginning of the affair but at each instant—] and ⑨[at the same time he wants this freedom to be captured *by itself*, to turn back upon itself, as in madness, as in a dream, so as to will its own captivity.] ⑩[This captivity must be a resignation that is both free and yet chained in our hands.] ⑪[In love it is not a determinism of the passions which we desire in the Other nor a freedom beyond reach; it is a freedom which *plays the role of* a determinism of the passions and which is caught in its own role.]

When we're faced with a difficult passage like this, often the best strategy is to first locate the final conclusion, then diagram any inferences which seem obvious, and finally put the pieces together as if they were a jigsaw puzzle. Read through this example again and see if you can spot the conclusion. If you do this carefully, I think you'll see that everything else in the passage functions either directly or indirectly as evidence for ① . Statement ①, then, is the final conclusion. Its number will go at the bottom of the diagram.

What other clues do we have to the argument's structure? Well, there's the conclusion indicator "thus" prefixed to statement ④. Normally this would indicate that ④ follows from previously stated premises. But there are some oddities here. First of all notice that ④ and ⑤ were originally a single sentence, which I broke up, leaving ⑤ as a mere fragment. Why? Well, for one thing, it doesn't do any harm, since ⑤ is easily regarded as the complete statement:

The lover is irritated by a pledge.

And Sartre clearly intends to assert both ④ and ⑤, so that breaking them up does not distort his intention. But the main reason is that I was looking ahead, and I noticed that the "thus" could not reasonably be regarded as applying to ④ and ⑤ in combination, but only, surprisingly enough, to ⑤ alone.

To see this, let's start by assuming, contrary to what I said above, that ④ and ⑤ constitute a single statement. We'll call this statement "④⑤." I'll show how this assumption leads to trouble, so that we have to wind up splitting ④⑤ into its components and considering the "thus" as applying to ⑤. So suppose that ④⑤ is a single statement. The "thus" indicates that it follows from what came before. But the sentences immediately preceding ④⑤ are both questions and not genuine premises at all. By now, however, you should know how to handle them. Both do in fact *suggest* premises. We'll regard ② as the premise:

No one would be content with a love given as pure loyalty to a sworn oath.

and ③ as the premise:

No one would be satisfied with the words, "I love you because I have freely engaged myself to love you and because I do not wish to go back on my word."

Each of these premises functions as evidence that the lover is irritated by a pledge, and so each supports ⑤. In fact, each seems to stand alone as evidence for ⑤. But neither is relevant to ④. Neither says or implies that the lover demands a pledge. Hence if we took them as evidence for the combined statement ④⑤ , we could not even begin to account for their relation to the first part, ④, of this statement. So it is best to take each by itself as evidence for ⑤. This means that we have to split ④⑤ up and treat

⑤ as the conclusion from ② and ③, as I said before. Thus part of our diagram will be:

Here is a case where mechanical application of the rules governing conclusion indicators would have led us astray. It shows the importance of thinking as opposed to applying rules.

There is another lesson to be learned here. You probably noticed that despite the fact that ③ contains two occurrences of the word "because," I did not break it up into separate statements. There are two reasons for this. First, "because" functions here as an explanation indicator, not an inference indicator. One person is *explaining* why he or she loves another. But second, and most importantly, "because" occurs inside a quotation, and breaking up the quotation would distort Sartre's thought. When a quotation occurs in an argument, the author is usually saying something about the words quoted. They are not the author's words and do not represent his or her reasoning. By indiscriminately breaking up the quotation, we treat it as if it were just another of the author's statements, and thus we misrepresent what the author is trying to say. Once again we see the importance of thinking about meaning in arriving at the correct bracketing of an argument.

So far, we have seen that ① is the final conclusion of Sartre's argument and that ② and ③ support ⑤. Where do we go from here? Let's turn our attention to ⑪, which consists of two statements joined by a semicolon. Generally, the rule is that we should break such sentences into their components, but I have not done so here. The reason, once again, is that I was looking ahead. Perusal of the argument gives one the impression that its flow is headed toward ⑪. That is, ⑪ seems to summarize and tie up much of what went before. It is therefore a conclusion. Now if we broke it up, we'd have two conclusions, and so since an argument can have only one conclusion, we'd have to split everything above it into two separate arguments. We can avoid this duplication by treating ⑪ as a unit, if no special problems result. I see no special problems, so I'm doing it.

Statement ⑪ seems to function in turn as evidence for ①. If what the lover desires in the Other is a freedom which plays the role of a determinism and is caught in its own role, as ⑪ asserts, then it would seem to follow that the lover would not be satisfied with pure, voluntary freedom, which is just what ① says. So we now have:

⑪
↓
①

We have now constructed the top and bottom of our diagram, but the middle is still missing. The central part of the argument consists of a series of sentences, ④–⑩, all making related points. Perhaps some of these statements are intended as evidence for others. But since there are no further indicator expressions and since the statements themselves are so vague that their interconnections are unclear, it is impossible to say with any certainty what the central structure of Sartre's argument really is. He just doesn't give us enough clues. The best I can do is simply this:

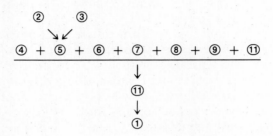

But I'm not at all sure that this accurately reflects Sartre's thinking. Perhaps you could do better.

The point of this example is that it is sometimes impossible to determine an argument's structure accurately. In such cases the fault lies not in logic or in our inability to comprehend, but rather in the author's failure to express his or her thinking clearly. We have some idea of the structure of Sartre's argument, but the details are murky. Good logical writing, by contrast, is as hard and sharp and clear as a diamond.

Exercise 2(a)   For each of the following argument diagrams, determine which numbers represent basic premises, which represent nonbasic premises, and which represent final conclusions. Which are diagrams of split-support arguments, and which are diagrams of normal arguments?

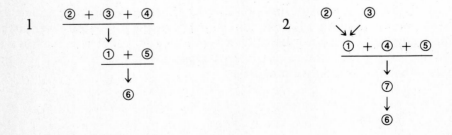

Exercise 2(b) For each of the diagrams above, construct an argument having the form indicated. If the argument is normal, write it in annotated standard form. If not, simply bracket and number each statement. Why is it difficult to represent split-support arguments accurately in annotated standard form?

Exercise 2(c) Some of the following passages contain arguments. Some do not. Copy those that do (either by hand or photostatically), circle all indicator words, bracket and number each statement, and construct the appropriate diagram.

1   Olaf is hairy and ugly as a wart hog. And besides, he never brushes his teeth. So he wouldn't be very pleasant to live with.

2   Since Olaf eats steak bones for dinner, we may infer that he doesn't have to brush his teeth. For the munching of steak bones is bound to have a pronounced cleansing effect.

3   Since steak bones are high in iron and Olaf eats large quantities of steak bones, it follows that Olaf ingests an adequate supply of iron. But anyone whose iron intake is adequate has healthy, deep red blood. So Olaf's blood must be healthy.

4   It is clear that Olaf's blood is healthy, for Ophelia stabbed him in the arm with a fork and it flowed deep red.

5   Olaf smashed Ophelia's favorite pitcher, and then Ophelia retaliated by breaking the horns off his Viking helmet.

6   There is snow in the mountains today. So you'll need a good pair of boots. And you can't expect to see any wildflowers, either.

7   She left because the pay was too low. So she obviously won't go back unless they offer her a raise.

8   If you knew some logic, then you'd see that this argument is valid. But you do know some logic. Therefore, you can see that it's valid.

9   You can see that this argument is valid, too. For anyone who knows some logic, as you do, can see that it is.

10 There are several reasons why I can't go with you tonight. First, I have a midterm tomorrow, and I have to study for it. Second, I can't afford to go. And third, I have to be here in case someone calls about the lost dog.

11 My battery is dead, which is why my car won't start. So I'll need to have it jumped before I can drive anywhere.

12 Only if he'd work blindfolded—and he won't—would there be good reason to believe that Shane is really telepathic. For when he can see the person he's interviewing, there's a good chance that he can pick up ordinary but subtle perceptual clues that help him guess what the person is thinking. So there is no good reason to believe that he has telepathic powers.

13 Solar power is better for the economy because it is labor intensive and therefore likely to stimulate employment. And solar power is much less likely to damage the environment or endanger human life than either nuclear power or coal. Moreover, the sun is a nearly inexhaustible energy source; it will continue to supply light and heat for billions of years to come. Thus solar power is by far the best choice as the major energy source for our nation's future.

14 When selecting tennis balls, you usually get what you pay for. Cheap balls don't last very long. They lose their bounce and cover sooner than quality balls. Any leading brand of top-grade balls will give you more enjoyment and last longer. (Clark and Carole Graebner with Kim Prince, *Mixed Doubles Tennis*)

15 Large diamonds are becoming rarer every day. That's why choosing a larger diamond makes good sense. For size affects value. So you shouldn't be too shy about looking for diamonds that are a bit bigger. (DeBeers diamond ad, *Mademoiselle,* April 1980)

16 No *object* can be in two places at the same time; no object can lie in both two- and three-dimensional space. Yet pictures are both visibly flat and three-dimensional. They are of a certain size, yet also the size of a face or a house or a ship. Pictures are impossible. (R. L. Gregory, *The Intelligent Eye*)

17 Gay people suffer a great deal of discrimination. In the past, gays were burned, hanged, or imprisoned for the crime of loving someone of the same sex. Even today, in what we call our permissive society, a gay person can be fired from a job or arrested for no greater crime than sexual preference. (Charles Silverstein, *A Family Matter: A Parents' Guide to Homosexuality*)

18 In the . . . future . . . people will still believe [in God]. Science will never be enough, because its revelations leave us outside of things, isolated and alone. We need a sense that we are part of something more than we are. Religion, even more than art, works through

emotion to make us whole. Recognizing our membership in mankind, it defines a place for us in the Universe. (Jack Williamson, "The God Instinct," *Science Digest,* summer 1980)

19 What is dreamt within a dream after waking from the 'dream within a dream,' is what the dream-wish seeks to put in place of an obliterated reality. It is safe to suppose, therefore, that what has been 'dreamt' in the dream is a representation of the reality, the true recollection, while the continuation of the dream, on the contrary, merely represents what the dreamer wishes. To include something in a 'dream within a dream' is thus equivalent to wishing that the thing described as a dream had never happened. (Sigmund Freud, *The Interpretation of Dreams*)

20 . . . logic is not much help in dealing with our own and other people's wants, motivations, and feelings. Logic and reasoning generally deal with yesses and noes, black or white, and all or nothing as input to the logical process. But in fact, our wants, motivations, and emotions are usually not apparent to us in terms of all or nothing. Often we have mixed emotions about things and people. Our emotions are felt in different degrees in different times and places. (Manuel J. Smith, *When I Say No, I Feel Guilty*)

21 So long as an opinion is strongly rooted in the feelings, it gains rather than loses in stability by having a preponderating weight of argument against it. For if it were accepted as a result of argument, the refutation of the argument might shake the solidity of the conviction; but when it rests solely on feeling, the worse it fares in argumentative contest, the more persuaded its adherents are that their feeling must have some deeper ground, which the arguments do not reach; and while the feeling remains, it is always throwing up fresh intrenchments of argument to repair any breach made in the old. (John Stuart Mill, "The Subjection of Women")

22 There is a beginning. There is not yet beginning to be a beginning. There is not yet beginning to be a not yet beginning to be a beginning. There is being. There is nonbeing. There is a not yet beginning to be nonbeing. Suddenly there is being and nonbeing. But between this being and nonbeing, I don't really know which is being and which is nonbeing. Now I have just said something. But I don't know whether what I have said has really said something or whether it hasn't said something. (Chuang Tzu)

23 Today, the male/female division of labor, with all its complicated psychological, political, economic and cultural elaborations, is obsolete. It has lost whatever correspondence with objective conditions it may once have had. In America today physical strength and speed of foot are of negligible importance, especially in more highly valued and rewarded work. Women spend only a small part

of their lives bearing children and even for the most part of that period are not incapacitated from tasks that men perform. (Marc Feigen Fasteau, *The Male Machine*)

24 One would know, for example, by examining the deceased, if a particular death was due to snake bite. But one would need to know the mourners in order to predict whether the snake was someone (a witch), or whether sorcery, genies, sprites, or something else had caused the snake to bite. Mystical explanations are not inherent in the symptoms of the misfortune, and there is thus little self-evident connection between a particular type of misfortune and a particular supernatural agency. (William S. Simmons, *Eyes of the Night: Witchcraft among the Senegalese People*)

25 Self-expression is impossible in relation with other men; their self-expression interferes with it. The greatest heights of self-expression—in poetry, music, painting—are achieved by men who are supremely alone. And it is for this reason that the idea of the 'beatific vision' is easier for the artist to grasp than for anyone else. He has only to imagine his moment of 'greatest aloneness' intensified to a point where it would fill up his life and make all other relations impossible or unnecessary. (Colin Wilson, *The Outsider*)

26 Since what we know of the future is made up of purely abstract and logical elements—inferences, guesses, deductions—it cannot be eaten, felt, smelled, seen, heard, or otherwise enjoyed. To pursue it is to pursue a constantly retreating phantom, and the faster you chase it, the faster it runs ahead. This is why all the affairs of civilization are rushed, why hardly anyone enjoys what he has, and is forever seeking more and more. Happiness, then, will consist, not of solid and substantial realities, but of such abstract and superficial things as promises, hopes, and assurances. (Alan Watts, *The Wisdom of Insecurity*)

27 To justify ethically any human activity, we must inquire—"Is this a means to good states of mind?" In the case of art, our answer will be prompt and emphatic. Art is not only a means to good states of mind, but, perhaps, the most direct and potent means that we possess. Nothing is more direct, because nothing affects the mind more immediately; nothing is more potent, because there is no state of mind more excellent or more intense than the state of aesthetic contemplation. This being so, to seek in art a means to anything less than good states of mind, is an act of wrong-headedness . . . .(Clive Bell, *Art*)

28 An object offers as much resistance to the air as the air does to the object. You may see that the beating of its wings against the air supports a heavy eagle in the highest and rarest atmosphere, close

to the sphere of elemental fire. Again you may see the air in motion over the sea, fill the swelling sails and drive heavily laden ships. From these instances, and the reasons given, a man with wings large enough and duly connected might learn to overcome the resistance of air, and by conquering it, succeed in subjugating it and rising above it. (Leonardo da Vinci, *Notebooks*)

3

Evaluating Arguments

Analyzing argument structure is of little intrinsic interest. But it is an essential preliminary to the more useful and engaging work of evaluation. In this chapter we'll begin to consider the question of argument quality in earnest. That question will occupy us for the rest of this book.

3.1 TRUTH OR FALSITY OF BASIC PREMISES

Argument evaluation, as we saw in Chapter 1, involves asking two fundamental questions: (1) Are the basic premises true? (2) How strong is the reasoning? Question (2) will be our main concern here. Answering question (1) is not usually a matter of logic, but of science and common sense. Of course, when we're not sure of the truth or falsity of a basic premise, one way to settle the matter is to provide a further argument to prove the premise. Logic does play a role, then, in evaluating this further argument. But this process of providing back-up arguments cannot go on indefinitely. At some point the reasoning must come to rest on some ultimate set of basic premises. At this point the domain of logic ends; we must thereafter rely on observation, education, and common sense.

Ideally, the basic premises on which an argument rests should be either common knowledge or else readily verifiable by observation. Further argument about their truth is then superfluous. But this ideal is not often achieved in practice. Basic premises may be so dubious and obscure that we won't be able to tell whether they are true. This makes evaluation difficult, but not necessarily hopeless. There are several things to keep in mind.

First, our lack of knowledge about certain assumptions does not mean that the facts themselves are indeterminate. If a pair of dice is rolled inside a sealed box, no one will know whether they show snake-eyes unless the box is opened. But still there is a fact of the matter. Either they do or they don't. So if we were to use the statement "The dice show snake-eyes" as an assumption of an argument, it would either be true or false despite the fact that we wouldn't know which. If the reasoning were deductive and all the basic premises true, then the argument would be sound—whether we knew it or not.

Second, even if we don't *know* whether an assumption is true, often we can make an educated guess. With respect to the concealed dice, it is most unlikely—assuming that the dice are fair—that they show snake-eyes. Not counting odd configurations in which they land on edges or corners, there are 36 ways for a pair of dice to fall. Snake-eyes is only one of them. Accordingly, the probability that the statement "The dice show snake-eyes" is true is very small. We can therefore judge with reasonable assurance that any argument which assumes this statement is unsound. Although we can't be absolutely sure, the chances are that this premise is false.

Finally, even without knowing whether the premises are true or even likely, we can still evaluate an argument's reasoning. For as we saw in Chapter 1, strength of reasoning has nothing to do with actual truth and falsity. Thus, we can obtain accurate estimates of the effectiveness of many arguments, even without knowledge of their premises. If an argument is fallacious, then it's weak no matter what the premises are. In other cases we have to make educated guesses. If an argument is inductive or deductive and the premises, though not known with certainty, seem probable, then we still have good reason to believe the conclusion. However, if the premises seem unlikely, then the argument is poor evidence, even if its reasoning is very strong. In the very worst cases, we won't have the slightest idea whether the premises are true or not. But still we can make some progress by evaluating the reasoning. If it is fallacious, we'll know that the argument is weak; if it is inductive or deductive, then at least we'll know that if we ever discover the premises to be true, then the conclusion will either probably or certainly be true as well. Thus, though uncertainty about premises is troubling, it is not crippling. We'll manage to work around it most of the time.

Moreover, as I mentioned already, our main job is not to worry about premises, but to evaluate reasoning. Logic is primarily the study of ways to answer question (2). Once we possess some initial information in the form of observation, common sense, or basic principles, logic tells what further conclusions can be drawn and with what degree of reliability we can draw them. Verification of this initial information is generally not a matter of logic.

3.2 POSSIBLE WORLDS AND THE TEST FOR VALIDITY

Answering question (2) involves estimating the strength of an argument's reasoning. As we saw in Chapter 1, that means classifying the argument as either deductive, inductive, or fallacious. Our task now is to develop a systematic method for making this classification. To simplify this task, we're going to start by considering only the problem of deciding whether or not an argument is deductive.

One way of defining deductiveness, you will recall, is this:

An argument is deductive if it is impossible for its basic premises to be true and its conclusion false.

We now need to say precisely what this means. When is something impossible? Is it impossible for you to run a three-minute mile? Is it impossible for the earth to repulse the moon, instead of attracting it? Is it impossible for all the residents of the state of Tennessee to suddenly and inexplicably turn a deep shade of blue? In a sense, all of these things are impossible. Yet in another sense they are not. We can imagine all of them happening. Of course, some of them violate the laws of physics and some go beyond all reasonable expectation, but still we can envision them. Who's to say that the laws of physics won't suddenly change? Who's to say that advances in medicine and physiology won't produce human beings who can run three-minute miles? In some sense, these things are indeed possible. There are other situations, however, which we simply cannot envision, no matter how fertile our imaginations are. These situations are absolutely impossible. Try to imagine, for example, a triangle with four sides. You'll find very quickly that the two ideas—triangularity and four-sidedness—are absolutely incompatible. You can't put them together, even in your imagination. Though you can perfectly well conceive or imagine hordes of people turning blue or the moon flying away from the earth, there is no coherent way to conceive or imagine a four-sided triangle. To take another example, try to imagine that all birds (without exception) are red, but that one is colorless; or that either Olaf or Ophelia owns a cat, but that neither of them owns a cat; or that all men are mortal and Socrates is a man, but that Socrates is immortal. In each of these cases there is an absolute inconceivability. These things are not only impossible in a practical or physical sense; they are **logically impossible.** Logical impossibility is absolute inconceivability—the most extreme form of impossibility. Therefore, the strongest reasoning occurs in arguments in which it is logically impossible for the basic premises to be true and the conclusion false. Logical impossibility, then, is the sort of impossibility relevant to our definition of deductiveness because, as I noted in Chapter 1, deduction is the very strongest kind of reasoning. To be precise, then, our definition should read:

> An argument is deductive if it is *logically* impossible for its basic premises to be true and its conclusion false.

Now since deductiveness is defined in terms of logical impossibility and since logical impossibility is the inability to be coherently conceived or imagined, it follows that coherent thought and imagination are central in determining whether or not an argument is deductive. In fact, the test for deductiveness is almost childishly simple: we try to imagine coherently a situation in which the basic premises are true and the conclusion is false. If we succeed, the argument is invalid. If we fail, then probably it is valid.

I say "probably" because it might be that something is coherently conceivable or imaginable but our mental powers are not sharp enough to conceive or imagine it. Four-dimensional objects are, for most of us at least, an example of this sort of thing. But imagination improves with practice. And after having thought through a number of examples, most people can apply the test fairly accurately, especially in practical, everyday cases.

There is another problem, too. You might think that you can coherently imagine something which in fact is not coherently imaginable. A subtle and unnoticed incoherence might lie concealed in the vagueness or ambiguity of your thought. It is impossible, for example, to coherently imagine a person who is taller than absolutely everyone, but you might not realize this at once. Clearly, however, such a person would have to be taller than him- or herself, and that is not coherently imaginable. (We can, of course, coherently imagine someone who is taller than everyone *else.*) Similarly, it is impossible to coherently imagine a plane (i.e., Euclidean) triangle whose interior angles do not add up to 180°. But if you allow your imagination a certain sloppiness and vagueness, you might think you could imagine it. Pinpointing such subtle incoherencies is sometimes tricky. To guard against them, it is important to imagine each possibility you consider as thoroughly and clearly as you can.

To summarize, then: In testing an argument for validity, what you're trying to do is to imagine coherently a situation in which the premises are true and the conclusion is false. If you succeed, then the inference is invalid. If not, it's probably valid. Let's consider a simple example:

Some reptiles are water-dwelling creatures.
Some water-dwelling creatures eat aquatic plants.
∴ Some reptiles eat aquatic plants.

All the statements in this inference happen to be true. (Turtles are water-dwelling reptiles which eat aquatic plants.) But that shows nothing about its validity, and we want to know whether the inference is valid. To find out, we apply the test. Can we coherently conceive or imagine a situation in which the premises are true and the conclusion false? This is not difficult. Just think, for example, of a universe in which the only water-dwelling reptiles are crocodiles, and they eat only fish, but the fish themselves live in the water and eat aquatic plants. In this universe the premises would both be true, but the conclusion would be false. So we know that the argument is invalid, even though all the statements it contains are actually true.

Universes which, like that of the previous example, are coherently conceivable or imaginable, are called **logically possible worlds,** or just **possible worlds** for short. The test for deductiveness is in effect an imaginative search for a possible world in which the basic premises are true and the conclusion is false. If such a world is found, the argument is invalid. If not, it's probably valid.

To demonstrate to others that an argument is invalid, we simply describe a possible world in which the basic premises are true and the conclusion is false, as I did in this example. Such a description is called a **counterexample.** Typically, each invalid argument has many associated counterexamples. Can you think of some others for the argument just discussed?

Now let's consider a different sort of inference:

The Easter Bunny exists.
∴ Something exists.

Here we have a false premise and a true conclusion. But once again this does not tell us whether or not the argument is valid, since the only combination of truth and falsity ruled out in a valid argument is all true assumptions and a false conclusion. So again we need to apply the test. Can we imagine a possible world in which it is true that the Easter Bunny exists and false that something exists? Obviously not! If the Easter Bunny exists, then something (namely, the Easter Bunny) exists. We cannot by the furthest stretch of the imagination dream up a counterexample here. So the argument is valid.

Let's try one more simple example:

All intelligent life forms perish quickly in the absence of an atmosphere.

There is no atmosphere in interstellar space, unless one is transported there by artificial means.

∴ No intelligent life forms can exist for long in interstellar space, unless protected by an artificially transported atmosphere.

Again, we test for validity by trying to imagine a world in which the premises are true and the conclusion is false. And in this example, too, we fail. In any situation in which the premises are true, it is inconceivable that the conclusion will simultaneously be false. The argument is valid.

Notice that it would be a misunderstanding here to object, "But I can imagine a possible world in which intelligent life evolves in such a way that it can survive unaided in interstellar space." Certainly we can imagine such a world. But all that shows is that it is logically possible for the first premise to be false. It tells us nothing about the validity of the argument, for it is not a description of a possible world in which the argument's premises are true and its conclusion false. For almost any argument, there are many possible worlds in which the premises are true and many in which some or all of them are false. But the only ones that tell us anything about validity are the worlds in which the basic premises are all true and the conclusion is false. If there are no such worlds, the argument is valid. If there are some, it is invalid. (If any of this puzzles you, review the discussion of this section until it becomes clear; from now on, everything we do will be based on it.)

Is the argument sound? I don't know. I'm pretty sure the second premise is true, but I doubt that anyone—on earth, at least—knows whether the first is. The only intelligent life forms we're acquainted with are those on earth. It may be that there are others which we don't know about whose physiology is completely different from ours. This, in effect, is what the objector in the last paragraph was pointing out. The argument is valid, but we can't tell whether it is sound, because we don't know whether the first premise is true. Logic alone can form no judgment here. We must await the verdict of scientific observation.

By now you may be wondering how a supposedly rigorous discipline like logic can make use of anything as subjective and ethereal as imagination. How can imaginative tests possibly yield objective results? Won't everyone disagree? Indeed, people do disagree—especially at first, when they are not used to exercising their imaginations. But with more experience opinion converges, and a consensus develops on most examples. People who initially can't grasp certain counterexamples begin to understand them. Certain patterns of reasoning which are always invulnerable to counterexamples begin to appear. After a lot of study and thought, it eventually becomes clear how certain words or expressions in these patterns determine validity or invalidity. This is the point at which formal logic begins and rigorous, mathematically precise treatment of inferences becomes possible. We'll arrive at this point in Chapter 10.

But logicians have achieved such rigor only for a fraction of the kinds of arguments encountered in daily life. So in practice the imaginative test is often our only recourse. It is not as precise as we'd like, but with experienced practitioners it does yield objective and fairly accurate results. We know this, because many of these results have been verified by formal techniques as logic has progressed.

This section has provided our first glimpse of the conceptual foundations of logic. Logic is the study of arguments and, more particularly, of the quality of their reasoning. Quality of reasoning, as we have begun to see, is circumscribed by what is logically possible. And what is logically possible is what can be coherently conceived or imagined. So in a sense logic is the study of the breadth and limits of coherent thought. But the realm of coherent thought can in turn be understood as the realm of logically possible worlds. And so we may understand logic—or at least a major part of it—as a study of logically possible worlds.

Exercise 3.2(a)   For each of the descriptions listed below, tell whether the situation described is logically possible or logically impossible.

1   Olaf leaps into the air. But instead of coming down, he floats momentarily and then begins to fly at will.
2   A drawer contains two separate pairs of socks. But there are only three socks in the drawer.
3   A starship travels faster than light.
4   Suddenly, in what had been empty space, an entire planet comes into being.
5   Ophelia is both taller and shorter than 5 feet, at the same time and measured in the same way.
6   All pizza is poisonous.
7   Olive has green eyes. Ophelia's eyes are not, never have been, and never will be green. Olive and Ophelia are the same person.
8    $2 + 2 = 27$
9   You put your hand in a fire, but it's not hot.
10   All cats torture mice, and Fuzzball is a cat. But Fuzzball does not torture mice.

Exercise 3.2(b) For each argument below, decide whether it is valid or invalid. If it is invalid, give a counterexample.

1   Ophelia is running swiftly.
    ∴ Ophelia is running.

2   All spiders have six legs.
    All six-legged creatures are insects.
    ∴ All spiders are insects.

3   Some elements are metals.
    Some metals are alloys.
    ∴ Some elements are alloys.

4   I dropped a stone.
    ∴ It fell to the ground.

5   Everything is conscious.
    I have a wart on my left big toe.
    ∴ The wart on my left big toe is conscious.

6   Neither Olaf nor Ophelia ever smoke.
    Someone is smoking in my basement.
    ∴ There is someone in my basement other than Olaf and Ophelia.

7   My car won't start.
    ∴ I can't go to work.

8   Fuzzball has an evil temperament.
    Fuzzball is a cat.
    ∴ All cats have evil temperaments.

9   Olaf usually sings as he wakes up.
    Olaf is waking up.
    ∴ Olaf is singing.

10 There are more people than hairs on any one person's head.
    ∴ Two people have the same number of hairs on their heads.

3.3   PROBABILITY AND THE TEST FOR INDUCTIVENESS

So far we've used our imaginative test only to decide between validity and invalidity. But the fact that an argument is invalid does not mean that we should reject it without further thought. There are two kinds of invalid arguments—fallacious and inductive. These stand on a continuum. At one end of this continuum are fallacies, which provide either no evidence or weak evidence for their conclusions. As we move toward the other end of the continuum, we encounter weak inductive arguments and then inductive arguments of increasingly greater strength. The very best inductive arguments are nearly as reliable as deductive ones. If their premises are true, their conclusions are almost certainly true.

Therefore we need a further test to distinguish inductive arguments from fallacies and to rank arguments within each classification. This test will be a simple generalization of the test for validity. Recall that in an inductive argument, the probability of the conclusion, given that the premises are true, is greater than 50 percent. In a fallacy it is 50 percent or less. Now probability depends on what is possible. One thing will be more probable than another if there are more possible ways for it to happen. Hence one way to estimate the probability of a conclusion, given a set of premises, is to determine from among all the possible ways in which these premises could be true the percentage of those in which the conclusion is true. Or to put it in the terminology of the last section, the probability of a conclusion, given a set of premises, is the percentage of possible worlds in which the conclusion is true among worlds in which all the premises are true. That is, an inductive argument is an argument whose conclusion is true in more than 50 percent of the logically possible worlds in which its premises are true. A fallacy is an argument whose conclusion is true in 50 percent or fewer. This will be the basis for our imaginative test of probability.

Unfortunately, there are some nasty problems with this notion of a percentage of possible worlds. The number of possible worlds in which a set of premises is true is generally infinite; and there is no single, precise idea of percentage in dealing with infinity. Logicians and mathematicians have worked for many years to clarify this idea, but many unsolved problems remain. We're going to sidestep these problems, since we're concerned with practical, informal logic. It would not serve our purposes to dwell on them, so we'll forge ahead, making do with a rough, intuitive idea of percentage. To see how this idea works in a very clear case, consider the fact that there are infinitely many natural numbers (i.e., positive whole numbers), and yet we can say, quite intelligibly, that precisely 10 percent of them (just the ones ending in 0) are evenly divisible by 10.

But we must be careful here. There is another sense in which there are just as many natural numbers divisible by 10 as not divisible by 10, since there are infinitely many of both. Looking at things this way, the proportion seems to be 50/50. Why this discrepancy? The difference is that in the first case we were looking at the **frequency of occurrence** of numbers divisible by 10 among the natural numbers in general. This frequency is 10 percent. If we run through the natural numbers in their usual order starting with 1, every tenth number will be divisible by 10. In the second case, we're looking at two complete infinite collections (the set of numbers divisible by 10 and the set of numbers not divisible by 10) and comparing them as if all the members of both were spread out before us at once. It's as if we were God, able to view all the numbers simultaneously in their magnificent infinitude.

From this point of view there is no difference in size; both collections are infinite.[1]

The appropriate viewpoint for evaluating reasoning is the first one. When we ask whether a statement is true in most of a certain set of possible worlds, we must imagine ourselves "running through" these worlds and estimating the frequency with which we encounter worlds in which the statement is true. Taking the "God's eye" view and noting that there are infinitely many worlds in which the statement is true and infinitely many in which it is false will not help in estimating probabilities. (Is there a theological lesson in this?)

Possible worlds, of course, are not lined up in a standard order like the numbers are. So there is no single natural way to "run through" them in imagination. But experience shows that for a given argument, virtually every reasonably natural way to do it yields roughly the same estimation of frequency. (You can, of course, "run through" the worlds in awkward and unnatural orders, directing your attention preferentially to some types and ignoring others, but this sort of bias is to be avoided. You should let your imagination wander through the various possibilities freely and at random.)

The test for inductiveness, then, is performed as follows. Consider the possible worlds in which the premises are all true. Be creative here; remember that what is logically possible far exceeds the range of what is practically or even physically possible, so that the range of worlds you survey will be vast and fantastic. Now imagine yourself running through these worlds, and estimate the frequency of those in which the conclusion is true. If the conclusion is true in most of them (where "most" is understood in the frequency sense), then the argument is inductive. If not, it's fallacious.

This test, used in conjunction with the test for validity, enables us to estimate the strength of any inference. Let's see how these tests work in application to a trio of arguments we've met earlier:

1   All elves drink stout.
     Olaf is an elf.
     ∴ Olaf drinks stout.

2   95 percent of elves drink stout.
     Olaf is an elf.
     ∴ Olaf drinks stout.

3   A few elves drink stout.
     Olaf is an elf.
     ∴ Olaf drinks stout.

---

[1]The way I've put this may puzzle you if you are aware that infinity comes in different "sizes" (i.e., cardinalities). But this curious fact is irrelevant here, since the set of natural numbers and the set of natural numbers divisible by 10 are equal in cardinality.

Consider the first argument. Applying the test for validity, we see at once that we cannot imagine a world in which the premises are true and the conclusion is false. No counterexample exists. This argument is valid. And of course, since it is valid, there is no need to apply the second test.

The second argument, however, fails the test for validity. We can imagine a world in which 95 percent of elves drink stout and Olaf is an elf but it is false that Olaf drinks stout. Olaf, in other words, is among the 5 percent of elves who shun that bitter brew. Having found a counterexample, we now apply the second test. Consider the possible worlds in which the premises are true. These are all the coherently imaginable worlds in which 95 percent of elves drink stout and Olaf is an elf. In some of these worlds, as we saw just now, Olaf will be among the 5 percent who don't drink stout (such worlds provide our counterexamples), and in some he will be among the 95 percent who do. But it is obvious that surveying at random the possible worlds in which these premises are true, we will more frequently encounter worlds in which the conclusion is true than in which it is false. This is because there are simply more ways for Olaf to be among the 95 percent of stout drinkers than among the 5 percent of abstainers. And each of these ways things could be is a possible world. In fact, we'd expect to find that about 95 percent of the worlds in which the premises are true are worlds in which the conclusion is also true. Thus the argument is inductive. Though invalid, it is still rational.

Finally, of course, it is ridiculously easy to dream up a counterexample to the third argument. (Do it yourself!) So this argument fails the first test. But it also fails the second. Let's check this out. Consider the possible worlds in which the premises are true. These will be worlds in which Olaf is an elf and a few elves drink stout. Among these will be some situations in which Olaf drinks stout and some in which he does not. Which are more frequent? Well, let's take a closer look. The premises tell us nothing about how many elves there are, so we can't make any special assumptions about this. There might be only three. But there might be 12 billion. Indeed, there could be any number at all. But if just a few elves drink stout and we're considering situations in which there could be any number of elves, then surely there are more possible situations in which Olaf the elf doesn't drink stout than in which he does. We conclude, then, that the argument is fallacious.

I think it's best when you're starting out to apply the two tests in sequence like this—first the test for validity and then the test for inductiveness. As you gain practice, you'll start taking shortcuts and doing certain things automatically. Actually, the two tests are so closely related that we could combine them into a single test. Simply examine the range of possible worlds in which the premises are true. If the conclusion is true in all of them, then the argument is valid. If it is true in most, then the argument is inductive. And if it is not true in a majority, the argument is fallacious.

(As usual, "most" and "majority" are to be understood in the frequency sense here.)

You should be aware that although our test for validity is fairly conventional, there is no consensus on methods for determining the probability of a conclusion, given a set of premises. Many logicians would reject the notion of percentages of possible worlds as theoretically indefensible. But there is little agreement on alternatives. Some logicians even argue that the very idea of the probability of a conclusion, given certain premises, is incoherent. I'll discuss their reasons in the Appendix.

Yet in spite of these doubts, we all seem to have a rough understanding of this kind of probability, and we can't avoid dealing with it if we wish to evaluate nondeductive arguments. Moreover, though the theoretical foundations of the possible-worlds test remain insecure, it is, as you will see, a convenient tool for organizing our understanding and systematizing argument evaluation. That is why I have adopted it in this book, although it belongs to one of the most hotly contested and highly controversial areas of modern logic.

Exercise 3.3   Using the tests discussed in the last two sections, decide for each of the arguments below whether it is deductive, inductive, or fallacious. If it is invalid, state a counterexample.

1   The moon is made of green cheese.
    ∴ It's edible.

2   Women usually live longer than men.
    Ophelia is a woman.
    Olaf is a man.
    ∴ Ophelia will live longer than Olaf.

3   This book has fewer than 400 pages.
    ∴ This book does not have 517 pages.

4   Olaf does not believe that the Yankees won the 1948 World Series.
    ∴ Olaf believes that the Yankees did not win the 1948 World Series.

5   Oscar is an old man.
    Very few old folks fly hang gliders.
    ∴ Oscar does not fly hang gliders.

6   It never rains in California.
    Santa Barbara is in California.
    ∴ It never rains in Santa Barbara.

7   Olaf is taller than Olive.
    Olive is taller than Ophelia.

Ophelia is taller than Oscar.
∴ Olaf is taller than Oscar.

8   Olive is Olaf and Ophelia's daughter.
∴ Olaf and Ophelia are Olive's parents.

9   Some elves are wicked.
All wicked things are foolish.
∴ Some elves are foolish.

10   Some senators are Democrats.
No Democrats are conservative.
∴ No senators are conservative.

11   A single die has six faces, labeled one through six.
If the die is tossed, exactly one face will land up.
Each face has an equal chance of landing up.
The die is being tossed.
∴ The face showing one will not land up.

12   Nearly all elves' names begin with "O."
Nearly all creatures whose names begin with "O" are objection-
ably odd.
∴ Some elves are objectionably odd.

3.4   EVALUATING THE REASONING
OF SIMPLE ARGUMENTS

Probably the most difficult thing to keep in mind when you first encounter
possible worlds is their diversity. Failure to imagine certain possibilities
frequently leads to overestimation of inferences. Consider, for example, the
following argument:

①[The room must have been colder than 32°F.] (For)
②[the water in the sink was frozen.]

This is a simple, one-premise inference:

Most people are initially inclined to call this inference inductive, perhaps
even deductive. And this inclination may persist even upon application of
the evaluative tests. "Surely," we may think, "among imaginable worlds in
which the water was frozen, the majority are worlds in which the room was
colder than 32°." But such thinking is the product of an unexercised imagination.

Consider carefully the worlds in which the premise is true. Certain counterexamples appear at once. Perhaps the water in the sink is ice, dumped there just a moment ago. Perhaps the sink has a built-in refrigeration unit. Perhaps the sink is next to an open window and therefore colder than the rest of the room. Or perhaps it has just been brought in from outdoors, where it accumulated the ice. In all these situations, the premise could be true and the conclusion false. But this is only the beginning. Nothing compels us to imagine the freezing point of water to be 32°. We can coherently imagine it to be anything we like. In some possible worlds water freezes at 32 thousand degrees—in some at 32 million! These worlds and countless others like them provide a host of additional counterexamples. So there are vastly many ways in which the premise could be true and the conclusion false. These certainly are at least as frequent as the possible worlds in which both the premise and conclusion are true. So contrary to appearances, this inference is fallacious.

But isn't all this just nit picking? If we went into a room and saw frozen water in the sink, we'd ordinarily conclude that the room was colder than 32°, and we'd probably be right. Why make the test of probability so whimsical and extreme?

The point is to sharpen awareness of the background knowledge we ordinarily bring to an argument. The reason this inference "feels" rational is that we unconsciously add a number of assumptions that are not actually given. We implicitly assume, for example, that water freezes only at or below 32° and that the temperature in the room was the same as the temperature of the sink. But this was not stated. Engaging the full force of imagination in the search for counterexamples brings these unconscious assumptions to light, thus intensifying critical awareness.

We'll see how to deal with these implicit assumptions in Chapter 4. But for now our goal is to avoid making them. We're going to try to assume nothing more than is given and to evaluate the argument accordingly. Ultimately this will help us appreciate the extent of what is tacitly assumed in ordinary reasoning.

Despite its tinge of whimsy, the process of imagining possible worlds is not as unfamiliar as it might seem. Every internally coherent work of fiction represents a possible world or at least some portion of one. When you are faced with a major decision and deliberate on its possible outcomes, you are also imagining possible worlds. If, for example, you are thinking about getting married, you will probably try to imagine what your life will be like if you do. You may construct very elaborate fantasies. These possible futures which you imagine are portions of possible worlds. They are especially interesting worlds, because they contain you. In general, the possible worlds you inhabit comprise the various courses your life could take.

Usually the worlds we imagine in decision making or fiction are not too different from the actual world. They may be romanticized or exaggerated, but they generally take the real world as a model. Logic requires a more radical departure from actuality. We must imagine worlds which violate the laws of physics, in which the superhuman and impractical is commonplace, and in which not only the future but also the past and the present bear no resemblance to what really happens.

The point of this, as we saw a moment ago, is to increase critical awareness. To understand an argument fully, we need to be aware of all its assumptions, both explicit and implicit, and only consideration of the wildest possibilities enables us to attain this awareness. But what do these flights of fancy have to do with reality? How can imagination have any relevance to what is actual?

The answer is quite simple. Our universe, the actual world, is also a possible world. What occurs in it can be coherently conceived or imagined. Of course, we do not always succeed in conceiving or imagining it coherently, but in principle it can be so conceived or imagined. (This is a fundamental presupposition of all rational knowledge. If it were false, coherent, systematic knowledge of our universe would be a forlorn hope.) Now we don't know everything about our world, so in a sense we don't know exactly which possible world it is. We don't know, for example, if it's one of the worlds in which intelligent life exists elsewhere than on earth. But suppose that we do know that the premises of a certain argument are true—that is, true in the actual world. If the argument is rational, then among the possible worlds in which the premises are true, all or most are worlds in which the conclusion is true. Thus we can see that our world is, or is likely to be, a world in which the conclusion is true. It all comes back to the actual world in the end.

One common source of confusion in thinking about possible worlds is that in other possible worlds words may have different meanings than they do in the actual world. To see how this causes trouble, suppose that someone suggests the following faulty, but rather ingenious "counterexample" to the Easter Bunny argument of Section 3.2:

> Imagine a world in which the word "something" means "Santa Claus," and in which the Easter Bunny, but not Santa Claus exists. In this world the premise "The Easter Bunny exists" is true, but the conclusion "Something exists" is false. Therefore the inference is invalid.

The mistake here is a failure to see that in arguing and in describing other possible worlds we always do so in ordinary English. So when we ask if the sentence "Something exists" is true in the world of this example, we are asking about this statement with its common English meaning. And of course, in that world it is true, not false, with its English meaning, regardless of what it means to the world's inhabitants. So this is not a legitimate counterexample. The Easter Bunny argument is in fact perfectly valid, and so, incidentally, is a proper translation of it into any other language. But if we confuse meanings by shifting languages, we'll lose sight of this fact and become hopelessly muddled.

By the way, one important consequence of the fact that we always use English to describe possible worlds is that our definitions hold in every possible world. We define "logic," for example, as the study of arguments. Thus, because we always employ this definition, no matter what world we are describing, it is true in all possible worlds that logic is the study of arguments. I'll discuss this matter in more detail in Section 8.7.

Just to make sure you've got the hang of it, let's apply the possible-worlds tests to a few more examples. Here's a kind of inference that is typically made in public-opinion polls:

> In a survey of 1000 randomly selected Americans, 33 percent considered the economy the biggest current political issue.
>
> ∴ About 33 percent of Americans consider the economy to be the biggest current political issue.

This is certainly not deductive. We can imagine a situation in which out of millions of Americans only 330 feel that the economy is the major issue and in which by sheer chance the pollsters talked to all 330. Here the premise is true and the conclusion false. But if we run through the worlds in which the premise is true in a fair and natural way, we'll more frequently encounter worlds in which the conclusion is true than worlds in which it is false. For of all the 1000-member random samples which the pollsters might pick, most would be fairly representative. Only a minority—like the sample in which they get all 330 who feel that the economy is the major issue out of millions who don't—would be radically unrepresentative. And only if they drew a radically unrepresentative sample would the conclusion be false, for it contains the word "about." Hence there are more possible ways for the conclusion to be true, given the premise, than for it to be false. The inference is inductive. (For a more detailed discussion of this sort of inference, see Section 6.4.)

Our imaginative tests, used properly, are very sensitive detectors of fallacy, as the next two examples illustrate. Here's the first:

> Mother told me that ghosts exist.
>
> ∴ They really do.

This one is fairly obvious. It's not deductive, because we can readily imagine worlds in which there are no ghosts but in which Mother is either mistaken or lying about this fact. And it's not inductive, either. Consider the range of possible worlds in which the premise is true. These include worlds in which Mother always tells the truth, worlds in which she is a pathological liar, and worlds in which her reliability is somewhere in between. Since the argument's premise contains no information about Mother's reliability, the worlds in which it is true and Mother is right are certainly no more frequent than the worlds in which it is true and Mother is wrong. So among the worlds in which the premises are true, those in which the conclusion is also true are not a majority. Thus the argument is fallacious. This type of fallacy is rather common, so much so that it has been given a special name: **the fallacy of appeal to authority.** I'll have more to say about it in Section 7.1.

Not all fallacious arguments are as simple and obvious as this one. Fallacies are disconcertingly common in much of our thinking and writing, and often they escape our attention. Even the most profound thinkers are not immune to bad reasoning, as is illustrated by this excerpt from the essay *A Confession*, by the great Russian writer Leo Tolstoy:

①[Whatever faith may be and whatever answers it may give, and to whomsoever it gives them, every such answer gives to the finite existence of man an infinite meaning, a meaning not destroyed by sufferings, deprivations, or death.] (This means that) ②[only in faith can we find for life a meaning and a possibility.]

This argument is a simple, single-premise inference:

But despite its impressive phrasing, it is fallacious. Before we perform our tests to see this, let's make sure we understand what Tolstoy is saying. The premise contains a long preamble of "whatever"s. They serve to indicate that Tolstoy wishes his point to be understood in an unqualified fashion but do not add anything substantial to the argument. Reduced to its bare bones, the argument is this:

Faith gives life an infinite, indestructible meaning.

∴ Only faith gives life a meaning.

(Check Tolstoy's wording to see that I haven't altered anything essential.) Now let's perform our tests. Is there a possible world in which the premise is true and the conclusion is false? Certainly. We can easily imagine that faith gives life an infinite and indestructible meaning, but that life's meaning can come from other sources as well—love, work, the grace of God, mystical union with the cosmos, sheer human determination, or any of a number of other possibilities. Under these circumstances the premise would be true, but the conclusion that *only* faith gives life meaning would be false. So the argument is not deductive.

And it's not inductive either. Consider the range of possible worlds in which the premise is true. In some of these worlds, faith will be the only source of meaning. But there are so many other conceivable sources that surely in the majority of these worlds there are several sources of meaning. In such worlds the conclusion is false. So the argument fails the test. It is quite clearly fallacious.

Exercise 3.4   For each of the following arguments:

A   Write the argument on a separate sheet of paper or copy it photo-statically.

B   Circle all inference indicators.

C   Bracket and number each statement.

D   Diagram the argument.

E   Use the tests for validity and inductiveness to evaluate the reasoning, and record your evaluation by placing either a "D," an "I," or an "F" next to the arrow representing the inference, to indicate whether the inference is deductive, inductive, or fallacious.

1   All pizza eaters are cowards, and some cowards drink beer. Therefore, all pizza eaters drink beer.

2   On the average, one out of every 2,000,000,000 people is killed by a falling meteor. I am a person. Therefore, I will not be killed by a falling meteor.

3   Grandma was either a mobster or a sweet old lady. But she was not a sweet old lady. Therefore, she was a mobster.

4   Olaf jumped out of a jet fighter at 30,000 feet yesterday. He had no parachute. Therefore, Olaf is dead.

5   If you eat an ox you will die. If you die you won't be able to disco anymore. Therefore, if you eat an ox you won't be able to disco anymore.

6   It is clear that those who hold that mathematical truths are not self-evident are wrong, for they are quibblers who will argue with any assertion, whether reasonable or not.

7   If we had received messages from deep space, we could be confident that alien civilizations exist on other planets. But we have received no such messages. Hence we cannot be confident of the existence of alien civilizations.

8   Olaf, Olive, Oscar, and Ophelia are the only elves. Exactly three elves drink stout. Therefore, Ophelia drinks stout.

9   ... Every being that is not God, is God's creature. Now *every creature of God is good* ... and God is the greatest Good. Therefore, every being is good. (St. Thomas Aquinas, *Summa Theologica*)

10   We build Super Sox for the runner. Which means we build them tougher—because running is tough work. (Super Sox ad, *Runner's World*, May 1980)

3.5   EVALUATING THE REASONING OF COMPLEX NORMAL ARGUMENTS

In our discussion of argument evaluation, we have so far considered only arguments consisting of a single inference. With complex arguments, arguments of more than one inference, things get trickier. There are two kinds of complex arguments: split-support and normal. (If you have forgotten this distinction, review Section 2.2.) To keep matters simple, we're going to confine the discussion in Sections 3.5 and 3.6 to normal arguments. In Section 3.7, we'll return to split-support arguments and see how they can be evaluated with slight modifications of the techniques developed in these earlier sections.

To understand the evaluation of complex arguments, we need to keep in mind the definitions of the three classes of reasoning: deductive, inductive, and fallacious. In all three, we are concerned with the relation of *basic* premises to a conclusion. Therefore, the most direct way to evaluate a chain of inferences is to treat it as a single inference, ignoring all the nonbasic premises. That is, we simply imagine the worlds in which the basic premises are true and determine the frequency among them of worlds in which the conclusion is true. This method works well if there are only a few basic premises, but if there are many, it is practically impossible to keep them all in mind at once. In that case, we must break the reasoning down into individual inferences and evaluate each separately. We then combine these separate estimates into an evaluation of the reasoning as a whole.

This procedure is not as simple as one might expect. Complex arguments exhibit many subtle variations, and virtually any generalization you can make about them is marred by exceptions. There is, however, one fact you can always count on: If all the inferences of a complex argument are deductive, then the argument itself is deductive. Recall that to say an argument is deductive means that there is no logically possible world in which the basic premises are true and the conclusion false. With this in mind it is not difficult to see why a whole argument is deductive if all its inferences are. Consider the possible worlds in which the basic premises are true. If each inference is deductive, then these must also be worlds in which the intermediate conclusions derived from these premises are true and hence in which any further intermediate conclusions derived from these intermediate conclusions are also true, and so on, until we reach the final conclusion. Thus every possible world in which the basic premises are true is also a world in which the final conclusion is true. So there is no possible world in which the basic premises are true and the conclusion is false. That is, there is no counterexample. Thus if each inference is deductive, the argument as a whole is deductive as well. Let's see how this works in an actual example:

①[No children are patient,] and ②[no impatient person can sit still.] (Therefore) ③[no children can sit still.] But ④[anyone who cannot sit still is mischievous,] and (so) ⑤[all children are mischievous.] Moreover, (since) ⑥[all mischievous creatures eventually become tiresome,] (we reach the unhappy conclusion that) ⑦[all children eventually become tiresome.]

This is a complex normal argument consisting of three inferences, related as follows:

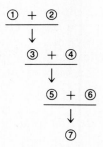

(Check to see that the diagram is correct.)

To determine whether the argument is deductive, we now examine each inference in turn. The first inference is from ① and ② to ③. To check it, we try to imagine a world in which no children are patient and no impatient person can sit still, but in which it's false that no children can sit still (i.e., in which some children can sit still). But we can't imagine this. If the premises are true, the conclusion must be true. So the inference is deductive. The second and third inferences are similar, and you can test them for yourself. Both are also deductive. Now according to the reasoning of the last paragraph, it follows that the argument as a whole is deductive or in other words, that there is no possible world in which the basic premises, ①, ②, ④, and ⑥, are true and the conclusion, ⑦, is false. While it's a bit difficult to keep all four basic premises in mind at once, with a little effort you should come to see that this is true; there is no such possible world— you absolutely cannot conceive it.

So for chains of deductive inferences at least, we have a simple and easily applied rule. Such chains are always deductive. There are no exceptions. When complex arguments contain invalid inferences, however, the picture becomes considerably more complicated. Consider, for example, complex arguments containing all inductive or a mixture of inductive and deductive inferences. Our first inclination is to say that such arguments should be inductive. But this is not always true. Sometimes, as in the following example, they are fallacious:

> Max is an animal.
> 60 percent of animals are mammals.
> ∴ Max is a mammal.
> 60 percent of mammals are felines.
> ∴ Max is a feline.
> 60 percent of felines are tigers.
> ∴ Max is a tiger.

The figures are fanciful, of course, but they illustrate the point. Each of the three inferences is inductive. But when all three are linked in sequence, a little certainty is lost with each step. In fact, given just these assumptions, the conclusion is quite improbable.

To see this, keep in mind that inductiveness is a relation between *basic* premises and conclusion. The basic premises here are:

> Max is an animal.
> 60 percent of animals are mammals.
> 60 percent of mammals are felines.
> 60 percent of felines are tigers.

It is simple mathematics to calculate from the last three of these that only 60 percent × 60 percent × 60 percent, or 21.6 percent, of animals are tigers. When we put this figure together with the first premise, we see that the chances of Max being a tiger, given all the basic premises, are just 21.6 percent—far too low to qualify the argument as inductive. There is no doubt, then, that the argument as a whole is fallacious. Though each inference by itself is inductive, when the three inferences are linked in a chain their weaknesses accumulate until the whole is too weak to support the conclusion.

In logic, a chain may be weaker than its weakest link. Arguments containing two or more inductive inferences are almost always weaker than the inferences they contain. Just how weak depends on the number of inferences and their individual strengths. A chain of inductive inferences need not always be a fallacy. If, for example, the figures in our last argument were all 90 percent, then the probability of the conclusion, given the basic premises, would be 90 percent × 90 percent × 90 percent, or 72.9 percent. Thus the argument as a whole would be inductive (though based on false premises). Still, even with figures as high as 90 percent the argument could be fallacious if we added more inferences. Most of the time, of course, we won't have precise figures to guide us. So the evaluation of arguments containing inductive inferences will involve some educated guesswork. Opinions will sometimes differ, but generally they won't differ much.

We have seen that an argument can be weaker than its weakest link, but it seems reasonable to think that it could be no stronger. If this were so, then any argument containing even one fallacious inference would automatically be fallacious, and so complex arguments containing fallacies would be easy to evaluate. In fact, if we could assume that an argument is no stronger than its weakest link, we could establish a straightforward set of rules which would enable us to evaluate any complex normal argument. The rules would look something like this:

1 If an argument contains only deductive inferences, then it is deductive.

2 If an argument contains only inductive or a mixture of deductive and inductive inferences, but no fallacies, then it is either inductive or fallacious, depending on the number and individual strengths of the inductive inferences.

3 If an argument contains even one fallacious inference, then the argument itself is fallacious.

As it turns out, these rules do give accurate results in almost all practical situations; unfortunately, however, rules 2 and 3 have exceptions. Contrary to Rule 3, some arguments are stronger than their weakest link. And, contrary to Rule 2, some containing only very strong inductive inferences (possibly mixed with some deductive ones) are fallacious. However, such arguments are so rare and peculiar that they are almost never encountered in practice. So we'll use the rules as they stand and not worry about exceptions for now. We'll return to the exceptions in Section 3.8.

Exercise 3.5 For each of the following arguments:

A Write the argument on a separate sheet of paper or copy it photostatically.

B Circle all inference indicators.

C Bracket and number each statement.

D Diagram the argument.

E Evaluate each inference, and record your evaluation by placing either a "D," an "I," or an "F" next to the arrow representing the inference.

F   Using the three rules above, evaluate the whole argument, and record your evaluation by placing one of the letters "D," "I," or "F" in a box next to the diagram. (Skip this step if the argument is a single inference.)

1   Because Olaf is in such good shape, he must play either tennis or handball. But he doesn't play tennis, for he never gets any sun. So he must play handball.

2   Jack Sprat could eat no fat;
His wife could eat no lean.
And so between the two of them
They licked the platter clean.

3   The deliciously creamy taste of Sealtest cottage cheese stands out no matter what you make with it. Because we make Sealtest cottage cheese with pure Sealtest sweet cream dressing for an outstandingly fresh natural flavor. That's why Sealtest cottage cheese is so good just by itself, or as a delicious ingredient. (Sealtest cottage cheese ad, *Redbook*, July 1980)

4   Consider that before long thou wilt be nobody and nowhere, nor will any of the things exist which thou now seest, nor any of those who are now living. For all things are formed by nature to change and be turned and to perish in order that other things in continuous succession may exist. (Marcus Aurelius, *Meditations*)

5   The thief got away, and there are only two ways he could have gone—to the left, down the long hallway, or to the right, down the shorter one. If he had gone down the long hallway, he would have been seen by the guard stationed there. But the guard saw nothing. So it is certain that he did not go down the long hallway. Therefore, he must have escaped by the shorter one.

6   Since smoking is detrimental not only to the health of those who smoke but also to the health of those who breathe their "exhaust fumes" and since what causes harm to self and others is a problem for society as a whole, it is clear that smoking is a social problem. It should therefore be made illegal.

7   If you search in your heart, you will find a yearning there, a deep unsatisfied longing which you do not understand. Thus you can feel that Lord Krishna is calling you to Cosmic Consciousness. If Lord Krishna calls to you and you follow his path, you will have abundant life. And surely you desire abundant life. Therefore, you should heed Lord Krishna's call and seek his Consciousness.

8   Moving just off a trail to avoid mud damages trailside wildlife and contributes to the widening of the trail. This sort of environmental damage should be avoided. Consequently, hikers should either walk

through the mud or take an alternative route. Often, however, no alternative is available. Therefore, hikers should be prepared to do some slogging in the mud.

9   The butler must have stabbed Rumsford. For only three people could have done it—the butler, the cook, or the maid. But it wasn't the cook, because he was probably away in London shopping at the time of the stabbing—at least 20 miles from the scene of the crime. And the maid didn't do it, because she almost surely lacked the necessary physical strength.

10   . . . human moods and reactions to the encounter with nothingness vary considerably from person to person and from culture to culture. The Chinese Taoists found the Great Void tranquilizing, peaceful, even joyful. For the Buddhists in India, the idea of Nothing evoked a mood of universal compassion for all creatures caught in the toils of an existence that is ultimately groundless. In the traditional culture of Japan the idea of nothingness pervades the exquisite moods of aesthetic feeling displayed in painting, architecture, and even the ceremonial rituals of daily life. But Western man, up to his neck in *things*, objects, and the business of mastering them, recoils with anxiety from any possible encounter with nothingness and labels talk of it as 'negative'—which is to say, morally reprehensible. Clearly, then, the moods with which men react to this Nothing vary according to time, place, and cultural conditioning. . . . (William Barrett, *Irrational Man*)

3.6   EVALUATING OVERALL ARGUMENT STRENGTH

The last three sections have been concerned exclusively with strength of reasoning. But the strength of an argument as a whole depends on more than just its reasoning; it also depends on the truth of the basic premises. (With inductive arguments, yet a third consideration is involved: the possibility of suppressed evidence. But we won't be concerned with that until Chapter 6.) It is important to distinguish between these two senses of "strength." We'll use the term **strength of reasoning** only to refer to the classification of arguments as deductive, inductive, or fallacious. When we use the expression **strength of an argument,** we'll mean its overall strength, taking into account not only the strength of its reasoning, but also the truth of basic premises and, eventually, the possibility of suppressed evidence.

In evaluating strength of reasoning, we are concerned with other possible worlds. In determining the truth of basic premises, we are concerned only with the actual world. These two stages of evaluation should not be confused. If, for example, we have an argument based on the assumption "All crows are black," we would evaluate the argument's reasoning by considering various possible worlds in which this was true, but we would determine the truth of the assumption itself by looking only at the actual world. This assumption is in fact false, for there are in the actual world albino crows, which are white. So any argument based on it is unsound.

To show that a premise is false, we find an actual fact or situation which falsifies it. That is just what I did here, by pointing out the fact that there are white crows as well as black ones. Such a falsifying fact or situation is often called a **counterexample to the premise,** but this term is confusing, since the term "counterexample" already has an importantly different meaning in application to reasoning. To avoid confusion, we'll use the term **exception** to designate an actual fact or situation which falsifies a premise. Evaluating premises, then, is a process of seeking exceptions. If there are any exceptions, the premise is false. If not, it is true.

Looking for counterexamples to passages of reasoning requires no knowledge of the actual world. Anyone with a good imagination can do it well. But looking for exceptions to premises does require specific knowledge. And this knowledge, as I noted in Section 3.1, may extend well beyond the domain of logic. Often we won't know enough to evaluate a basic premise accurately. But we'll do the best we can with what we do know.

Let's now summarize the procedure we have developed for evaluating arguments. The preliminary steps were dealt with in Chapter 2: circle all indicators, bracket and number each statement, and construct a diagram. The next stage, evaluation of the reasoning, was discussed in sections 3.2–3.5. We perform imaginative tests on each inference and record the result by writing either "D," "I," or "F" next to the arrow representing the inference on the diagram. (This accounting procedure was introduced in Exercises 3.4 and 3.5.) Then if the argument is complex, we combine our estimates of the individual inferences into a single estimate of the argument's reasoning, using the three rules provided at the end of Section 3.5. This final estimate is recorded in a box next to the diagram. (This is unnecessary, of course, if the argument consists of a single inference, since then the overall strength of its reasoning will coincide with the strength of reasoning of the inference.) The last step in the evaluation procedure is to determine the truth or falsity of the basic premises. Putting this determination together with our evaluation of the argument's reasoning, we obtain an estimate of the argument's overall strength. Our evaluation of the premises and our final estimate of the argument's strength should be summarized in a short note accompanying the diagram.

To demonstrate this procedure, we're now going to put it to work on an old, important, and controversial argument against the existence of God. This argument is a focus of contention in what has come to be known as the **problem of evil,** the problem of how belief in an omnibenevolent (supremely good) and omnipotent (supremely powerful) God is to be reconciled with the existence in our world of suffering, turmoil, and evil. This difficulty has troubled religious thinkers since the dawn of monotheism, but its classic statement occurs in the writings of St. Augustine (A.D. 354–430). Augustine worked out a solution to the problem, as we'll see later, but its adequacy remains subject to debate even to the present day. Here's the argument in one of its simplest forms:

①[What an omnipotent being wills is always achieved.]②[Any omnibenevolent being would will the complete and immediate nonexistence of evil.] (Therefore), ③[if there were an omnipotent, omnibenevolent being, evil would not exist.] But ④[evil does exist.] (So) ⑤[there is no omnipotent, omnibenevolent being.]

Notice that statement ③ is a conditional and thus is not broken into its components. The argument should be diagramed as follows:

$$
\begin{array}{c}
① + ② \\
\downarrow \\
③ + ④ \\
\downarrow \\
⑤
\end{array}
$$

It starts from three basic premises—①, ②, and ④—and moves through two inferences to the final conclusion.

We now evaluate the inferences. Is there a possible world in which ① and ② are true but ③ is false? No; it is absolutely impossible for a being whose will is always achieved to will the complete and immediate cessation of evil and yet for evil to exist. Therefore, this inference is deductive. The second inference is likewise deductive. In any world in which it is true that if there were an omnipotent, omnibenevolent being, then evil would not exist, and also true that evil exists, then it is true as well that there is no omnipotent, omnibenevolent being. Once again, there is no counterexample.

Since both inferences are deductive, the entire argument is deductive. We therefore complete the diagram by recording the results of our evaluative tests as follows:

$$
\boxed{D} \quad
\begin{array}{c}
① + ② \\
\mathbf{D} \downarrow \\
③ + ④ \\
\mathbf{D} \downarrow \\
⑤
\end{array}
$$

We have shown that the reasoning is flawless. If this argument has a fault, it must lie in the premises.

Consider premise ①, "What an omnipotent being wills is always achieved." This seems true enough. We sometimes speak of people acting against God's will, but here "will" means something like "commandment." Those who believe in the omnipotence of God generally hold that he permits us the freedom to act against his commandments, but if he actually made the decision (i.e., willed) to stop us, we'd be stopped dead in our tracks. When "will" is taken in the sense of "decision" or "choice," as it is intended to be in this argument, then it is clear that whatever an omnipotent being wills must be carried out. So there is no problem with premise ①.

Premise ②, however, is far more controversial. It is based on the idea that a good being always strives to eliminate evil. But Augustine and others have argued that this is not so. God allows some evil, says Augustine, so that the world as a whole will be more perfect. The evil we experience now is necessary so that a higher good can be achieved in the end. If Augustine is right, this fact would constitute an exception to the premise. But opponents have replied that there is no reason to believe that current evils really do contribute to a greater good. There seems to be no reliable way of determining the truth here, so the best we can say is that premise ② remains in doubt.

Premise ④ has also been disputed, though not so widely. Some theologians and mystics have held that though evil appears to exist, a deeper understanding of the world reveals its absolute goodness. Their opponents have argued that this claim is ludicrous in light of the hideous violence, suffering, and inhumanity we have witnessed, particularly in the twentieth century. One cannot say with utter certainty, but the bulk of the evidence surely favors premise ④.

Now what has our evaluation revealed? We have seen that the argument is deductive, so that if the basic premises are true, the conclusion must be true. Two of the basic premises are very plausible. Premise ②, however, is open to serious doubt. If all three of the premises are true, then we have a sound argument showing that no omnipotent, omnibenevolent being exists. But in the absence of a clearer assessment of premise ②, we simply cannot tell whether the argument is sound or not. We should record these findings by attaching a brief note to the diagram. Something like this would be appropriate:

Premises ① and ④ are plausible, but ② is questionable. Argument is therefore inconclusive.

Indeed, so far as I know, there is no clearly sound argument either for or against the existence of God. We'll examine several more arguments on both sides of this question in later chapters. But like this one, none of them settles the issue.

Perhaps by now you're beginning to experience a sense of frustration. We've seen a great many arguments so far, but few, if any, have been clearly sound. So you may be inclined to ask, in a somewhat irritated tone, "Does logic ever prove anything?" It's a fair question. The scarcity of nontrivial, obviously sound arguments is not just a quirk of this textbook; they are genuinely rare. But it doesn't follow that they are unimportant or even that they are not common in certain fields of thought. In mathematics, for example, where great clarity and rigor is possible, sound arguments abound. And though they are less common in other fields, they can occur anywhere, sometimes with very surprising results. In Section 5.4, for example, I'll present a sound argument to show that you can't like just the people who don't like themselves.

In fact, when you think about it, what is surprising is not that there are so few obviously sound arguments, but that there are any at all. Soundness is an extremely high standard. It requires both the truth of all basic premises and the absolute logical impossibility of having true premises and a false conclusion. The fact that a great deal of our knowledge, particularly in mathematics, is firmly established by verifiably sound arguments is actually quite remarkable.

In the natural sciences and in everyday life, we must often settle for something less than soundness. In these areas, inductive arguments are more common. Sometimes the probabilities involved in inductive arguments are quite high, even approaching certainty; but even the best inductive argument could lead us astray. In science and everyday life, we are for the most part gamblers, constantly playing the odds.

Here's an example of a fairly strong inductive argument with a rather interesting conclusion:

①[Backward time travel will never be developed and used extensively by human beings at any time in the future.] (For) ②[if it were to be, then travelers from the future would be likely to visit our own time and times already past.] But (since) ③[such visits should be readily detectable] and (since) ④[we have no evidence of them,] (we can only conclude that) ⑤[they don't occur.]

The argument's diagram is as follows:

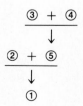

There are three basic premises, statements ②, ③, and ④. All three are quite likely to be true. If backward time travel were to be developed and used *extensively* in the actual future, then it does seem likely that time travelers would often visit our own time and times past. Perhaps their time machines, once invented, would have some inherent limitation to prevent them from going very far back. But there is no evidence whatsoever to think that this is true, and it seems improbable. Thus we can be fairly sure of premise ②. Likewise, premise ③ seems highly probable. Even if the time travelers all went to the trouble of devising elaborate means of disguise or camouflage (which in itself seems unlikely—why should they?), still if time travel were employed *extensively*, somewhere along the line there ought to be some slip-ups, so that the visitors would be detected. Finally, premise ④ is certainly true; we have no evidence of time travelers. So the basic premises are all acceptable.

Moreover, both the inferences are strongly inductive. (I'll leave it to you to formulate counterexamples to show that they are not deductive. I'll discuss only the test for inductiveness.) To test the first inference, consider the range of possible worlds in which premises ③ and ④ are true (i.e., in which hypothetical visits from the future should be readily detectable, but are in fact not detected). Among these are some worlds in which there are visitors from the future and some in which there are not. But the latter are clearly in the majority, since we're looking at situations in which if the travelers were present, they should be detectable. There are more ways to imagine them not there and not detected than there are ways to imagine them there and not detected. Accordingly, given ③ and ④, the conclusion ⑤ that such visits do not occur is probable, and so the inference is inductive.

Similar considerations reveal that the inference from ② and ⑤ to ① is inductive. (Think this one through for yourself.)

Now we don't have any percentages here to make things precise, so evaluation of the whole argument is going to involve some guesswork. But each inference by itself seems pretty strong, and since there are only two of them, the decrease in certainty resulting from their combination seems unlikely to drop the probability of the conclusion relative to the basic premises to 50 percent or less. It seems fairly clear, then, that the whole thing is inductive. Since the basic premises are themselves quite likely, this means that the argument is probable evidence for its conclusion. There really is reason, then, to believe that backward time travel will never be developed and used extensively. To complete the diagram, we add evaluations and a summary, as follows:

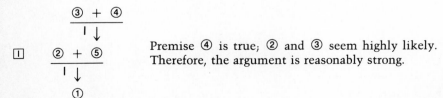

Premise ④ is true; ② and ③ seem highly likely. Therefore, the argument is reasonably strong.

As a final example of evaluating complex normal arguments, consider this complex and controversial chain of reasoning:

①[There is nothing immoral about abortion when it contributes to a woman's well-being.] (Since) ②[consciousness is a function of brain structure] and ③[the brain structure of a fetus is akin to that of a nonhuman animal,] (it follows that) ④[a fetus's consciousness is similar to that of a nonhuman animal.] And (since) ⑤[the value of an organism's life depends on the nature of its consciousness,]⑥[the value of a fetus's life is (therefore) similar to the value of the life of a nonhuman animal.] Now ⑦[the well-being of a fully conscious woman is surely more valuable than the life of an animal,] (as is amply demonstrated by the fact that) ⑧[we do not hesitate to kill animals if doing so contributes to our well-being.] (Accordingly), ⑨[the well-being of a woman is of greater moral value than the life of a fetus.] And obviously, ⑩[if the woman's well-being is more valuable than the fetus's life, then there is nothing wrong with taking the fetus's life for the sake of that well-being.]

The diagram of this argument is long, but fairly straightforward:

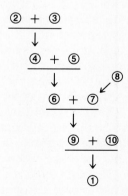

Once again, you should check it carefully by reading the arrows as "is intended as evidence for."

Now let's examine the inferences. What about the first one, the step from ② and ③ to ④? Can we imagine a world in which the premises are true and the conclusion is false? In this case, it is not easy to tell because of the vagueness of the phrase "is a function of." We're not told specifically what this means. Nevertheless, our imaginative test does produce an answer. We can imagine that consciousness is in some sense a function of brain structure and yet that very minute changes in brain structure produce vast differences in the nature of consciousness. If this is so, then ② and ③ could be true but ④ false. This is a counterexample. So the first inference is invalid. However, it is not irrational, for in most possible situations in which consciousness depends on brain structure and two organisms are similar in brain structure, we'd expect that their consciousnesses would be similar, at least to some degree. The inference from ② and ③ to ④ is therefore best classified as inductive.

What about the inference from ④ and ⑤ to ⑥? As far as logic goes, this one is a carbon copy of the last, and we can construct a counterexample in precisely the same way. Imagine a world in which the value of a life depends on the nature of consciousness but in which small differences in consciousness entail large differences in life's value. In such a world, ④ and ⑤ would be true and ⑥ false. Again, however, it seems clear that in most possible situations in which the premises are true the conclusion is true as well. So again we classify the inference as inductive.

Next we consider the inference from ⑥ and ⑦ to ⑨. Again there is a counterexample. Imagine a world in which a fetus's life is somewhat more valuable than the life of an animal but in which the two values are still *similar*. And imagine that in this same world a woman's well-being is more valuable than the life of an animal but less valuable than the life of a fetus. In this world, ⑥ and ⑦ would be true, but ⑨ would be false. Again, however, among possible situations in which the value of a fetus's life is similar to that of the life of an animal and the value of a woman's well-being is greater than the value of an animal's life, the majority are situations in which the value of a woman's well-being is also greater than the value of a fetus's life. So again we have an inductive inference.

The inference from ⑧ to ⑦, however, is fallacious. Among the possible situations in which we do not hesitate to kill animals for our well-being, we can imagine at least as many in which the lives of animals are no less valuable than the well-being of women as we can imagine situations in which the reverse is true. (This may seem outrageous, but don't let your imagination be bound by the facts; we can imagine, for example, that animals are very special and valuable creatures, despite what we do to them.) There is in fact no logical connection between moral value and our actions or beliefs about moral value. This inference is a fallacy. (For a more detailed discussion of fallacious appeals to popular opinion, see Section 7.1.)

Finally, let's consider the inference from ⑨ and ⑩ to ①. Can we imagine the premises to be true and the conclusion false? No; granting that if a woman's well-being is more valuable than a fetus's life, then there is nothing wrong with abortion, and that a woman's well-being is in fact more important than a fetus's life, then it must be true that there is nothing wrong with abortion. There can be no counterexample here. So this final inference is valid. We now add our evaluations of individual inferences to the diagram and evaluate the reasoning as a whole:

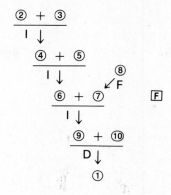

Since the argument contains a fallacious inference, it is itself fallacious, and I have recorded this fact by placing an "F" in the box next to the diagram.

We could stop here. Since the argument is fallacious, it is a bad argument, even if all the premises are true. But sometimes, if we're really interested in the truth and not just in refuting somebody's argument, it's best to look a little further. This argument has only one fallacious inference, the one supporting ⑦. Now ⑦ itself seems fairly plausible. Perhaps we could just omit the fallacious inference and allow ⑦ to stand as a basic premise. This produces a new argument; we're no longer dealing with the argument we were given. But perhaps this new argument is stronger and more interesting than the original. Let's take a moment to examine it.

Our new argument has three inductive inferences and one that is deductive. Since some certainty is lost with each inductive inference, only if all three are very strong can we conclude that the argument as a whole is inductive. (It's obviously not deductive.) The strengths of these inferences are difficult to judge; they all contain some vague language, and none of them seems outstandingly strong. It's a close call, but I'd say that on the basis of our evaluation of the inferences either "inductive" or "fallacious" is a reasonable classification. The argument itself is too vague to permit a more precise determination.

Let's suppose, just for the sake of discussion, that the argument as a whole is inductive. Then, of course, we need to look seriously at the basic premises. For if they are true, then we have established that probably there is nothing wrong with abortion if it contributes to a woman's well-being. This would be quite important, in view of the social and moral significance of this issue. However, some of the basic premises are dubious—especially ⑤, which asserts that the value of an organism's life depends on the nature of its consciousness. After all, there are people in temporary comas who lack consciousness, and yet—since the coma is temporary—their lives seem as valuable as anyone else's. They are apparent exceptions to premise ⑤. Can you think of any others? Still, the term "nature" in premise ⑤ is vague enough that the author might use it to discount these exceptions. Perhaps he or she would claim that coma does not change the essential nature of a person's consciousness, that something of this nature remains even when the person is completely blacked out. That seems unlikely, but it's hard to refute.

Many opponents of abortion would consider ⑤ false for a quite different reason. They hold that an organism has value in proportion to its *potential*, not in proportion to the nature of its consciousness at any given moment. In other words, they say that since a fetus has the potential to become an adult human being, it is just as valuable as an adult, even though its current consciousness and brain structure may be quite different. If they are right, the fetus itself constitutes an exception to ⑤.

These matters are quite complicated, and obviously a lot more could be said. But it should be clear by now that ⑤ is at least doubtful.

To sum up, then: The reasoning of this revised version of the argument is fairly weak, either weakly inductive or fallacious. Moreover, at least one of the premises, ⑤, is controversial and of doubtful truth. Therefore, even this revised version is a weak argument, and it should not convince anyone that abortion is right.

Does it follow that abortion is wrong? Certainly not, as you should know by now. All we've done here is to show the weakness of one particular proabortion argument. We've shown nothing about the moral status of abortion itself. To do that we'd need a sound argument or at least an inductive argument with true premises. I do not know of any, but it may be that among the arguments now being offered for and against abortion there is one that is sound. If so, we can be sure it contains the truth.

Omitting premise ⑧ from the preceding argument illustrates the sensitivity and flexibility of good argument analysis. Frequently an argument containing a bad inference or a false premise can easily be reworded or reorganized to avoid the mistake. Such is often the case, for example, with arguments which can be classified either as split-support or normal. Even if some of the premises of such an argument are false, the others may still be strong enough to provide good evidence for the conclusion.

Don't be rigid and mechanical in argument analysis. If the author makes a small mistake which can be corrected by minor revision, take note of this fact. Your understanding will be deeper and fairer if you do.

So far we have discussed strength or reasoning and argument strength, but there is a third sort of strength we have neglected—**statement strength.** The strength of a statement is, roughly, the amount of information it contains. A stronger statement tells us more than a weaker one. For example, the statement:

Olaf is a spritely green elf with red hair, blue eyes, and an orange beard.

is stronger than the less informative statement:

Olaf is an elf.

And the statement:

All elves drink stout.[2]

is stronger and more informative than the statement:

At least some elves drink stout.

A more useful way of characterizing statement strength is in terms of possible worlds. Notice that the more information a statement contains, the more inherently improbable it becomes. Even without knowing anything about elves, we can sense that it's less probable that all elves drink stout than that at least some do. The **inherent probability** of a statement is the proportion of worlds in which it is true among all possible worlds. Thus the stronger a statement is, the fewer are the worlds in which it is true; and the weaker it is, the more frequent among all worlds are the worlds in which it is true. The statement "All elves drink stout" is true in fewer worlds than is the statement "At least some elves drink stout," because the latter is true in all the worlds in which the former is true and in some others besides.

The importance of statement strength lies in its relation to strength of reasoning. Since a strong statement is true in few worlds, an argument which assumes it is more likely to have strong reasoning than one which assumes a weaker premise. That is, since strength of reasoning depends on the proportion of possible worlds in which the conclusion is true among those in which the premises are true, if we minimize the number of worlds in which the premises are true, we'll maximize this proportion and hence maximize strength of reasoning. Thus, for example, of the following pair of arguments, the first has stronger reasoning, because its first premise is stronger:

All elves are between 8 and 16 inches tall.
Ophelia is an elf.
∴ Ophelia is between 10 and 14 inches tall.

All elves are between 6 and 18 inches tall.
Ophelia is an elf.
∴ Ophelia is between 10 and 14 inches tall.

Conversely, since a weak statement is true in a large proportion of possible worlds, an argument with a weak conclusion is more likely to have strong reasoning than one with a strong conclusion. That is, by weakening the conclusion we increase the number of worlds in which it is true, and

---

[2] I am assuming that in using the term "all elves" we assert that there are elves. In formal logic there is a use of "all" according to which this needn't be so. But that is not the meaning intended here.

this generally increases the proportion of these worlds among those in which the premises are true, thus strengthening the reasoning. The following pair of arguments illustrates this:

> Many elves wear green hats.
> Many elves wear red trousers.
> Olaf is an elf.
> ∴ Olaf wears a green hat or red trousers or both.

> Many elves wear green hats.
> Many elves wear red trousers.
> Olaf is an elf.
> ∴ Olaf wears both a green hat and red trousers.

Though both arguments are fallacious ("many" is not "most"), the reasoning of the first is stronger, because its conclusion is weaker.

We may summarize these findings as follows: *strength of reasoning tends to vary in direct proportion to the strength of the basic premises and in inverse proportion to the strength of the conclusion.* This principle will prove useful from time to time.

It is not always possible to compare strengths of statements. Given the following pair of statements, for example:

> Some cows are purple.
> Olaf smokes a pipe.

we are at a loss to say which is stronger. For the most part, comparisons of strength are possible only between closely related statements. But usually, comparisons between closely related statements are all that interest us anyway, since statement strength is important mainly as a guide to strength of reasoning. When we wish to make a line of reasoning stronger by strengthening its assumptions or weakening its conclusion, we will generally only make minor modifications of these statements. For minor modifications of this sort, comparisons of strength are usually easy.

Exercise 3.6(a)   For each of the following pairs of statements, tell which of the pair is stronger.

1   Some elves drink stout.
    Exactly one elf drinks stout.
2   More than two elves drink stout.
    More than seven elves drink stout.

3   The President is either a man or a woman.
    The President is a woman.

4   All crows are black.
    Most crows are black.

5   Most crows are black.
    Some crows are black.

Exercise 3.6(b)   For each of the following arguments:

A   Copy the argument by hand or photostatically, circle indicators, bracket and number statements, and diagram as usual.

B   Evaluate each inference and record your evaluation by writing either "D," "I," or "F" next to the arrow representing the inference.

C   Estimate the strength of reasoning of the argument as a whole, and record this estimate by writing either "D," "I," or "F" in a box next to the diagram.

D   Evaluate each basic premise to the best of your knowledge in order to determine the strength of the argument. Record this determination in a brief note beside the diagram.

1   The population of the earth is over two billion, and since most people sleep about a third of the time and people on different parts of the earth sleep at different times, at any given moment someone is asleep.

2   . . . We know that the brain is not immortal, and that the organized energy of a living body becomes, as it were, demobilized at death. . . . All the evidence goes to show that what we regard as our mental life is bound up with brain structure and organized bodily energy. Therefore it is rational to suppose that mental life ceases when bodily life ceases. (Bertrand Russell, "What I Believe")

3   If the Loch Ness monster exists, it is either a mammal, a reptile, or an amphibian; for no other sorts of animals could be responsible for the sightings reported at the Loch. But it is not a mammal or a reptile, since if it were, it would have to surface frequently for air, and it does not do so. Moreover, it is not an amphibian, for no amphibian is large enough to be the monster. Thus the monster does not exist.

4   A computer is a machine—an artificial assembly of electronic and mechanical components. Therefore, all its operations are predictably determined by physical laws. But the operations of a mind cannot be predictably determined by physical laws. Consequently, computers do not have minds.

5 A line segment is a subset of a line consisting of two distinct points of the line and all points of the line between these two points. Since there are infinitely many points between every two distinct points of a line, every line segment is an infinite set of points. And since a polygon is the union of three or more line segments, it follows that a polygon, too, is an infinite set of points.

6 Anything which causes avoidable harm to human beings is immoral. Now complete sexual abstinence is harmful, because without sexual activity there is an increase in irritation and tension, which in some cases even leads to serious psychological or psychosomatic disorders. And even minor irritation and tension (not to mention mental illness) is a form of harm. This harm is avoidable by any of a variety of sexual activities. It follows that complete sexual abstinence is immoral.

7 . . . if the universe were to crush him, man would still be more noble than that which killed him, because he knows that he dies and the advantage which the universe has over him; the universe knows nothing of this. All our dignity consists, then, in thought. (Blaise Pascal, *Pensées*)

8 Undeniably a large part of our calculations in choosing lovers and mates consists of how much we think others will be impressed by our having caught him or her. How envious we predict others will be plays a central role in our selections.

So . . . the woman you couldn't get anywhere with . . . may start desiring you if her friends, whose opinions she trusts, think you're an exceptional catch. By putting the relationship with the woman you want on the back burner and charming her friends for awhile, you may very well wind up with the woman you wanted, plus her friends. (R. B. Sparkman, *The Art of Manipulation*)

9 Creating is obviously present in the universe. Life is more than bare matter, yet emerged from it in the temporal process; mind is more than life, yet appeared in the evolutionary scale. Time must therefore be conceived of not merely as change, but as *creative* change; not merely as replacement of specific qualities by other specific qualities, but as the origination of new genera. Hence something comes from nothing. (A. Cornelius Benjamin, "Ideas of Time in the History of Philosophy")

10 There is much controversy about the delivering up of fugitives from service or labor. The clause I now read is as plainly written in the Constitution as any of its other provisions:

"No person held to service or labor in one State, under the laws thereof, escaping into another, shall in consequence of any law or regulation therein be discharged from such service or labor, but shall be delivered up on claim of the party to whom such service or labor may be due."

It is scarcely questioned that this provision was intended by those who made it for the reclaiming of what we call fugitive slaves; and the intention of the lawgiver is the law. All Members of Congress swear their support to the whole Constitution—to this provision as much as any other. To the proposition, then, that slaves whose cases come within the terms of this clause, "shall be delivered up," their oaths are unanimous. (Abraham Lincoln, first inaugural address, 1861)

3.7 EVALUATING SPLIT-SUPPORT ARGUMENTS

The rules at the end of Section 3.5 provide guidelines for evaluating the reasoning of normal arguments, but these rules do not apply to split-support arguments. To see why, consider the following example:

①[Cats are a nuisance] (because) ②[they are furtive and sneaky;] besides, ③[they always have fleas,] and ④[anything which has fleas is a nuisance.]

The antifeline conclusion is supported by two lines of reasoning—one having to do with furtiveness and the other with fleas. The diagram is as follows:

$$\begin{array}{ccc} ② & ③ & + & ④ \\ F \searrow & \overline{} & \nearrow & \\ & ① & & D \end{array}$$

I've already evaluated the inferences. The first one, from ② to ①, is clearly invalid, since we can imagine a world in which cats are so furtive and sneaky that they or their acts are never noticed—in which case they could hardly be a nuisance. But I'm not sure whether to class this inference as inductive or fallacious. Its premise and conclusion are so vague that I'm very hesitant to say that there's a connection of probability between them. Therefore, I've decided to call it fallacious rather than inductive. But if you think that "sneaky" connotes troublesomeness, then you may be inclined to call it inductive. Either evaluation is reasonable.

The second inference, however, is unquestionably deductive. We certainly can't imagine a world in which cats always have fleas and everything which has fleas is a nuisance, but cats are not a nuisance.

By the rules at the end of Section 3.5, the whole thing should be either inductive or fallacious, depending upon how we judge the first inference.

But both these evaluations are mistaken. The argument is actually deductive. Since we have a deductive chain of reasoning leading from basic premises ③ and ④ to the conclusion, ①, we know that if the argument's basic premises—including ③ and ④—are true, then ① must be true. Hence there is no counterexample to the argument as a whole.

We can perhaps best conceive this situation by means of an analogy. The conclusion of this argument is like a weight suspended from two chains. One of the chains is weak—so weak, perhaps, that it would break if it were supporting the weight alone. But the other is quite strong, strong enough to support the weight all by itself. The weight, then, clearly has adequate support; it will not fall. By now you've seen the analogy: the two chains are the two lines of reasoning supporting the conclusion; the weakness of the first is the weakness of the first inference; and the strength of the second is the strength of the second inference. The analogy points to the principle that the reasoning of a split-support argument will generally be as strong as the strongest chain of reasoning it contains. Of course, if each of the chains is fallacious then the argument as a whole will be fallacious. But if there is just one deductive chain from basic premises to conclusion, then the whole argument is deductive, no matter how bad the reasoning is in other chains; likewise, if there is just one inductive chain (and none that are deductive) then the argument will be inductive.

Just as the reasoning of a split-support argument is as strong as its strongest chain, so too the overall strength of the argument is as great as the overall strength of its strongest chain. If one chain is sound, then the whole argument, while not technically sound unless all other basic premises are true, still proves its conclusion. If all chains are weak, so is the argument as a whole. There are many possible variations here.

There remains one unanswered question in this discussion: What, exactly, is a "chain" of reasoning? Well, you probably have a pretty good idea already, though in complicated arguments chains may be difficult to identify. The best way to identify a complete chain is to think of it as being represented by as big a chunk of the diagram as is normal—that is, as big a chunk of the diagram as you can mark off without including two arrows pointing to the same conclusion. I have circled all the complete chains of reasoning in the following split-support diagrams.

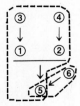 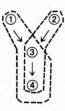 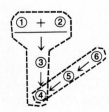

By contrast, the chunks marked off in the following normal diagram are *not* complete chains, because they do not contain as much of the diagram as can be marked off without including two arrows pointing to the same conclusion:

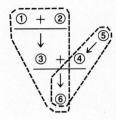

The only complete chain in this case (and in any normal argument) is the whole argument.

Exercise 3.7 Some of the following arguments are split-support. Some are normal. Copy and diagram each, and evaluate the reasoning.

1 Olaf is a sparkling conversationalist, because he is a logician and because he has nice eyes.

2 Not everyone enjoyed the party. Ophelia was there, and she was completely miserable.

3 Since too much sun dries your skin and can even cause cancer, to maintain healthy skin you should avoid the sun.

4 I couldn't have told Bill what you said, because I never heard you say it. And anyway, I never met Bill in my life.

5 In order to evaluate arguments well, you need a vivid imagination. Some people don't have vivid imaginations. Therefore, some people can't evaluate arguments well. Now clearly no drunkard can evaluate arguments well. Therefore, some people are drunkards.

6 The planet you see up there is either Jupiter or Venus, because they are the only ones that shine so brightly. But it's not Venus, because Venus never appears that high in the sky. And Venus is not visible now anyway, since it's almost directly in line with the sun. So the planet you see must be Jupiter.

7 Since it was cold, if any of the party survived the avalanche, they would have built a fire. If there were any survivors, then, they should have been easy to spot. Another reason for thinking this is that they

were all wearing orange coats. But the searchers saw nothing. So probably no one survived.

8 Precisely because the tyranny of opinion is such as to make eccentricity a reproach, it is desirable, in order to break through that tyranny, that people should be eccentric. Eccentricity has always abounded when and where strength of character has abounded; and the amount of eccentricity in a society has generally been proportional to the amount of genius, mental vigor, and moral courage which it contained. (John Stuart Mill, *On Liberty*)

3.8 SELF-WEAKENING AND FORTUITOUS STRENGTH

When I stated the rules for evaluating complex normal arguments at the end of Section 3.5, I noted that there are some rare exceptions to rules 2 and 3. In this section we'll examine these exceptions. Rules 2 and 3, you should recall, are as follows:

2 If an argument contains only inductive or a mixture of deductive and inductive inferences, but no fallacies, then it is either inductive or fallacious, depending on the number and individual strengths of the inductive inferences.

3 If an argument contains even one fallacious inference, then the argument itself is fallacious.

The exceptions are of two types: either the reasoning is stronger than the rules predict, in which case we shall say that it is **fortuitously strong,** or it is weaker than Rule 2 predicts, in which case we shall call it **self-weakening.** (There are no arguments whose reasoning is weaker than Rule 3 predicts, for there is no category weaker than "fallacy.") We'll consider fortuitously strong arguments first.

Fortuitously strong reasoning arises when basic premises alone provide stronger support for the conclusion than do the chains of inference linking them to the conclusion. Such arguments are always poorly constructed and in need of revision. Here's an example:

①[Every hard worker benefits from his or her own labor,] and ②[Olaf's sister is a hard worker.] (So it follows that) ③[Olaf benefits from his sister's labor.] But ④[Olaf's sister is Olivia.] (Therefore) , ⑤[Olivia benefits from her own labor.]

According to the inference indicators, the argument's diagram is as follows:

$$\frac{① + ②}{\downarrow F}$$
$$\frac{③ + ④}{\downarrow F}$$
$$⑤$$

Each of the two inferences is fallacious, as my evaluations indicate. Yet if we examine the relation between the basic premises:

> Every hard worker benefits from his or her own labor.
> Olaf's sister is a hard worker.
> Olaf's sister is Olivia.

and the final conclusion:

> Olivia benefits from her own labor.

we see that it is impossible for these premises to be true and the conclusion false. There is no counterexample. Thus, despite the fact that it consists of two fallacious inferences, the argument as a whole is deductive. The chain is stronger than its weakest link; Rule 3 is violated.

What this shows is that the argument is shoddily crafted. It is a defective argument, despite its validity, because the inference to the intermediate conclusion ③ that Olaf benefits from his sister's labor is both unnecessary and fallacious. We get a well-constructed argument if we eliminate this intermediate conclusion and use all three basic premises together in a single inference, as follows:

$$\frac{① + ② + ④}{\downarrow D}$$
$$⑤$$

This is the way the argument should have been formulated in the first place. What we have instead is a mess. Here, incidentally, is the way you should diagram and evaluate the argument if you encounter it in an exercise:

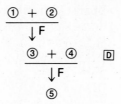

This example makes it clear why fortuitously strong arguments are rare. People generally try to offer arguments which are as convincing as possible. Fortuitously strong arguments are not convincing, because they contain inferences which are unnecessarily weak. So people seldom reason this way. It's not a natural sort of mistake to make.

Self-weakening arguments, like fortuitously strong ones, are seldom encountered in practice. They are arguments which should be classified as inductive according to Rule 2, but which are actually weaker. Such arguments occur when a premise contained in one inference undercuts the probability of a conclusion drawn inductively in another inference. Here's an example:

①[Igor is silent, but hideously destructive.] ②[He is hideously destructive,] (because) ③[he is a monster] and ④[nearly all monsters are hideously destructive.] And ⑤[he is silent,] (because) ⑥[he does nothing] and ⑦[all creatures that do nothing are silent.]

The argument should be diagramed as follows:

$$
\begin{array}{ccc}
③ + ④ & & ⑥ + ⑦ \\
\hline
\ \downarrow & & \downarrow D \\
② & + & ⑤ \\
\hline
& \downarrow D & \\
& ① &
\end{array}
$$

According to Rule 2, this argument should be inductive, but in fact it's fallacious. The basic premises:

Igor is a monster.

Nearly all monsters are hideously destructive.

Igor does nothing.

All creatures that do nothing are silent.

do not even make it probable that Igor is silent but hideously destructive. This is because the premise that Igor does nothing undercuts the inductive inference from ③ and ④ to ②, making it probable, despite ③ and ④, that Igor is *not* hideously destructive.

Self-weakening arguments are unusual, because people generally strive for coherence in their reasoning and tend not to employ premises which undercut their own inferences. But self-weakening does sometimes occur. So if you suspect that something said in an argument undercuts one of its inductive inferences, don't rely on Rule 2 alone, but check for self-weakening by examining the relation between the argument's basic premises and final conclusion directly.

I have not been very precise here about what it means for a statement to "undercut" an inductive inference. What it means is that the statement functions as contrary evidence, a concept I'll explain more fully in Section 6.2.

Exercise 3.8   Some of the following arguments are self-weakening or fortuitously strong. Others are not. Copy and diagram each, and evaluate the reasoning.

1   Olaf and Ophelia really are elves. Thus there are some intelligent creatures less than 2 feet tall, from which it follows that elvish folk really do exist.

2   Ophelia has only two or three cats. For she has fewer than four and yet more than one. She has fewer than four, because she has fewer than seven. And she has more than one, because she has more than two.

3   Without natural selection, evolution would cease. But natural selection no longer operates in human beings, for it requires that a greater proportion of weak individuals than strong ones perish before reproducing. Modern medicine, however, permits the weak to survive and reproduce as readily as the strong. Human evolution has therefore come to a standstill.

4   I took the jewelry, all right. But there was nothing wrong with my taking it, because I almost always do the right thing. Of course, for most people taking it would have been wrong. But that just goes to show that I'm different from most people.

5   Since Olaf delivers letters and at least 90 percent of letter deliverers are postal employees, it seems likely that Olaf is a postal employee. It is nearly certain that he delivers letters, since he is a mailman and almost all mailmen deliver letters. And certainly at least 90 percent of letter deliverers are postal employees, because all mailmen are postal employees and 90 percent of letter deliverers are mailmen.

6   Happiness in marriage requires that both partners have a clear sense of self-worth. For if one or both of the partners feel insecure or unworthy, the likely result is frustration, resentment, and ultimately a burning irrational anger. This anger is either suppressed, darkening and festering in silence, or released in a torrent upon the other partner or suppressed and released in alternation. Each of these patterns of behavior is incompatible with happiness. Now a sense of self-worth is acquired only through experience and maturity. Hence it is essential to a happy marriage that both partners be experienced and mature.

4

Implicit Premises and Conclusions

In Section 3.4 we noted that some arguments harbor tacit assumptions. There are many reasons for this. Sometimes authors want to conceal premises which are embarrassingly dubious. In contrast, some assumptions are so obviously true that there is no need to mention them. And sometimes it is redundant, stylistically awkward, or just plain boring to state an argument in full. Tacit statements are therefore pervasive in practical reasoning, and we need a fair and enlightening policy for dealing with them.

4.1   CRITERIA FOR ADDING PREMISES AND CONCLUSIONS

Let's begin with a very simple example:

>   Olaf won't like Oscar, because Oscar's a Republican.

As stated, this argument has only one premise, and its inference is fallacious:

Oscar is a Republican.

∴ Olaf won't like him.

But it's evident that anyone who would argue this way is assuming something that's not being said—namely that Olaf won't like anyone who is a
Republican. Therefore, the argument in full is:

Oscar is a Republican.

Olaf won't like anyone who is a Republican.

∴ Olaf won't like Oscar.

But if this is what the author meant, why didn't he or she say it? Undoubtedly
you see the reason. With the second premise added, the argument sounds
stiff, formal, and redundant. Besides, we can see that the premise is intended
even if it is not stated. So there was no real reason to mention the premise,
and a perfectly good reason not to. It seems likely, too, that this argument
would have been spoken to listeners who were already familiar with Olaf's
political leanings—listeners who could be expected to assume the missing
premise automatically.

Our policy with missing statements will be to write them at the end
of the argument and label them with letters, like this:

①[Olaf won't like Oscar,] (because) ②[Oscar's a Republican.] Ⓐ[Olaf
won't like anyone who is a Republican.]

The missing statements can then be included in the argument diagram, just
as stated premises and conclusions are. The reason for using letters instead
of numbers is that it tells us at a glance which statements were added and
which are original. Writing the extra statements at the end helps avoid the
crowded mess which might develop if we put them in the middle. (Their
order doesn't matter, since our diagram will reveal their logical place in the
argument.) In this case the diagram is quite simple:

$$\frac{② \; + \; Ⓐ}{\underset{①}{\downarrow \; D}}$$

Adding the premise has made the evaluation fairer and more accurate.
We now see that there was no fallacy in reasoning, though of course we
still need to ask whether the premises are true. But at least we will not
falsely accuse the speaker of irrationality.

Knowing that some arguments have missing premises presents us with
a problem: How can we decide which seemingly fallacious inferences are

genuinely fallacious and which are really rational but lacking a premise or two? The answer, I'm afraid, is that we must try to divine the author's thoughts. An argument, after all, is its author's creation. If it contains more than is actually stated, that is because the author would have expected the unstated parts to be taken for granted and thus did not verbalize them. Therefore, the only way to know for sure whether an argument is genuinely fallacious or merely incomplete is to ask the author what he or she had in mind. Since we usually can't do that, we are reduced for the most part to making educated guesses, as we did in the last example. Of course we could stubbornly resolve to take every argument at face value and never add anything. But implicit statements are so common that such stubbornness would condemn us to frequent misunderstanding. We'll understand more if we try to fill in the author's thoughts whenever we have a reasonable chance of doing so correctly. The following criteria are useful in deciding when and how to do this:

(1) *Add only statements which the author would have intended to be taken for granted.* There are generally three sources of evidence about an author's intentions: (i) the way in which the argument itself is worded, (ii) our knowledge of the context, and (iii) our knowledge of the author's beliefs apart from the argument. Consider our example again. There are many premises besides "Olaf won't like anyone who is a Republican" which would have made the argument rational. The premise-pair "Olaf won't like any members of political parties" and "Republicans are members of a political party" would do the job. So would "Olaf never likes anyone at all." But although each of these choices would have improved the reasoning, the wording of the argument provides no evidence that the author intended us to assume either of them. There is a strong indication, however, that the author specifically expected listeners to assume that Olaf won't like Republicans. Why else would he or she employ the premise that Oscar is one? The wording of the argument suggests the author's intention very clearly.

Our overall knowledge of the context and of the author's beliefs also plays a role in filling in missing statements. If we knew that Olaf was a passionate and irascible Democrat—and suspected that the author knew this as well—then our knowledge would rightfully reinforce the conviction that the hidden premise is "Olaf won't like anyone who is a Republican." However, if we knew that Olaf himself was a Republican and had many Republican friends and that the argument's author knew this, then we would be puzzled by this conflict and unable to make much sense of the argument. Here our general knowledge makes it seem unlikely that the author would have intended it to be taken for granted that Olaf won't like Republicans. So by criterion (1) we should not add this premise. Under these circumstances, the best we can do is register puzzlement and treat the argument as a fallacy.

(2) *Add premises only if they strengthen the reasoning.* There are many things an author intends us to take for granted which play no logical role

in the argument. The author of our example probably would have intended us to take it for granted, for instance, that Oscar is a living person. But adding the premise "Oscar is a living person" does nothing to strengthen the argument. Once we have assumed that Oscar is a Republican and that Olaf won't like Republicans, it follows that Olaf won't like Oscar, whether Oscar is a living person, an elf, an automaton, or a lump of Gruyère cheese. Of course it's unlikely that cheese could hold membership in the Republican party, but you see the point. The assertion that Oscar is a living person plays no role in the argument. So we shouldn't add this assertion even if the author intends it to be taken for granted.

(3) *Do not add premises which merely embody a stated inference.* It is possible to make any inference valid by an unsubtle trick called **condition-alization.** You simply add a conditional premise of the form "If _____, then _____," where the first blank is filled in by all the premises actually stated and the second is filled in by the inference's conclusion. For example, instead of adding the premise "Olaf won't like anyone who is a Republican," we could have added "If Oscar is a Republican, then Olaf won't like him." The argument would then be:

If Oscar is a Republican, then Olaf won't like him.

Oscar is a Republican.

∴ Olaf won't like him.

This is valid and perfectly clear, so why not take it to be the actual structure of the argument?

Well, let's consider what we've done. In effect we have just reformulated the original inference as a premise and tacked it on to the argument. We have not added anything substantial, nor have we deepened our understanding of what the author was saying. We have only managed to complicate the argument. So there is a loss of simplicity without any palpable gain.

But is there really no palpable gain? After all, the original argument was fallacious and the new one is valid. Haven't we increased the argument's strength? No, we haven't. We have only shifted the location of its weakness. The conditional premise which we added is no more reliable than the invalid inference it embodies. It therefore stands a good chance of being false. Thus we have merely converted a fallacious argument into an argument which is valid but of questionable soundness. We haven't really strengthened it at all.

Notice, by contrast, what happens when we add the more satisfactory premise "Olaf won't like anyone who is a Republican." We are not just making a premise out of an inference which was already there; we are adding a substantive new thought—a thought, moreover, for which there is evidence in the author's wording. This genuinely deepens our understanding of what the author was saying, instead of just needlessly complicating things. And if the premise is true, it genuinely strengthens the argument.

There is in a sense nothing wrong with conditionalization. It does legitimately make valid arguments out of invalid ones. But it doesn't affect our overall evaluation of an argument. It only complicates the argument and shifts the location of its weakness. So in the end it just adds extra work. It should therefore be avoided. If conditionalization seems to be the only way to make a fallacious inference rational, then regard that inference as a genuine fallacy.

As we'll see in Section 5.2, there are a number of ways of expressing conditional statements and hence a number of variants of conditionalization. But don't worry about these variants for now. Just keep in mind that it is pointless to add any premise which merely embodies a stated inference.

(4) *If several different sets of premises satisfy criteria (1)–(3), add the premise or set of premises which make the argument strongest.* Notice that I'm talking about strength of an *argument* here. (Recall the distinction between argument strength and strength of reasoning made in Section 3.6.) Strength in this sense takes into account the reliability of both inferences and premises. Thus, for example, adding a true premise which makes an inference inductive produces a stronger argument than adding a false premise which makes the inference deductive. The idea behind this criterion is to give the author the benefit of the doubt—that is, to assume that he or she made the best possible case for the conclusion within the bounds of what was actually stated. The criterion itself is often called the **principle of charity,** because of the spirit of magnanimity—charity—which it urges toward the author. The real point, however, is not charity toward the author (though that may be an incidental benefit) but efficient enhancement of our own understanding. If we violate the principle by constructing a weaker version of the argument than necessary, then it is open to the author or someone who shares the author's view to respond with a more powerful version. Now we have this more powerful version to contend with. If it too has missing premises and if we violate the principle again by filling them in haphazardly, then again we can expect a more powerful reply. Such foolish and tiresome haggling can be drawn out indefinitely, without ever getting to the heart of the matter. The principle of charity aims to forestall this foolishness by responding immediately to the best possible version of the argument.

The principle also has a subtler justification. It may be that the author didn't have the best possible version of the argument in mind. In fact, it may even be that he or she had no clear idea of what the missing statements should be. If so, and if we are content merely with refuting the author, then restricting attention to weak forms of the argument might serve our purpose (though we still run the risk that someone will respond with a stronger version which we have attempted to ignore). But if we sincerely want to know whether the conclusion is true, then it is in our interest to examine the strongest argument possible—even if it isn't exactly what the author had in mind. For if the conclusion happens to be true, only a strong argument will prove it and thereby enable us to know.

Therefore the principle of charity has at least two justifications: it short-circuits pointless debate, and it helps to direct us toward truth. In logic, as elsewhere, charity returns to the giver.

But doesn't the principle violate the original purpose of our criteria, which was to provide guidelines for determining which argument *the author intended?* Not really. Criterion (1) tells us to add only premises which the author expects us to take for granted. The principle of charity, criterion (4), applies only if the other criteria fail to narrow the range of choices down to one. Thus it tells us to construct the best possible argument *within what we know of the author's intentions.* Since authors generally try to make the best case they can for their conclusions, to the degree that they succeed the principle of charity actually helps in capturing their intentions.

The principle of charity seems at first not to apply to our sample argument. The premise "Olaf won't like anyone who is a Republican" seems an obvious choice by criterion (1). What other possibilities could there be? But closer consideration reveals that there are indeed other possibilities. Perhaps the most obvious is simply "Olaf doesn't like Republicans." The main difference between this and "Olaf won't like anyone who is a Republican" is the element of time. The first says that Olaf doesn't like Republicans *now.* The second says that he won't like them *in the future.* Adding the first strengthens the argument slightly but fails to make it rational. (It is not a good bet that a current condition will remain unchanged—unless we know something about the stability of the condition and the time period involved.) Adding the second makes the argument valid. What is interesting about this case is that the author probably intended us to take both for granted, so that criterion (1) provides no grounds for choosing between them. To make the choice we have to apply the principle of charity, which is precisely what I did. I chose "Olaf won't like anyone who is a Republican" instead of "Olaf doesn't like Republicans," because the former makes a stronger argument.

Which premise did the author intend us to assume? It is impossible to tell from the argument alone. Frequently, in fact, the author has no single premise clearly in mind. Perhaps he or she was just thinking in general about Olaf's negative attitude toward Republicans. If so, then our reconstructed argument represents not the author's actual intentions, but what the author's thoughts would be if strengthened and clarified. That's just what we want, as I argued earlier.

There is, however, yet another way in which we might formulate the missing premise: "Olaf will *probably* not like anyone who is a Republican." This premise, which is just like the original one except for the addition of the word "probably," makes the argument inductive rather than deductive. Its advantage over the original premise is that it is weaker and hence more likely to be true. Its disadvantage is that it weakens the reasoning. There is an evident tradeoff here: with the weaker premise we can be surer of truth but less sure of our reasoning; with the stronger, we are less sure of truth but quite confident in our reasoning. Neither choice seems to make the argument as a whole significantly stronger than the other. So even the principle of charity does not enable us to decide between them.

Since our overall estimate of the argument's strength will be the same whichever premise we choose, we can safely choose either. Our goal is to find out how close the author has come to proving the conclusion. If the answer comes out the same either way, then for our purposes either premise is as good as the other. I chose the one that makes the argument deductive because I think that deductive arguments are more beautiful than inductive ones. But your choice could go the other way. It doesn't matter.

There is one more point to be made in connection with the principle of charity: sometimes it is possible to weaken an added premise without affecting the strength of the reasoning. We saw, for example, that both "Olaf won't like anyone who is a Republican" and "Olaf never likes anyone at all" make the argument deductive. The second of these, as we also saw, is ruled out by criterion (1). But if it weren't, it would be ruled out by the principle of charity. For the following argument:

> Oscar is a Republican.
> Olaf won't like anyone who is a Republican.
> ∴ Olaf won't like Oscar.

is stronger overall than:

> Oscar is a Republican.
> Olaf never likes anyone at all.
> ∴ Olaf won't like Oscar.

since, although both are deductive, the second premise of the first argument is weaker, and hence more likely to be true, than the second premise of the second argument. Thus we can state the following principle as a corollary to the principle of charity: *If two or more premises of unequal strength all satisfy criteria (1)–(3) and all make the argument valid, add the weakest.* **Corollary** means "obvious consequence." This corollary is not a new criterion in addition to the four already stated; rather, it is merely an application of criterion (4).

So far we've talked mainly about missing premises, but sometimes conclusions are missing as well. Often this is for dramatic effect. The author sets up all the premises and the reader is left to draw the conclusion. This is especially effective in advertising and propaganda, for it gives unwary readers or listeners the feeling that the conclusion is their own idea and thus makes them more receptive to it. One example from a 1970s advertising campaign is this:

The bigger the burger the better the burger. The burgers are bigger at Burger King.

Your mind jumps automatically to the implied conclusion: "The burgers are better at Burger King." And this, of course, is exactly the effect the ad writer intended. Is the argument any good? Hardly. The second premise and conclusion are practically meaningless, since they don't tell us what the burgers are supposed to be bigger or better than. This makes accurate evaluation difficult. The most obvious problem, however, is that the first premise is clearly false.

When a conclusion is missing, the wording of the premises usually makes its structure obvious. When in doubt, we should apply criteria similar to those which guide addition of hidden premises—that is, we should add only conclusions which the author obviously intended us to infer, and if we can't decide among several of these we should charitably supply the weakest (the one that makes the argument strongest).

Sometimes both premises and conclusion are missing. In fact, an entire argument can be suggested by a single sentence. This happens frequently with conditionals, as when someone says, "If you really loved me, you'd do what I ask." If this sentence were uttered during a lovers' quarrel in which one of the parties was refusing the other's request, both antagonists would probably have in mind the additional premise "You aren't doing what I ask," and both would automatically understand the intended conclusion, "You don't love me." But neither this second premise nor the conclusion need be stated for communication of the entire argument to occur. When completed and diagramed, the argument looks like this:

①[If you really loved me, you'd do what I ask.] Ⓐ[You aren't doing what I ask.] Ⓑ[You don't love me.]

$$\frac{① + Ⓐ}{\underset{Ⓑ}{\downarrow \text{D}}}$$

Incidentally, notice that although the reconstructed argument has a conditional premise, it is not an instance of conditionalization. Conditionalization occurs only when we add a conditional embodying a previously stated inference. Here the conditional was given as part of the argument; we did not add it. The premise and conclusion which we did add conform to all our criteria, as you can check for yourself.

Exercise 4.1 Copy each of the following arguments, circle all inference indicators, bracket and number each statement, add implicit premises and conclusions, and diagram and evaluate the argument's reasoning.

1   She's human, so she's bound to make a mistake sooner or later.

2   If that's not weird, nothing's weird.

3   Wisdom is a product of good judgment. Good judgment is a product of experience. And experience is a product of bad judgment.

4   Money is power, and power corrupts.

5   When guns are outlawed, only outlaws will have guns.

6   You deserve a break today. So get out and get away to McDonald's.

7   I said I'd do the job. So if I didn't do it I'd be a liar. Don't you worry; it'll get done.

8   It's windy out. Just look at the way those trees are moving.

9   Ophelia must be a Scorpio. She's so clever and strong willed.

10 Nothing can be more vital in these days of chaos and confusion than a return to the values of our great American heritage. And nothing can accomplish this more efficiently than the promotion of discipline, patriotism, and respect for authority in our public schools.

11 The film must have been exposed either to excessive light or to radiation, for the negatives are all completely dark. But it wasn't exposed to light, for it remained sealed in my camera from the time I opened the package until the time I developed it. Therefore, it must have been exposed to some sort of radiation.

12 You may rightfully suspect any scientific researcher whose résumé contains an awesome list of publications. He is either a writer of trash, a genius, or a scoundrel. And genius is in short supply. (from a letter to the editor, *Time*, December 28, 1981)

13 There can be no voice where there is no motion or percussion of the air; there can be no motion or percussion of the air where there is no instrument; there can be no instrument without a body; and this being so, a spirit can have neither voice, nor form, nor strength. (Leonardo da Vinci, *Notebooks*)

14 Militarily, the MX would actually diminish our security. It is simply not needed for defense. The Pentagon's own 1982 report shows that the United States already has over 9000 strategic nuclear warheads, compared to approximately 7000 for the Soviet Union. We can destroy every Russian city dozens of times. If we build new missiles the Soviets will do likewise, and the end result will be more missiles pointed at both sides—and greater insecurity all around. (Ted Weiss, board member, SANE, a citizens' group for nuclear disarmament)

15 Atheists ought to say what is perfectly evident; now it is not perfectly evident that the soul is material. (Blaise Pascal, *Pensées*)

4.2 APPLYING THE CRITERIA

Criterion (1) should be applied conservatively. That is, we should not add a premise unless we are fairly certain that it expresses the author's intent. Applying the criterion too liberally may result in the addition of unintended premises and consequent distortion of the author's thought. We can reasonably assume that the author intended at least as much as was written or spoken. If beyond that we are not sure, the safest course is to stick with what we know. In other words, when in doubt add nothing. We should keep in mind, of course, that the author might have intended something we missed. But the chances are equally great, and perhaps greater, that the author had no extra premise in mind, but simply committed a fallacy in reasoning. The following example illustrates this point:

①[There is no proof that the senator didn't take the money.] (Therefore) ②[she took it.]

You can see at once that this inference is fallacious as it stands. Our inability to prove that something didn't happen does not even make it probable that it did. There may simply not be enough evidence, no matter how hard we look—or perhaps no one has tried hard enough to disprove the charge, or no one has the skill, and so on.

But could a hidden premise block these counterexamples? The first thing that comes to mind is probably this:

If there is no proof that the senator didn't take the money, then she took it.

But this is just conditionalization, and as we saw earlier, conditionalization does not illuminate the author's intentions. Thus, this premise is ruled out by criterion (3).

What about the following statement?

Anything not disproved happened.

This is not a form of conditionalization, but it's so obviously false that it is unlikely that any author would expect it to be taken for granted. Thus, despite the fact that it is vaguely suggested by the wording of the argument, this premise violates criterion (1) and must be rejected as well. The same goes for the weaker but still blatantly false premise:

Anything not disproved probably happened.

It's not very likely that anyone would soberly intend us to assume this, either. What seems most probable, or at least equally probable, in this case is that the author had no extra premise in mind, but simply committed a fallacy. Of course, we can't be certain, but under these conditions the best we can do is add nothing. We'll diagram the argument, then, as follows:

$$①$$
$$↓\ F$$
$$②$$

Incidentally, the fallacy committed here is called the **fallacy of ignorance.** We'll examine it more closely in Section 7.4.

We are now ready to take up some more complicated examples. The first is from the Bible. Some people might think it impious to analyze the Bible logically. I disagree. Logic, particularly when used to uncover hidden premises, is a powerful tool of understanding. And the fact that the Bible's authors took the trouble to record their thoughts is good evidence that they wanted to be understood. Indeed, if impiety is the issue, we ought to reflect on the possible impiety of not reading the Bible with the care, charity, and nonlinearity which logic demands.

Our example is from Romans 14:10–13. Its author is the apostle Paul:

①[We shall all stand before God's tribunal.] (For) ②[Scripture says, 'As I live, says the Lord, to me every knee shall bow and every tongue acknowledge God'.] (So) , you see, ③[each of us will have to answer for himself.] ④[Let us (therefore) cease judging one another . . .]

The first thing to notice is that ④, which functions as the final conclusion, is a command, not a declarative statement. So technically speaking, it cannot be part of the argument. We can, however, regard it as the related declarative statement "We should cease judging one another." This doesn't change the meaning in any essential way, and it allows us to treat the final sentence as part of the argument, which certainly seems to have been Paul's intention. If we now diagram the argument as it stands, we get this:

$$②$$
$$↓\ F$$
$$①$$
$$↓\ F\quad \boxed{F}$$
$$③$$
$$↓\ F$$
$$④$$

As stated, each inference is fallacious. Some sceptical and self-indulgent souls might wish to stop here and declare the Bible to be full of fallacies. But if we are seeking understanding, the possibility of hidden premises makes it necessary to look deeper.

Consider the inference from ② to ① . The quotation mentioned is from the Old Testament, most probably Isaiah 45:23. The inference is fallacious as it stands, because in the absence of further information what Isaiah says does not make our standing before God's tribunal even probable. But Paul clearly intended his readers to assume more than he says. His epistle, as its title informs us, was addressed to the Christians in Rome. They would obviously share his belief in the truth of the Old Testament. And so it is clear that one of the things he expected them to take for granted is this:

    Ⓐ   This scriptural passage is true.

Notice that I have chosen this relatively specific premise and not the stronger and more general "Everything the Old Testament says is true," even though Paul intends both, because Ⓐ, though weaker, serves just as well in the argument. This keeps us within the bounds of the corollary to the principle of charity.

But even with Ⓐ added, the inference from ② to ① is not valid, for ② asserts that God *says* we will all stand before his tribunal. We could imagine that what God says is false, so that ② and Ⓐ could both be true and yet ① be false. Paul obviously had something else in mind here:

    Ⓑ   What God says in this passage is true.

Again, Paul probably intended his readers to assume that everything God says is true. But Ⓑ is all the argument requires, so we'll add no more.

Have we now made the inference valid? Not quite. There's yet another counterexample. All three premises—②, Ⓐ, and Ⓑ—could be true and yet we might not bow and acknowledge God *before his tribunal.* What is being assumed, but not stated, is this:

    Ⓒ   This bowing and acknowledgment will take place before God's tribunal.

The wording of the argument strongly suggests that Paul intended his readers to take this assumption, too, for granted.

With this third addition the inference at last becomes valid. Someone could quibble about the phrase "as I live," which implies that what God is saying is just as certain as his living. In that case, we might want to add the further premise "God lives." But I think it is better to regard this phrase as a rhetorical flourish. The essential point of the Isaiah passage is that God says we should all bow and acknowledge him. The first inference, then, is this:

$$\frac{②\ +\ ⓐ\ +\ ⓑ\ +\ ⓒ}{\underset{①}{\downarrow\ \text{D}}}$$

It is clear that Paul intended ⓐ, ⓑ, and ⓒ all to be taken for granted and that their addition strengthens the argument. Moreover, we have not conditionalized, and there seems to be no other choice of premises that would do as well. So all our criteria are met. This is our best guess as to what Paul had in mind.

Now let's stop a minute and consider what we have accomplished. Our analysis just of the first inference has brought to light three of Paul's implicit thoughts. These thoughts probably would have escaped our notice if we had not slowed down and considered this passage carefully. This is part of what I meant when I spoke in Section 1.4 of the power of nonlinear reading and a lot of what I meant when I said just recently that logic is a powerful tool of understanding.

But isn't it obvious that Paul believed these things? Has logic really helped us to uncover anything of value here? I think it has. It is, of course, news to no one that Paul believed premises ⓐ and ⓑ. Premise ⓒ, however, reveals an interesting fact about Paul's interpretation of an Old Testament passage—a fact which is not obvious and which we almost certainly would have overlooked on a quick linear reading. The Isaiah passage itself does not mention a tribunal. Yet Paul, reading between the lines, sees in it a discussion of God's tribunal—the Last Judgment.

Is Paul's interpretation correct? I don't know. But knowing that it *is* his interpretation adds to our understanding of his conception of the Old Testament.

Now that we've wrung all this out of the first inference, let's move on to the second, the inference from ① to ③. As it stands, it too is a fallacy; the fact that we will all stand before God's tribunal does not even make it probable that each of us will have to answer for himself. We could imagine God forcing some to answer for others or simply passing judgment arbitrarily without demanding an account of anyone. But the wording of ① and ③ strongly suggests that Paul intended us to assume the following:

ⓓ   All who stand before God's tribunal will have to answer for themselves.

The addition of ⓓ now makes the second inference valid—and helps us penetrate a little further into Paul's thinking.

It is not quite so easy to see what Paul had in mind with respect to the inference from ③ to ④. What connection was he trying to make between answering to God and judging others? The argument itself gives no solid clues; fortunately, however, in this case we can fill in the missing thought from another source. In the Sermon on the Mount, Jesus is reported to have said, "Pass no judgment, and you will not be judged. For as you judge others, so you will yourselves be judged" (Matthew 7:1). These words would have been familiar both to Paul and his readers, and Paul could no doubt have counted on his readers to take their truth for granted. Moreover, he undoubtedly assumed that God's judgment would take place at the aforementioned tribunal. Thus his implicit thought was probably something like this:

Ⓔ   When we answer for ourselves, God will judge us as we have judged others.

This is a good example of a premise added on the basis of general knowledge about context and the author's beliefs (see the discussion of criterion (1) in the previous section).

Finally, to cinch the validity of this inference, we need the following premise, which Paul also clearly intended to be taken for granted:

Ⓕ   We should not do anything which would bring God's judgment upon us.

(It is obvious that the term "judgment" in all three statements—Ⓔ, Ⓕ, and ④—has the connotation of "negative judgment.") Diagramed in full, the argument now is as follows:

$$
\begin{array}{c}
② \;+\; Ⓐ \;+\; Ⓑ \;+\; Ⓒ \\
\hline
\downarrow \text{D} \\
① \;+\; Ⓓ \qquad\qquad \boxed{\text{D}} \\
\hline
\downarrow \text{D} \\
③ \;+\; Ⓔ \;+\; Ⓕ \\
\hline
\downarrow \text{D} \\
④
\end{array}
$$

Only careful reading and thinking enable us to see this entire structure. There is a great deal more to many arguments than meets the eye.

We can now see that Paul committed no fallacies here; his reasoning is fine, though there is still, of course, the question of the truth of the premises. I'll leave that for you to ponder.

Our last, and most complex, argument in this section is taken from a transcript of a conversation with a school official of an American city. The text is verbatim:

Well, ①[one of the major problems in the city school system right now . . . (is) that we have a number of schools that are underpopulated.] ②[We have elementary schools with as few as 200 students, junior highs with 300 students, and actually senior highs with 400 students.] ③[Programs are terribly limited when there are too few students] (because) ④[you have students bring in money from the state] and ⑤[if you don't have enough students you cannot have a sufficient number of teachers.] (As a consequence), ⑥[we have to bring more students into the schools that are underpopulated.]

Let's take this argument one step at a time. A good place to start is with the premise indicator "because." This indicator shows that ④ and ⑤ are given as evidence for ③. But a closer look reveals that ④ is not evidence for ③ directly. Rather, ④ is a justification for ⑤, which in turn leads to ③. Statement ④ explains why it is that if you don't have enough students you can't have enough teachers. The reason is that state funds are linked to student population (which is just what premise ④ asserts). Hence we have:

Both inferences are fallacious as stated. The inference from ④ to ⑤ is curious, for one would think that reduction of students would also result in a proportionate reduction in the need for teachers. But the author is evidently denying this. Crucial to the inference, then, is the assumption:

Ⓐ   When there are too few students, this money is reduced so much that it is no longer possible to employ enough teachers for the students who remain.

The structure of the argument suggests this premise, and the author seems to have wanted listeners to take it for granted. So we'll add it. It's certainly something we'd need to investigate, though. Its truth is not obvious, and it might turn out to be a major point of contention. Notice, too, that we might not have spotted this assumption if we were not performing a logical analysis.

With Ⓐ added, the inference from ④ to ⑤ becomes valid.

The inference from ⑤ to ③ also has a missing premise:

Ⓑ   If there are too few teachers, programs are terribly limited.

This is a conditional premise, but it is not conditionalization, for it does not embody the stated inference. Rather, it adds a substantial and plausible thought—one which the author probably did expect to be taken for granted. The argument so far can be diagramed as follows:

$$\frac{④ + Ⓐ}{↓ \ D}$$
$$\frac{⑤ + Ⓑ}{↓ \ D}$$
$$③$$

Now where is this reasoning going? Notice that premise ② lists enrollment figures for various schools. These figures sound very small and therefore in this context are evidently intended to show that enrollment in city schools is too low. Together with ③, this would lead to conclusion ①, that underpopulation is a major problem. So apparently there is an inference from ③ and ② to ①. This inference, however, embodies two additional assumptions, without which it would not be valid:

Ⓒ   These figures are too low.

Ⓓ   Whatever results in a terrible limitation of programs is a major problem.

Again, both assertions are plausible, and there is every reason to think that they reflect the author's intentions. So the inference becomes:

$$\frac{② + Ⓒ + ③ + Ⓓ}{↓ \ D}$$
$$①$$

The only statement which remains is ⑥, and the inference indicator "as a consequence" shows that it is the final conclusion. There is, therefore, an inference from ① to ⑥. But this inference, like the others, is invalid as it stands. We can imagine having this problem and simply not wanting to do anything about it. Perhaps no one cares whether it is solved or not. But this is clearly not the author's view. The author is assuming that:

    Ⓔ   This problem must be solved.

Again, there is no question that the author intends this to be taken for granted. But even so, the inference is still not valid. The problem might be soluble in a variety of ways. We might, for example, simply close all the underpopulated schools and send all the students elsewhere. But the author concludes that the solution is to bring more students to the underpopulated schools. It is not clear why this solution is to be preferred over any other, and we do not know enough of the author's thinking to make an accurate guess. But we do know that the author seems to take it for granted that:

    Ⓕ   Solving this problem requires bringing more students to underpopulated schools.

Perhaps the author has reasons to back up this claim, but as with Ⓐ, I'd be wary and would want to examine all the alternatives before accepting it as true. It does, however, make the inference valid, and so we have:

$$\frac{① + Ⓔ + Ⓕ}{\underset{⑥}{\downarrow\ D}}$$

Putting everything together, we can now construct the final argument diagram:

$$
\begin{array}{c}
\dfrac{④ + Ⓐ}{\downarrow\ D} \\
\dfrac{⑤ + Ⓑ}{\downarrow\ D} \\
\dfrac{② + Ⓒ + ③ + Ⓓ \qquad \boxed{D}}{\downarrow\ D} \\
\dfrac{① + Ⓔ + Ⓕ}{\underset{⑥}{\downarrow\ D}}
\end{array}
$$

The argument is deductive, but as I noted earlier, we'd want to take a long, hard look at the premises—especially Ⓐ and Ⓕ—before accepting it as sound.

Exercise 4.2   Copy each of the following arguments, circle all inference indicators, bracket and number each statement, add implicit premises and conclusions where necessary, and diagram and evaluate the reasoning.

1   You'd better not ask for a raise today. The boss is still beet-faced crazy mad about what Olaf did this morning.

2   Ophelia couldn't have driven her car home from the shopping center in 15 minutes. The distance is fully 10 kilometers, and her car won't go over 60 kilometers per hour.

3   It is preposterous to speak of poverty in America. After all, we are the richest nation in the world.

4   We should refrain from breaking the law both because we should seek to avoid punishment ourselves and because we should seek to avoid harm to others.

5   . . . if thine enemy hunger, feed him; if he thirst, give him drink: for in so doing thou shalt heap coals of fire on his head. (Romans 12:20, King James Version)

6   Friendship requires for its existence two or more persons having common interests and pursuits and cooperating in their fulfillment; it also requires, of course, frequent association for a considerable time. . . . It is for these reasons—the possession of common interests, cooperation, and frequent association—that no one could truly declare the entire world, or even any considerable part of it, to be his friend. (Richard Taylor, *Good and Evil*)

7   Now do you say you are going to make Right your master and do away with Wrong, or make Order your master and do away with Disorder? If you do, then you have not understood the principle of heaven and earth or the nature of the ten thousand things. This is like saying that you are going to make Heaven your master and do away with Earth, or make Yin your master and do away with Yang. Obviously it is impossible. (Chuang Tzu)

8   People feel that they want and "need" indoor plumbing, central heating, refrigerators, penicillin, education, movies, radios, records, television, green lawns, books, autos, travel, sports and concerts, music, chic clothes, and so forth. The biological scientist tells them that they can be well nourished on a thin porridge for a few cents a day, but that leaves them as cold as the information that the chemicals in their bodies are worth only a couple of dollars. . . . the necessities of life—the absolute musts—have little to do with the minimum *physiological* needs of food, clothing, and shelter. (Paul A. Samuelson, *Economics*, 9th ed.)

9   The other conceivable use of a space-based laser weapon is as an antisatellite system. The practicality of the concept is highly questionable. In the first place, satellites in orbit are already vulnerable to explosive weapons, which can be placed accurately in space or even made to home in on a warm object in orbit. A space-based antisatellite laser would itself be vulnerable to the same weapons. The laser system would also be complex and fragile and therefore expensive and difficult to maintain. It is highly unlikely that antisatellite lasers will ever become more cost-effective than mechanical satellite killers launched from the earth. (Kosta Tsipis, "Laser Weapons," *Scientific American*, December 1981)

10 You are not the deputies of a district or of a certain tribe, you are not the representatives of particular interests, but you are first of all the chosen delegates of the whole great German nation. You are thus guarantors of that German Reich which National Socialism has made possible and created. You are therefore duty bound to serve with the deepest loyalty the movement which paved the way for and realized the miracle of German history in the year 1938. In you must be incorporated in the most superlative form the virtues of the National Socialist Party: loyalty, comradeship, and obedience. (Adolph Hitler, speech to the German Reichstag, January 30, 1938, shortly after Nazi invasions of Austria and Czechoslovakia)

11 [The people] . . . considered that the Congress [of 1774] was composed of many wise and experienced men. That being convened from different parts of the country, they brought with them and communicated to each other a variety of useful information. That in the course of the time they passed together in inquiring into and discussing the true interests of their country, they must have acquired some very accurate knowledge on that head. That they were individually interested in the public liberty and prosperity, and therefore that it was not less their inclination than their duty, to recommend only such measures as after the most mature deliberation they really thought prudent and advisable.

   These and similar considerations then induced the people to rely greatly on the judgment and integrity of the Congress; and they took their advice, notwithstanding the various arts and endeavors used to deter and dissuade them from it. But if the people at large had reason to confide in the men of that Congress, few of whom had been fully tried or generally known, still greater reason have they now to respect the judgment and advice of the Convention, for it is well known that some of the most distinguished members of that Congress, who have since been tried and justly

approved for patriotism and abilities, and who have grown old in
acquiring political information, were also members of this Convention, and carried into it their accumulated knowledge and experience. (John Jay, *The Federalist*, written in support of the results
of the Constitutional Convention of 1787)

4.3   REWRITING ARGUMENTS

Sometimes an argument is so poorly stated or so complex that there is no
reasonable way to bracket off its component statements. In such cases, we
may not only have to add missing statements, but we may also have to
rewrite portions of the argument itself before a coherent bracketing scheme
is feasible. Of course, in doing so our aim is only to clarify structure. We
must be careful not to distort the meaning. The following argument will
serve as an illustration. It is from the prosecutor's speech in the trial scene
of Dostoyevski's magnificent novel *The Brothers Karamazov.* Fyodor Karamazov has been murdered, and his son Dimitri, the prisoner, stands ac-
cused.

> You see, gentlemen of the jury, on the night of the murder there were five
> people in Fyodor Karamazov's home: Fyodor Karamazov himself (but he did
> not kill himself, that's evident); then his servant, Gregory, but he was almost
> killed himself; the third person was Gregory's wife, Marfa, but it would be
> simply shameful to imagine her murdering her master. Two people are left—
> the prisoner and Smerdyakov . . . if we are to believe the prisoner's statement
> that he is not the murderer, then Smerdyakov must be the murderer. . . .

This, of course, is only part of the prosecutor's argument. The whole is
considerably longer and more complicated. In this section the prosecutor
reaches the conclusion that if the prisoner is not the murderer, then Smerdyakov is. Then, in an intricate argument which I have not included here,
he tries to show that Smerdyakov could not be the murderer. The ultimate
conclusion? That the prisoner is the murderer, which of course is just what
we would expect a prosecutor to conclude. But let's confine our attention
to the fragment stated here.

The first statement consists of a list of possible suspects, interspersed
with reasons for eliminating some of them. If we set out to bracket and
number it as usual, we immediately run into two problems: (1) the interspersed reasons function as separate premises and (2) not all five suspects
are listed in the first statement, so that when we diagram the argument,
the second statement (that only the prisoner and Smerdyakov are left) does
not follow from the first, as it obviously is supposed to do. The prosecutor
clearly intends the prisoner and Smerdyakov to be counted among the five,
but for stylistic reasons he neglects to mention them in the first statement.
These problems, especially the second, make it impossible to bracket and

number in the usual way and still come up with a reasonable diagram. (If you can't see why, try making the diagram.) We need to rewrite the argument to clarify its structure. This will involve adding the names of Smerdyakov and the prisoner to the first statement and writing the interspersed statements separately so that their role as independent premises is made apparent. We should wind up with something like this:

①[On the night of the murder, there were five people in Fyodor Karamazov's home: Fyodor Karamazov himself; his servant, Gregory; Gregory's wife, Marfa; the prisoner; and Smerdyakov.] ②[Fyodor Karamazov did not kill himself.] ③[Gregory was almost killed himself.] ④[It would be shameful to imagine Marfa murdering her master, Fyodor.] ⑤[Only two people are left who could have committed the murder—the prisoner and Smerdyakov.] ⑥[If we are to believe the prisoner's statement that he is not the murderer, then Smerdyakov must be the murderer.]

Notice that all I've done here is to rearrange things, drop some irrelevant phrases, and expand some statements to make their meaning clearer. I haven't changed anything essential to the argument's meaning.

However, some of the thought is still missing. Statement ⑤ is evidently supposed to follow from ①, ②, ③, and ④, but how? Well, ① sets up five possibilities, and ②, ③, and ④ knock down three of them. Statement ② tells us that Fyodor did not kill himself and thus eliminates him as the murderer. Statement ③, however, doesn't say that Gregory didn't do it; rather, it functions as evidence that he didn't. In other words, it is a premise for the implied conclusion:

Ⓐ   Gregory is not the murderer.

Likewise, ④ is given as evidence for the implied conclusion:

Ⓑ   Marfa is not the murderer.

These implied conclusions, together with ① and ②, are used to establish ⑤ as follows:

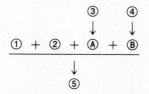

But notice that ⑤ does not follow validly from ①, ②, Ⓐ, and Ⓑ without the additional assumption:

Ⓒ   Fyodor was murdered by someone in his house.

The prosecutor obviously expects us to take this for granted, but we ought to be wary, for murder at a distance is possible by various means. If we had not analyzed this argument, this assumption could well have escaped our attention. And if it were a real trial and this assumption were false, this oversight could be a matter of life or death. (As it turns out in the novel, Fyodor was murdered by someone in his house, though not by Dimitri. But you see the point.) Hence we must add Ⓒ to ①, ②, Ⓐ, and Ⓑ. The rest of the argument is now straightforward, and the full diagram is this:

$$
\begin{array}{cc}
③ & ④ \\
\downarrow F & \downarrow F
\end{array}
$$

$$
\underline{① \;+\; ② \;+\; Ⓐ \;+\; Ⓑ \;+\; Ⓒ} \qquad \boxed{F}
$$
$$
\downarrow D
$$
$$
⑤
$$
$$
\downarrow D
$$
$$
⑥
$$

The inferences from ③ to Ⓐ and ④ to Ⓑ are weak links in the argument. In neither case is there any natural way, apart from conditionalization, of supplying premises that clearly capture the prosecutor's intention. His reasoning in both cases is rhetorically powerful, but logically fallacious.

   The prosecutor's argument—at least the portion of it we analyzed—was relatively simple to rewrite once we understood its organization. Often, however, rewriting is considerably more difficult. This is especially true when the argument is loosely organized, rambling, and repetitive. Under such conditions the burden is on us to edit, reorganize, and simplify, while remaining faithful to the author's thought, until a coherent argument emerges. That's hard work, but it's the price we must pay for thorough understanding. Our next example has all these negative features; it is indeed loosely organized, rambling, and repetitive. Nevertheless, it manages to communicate something, and we will be able to glean considerable understanding from it. The argument is from a speech made by Mao Zedong on February 27, 1957, to the Eleventh Session of the Supreme State Congress of the People's Republic of China:

   ①[The policy of letting a hundred flowers blossom and a hundred schools of thought contend is designed to promote the flourishing of the arts and the progress of science;]   ②[it is designed to enable a socialist culture to thrive in our land.] ③[Different forms and styles of art can develop freely and different schools in science can contend freely.] We think that ④[it is harmful to the growth of art and science if administrative measures are used to impose one particular style of art or school of thought and to ban another.] ⑤[Questions of right and wrong in the arts and sciences should be settled through free discussion in artistic and scientific circles and in the course of practical work in the arts and sciences.] ⑥[They should not be settled in summary fashion.] ⑦[A period of trial is often needed to determine whether something is right or wrong.] ⑧[In the past, new and correct things often failed at the outset to win recognition from the majority of people and had to develop by twists and turns in struggle.] ⑨[Correct and good things have often at first been looked upon not as fragrant flowers but as poisonous weeds.] ⑩[Copernicus' theory of the solar system and Darwin's theory of evolution were once dismissed as erroneous and had to win over through bitter opposition.] ⑪[Chinese history offers many similar examples.] ⑫[In socialist society, conditions for the growth of new things are radically different from and far superior to those in the old society.] ⑬[Nevertheless it still often happens that new, rising forces are held back and reasonable suggestions smothered.]

⑭[The growth of new things can also be hindered, not because of deliberate suppression, but because of lack of discernment.] (That is why) ⑮[we should take a cautious attitude in regard to questions of right and wrong in the arts and sciences, encourage free discussion, and avoid hasty conclusions.]

I have numbered the statements here to facilitate the following discussion, but before we are through we will rewrite and renumber the entire passage.

The argument is a justification for Mao's policy of "letting a hundred flowers blossom and a hundred schools of thought contend," a policy which, incidentally, was abandoned during the so-called Cultural Revolution of the late 1960s and early 1970s and since has had an uneven history. The essence of this policy is expressed in statement ⑮, which is also the main conclusion: "We should take a cautious attitude in regard to questions of right and wrong in the arts and sciences, encourage free discussion, and avoid hasty conclusions." The rest of the argument supports this conclusion.

The only statements in the passage which clearly do not contribute evidence for ⑮ are statements ①, ②, and ③. Statements ① and ② explain what Mao's policy is designed to accomplish, and statement ③ tells what will be allowed under the policy, but none of the three actually functions as evidence that the policy is correct. Thus they are not components of the argument and should be omitted. Statement ⑨ can also be omitted. It is just a metaphorical restatement of ⑧. These omissions simplify our work.

Now let's start with the obvious. There is a clear and valid inference from ⑩ and ⑪ to ⑧, given the obviously implicit premise:

Ⓐ   Copernicus' theory of the solar system and Darwin's theory of evolution are now known to be correct.

Moreover, ⑧ leads to ⑦, via the tacit assumption:

Ⓑ   The future is likely to resemble the past.

This assumption is needed because ⑦ asserts that a period of trial is often needed *in general* (i.e., both in the past and in the future). I said "likely," because it is not true that the future invariably resembles the past. Thus I chose to add a plausible assumption that makes the inference inductive, rather than a false one that would make it valid. This accords with the principle of charity. Assumption Ⓑ, by the way, is a version of the principle of the uniformity of nature, which I'll explain more thoroughly in Section 6.5. So far we have:

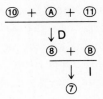

But now things get difficult. The argument must ultimately lead from ⑦ to the conclusion ⑮, which makes three assertions:

(i)   We should take a cautious attitude in regard to questions of right and wrong in the arts and sciences.
(ii)   We should encourage free discussion.
(iii) We should avoid hasty conclusions.

The premises directly prior to the conclusion presumably provide evidence for all three. Assertion (i), which urges caution, could conceivably be supported by any of ④, ⑤, ⑥, ⑦, ⑬, or ⑭. Assertion (ii) is certainly best supported by ⑤. And assertion (iii) could be supported by ⑤, ⑥, or ⑦—and possibly ⑭. Do all these premises directly support ⑮, or do some support others? One can see a number of possible patterns of inference: ⑦ could support ④, ⑤, or ⑥; ④ could support ⑥ and perhaps ⑤; ⑤ could support

⑥. But what did Mao intend? Unfortunately he has not provided enough inference indicators to make his intentions clear. And after some deliberation one gets the impression that this passage expresses a complex web of inferences, not a single line of argument. One also begins to suspect that Mao himself had no clear idea of what the logical order of the premises was supposed to be. If we throw together in one diagram all the inferences suggested by what he says, we get the following atrocity:

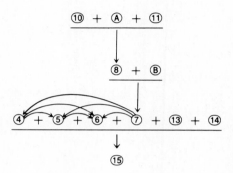

Since at several points more than one arrow emerges from a single circle, *this is not a correct argument diagram* (see Section 2.7). It is impossible to evaluate by our procedures and therefore of no use to us. But it does illustrate what I mean by a "web" of inferences.

It should not be construed, either, as an accurate portrayal of Mao's inferential intentions. Mao's intentions, as I noted above, were probably indeterminate and thus incapable of being captured by any diagram. This indeterminacy, while extremely frustrating from a logician's point of view, would not even be noticed by a general audience. It is therefore not a hindrance to communication; Mao manages to express his overall point rather effectively. Moreover, Mao is not alone in reasoning this way; a great deal of argumentative thought and discourse is weblike or indeterminate in character. We should therefore have a workable policy for dealing with it.

My suggestion is that we try to unravel from the web of the author's possible intentions the strongest and most reasonable strand of argument. While there is no guarantee that this will capture the author's actual thought, it does accord with the spirit of the principle of charity and may well bring us close to what the author wishes us to understand.

Let us, then, return to an examination of Mao's conclusion and try to determine how best to support it, given the premises at hand. The one premise which appeared as plausible support for all three components of the conclusion was premise ⑤. That's good reason to place it immediately prior to the conclusion in our diagram. But ⑥ also supports assertions (i) and (iii) of the conclusion, and it seems to follow from ⑤, which suggests that ⑥, not ⑤, should immediately precede the conclusion. One way to resolve this conflict is to combine ⑤ and ⑥ into a single premise, as follows:

(5,6)   Questions of right and wrong in the arts and sciences should be settled, not in a summary manner, but through free discussion in artistic and scientific circles and in the course of practical work in the arts and sciences.

This combined premise, then, will directly support ⑮. Now there are two possibilities for the derivation of (5,6) . Either it comes directly from ⑦, or it is inferred from ④, which in turn is inferred from ⑦. I think that the direct connection with ⑦ is stronger. For ④ says only that administrative control is harmful to science and art. From that it doesn't follow that artists and scientists should engage in free discussion. (Perhaps they should roll dice, consult the *I Ching*, or take a vote.) If, however, we start from the idea of needing a period of trial—where it is assumed that by "trial" is meant controversy in the course of practical work—then (5,6) follows with little difficulty. The inference does, however, require the extra premise:

Ⓒ   We should do what promotes, and not what hinders, determination of right and wrong in the arts and sciences.

Mao surely intended this. So now we have:

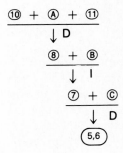

This neglects ④, but it does make a strong line of reasoning, and that is what we set out to do.

The rest is relatively easy. Statements (5,6) , ⑬, and ⑭ all directly support ⑮. And though I'm not absolutely sure, I'd judge this inference to be inductive. See what you think. Statement ⑫, the only statement which remains, serves only to introduce ⑬. It plays no direct role in the argument. Thus our final diagram is:

$$\frac{\text{⑩} + \text{Ⓐ} + \text{⑪}}{\downarrow \text{ D}}$$

$$\frac{\text{⑧} + \text{Ⓑ}}{\downarrow \text{ I}}$$

$$\frac{\text{⑦} + \text{Ⓒ}}{\downarrow \text{ D}}$$

$$\frac{\text{⑤,⑥} + \text{⑬} + \text{⑭}}{\downarrow \text{ I}}$$

$$\text{⑮}$$

I have changed and omitted so much, however, and the original argument was stated so long ago, that it seems worthwhile now to renumber and rewrite it, so that we can more easily appreciate the final product. Here it is, renumbered and rewritten in annotated standard form:

1   Copernicus' theory of the solar system and Darwin's theory of evolution were once dismissed as erroneous and had to win over through bitter opposition.

*2   These theories are now widely known to be correct.

3   Chinese history offers many similar examples of correct theories which were at first widely opposed and had to gain acceptance through struggle (i.e., controversial discussion).

∴ 4   In the past, new and correct things have often failed at the outset to win widespread recognition and have had to develop by struggle (controversial discussion).   1,2,3

*5   The future is likely to resemble the past.

∴ 6   A period of trial (controversial discussion) is often needed to determine (establish widespread recognition of) whether something is right or wrong.   4,5

*7   We should do what promotes, and not what hinders, determination (widespread recognition) of right and wrong in the arts and sciences.

∴ 8   Questions of right and wrong in the arts and sciences should be settled, not in a summary manner, but through free discussion in artistic and scientific circles.   6,7

9   Even in socialist society it still often happens that new, rising forces are held back and reasonable suggestions smothered.

10   The growth of new things can also be hindered, not because of deliberate suppression, but because of lack of discernment.

∴ 11   We should take a cautious attitude in regard to questions of right and wrong in the arts and sciences, encourage free discussion, and avoid hasty conclusions.   8,9,10

(Numbers preceded by asterisks indicate premises I have added.) The diagram is now:

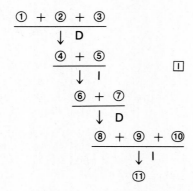

In this final version, I have reordered the premises and made a number of simplifying and clarifying changes in the wording, but I have tried, while building a strong argument, to stay as close as possible to Mao's thought. The result, as you can see, is a clear, rational argument, whose premises are all fairly plausible. It's a good argument, and it establishes its conclusion with a substantial degree of probability. It is certainly not precisely what Mao had in mind, but it's a reasonable and charitable interpretation of what he said, and it shows that his thought was essentially rational. Mao should have listened to his own advice.

In practical life you will never go to this much trouble to analyze and reconstruct an argument. But I think it's worthwhile to see it done and to try a few examples for yourself, if only to gain a realistic appreciation of the complexities of human reasoning.

You might have noticed that I followed a different strategy in each of the last two examples. In the prosecutor's argument, where the problem merely concerned the form of existing premises and the argument was simple enough to keep in mind all at once, I just rewrote the whole thing and then worried about where to add premises. With Mao's speech, I jumped right in in the middle, reconstructing inferences and adding premises, until I got a clear idea of what the argument was. Only then did I rewrite and reorganize. In the next example, I'm going to use an even more radical version of this second strategy. This argument is so long that I'll start just by listing what I think *could be* the relevant statements. Then I'll pare, juggle, and clarify this list, adding premises where necessary, until the argument emerges in its purest and simplest form. Which strategy works best depends largely on the argument's length and complexity. The first works better for short and simple arguments, the second for long and complex ones. But experiment and decide! With practice you'll develop your own feeling for strategy.

The argument is from the *Republic*, written by the Greek philosopher Plato in the fourth century B.C. It takes the form of a dialogue, or conversation, between Socrates, who was Plato's teacher, and Glaucon, a friend and pupil of Socrates. The topic is the immortality of the soul. Socrates speaks first.

Are you not aware that the soul is immortal and never perishes?

Glaucon looked at me in astonishment. Indeed I am not, he replied. Are you prepared to assert that?

I ought to be; and so, I think, ought you. There is no difficulty.

There is for me; but if you find it so easy a matter, I should like to hear your account.

You shall. When you speak of a certain thing as 'a good', and of another as 'an evil', do you agree with me in thinking of the evil as always being the thing which corrupts and destroys, and of the good as that which benefits and preserves?

Yes.

And would you say that everything has its peculiar evil as well as its good, for instance, opthalmia for the eyes, disease for the body in general, mildew for grain, rot for timber, rust for iron and copper—and, as I say, that almost anything has some special evil or malady, which impairs the thing it attacks and ends by breaking it up and destroying it altogether?

Yes, no doubt.

Everything, then, is destroyed by its own peculiar evil or corruption; or if that will not destroy it, there is at any rate nothing else that can bring it to an end; for clearly what is good for it will never destroy it, not yet what is neither good nor evil. Hence if we find that there is a thing whose peculiar evil does indeed deprave it but cannot bring about its utter dissolution, shall we not at once be sure that it is by nature indestructible?

That seems likely.

What of the soul, then? Has it not some special evil which depraves it?

Certainly; there are all the vices we have been speaking of, injustice, intemperance, cowardice, ignorance.

And does any of these vices work its complete destruction? We must be careful here not to be misled into supposing that when a wicked and foolish man is

found out, he has been destroyed by his wickedness, which is a depraved condition of his soul. Think of it rather in this way. It is true of the body, is it not?
that physical evil, namely disease, wastes and destroys it until it is no longer
a body at all, and all the other things we instanced are annihilated by the
pervading corruption of the evil which peculiarly besets them. Now is it true
in the same way of the soul that injustice and other forms of vice, by besetting
and pervading it, waste it away in corruption until they sever it from the body
and bring about its death?

No, certainly not.

On the other hand, it would be unreasonable to suppose that a thing which
cannot be destroyed by its own vice should be destroyed by the vicious condition
of something else. Observe that we should not think it proper to say of the
body that it was destroyed simply by the badness of its food, which might be
rotten or mouldy; only when such food has induced a bad condition of the body
itself do we say that the body is destroyed by its own diseased state, occasioned
by the bad food. The body is one thing, the food another; and we shall not allow
that the evil belonging to that other thing can ever destroy the body, unless it
engenders the body's own peculiar evil. By the same reasoning, if bodily evil
does not engender in the soul the soul's peculiar evil, we must never allow that
the soul is destroyed merely by an evil peculiar to something else.

That is reasonable.

. . . So, since the soul is not destroyed by any evil, either its own or another's,
clearly it must be a thing that exists for ever, and is consequently immortal.

Before we try to do any analysis, let's simply list the major points of
this dialogue so that we get a clearer idea of what we have to work with:

1 Evil is that which corrupts and destroys.
2 Good is that which benefits and preserves.
3 Everything has its peculiar evil.
4 What is good will never destroy a thing, nor will what is neither
   good nor evil.
5 If a thing is not destroyed by its peculiar evil, nothing can destroy
   it.
6 The peculiar evils of the soul are the vices of injustice, intemperance, cowardice, and ignorance.
7 These vices do not destroy the soul.
8 If bodily evil does not engender the soul's peculiar evil, then the
   soul is not destroyed by it.
9 The soul is not destroyed by anything.

10   The soul exists forever.

11   The soul is immortal.

This is not yet a summary of the argument, but only a compilation of the major points of the dialogue. We have not yet determined which of these statements actually function in the argument and which of them are inessential.

The next step is to pick out the inferences. Statement ⑪, of course, is the conclusion, and the most obvious line of inference leads from ⑨ through ⑩ to ⑪. The inference indicators "so," "since," and "consequently" in the final paragraph of the passage confirm this. But each of these inferences requires an extra premise.

Consider first the inference from ⑨ to ⑩. We could imagine that the soul is not destroyed by anything and yet that it would wink out of existence for no reason. But this seems terribly unlikely, as Socrates knew. He was evidently assuming:

Ⓐ   A thing can cease to exist only if something destroys it.

This makes the inference valid.

The inference from ⑩ to ⑪ also contains a hidden thought. To say that something exists forever is to say that it *lasts* forever; to say that it is immortal is to say that it *lives* forever. Something could therefore exist forever without being immortal. What Socrates is assuming is this:

Ⓑ   The soul lives so long as it exists.

It is evident from other passages in Plato's writings that Socrates believed this. He thought that the soul was the principle of life and therefore that a soul could not exist without being alive. So we are warranted in adding this premise. What we have so far is this:

$$\frac{⑨ \; + \; Ⓐ}{\downarrow \;\; D}$$

$$\frac{⑩ \; + \; Ⓑ}{\downarrow \;\; D}$$

$$⑪$$

Now where did ⑨ come from? That's not too difficult to see. There is a clear and valid inference from ⑤, ⑥, and ⑦ to ⑨. This inference is perfectly correct as it stands and requires no additions. Thus we have:

And what of the statements that remain? Well, there seems to be an inference from ① and ② to ④ and one from ④ to ⑤, like this:

$$① + ②$$
$$↓$$
$$④$$
$$↓$$
$$⑤$$

But there are difficulties with both inferences.

The inference from ① and ② to ④ seems open to the following counterexample: Nourishment is good, because it benefits and preserves us; but it destroys the plants and animals which we eat. Therefore, we can imagine that ① and ② are true but ④ is false. What is good (nourishment) destroys a thing (food). On second thought, however, this seems to violate the intended meaning of these statements. Nourishment is good *for us*, but evil *for the things we eat*. What is good for the food itself would never destroy it. When speaking of good and evil, we have to be specific about what a thing is good or evil for. So let's modify ①, ②, and ④ slightly, so that they say specifically what Socrates seems to have had in mind:

①'   What is evil for a thing is that which corrupts and destroys it.

②'   What is good for a thing is that which benefits and preserves it.

∴ ④'   What is purely good for a thing will never destroy it, nor will what is neither good nor evil.

This rules out the counterexample and makes the inference valid. Notice, however, that what I've done is not to add premises, but to rewrite existing ones to bring out their intended meaning. That's why I've numbered these premises with their original numbers followed by a prime mark. (I'll renumber before I'm through, but this helps keep track of what I'm doing.)

Finally, we must examine the inference from ④′ to ⑤. The validity of this inference depends upon what is meant by "peculiar evil." If "peculiar evil" means whatever is evil to a thing in any way (even if it also has good effects), then the inference is valid. Since what is purely good for a thing won't destroy it and neither will what is neither good nor evil, it does follow deductively that only something which is in some way evil for it can destroy it.

If, however, by "peculiar evil" Socrates means whatever is purely evil for a thing—and his examples of peculiar evils seem to suggest this—then the inference is invalid. For there are things, like chemotherapy for cancer, which are both good and evil to something (in this case a human patient). Chemotherapy benefits and preserves, but it also corrupts (through unhealthy side effects) and may eventually even destroy (i.e., kill) the patient. Hence it may be true that what is purely good or neither good nor evil would never destroy a thing (premise ④′), but false that only its peculiar evil could destroy it (premise ⑤). For it could also be destroyed by something that was not its peculiar evil—that is, not purely evil for it, but something both good and evil, like chemotherapy. So under this interpretation of "peculiar evil" the inference is invalid, indeed fallacious.

Which meaning of "peculiar evil" should we choose? I have a hunch that by "peculiar evil" Socrates meant something purely evil; if so, his reasoning, as we just saw, is fallacious. Yet the argument is so interesting and the topic such a vital one that it would be a shame if we didn't examine the strongest version. So despite my hunch, let's go ahead and make the assumption required to validate the inference. We'll assume, in other words:

ⓒ   A thing's peculiar evil is anything which is evil to it in any way (even if it also has good effects).

We now have:

$$
\begin{array}{c}
① ' \ + \ ② ' \\
\downarrow \ \text{D} \\
④ ' \ + \ ⓒ \\
\downarrow \ \text{D} \\
⑤ \ + \ ⑥ \ + \ ⑦ \\
\downarrow \ \text{D} \\
⑨ \ + \ Ⓐ \\
\downarrow \ \text{D} \\
⑩ \ + \ Ⓑ \\
\downarrow \ \text{D} \\
⑪
\end{array}
$$

The only statements in our original list which remain unused are ③ and ⑧. Statement ③ is not needed anywhere and can be omitted. Statement ⑧, however, at least at first glance, seems to support ⑤. But it does so only as an answer to a possible objection—namely, that bodily evils like disease or injury seem to destroy the soul. It would not, without a good bit more reasoning, actually imply ⑤. Since Socrates has not supplied any such reasoning and since ⑤ is already adequately supported by other premises, we can leave ⑧ out as well.

We are at last ready to renumber and rediagram. The argument is this:

  1   What is evil for a thing is that which corrupts and destroys it.
  2   What is good for a thing is that which benefits and preserves it.
∴ 3   What is purely good for a thing will never destroy it, nor will what is neither good nor evil.   1,2
 *4   A thing's peculiar evil is anything which is evil to it in any way (even if it has good effects).
∴ 5   If a thing is not destroyed by its peculiar evil, nothing can destroy it.   3,4
  6   The peculiar evils of the soul are the vices of injustice, intemperance, cowardice, and ignorance.
  7   These vices do not destroy the soul.
∴ 8   The soul is not destroyed by anything.   5,6,7
 *9   A thing can cease to exist only if something destroys it.
∴ 10   The soul exists forever.   8,9
 *11   The soul lives so long as it exists.
∴ 12   The soul is immortal.   10,11

(Once again, asterisks indicate added premises.) The diagram is:

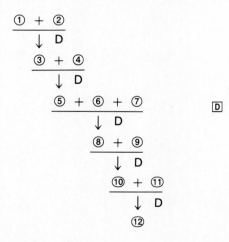

This argument is logically superb, and except perhaps for premise ④, I think it accurately reflects Socrates' thought. (Recall that if we don't assume ④ the step from ③ to ⑤ is fallacious.) Different logicians working with the same material might have come up with slightly different analyses (different wording, greater or lesser elaboration of the reasoning, etc.) but any good analysis would come out something like this. We have deviated very little from what Socrates actually said.

Is the argument sound? Unfortunately not. The weak point is premise ⑥. Surely the soul has other peculiar evils besides the vices of injustice, intemperance, cowardice, and ignorance. These include senility, madness, coma—and perhaps even death itself. And among these other peculiar evils may be some that destroy the soul; this possibility has not been ruled out. So ⑥ is false, and the argument fails to establish its conclusion.

The immortality of the soul, like the existence of God, is a proposition which has never been successfully proved or disproved. Logic has its achievements, but it also has its limitations.

Exercise 4.3   Rewrite each of the following arguments in annotated standard form (see Section 2.1), making minor changes and adding statements where necessary to clarify the author's thought. Then diagram and evaluate as usual. Take your time; one of the longer examples is plenty for an evening's work. Also, write on only one side of your paper. You'll save a lot of bother for yourself and anyone who reads your work.

1   . . . whatever I'm telling you about the *tonal* and the *nagual* could not possibly have been told to you before. Any idiot would know that you know nothing about them, because in order to be acquainted with them, you would have to be a sorcerer and you aren't. Or you would've had to talk about them with a sorcerer and you haven't. So disregard everything you've heard before, because it is inapplicable. (Don Juan, Yaqui Indian sorcerer, quoted by Carlos Castaneda in *Tales of Power*)

2   These times demand a magazine be read in an environment of tranquility.

The premise is a simple one. When people have the time to read a magazine, they have the time to read your ad. So when do they have the time? Sunday morning. And what do they read? *The New York Times Magazine.*

It arrives in an environment of tranquility. And arrives surrounded by a unique environment of integrity: The Sunday New York Times.

The right time. And the right place. No wonder the ads get read.

These times demand the Times. (Advertisement in Sunday *New York Times*, December 6, 1981)

3   ... in the development of this organization rests the only true alternative to war—and war appeals no longer as a rational alternative. Unconditional war can no longer lead to unconditional victory. It can no longer serve to settle disputes. It can no longer concern the great powers alone. For a nuclear disaster, spread by wind and water and fear, could well engulf the great and the small, the rich and the poor, the committed and the uncommitted alike. Man must put an end to war—or war will put an end to mankind.

   ... This will require new strength and new rules for the United Nations. For disarmament without checks is but a shadow—and a community without law is but a shell. (John F. Kennedy, address to U.N. General Assembly, September 25, 1961)

4   Sometimes it is suggested ... that there are *two kinds of arguments*, deductive arguments, on the one hand, and inductive arguments on the other. This 'distinction', at least as it is usually explained, only confuses matters. One is told that 'deductive arguments' are 'explicative' or 'non-ampliative', that is, they 'contain nothing in the conclusion not already contained in the premises'. If this is, as it seems to be, intended as an explanation of what it is for an argument to be *deductively valid*, it is apt to turn out either false, if 'contains nothing in the conclusion not already contained in the premises' is taken literally (for while '*A* and *B*, so *A*' meets this condition, '*A*, so *A* $\lor$ *B*', which is also deductively valid, does not) or else trivial, if 'contains nothing in the conclusion not already contained in the premises' is taken metaphorically (for what is the test for '*A* $\lor$ *B*' being *implicitly* 'contained in' '*A*', if not that '*A* $\lor$ *B*' follows deductively from '*A*'?). 'Inductive arguments', by contrast, one is told, are 'ampliative' or 'non-explicative', that is to say, 'their conclusions go beyond what is contained in their premises'. This makes matters worse, because it cannot be taken, symmetrically with the explanation of 'deductive argument', as an explanation of what it is for an argument to be inductively strong. For all it says about inductive arguments is that they are not deductively valid; but not all deductively invalid arguments are inductively strong. (Susan Haack, *Philosophy of Logics*)

(Note: The definitions Haack is discussing in this excerpt are used in some traditional logic books, but are seldom nowadays taken seriously because of the problems she mentions. They are not, of course, the definitions used in this book. The symbol "$\lor$" means "or." We'll meet it again in Chapter 10.)

5   In the entire water-pollution problem, there is probably nothing more disturbing than the threat of widespread contamination of groundwater. It is not possible to add pesticides to water anywhere without threatening the purity of water everywhere. Seldom if ever

does Nature operate in closed and separate compartments, and she has not done so in distributing the earth's water supply. Rain, falling on the land, settles down through pores and cracks in soil and rock, penetrating deeper and deeper until eventually it reaches a zone where all the pores of the rock are filled with water, a dark, subsurface sea, rising under hills, sinking beneath valleys. This groundwater is always on the move, sometimes at a pace so slow that it travels no more than 50 feet a year, sometimes rapidly, by comparison, so that it moves nearly a tenth of a mile in a day. It travels by unseen waterways until here and there it comes to the surface as a spring, or perhaps it is tapped to feed a well. But mostly it contributes to streams and so to rivers. Except for what enters streams directly as rain or surface runoff, all the running water of the earth's surface was at one time groundwater. And so, in a very real and frightening sense, pollution of groundwater is pollution of water everywhere. (Rachel Carson, *Silent Spring*)

6 Skyscraper curtain walls are no longer designed by architects, but by real estate salesmen; today, the rentable square footage in an American office tower is measured from glass skin to glass skin (not from the edge of the interior, carpeted floor to the opposite edge). This means that every skyscraper developer insists upon pushing the glassline of his building out as far as the laws determining the shape of the "envelope" will permit, with no projections beyond that line. The result is a building package, tightly and smoothly wrapped in glass, that will generate as much rentable interior space as possible. Any building that boasts an irregular exterior wall, with projections and indentations that might cast interesting shadows (and disperse high-velocity up- and down-drafts), may generate as much as 8 to 10 percent less in rentable floor area than a building with a sheer, smooth skin that projects blandness and boredom to the outside world (and helps generate fierce mini-tornadoes at sidewalk level).

So the modern movement, which grew out of a passionate involvement with the human condition, has, via the skyscraper, become the chief apologist for the real estate speculator. (Peter Blake, *Form Follows Fiasco: Why Modern Architecture Hasn't Worked*)

7 . . . it is not difficult to see that during every transition from capitalism to socialism, dictatorship is necessary for two main reasons, or along two main channels. First, capitalism cannot be defeated or eradicated without the ruthless suppression of the resistance of the exploiters, who cannot at once be deprived of their wealth, of their advantages of organization and knowledge, and consequently for a fairly long period will inevitably try to overthrow the hated rule of the poor; second, every great revolution, and a socialist

revolution in particular, even if there is no external war, is inconceivable without internal war, that is, civil war, which is even more devastating than external war, and involves thousands and millions of cases of wavering and desertion from one side to another, implies a state of extreme indefiniteness, lack of equilibrium, and chaos. And of course, all the elements of disintegration of the old society, which are inevitably very numerous and connected mainly with the petty bourgeoisie (because it is the petty bourgeoisie that every war and every crisis destroys first), are bound to "reveal themselves" during such a profound revolution. And these elements of disintegration *cannot* "reveal themselves" otherwise than in an increase of crime, hooliganism, corruption, profiteering, and outrages of every kind. To put these down requires time and *requires an iron hand.* (V. I. Lenin, "The Immediate Tasks of the Soviet Government," *Izvestiya,* April 28, 1918)

8   As geology plainly proclaims that each land has undergone great physical changes, we might have expected to find that organic beings have varied under nature, in the same way they have varied under domestication. And if there has been any variability under nature, it would be an unaccountable fact if natural selection had not come into play. It has often been asserted, but the assertion is incapable of proof, that the amount of variation under nature is a strictly limited quantity. Man, though acting on external characters alone and often capriciously, can produce within a short period a great result by adding up mere individual differences in his domestic productions; and every one admits that species present individual differences. But, beside such differences, all naturalists admit that natural varieties exist, which are considered sufficiently distinct to be worthy of record in systematic works. No one has drawn any clear distinction between individual differences and slight varieties; or between more plainly marked varieties and subspecies and species. On separate continents, and on different parts of the same continent, when divided by barriers of any kind, and on outlying islands, what a multitude of forms exist, which some experienced naturalists rank as varieties, others as geographical races or subspecies, and others as distinct, though closely allied species.

If, then, animals and plants do vary, let it be ever so slightly or slowly, why should not variations or individual differences, which are in any way beneficial, be preserved and accumulated through natural selection, or the survival of the fittest? If man can by patience select variations useful to him, why, under changing and complex conditions of life, should not variations useful to nature's living products often arise, and be preserved or selected? What limits can be put to this power, acting during long ages and rigidly scrutinizing the whole constitution, structure and habits of each creature, favoring the good and rejecting the bad? I can see no limit to this power, in slowly and beautifully adopting each form to the most complex relations of life. The theory of natural selection, even if we look no further than this, seems to be in the highest degree probable. (Charles Darwin, *The Origin of Species by Means of Natural Selection*)

9 ... The question facing us today is: Now that we are in the war, what is the best way to end it?

In January I could only conclude that the precipitate withdrawal of American forces from Vietnam would be a disaster not only for South Vietnam but for the United States and for the cause of peace.

For the South Vietnamese, our precipitate withdrawal would inevitably allow the communists to repeat the massacres which followed their takeover in the North fifteen years before.

They then murdered more than fifty thousand people, and hundreds of thousands more died in slave labor camps.

We saw a prelude of what would happen in South Vietnam when the communists entered the city of Hue last year. During their brief rule, there was a bloody reign of terror in which three thousand civilians were clubbed, shot to death, and buried in mass graves.

With the sudden collapse of our support, these atrocities of Hue would become the nightmare of the entire nation—and particularly for the million and a half Catholic refugees who fled to South Vietnam when the communists took over in the North.

For the United States, this first defeat in our nation's history would result in a collapse of confidence in American leadership, not only in Asia but throughout the world.

Three American presidents have recognized the great stakes involved in Vietnam and understood what had to be done.

In 1963 President Kennedy, with his characteristic eloquence and clarity said, "We want to see a stable government there carrying on the struggle to maintain its national independence. We believe strongly in that. We're not going to withdraw from that effort. In my opinion, for us to withdraw from that effort would mean a collapse not only of South Vietnam, but Southeast Asia, so we're going to stay there."

President Eisenhower and President Johnson expressed the same conclusion during their terms in office.

For the future of peace precipitate withdrawal would thus be a disaster of immense magnitude.

A nation cannot remain great if it betrays its allies and lets down its friends.

Our defeat and humiliation in South Vietnam would without question promote recklessness in the councils of those great powers who have not yet abandoned the goals of world conquest.

This would spark violence wherever our commitments help maintain peace—in the Middle East, in Berlin, eventually even in the Western Hemisphere.

Ultimately, this would cost more lives.

It would not bring peace but more war.

For these reasons I rejected the recommendation that I should end the war by immediately withdrawing all our forces. (Richard M. Nixon, nationwide radio and television address, November 3, 1969)

10 Had we but World enough and Time,
This coyness Lady were no crime.
We would sit down, and think which way
To walk, and pass our long Love's Day.
Thou by the *Indian Ganges'* side
Should'st Rubies find: I by the Tide
Of *Humber* would complain. I would
Love you ten years before the Flood:
And you should, if you please, refuse
Till the Conversion of the Jews.
My vegetable Love should grow
Vaster than Empires, and more slow.
An hundred years should go to praise
Thine eyes, and on thy Forehead Gaze.
Two hundred to adore each Breast:
But thirty thousand to the rest.
An Age at least to every part,
And the last Age should show your Heart.
For Lady you deserve this State;
Nor would I love at lower rate.
But at my back I alwaies hear
Time's winged Charriot hurrying near:
And yonder all before us lye
Deserts of vast Eternity.
Thy beauty shall no more be found;
Nor, in thy marble Vault, shall sound
My echoing Song: then Worms shall try
That long preserv'd Virginity:
And your quaint Honour turn to dust;
And into ashes all my Lust.
The Grave's a fine and private place,
But none I think do there embrace.
Now, therefore, while the youthful hew
Sits on thy skin like morning dew,
And while thy willing Soul transpires
At every pore with instant Fires,

Now let us sport us while we may;
And now like am'rous birds of prey,
Rather at once our Time devour,
Than languish in his slow-chapt pow'r.
Let us roll all our Strength, and all
Our sweetness, up into one Ball:
And tear our Pleasures with rough strife,
Through the Iron gate of Life.
Thus, though we cannot make our Sun
Stand still, yet we will make him run.
(Andrew Marvell, "To His Coy Mistress")

4.4 LENGTHY PASSAGES OF REASONING

Some arguments extend through an entire article or even an entire book. Plato's *Republic*, for example, which is the dialogue containing the argument for immortality discussed in the last section, is itself a book-length argument, whose ultimate conclusion is that the just person is happier than the unjust person. (The argument for immortality contributes to this conclusion by introducing a discussion of the rewards of justice in the afterlife.) In fact, practically any nonfiction book or article that purports to establish a specific thesis can be regarded as an argument. There are article-length or book-length arguments which attempt to show that nuclear war is winnable or that it is unwinnable, that certain diets are safe and highly effective or that these same diets are fraudulent and harmful, that sex is the fundamental source of human motivation or that sex is unimportant, that a new ice age is coming or that the world will overheat, that supply-side economics can restore healthy economic growth or that it is the greatest boondoggle since the Edsel, that Americans are the world's most selfish people or that they are the most generous, that computers can't think or that they can think better than people and will eventually replace us—in short, just about any thesis you can imagine.

Some of these arguments are careful, rational, and convincing. Others are monuments to human credulity and stupidity. Most fall somewhere in between. Generally they can be evaluated by the techniques we've discussed here, but length induces some special problems—and of course, it makes for more work.

Even in a very lengthy argument it is often possible to list the major points and reconstruct the argument from them as we did with the argument for immortality in the last section. There are several things to look for in doing this. Often the argument as a whole is summarized at the beginning or end of the piece. For example, the argument from Darwin's famous book *The Origin of Species* in the last exercise set was taken from the final chapter, entitled "Recapitulation." It is a summary of a major portion of

Darwin's argument for his theory of evolution. By reading that chapter, we get an overview of the entire book and thus perceive the outlines of its reasoning. Each of the stated premises in this summary is supported by scores of pages of evidence elsewhere in the book. It would, of course, be totally impractical to make an argument diagram which included all this evidence. But we can diagram the core of the argument and then evaluate the truth of its premises in the light of our general understanding of this evidence.

Chapter and section headings are also clues to argument structure. In a very tightly organized work, these headings will reflect the major premises of the argument; and sometimes, though not often, the outline of the argument can even be reconstructed simply by listing the headings. More frequently, chapter and section titles give us only general clues about the argument's structure, and we have to rearrange and rework them and add statements from other parts of the work to produce a clear argument.

Frequently, lengthy arguments contain refutations of objections or opposing views. These may or may not be part of the main argument. A systematic refutation of all known opposing views provides inductive evidence for the author's position and thus can be regarded as central to the argument. Isolated refutations of some opposing views or answers to isolated objections, though perhaps crucial to our understanding of an argument, are not central to its logic and may be omitted. (Incidentally, whenever an author refutes an opposing view, it's worthwhile to ask whether the same or a similar refutation applies to the author's own thought. It is a common human foible to have an eagle's eye for the mistakes of others but to be utterly oblivious when making the same mistakes ourselves.)

Many argumentative works are so poorly organized that no overall argument is discernible. There is instead a web of loosely connected inferences, all roughly directed toward the same conclusion. Instead of trying to summarize the central argument where no central argument exists, the best we can do with such works is to follow out one or more strands of reasoning, as we did with Mao's argument in the last section, and thereby get a general feeling for the author's reasoning ability. We will, of course, also want to check the accuracy of the statements on which the reasoning is based.

Typical among works whose reasoning is loosely organized are those which construct accounts of vast and intricate conspiracies by obscure and often fallacious inferences from thin evidence. Such, for example, were the writings of those political extremists of the late 1950s and early 1960s who argued that fluoridation of water was part of a gigantic communist plot to destroy America. You can probably think of several other examples of this paranoiac-conspiratorial genre. Pseudoscientific works, such as those of diet faddists, religious creationists, pop psychologists, spiritualists, Atlanteans, and so on, often have this loosely knit character. Their irrationality quickly becomes obvious if you take the trouble to evaluate a few representative passages of reasoning.

Often an article or book purporting to prove some controversial point contains virtually no reasoning at all—just a series of unsupported statements. In such cases there is nothing to diagram, though we can still inquire about the truth of the evidence.

Occasionally a work containing little argument will present a collection of evidence so massive that it seems incontrovertible. There are, for example, books purporting to prove the existence of ghosts, flying saucers, innumerable species of monsters, assorted miracles, various psychical phenomena, and so on, on the basis of hundreds of anecdotes from "reliable" witnesses. If the evidence is as reported by these witnesses, then the conclusion seems to follow with a high degree of probability. The real question then becomes, How accurate is the evidence?

It would be utterly naïve to accept such evidence at face value, for there are many ways in which evidence can be falsified or distorted. Such falsification and distortion is a frequent product of wishful thinking. Human delight in mystery is unbounded. Witness the eagerness with which we receive reports of extraordinary events and the extra zest involved if we think these reports are true. Most of us, in fact, are somewhat disappointed by our daily lives and secretly yearn for something more awesome, resonant, and powerful. When counterbalanced by reason, this yearning can stimulate the highest human achievements. But in the absence of reason it fosters only gullibility and self-deception.

Such gullibility acts on many levels. For one thing, desires, both conscious and unconscious, can influence a witness' interpretation of what has been observed. I once was walking at night with a woman who believed herself to be haunted by a demon. Suddenly she gasped in terror at what she thought was the demon's face peering out at her from a darkened window. It was, however, only a window fan. Had she been alone, I am certain that she would have run away and never recognized her mistake. For in a way she needed to believe in this demon. The belief solved certain personal problems for her. But it also led her to falsify her experiences. Even outward sceptics may have unconscious desires to believe in the extraordinary, and these desires may influence their interpretation of experiences, just as this woman's desires did.

Another source of falsification is the natural pleasure—and in some circles, social prestige—of relating fantastic tales. Most people, including professed sceptics, thoroughly enjoy hearing such tales and reward the teller with eager attention. The result is temptation on the part of the teller to embellish, exaggerate, and even lie. That people often do so is an established fact. Travel books from the middle ages are full of purportedly true accounts of fantastic animals, some of which are obviously distorted descriptions of real creatures, but many of which are pure fictions. And almost anyone can readily call to mind several personal examples. Perhaps on occasion even you have embroidered or exaggerated the truth!

Falsehood, distortion, and omission can also enter in when an author reports the experiences of witnesses. Here, in addition to the natural desire to believe in the marvelous and, perhaps, the passion for notoriety, there is also the temptation of profit. The better an author's evidence appears, the more salable it is, and thus the more likely it is to bring financial reward. This can be a powerful motive for "doctoring" weak evidence—or even manufacturing evidence out of thin air.

Finally, falsehood and misrepresentation can creep into your interpretation of what an author says. If you are already predisposed to believe the author, you may unconsciously filter out inconsistencies, inaccuracies, vagueness, spurious inferences, and other indications of falsehood and distortion in the author's work. You may read only what you want to read and hear only what you want to hear—and you may be entirely unconscious of doing so. We almost always underestimate our own capacity for self-deception.

However, it is irrational to infer that all accounts of the marvelous or unusual are false just because there *could have been* ample motivation for distortion. Therefore, if an author amasses what appears to be considerable evidence for an unusual thesis and this evidence is not obviously false or inconsistent with anything you know to be true, the reasonable response is neither to believe nor to disbelieve, but to suspend belief—in other words, to maintain an open mind.

If you want to know more, than you have to do more. Check out the evidence yourself in every way you can. Are the witnesses still alive? Call or write them. Try to find other witnesses. Investigate the general reliability of the author. Examine conflicting views. Perform observations yourself on whatever aspects of the evidence you can verify or disprove. Read whatever is available on the subject. Analyze whatever arguments you can find. Maintain a constant awareness of your own motives to avoid self-deception.

All of this will help you get closer to the truth. Without this sort of effort, if the topic is greatly controversial, you cannot reasonably claim to know the truth.

5

Deductive Arguments

Now that you have a good idea of how to evaluate arguments in general, we're going to apply the techniques developed in the last four chapters to the detailed analysis of specific types of arguments. This and the next two chapters examine common varieties of deductive, inductive, and fallacious reasoning, respectively, and lay out some of the fundamental principles applicable to each.

5.1 VALIDITY AND ARGUMENT FORM

So far the only method we have discussed for determining the validity of arguments is the possible worlds test. But in some cases there are easier and more reliable procedures. One remarkable and extremely useful fact about validity is that it sometimes depends on the form of an argument alone and not on the meanings of the individual terms. Recognizing this enables us to see that whole classes of arguments are valid and thus spares us the effort of applying the possible worlds test in every case. Consider these three inferences:

> If fire burns, then it can hurt you.
> Fire burns.
> ∴ It can hurt you.

> If nobody loves me, I'll go drown myself in a lake.
> Nobody loves me.
> ∴ I'll go drown myself in a lake.

> If you read Aristotle in the original Greek, then you are wise.
> You are reading Aristotle in the original Greek.
> ∴ You are wise.

All three are valid, as you can check by using the possible worlds test, though their premises vary in truth and falsity. Moreover, all three are strikingly similar in form. In each case, the first premise is a conditional statement, the second is the part of the conditional following the "if" (this is called the **antecedent** of the conditional), and the conclusion is the part of the conditional following the "then" (which is called the **consequent**). The form of all three arguments can be represented like this:

> If p, then q
>
> p
>
> ∴ q

Here the letters p and q function like the variables x, y, and z in algebra. In algebra, however, when we want to make a definite statement out of a schema like "$x + y = y + x$," we replace the variables with numerals—so that we get, for example, something like this: $2 + 3 = 3 + 2$. The variables p and q, however, are to be replaced, not by numerals, but by declarative sentences. Just as mathematical formulas like "$x + y = y + x$" stand for indefinitely many different mathematical statements, so the logical schema above stands for indefinitely many different arguments. What is noteworthy about the formula "$x + y = y + x$" is that every possible replacement of its letters with numerals (each occurrence of the same letter being replaced by the same numeral) results in a true statement. Similarly, what is noteworthy about the logical schema above is that each of its indefinitely many instances is a valid argument. These arguments are valid in virtue of form alone; the meanings of the particular statements they contain do not matter. (If you doubt this, try to find an invalid argument having this form.) In Chapter 10 we'll see more clearly why this is true, but for now you'll have to take it on faith or convince yourself by testing many examples. Knowing that all arguments of this form are valid saves work by enabling us to classify them as valid automatically, without having to perform the possible worlds test.

Just as "$x + y = y + x$" is not the only mathematical formula all of whose instances are true, so the schema above is not the only argument schema all of whose instances are valid. Many of these schemata, or **valid argument forms,** are known to logicians, and the most common have been named. The one we've been considering is called **modus ponens,** a Latin term meaning "mode of affirming." It is also called **affirming the antecedent.** Both names allude to the fact that the second premise of this form affirms the antecedent of the first premise.

Another valid form, closely related to modus ponens, is this:

If p, then q

Not-q

∴ Not-p

Again, any argument having this form is valid—for example:

If my alarm clock had been trampled by buffalo, it would have been destroyed.

It has not been destroyed.

∴ It has not been trampled by buffalo.

Try to imagine a world in which the premises are true and the conclusion is false. Again, you will soon see that you can't do it. Moreover, no matter what statements you substitute for p and q, you still won't be able to do it. The form is always valid. It is called **modus tollens** (mode of denying) or **denying the consequent,** because its second premise denies what was said in the consequent of the conditional.

But just as there are many mathematical formulas which have some false instances—"$x + y = x - y$," for example—so there are many argument forms which have some invalid instances. These are called (appropriately enough) **invalid argument forms.** Here are two invalid argument forms which are often confused with modus ponens and modus tollens:

If p, then q If p, then q

q Not-p

∴ p ∴ Not-q

The first is called **affirming the consequent** and the second **denying the antecedent.** Again the names of these forms are based on what occurs in the second, or nonconditional, premise. Most arguments having these forms are fallacies. Consider, for example, this instance of affirming the consequent:

> If you play loud music, Olaf goes stark raving mad.
> Olaf is going stark raving mad.
> ∴ You are playing loud music.

This is invalid, and to show it we need to describe a possible world in which the premises are true and the conclusion false. What sort of world should we consider? Well, imagine a world in which Olaf is pathologically sensitive to loud music, but in which you are 1000 miles away from Olaf and not playing music at all and in which Olaf is going stark raving mad for other reasons. (Perhaps he's just lost his shirt in the stock market, Ophelia has left him, and underworld thugs have burned down his house.) In such a world, the premises would be true and the conclusion false, and so the argument is invalid. Moreover, it's not difficult to see that it's not inductive either. Given all the possible ways in which a person can go insane, the truth of the premises does not make the conclusion even probable. Thus the argument is completely fallacious.

I'll leave it up to you to construct a counterexample to show that denying the antecedent is an invalid form. All you have to do is invent some declarative sentences to put in place of p and q (almost anything you try will work) and then describe a world in which the premises are true and the conclusion is false. I said *almost* any declarative sentences would work, because there are some that won't. In other words, some instances of denying the antecedent are valid. (Remember that an invalid form is a form *some* of whose instances are invalid; thus there's no inconsistency in the thought that some are valid as well.) Valid instances of invalid argument forms are, however, unusual. Their validity results, not from having these forms (as it does in modus ponens or modus tollens) but from something extraneous to the form. Here's an example:

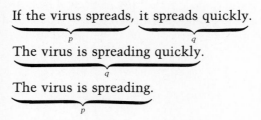

This is a valid instance of affirming the consequent. Its validity results from the fact that it is impossible for the second premise to be true and the conclusion false. That is, the inference:

The virus is spreading quickly.

∴ The virus is spreading.

is valid all by itself. Hence it is obviously impossible for both premises to be true and the conclusion false. The conditional premise is superfluous.

It is only in cases like this, where the validity depends on something other than the main argument form, that affirming the consequent and denying the antecedent are valid. We can summarize the results of our discussion in the following table:

Always Valid	*Usually Not Valid*
Affirming the antecedent (modus ponens)	Affirming the consequent
Denying the consequent (modus tollens)	Denying the antecedent

These four, of course, are by no means the only possible argument forms. The number of argument forms, both valid and invalid, is infinite. Logicians have developed a variety of exact techniques for classifying them and testing their validity. These techniques constitute the subject matter of **formal logic,** which we will examine briefly in Chapter 10. Formal logic is extremely useful where arguments are capable of precise formulation, as in mathematics, but in ordinary reasoning we constantly encounter new forms for which no formal techniques have been developed. The only way to determine their validity is to use something like the possible worlds tests, and that is why informal logic remains important.

Nevertheless, it will be useful for us now to take note of some of the valid forms which have been studied in formal logic, because as I noted above, knowing these forms saves work. Here are some of the more common valid argument forms:

Hypothetical Syllogism

If p, then q

If q, then r

∴ If p, then r

Disjunctive Syllogism

p or q

Not-p

∴ q

Simplification

p and q

∴ p

Conjunction

p

q

∴ p and q

Contraposition	**Constructive Dilemma**
If p, then q	p or q
∴ If not-q, then not-p	If p, then r
If not-q, then not-p	If q, then s
∴ If p, then q	∴ r or s

All the forms listed above are single inferences. None is a complex argument, though of course any of them can occur in complex arguments.

Notice that there are two forms of contraposition. Notice, too, that in simplification and conjunction a compound sentence formed by "and" is treated as a single conclusion or premise. Our policy (adopted in Section 2.1) has generally been to break such sentences into their components. This is mainly for convenience. It is usually easier to deal with two simple statements than with one complicated one. But where "and" plays a crucial role in the reasoning, as it obviously does in simplification and conjunction, it is more illuminating not to split the compounds it forms. Thus we will treat these uses of "and" as exceptions to our policy.

The order of premises in an argument form is of no importance. Although the premises of the forms I've discussed are most commonly listed in the order in which I've written them, this order is arbitrary and makes no difference to the form or validity of the argument. Thus, for example, the schema:

p

If p, then q

∴ q

is also modus ponens and is also valid.

> **Exercise 5.1** Copy each of the following arguments, bracket statements, circle indicators, supply missing statements, and diagram and evaluate as usual. If any inference has one of the following forms, write the name of the form next to the arrow representing the inference:

Modus ponens (affirming the antecedent)	Disjunctive syllogism
Modus tollens (denying the consequent)	Simplification
Affirming the consequent	Conjunction
Denying the antecedent	Contraposition
Hypothetical syllogism	Constructive dilemma

1   If he kidnapped the maiden, then he's the vilest of villains. But he did not kidnap the maiden. Therefore, he is not the vilest of villains.

2   Either you're going to have to put up with that jerk or you're going to have to leave him, and you know you can't put up with him any longer.

3   If he moves, I'll see him, and if I see him I'll squash him like a bug; so if he moves, I'll squash him like a bug.

4   Since you went shopping *and* went to the swimming pool, you went to the swimming pool. So you disobeyed me. I don't care if you go shopping, but I told you not to go to the swimming pool.

5   If she had talked to him, she would have told him the news. But she didn't tell him the news, because he didn't know it. Therefore, she didn't talk to him.

6   If food is not exposed to bacteria, it will not rot. It follows that if it does rot, it has been exposed to bacteria. Now I have exposed this food to bacteria. Therefore, it will rot.

7   Ron loves either you or Samantha. Now if he loved Samantha, he would help her with her homework. But he doesn't, because her sister says so and she's telling the truth. So it's not Samantha that he loves. Therefore, it must be you.

8   If she's strong and has the will, she'll live. And she has the strength and the will. She has the strength, because she has always kept herself fit and healthy. And she has the will, because of her deep and abiding love for life. There's no doubt that she'll make it.

9   If you wait for me in the rain, you'll get soaked; and if you get soaked, you'll get sick. So if you wait for me in the rain, you'll get sick. Now I don't want you getting sick. Therefore, you shouldn't wait for me in the rain.

10 In a practical sense, it is never wrong to assume that we have free will. For either we have free will or we do not. If we do, then the assumption that we do is true. If we don't, then all our actions are determined. Hence either the assumption that we have free will is true or all our actions are determined. But if the assumption that we have free will is true, then it makes sound, practical sense to believe it. And if all our actions are determined, then we can't help ourselves, whatever we assume. Hence either it makes good practical sense to assume that we have free will or else we can't help assuming what we do. And in neither of these cases, obviously, would the assumption of free will be a practical error.

148

5.2   CONDITIONALS

You have probably noticed how often conditionals occur in arguments. Clearly they play a very important role in logic. Unfortunately—at least for the logician—this role is complicated by the fact that they can be expressed in many ways besides "If p, then q." We can, for example, invert word order, so that instead of saying "If it's an aardvark, it's an animal," we would say "It's an animal if it's an aardvark." These two sentences mean exactly the same thing. More generally, any sentence of the form "If p, then q" can also be expressed as "q if p."

Another way of saying "If p, then q" is "p only if q." (Note that in this case the order of the letters does not change.) This is harder to understand at first. It's easy to confuse "only if" with "if," so you need to be careful to keep the difference in mind. The statement "It's an aardvark only if it's an animal" means the same as "If it's an aardvark, it's an animal" and "It's an animal if it's an aardvark." "Only if" can also occur in inverted word order, so that "Only if it's an animal is it an aardvark" is another way of saying "It's an aardvark only if it's an animal." In general, then, all of the following sentence forms are equivalent:

If p, then q

q if p

p only if q

Only if q, p

In each case, of course, the letters are to be replaced by sentences. Try making some replacements, and see if you can recognize that all these forms express the same thing. (Be careful always to replace the same letter with the same sentence.) These are not the only ways of expressing conditionals, but they are perhaps the most common.

Corresponding to various versions of the conditional, there are various ways of expressing each argument form containing a conditional. Thus the following forms, for example, are all modus ponens:

p only if q	p	Only if q, p
p	q if p	p
$\therefore$ q	$\therefore$ q	$\therefore$ q

The order of individual letters within the statements is crucial. The following forms, for example, though they resemble those above, are not modus ponens, but versions of affirming the consequent:

q only if p	p	Only if p, q
p	p if q	p
$\therefore\ q$	$\therefore\ q$	$\therefore\ q$

They are all invalid, as you can verify by constructing counterexamples.

Sometimes you will encounter the expression "if and only if," as in the sentence, "You own the property if and only if you hold the deed." Breaking this into its components, we see that it means:

> You own the property if you hold the deed, and you own the property only if you hold the deed.

Given the equivalences noted above, this complex sentence in turn means:

> If you hold the deed, then you own the property, and if you own the property, then you hold the deed.

Now clearly there is no change of meaning if we exchange the two sentences joined by "and." So we can also say the same thing this way:

> If you own the property, then you hold the deed, and if you hold the deed, then you own the property.

This illustrates the general fact that "p if and only if q" means "If p, then q, and if q, then p." Statements of the form "p if and only if q" are called **biconditionals.** I'll have more to say about them in Section 10.3.

Exercise 5.2(a)   Which of the following statements are ways of expressing the conditional "If he's full, then he's contented"?

1 He's contented if he's full.
2 He's full if he's contented.
3 He's contented only if he's full.
4 He's full only if he's contented.
5 If he's contented, he's full.
6 Only if he's full is he contented.
7 Only if he's contented is he full.
8 He's contented, provided that he's full.
9 Being full is sufficient to make him contented.
10 He's only full if he's contented.

Exercise 5.2(b) Copy each of the following passages, bracket statements, circle indicators, supply missing statements, and diagram and evaluate as usual. If any inference has one of the following forms, write the name of the form beside the arrow representing the inference:

Modus ponens (affirming the antecedent)   Disjunctive syllogism
Modus tollens (denying the consequent)   Simplification
Affirming the consequent   Conjunction
Denying the antecedent   Contraposition
Hypothetical syllogism   Constructive dilemma

1 Truth would matter to poetry if poetry described the world. But since the function of poetry is to express emotion, it does not describe the world. Therefore, truth does not matter to poetry.

2 World conflict will cease only if something is done to equalize the disparity between developed and underdeveloped nations. But something is being done to equalize this disparity, for we provide massive amounts of foreign aid to underdeveloped countries. Therefore, world conflict will cease.

3 If there were gods, how could I endure not to be a god? *Hence* there are no gods. (Friedrich Nietzsche, *Thus Spoke Zarathustra*)

4 If she knew who I am, then I'd be in danger. But she doesn't, because she could know only if she'd seen my identification papers, and she hasn't seen them. Therefore, I'm in no danger.

5 Only if the burglars were sophisticated professionals could they have successfully dismantled the alarm system. Hence they were not sophisticated professionals, for they were unable to dismantle it.

6 The precipitate forms only if the reaction occurs, and the reaction occurs only if a catalyst has been added to the solution. Therefore, the precipitate forms only with the addition of a catalyst. It follows that the precipitate will not form if no catalyst is added.

7 An eruption would have occurred if and only if the pressure of the lava exceeded the strength of the overlying rock. Therefore, since there was no eruption, we may infer that the pressure of the lava did not exceed the strength of the rock mantle above it.

8 Either her madness was due to an organic deterioration of the brain, or it was caused by one or more traumatic childhood experiences. We could have detected organic deterioration if it were present. But if the cause were some childhood trauma, it would lie deeply submerged in her subconscious memory. All efforts to discover an

organic cause failed. Therefore, it became necessary to probe her subconscious mind.

9   If the future holds travail and anguish in store, the self must be in existence, when that time comes, in order to experience it. But from this fate we are redeemed by death, which denies existence to the self that might have suffered these tribulations. Rest assured, therefore, that we have nothing to fear in death. (Lucretius, *On the Nature of the Universe*)

10   I am sure that you have read of the charge that I, Senator Nixon, took $18,000 from a group of my supporters.

Now was that wrong? . . . The question is, was it morally wrong?

I say that it was morally wrong if any of that $18,000 went to Senator Nixon for my personal use. I say it was morally wrong if it was secretly given and secretly handled. And I say that it was morally wrong if any of the contributors got special favors for the contributions that they made.

And now to answer those questions let me say this:

Not one cent of the $18,000 or any other money of that type ever went to me for my personal use. Every penny of it was used to pay for political expenses that I did not think should be charged to the taxpayers of the United States.

It was not a secret fund. As a matter of fact, when I was on *Meet the Press*—some of you may have seen it last Sunday—Peter Edson came up to me after the program and said, "Dick, what about this fund we hear about?" And I said, "Well, there's no secret about it. Go out and see Dana Smith, who was the administrator of the fund." And I gave him his address, and I said that you will find that the purpose of the fund was simply to defray political expenses that I did not feel should be charged to the government.

And, third, let me point out—and I want to make this particularly clear—that no contributor to this fund, no contributor to any of my campaigns, has ever received any consideration that he would not have received as an ordinary constituent. (Vice presidential candidate Richard M. Nixon, from the nationally televised "Checkers speech," September 23, 1952)

5.3   CONDITIONAL PROOF

We're now going to consider a distinctive valid argument form which requires a novel sort of diagram. The valid forms we've discussed so far are all single inferences, and their diagrams all contain just a single arrow. Diagrams of this new form, **conditional proof,** are more complex and variable.

Conditional proof is, unsurprisingly enough, a method for proving conditional conclusions. We've already seen two ways of doing this—hypothetical syllogism and contraposition (Section 5.1)—but conditional proof is a more powerful and generally more useful strategy. Here's how it works. To prove a conditional, we assume its antecedent (regardless of whether or not this antecedent is true) and then provide a valid argument of any form whatsoever from this assumption to the conditional's consequent as conclusion. Since this argument is valid, if all its basic premises were true, its conclusion would have to be true. So assuming that all its basic premises apart from the conditional's antecedent are true, we know that if the antecedent is true, then the consequent must be true as well. But this is just to say that the conditional itself is true, and so we have in effect proved the conditional. This may sound confusing when stated in the abstract, but it's fairly easy to understand when applied to a particular example. Consider this one:

① [If Fuzzball is a living cat, then Fuzzball is not at the center of the sun.] (For) suppose ② [Fuzzball is a living cat.] Now ③ [no cat can be vaporized into incandescent plasma and survive.] But ④ [any object located at the center of the sun is immediately vaporized into incandescent plasma.] (Hence) ⑤ [there are no living cats at the center of the sun.] But (we assumed that) ② [Fuzzball is a living cat.] (Therefore), ⑥ [Fuzzball is clearly not at the center of the sun.]

Notice that premise ② occurs twice. Repetition is common in conditional proofs. The conclusion of the entire argument is ①. This is the conditional the author wants to prove. Its consequent, ⑥, is deduced from its antecedent, ②.

We'll use the term **hypothetical argument** to designate the argument leading from the antecedent to the consequent of the conditional to be proved. In our example, the hypothetical argument is this:

$$\frac{③ \ + \ ④}{\downarrow \ D}$$
$$\frac{② \ + \ ⑤}{\downarrow \ D}$$
$$⑥$$

I've supplied evaluations. As you can see, the argument is deductive. But notice that this hypothetical argument does not contain the main argument's final conclusion, ①. How does ① fit into the diagram? We can't just draw an arrow from ⑥ to ①, for surely the conditional is not derived merely from its consequent. The solution to this puzzle becomes apparent when we realize that our confidence in ① is based, not on ⑥, but on the entire chain of reasoning leading from ② to ⑥—that is, on the entire hypothetical argument. Statement ① follows, in other words, from the hypothetical argument as a whole. To symbolize this peculiar evidential arrangement, we enclose the hypothetical argument in a box and then draw an arrow to ①, as follows:

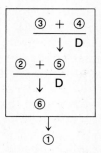

The diagram indicates that the author intends to prove the conditional conclusion, ①, by assuming its antecedent and validly deducing its consequent by means of the hypothetical argument represented in the box.

There's one more tricky point about conditional proofs, and it has to do with the assumption of the antecedent—in this case, ②. In offering the argument, the author is not really asserting that ② is true, as is the case with a normal premise. Instead, he or she is saying, "Suppose that it were true; let's see what follows." Statement ② is assumed only "for the sake of argument." It is what is called a **hypothetical assumption.** The other assumptions of the argument, ③ and ④, are not hypothetical; the author asserts them straightforwardly. In conditional proof generally, the assumption of the antecedent, and it alone, is hypothetical.

Since the author makes no claim about the truth of the hypothetical assumption, it, unlike the other assumptions of the hypothetical argument, does not function as evidence for the main argument's final conclusion. Therefore, although it is obviously a basic premise of the hypothetical argument, it does not count as a basic premise of the argument as a whole. We indicate this by crossing out its number in the diagram:

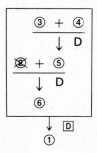

The diagram is now complete.

Notice that I've also placed a "D" in a box next to the arrow leading from the hypothetical argument to ①. This is to show that the whole argument is deductive. A conditional proof is always deductive if its hypothetical argument is. To see that this is true in our example, note that if the hypothetical argument is deductive and the basic premises, ③ and ④, are true, then it must be that if ② is also true, ⑥ is true as well. Now since ① is just the conditional statement "If ②, then ⑥," this means that if the hypothetical argument is deductive and ③ and ④ are true, then ① must be true. But this is just to say that if the hypothetical argument is deductive and the argument's basic premises are true, then the conclusion ① must be true, which is exactly what it means for the argument as a whole to be valid.

If at first you are a bit flummoxed by this conditional reasoning about conditional proofs, don't worry. But go over it again. Get a feel for how each step leads inevitably to the next, and keep at it until the ideas involved become crystal clear. One of the beauties of deductive logic is that its precision makes this crystalline clarity possible. It takes some effort to achieve it, but when you do it's an exquisite experience!

Now that we've seen that our sample argument is valid, we might as well ask whether it is sound. I believe it is. Premises ③ and ④ are to the best of my knowledge true, and since they are the only basic premises, it follows that the argument is sound. So it proves that if Fuzzball is a living cat, then Fuzzball is not at the center of the sun. Not a very startling conclusion, but certainly a true one!

How can you recognize a conditional proof when you see one? That's usually easy. There are three things to look for. First, the final conclusion will always be a conditional statement. Second, the antecedent of this conditional will be assumed somewhere in the argument. And third, there will be a chain of reasoning starting from the antecedent and leading to the consequent. (This is the hypothetical argument.) All three features are present in every conditional proof, though sometimes only implicitly. In addition, there is a fourth clue which also ought to spark your attention; often, the hypothetical assumption is preceded by a **hypothetical-assumption indicator.** Hypothetical-assumption indicators are words or phrases like:

> Suppose
>
> Suppose that
>
> Assume
>
> Assume that
>
> Suppose for the sake of argument that
>
> Let it be granted that

and so on. These expressions generally signify the presence of a hypothetical assumption, but they do not always indicate the presence of conditional proof, since there are other argument forms which employ hypothetical assumptions as well, as we'll see in the next section.

Before going on, however, let's look at one more conditional proof, this one from geometry:

①[If *ABCD* is a four-sided polygon, then the sum of its interior angles is 360°.] (For) let ②[*ABCD* be a four-sided polygon.] (Then) ③[drawing a diagonal between two opposite corners of *ABCD* produces two distinct triangles, the sum of whose interior angles is equal to the sum of the interior angles of *ABCD*.] (See figure at right.) But ④[the sum of the interior angles of any triangle is 180°.] (Hence) ⑤[the sum of the interior angles of two distinct triangles is 360°.] (Therefore) ⑥[the sum of the interior angles of *ABCD* is 360°,] which was to be proved.

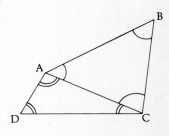

There are several points to be made here. First, a polygon, in case you don't remember from geometry, is a closed plane figure composed of straight lines. Second, the incomplete phrase which I have labeled ② should be understood as the statement:

ABCD is a four-sided polygon.

Third, notice that I have not bothered to number the parenthetical remark, "(See figure at right.)." This remark is obviously not a part of the argument, but merely a command or direction calling our attention to the appropriate figure. Finally, note that all the clues for identifying conditional proofs are apparent here. Statement ② is preceded by the premise indicator "for," showing that it is a premise, and by the hypothetical-assumption indicator "let," which signifies that it is a hypothetical assumption. This should alert us to the possibility of conditional proof at first glance. Looking more closely, we see that the final conclusion is ①, and it is a conditional. That is another clue. Moreover, the antecedent of ① is the hypothetical assumption, ②, and the consequent of ①, which is ⑥, is deduced from ② by a chain of reasoning. That cinches it; we know we have a conditional proof.

Our next problem is to discern the structure of the hypothetical argument. Using the inference indicators provided, we can see that it is:

And so, supplying the box and the final conclusion and crossing out the hypothetical assumption, we have:

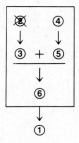

The diagram is now complete, except for evaluations.

Is the argument valid? As we noted before, it is valid if the hypothetical argument is. The hypothetical argument itself is valid if each of its inferences is valid. So let's check each in turn. Consider the inference from ② to ③. Can we imagine a situation in which *ABCD* is a four-sided polygon but it's not possible to draw a diagonal dividing it into two triangles, the sum of whose interior angles is equal to the sum of the interior angles of *ABCD*? Evidently not; so this inference is valid. You should also be able to see the validity of the inferences from ④ to ⑤ and from ③ and ⑤ to ⑥. It should be clear, then, that the whole argument is valid.

This example illustrates the importance of imagination, not only in logic, but in geometry as well. The imagination of geometrical figures, so essential to the concrete understanding of geometrical reasoning, can be regarded as a special case of the imagination of possible worlds. For geometrical figures are possible objects, and such possible objects are components of some of the possible worlds.

While we're at it, we might as well check for soundness. There is only one basic premise, ④. So if ④ is true, the argument is sound. As it turns out, if we're talking about triangles in flat space, ④ is perfectly correct. But the space of our world is curved; so strictly speaking, ④ is false. Thus the argument is unsound. That, however, is a matter of physical geometry, not of logic, and so it need not concern us here. What is important from a logical viewpoint is that the argument is valid. If you still haven't seen clearly why it is valid, read through this section again—slowly and nonlinearly.

To finish the diagram, we should of course put "D"s beside all the arrows in the box and a "D" enclosed in a box beside the arrow leading to ①. But you can do this in your imagination.

Conditional proof is always deductive when the hypothetical argument is deductive, but what about cases in which the hypothetical argument is inductive or fallacious? In these cases the conditional proof is correspondingly weak. If the hypothetical argument is inductive, then given the whole argument's basic premises, if the antecedent of the conditional conclusion is true, then its consequent is probable. So the conditional itself is probably true, given these premises, and hence the whole argument is inductive. Likewise, if the hypothetical argument is fallacious, so is the argument as a whole.

Exercise 5.3   All of the following passages either are or suggest conditional proofs, though some of them are incomplete as stated. Copy each, bracket and number statements, add missing statements, construct a diagram, and evaluate the reasoning.

1   If you get flattened by a steam roller, you will die. For suppose a steam roller flattens you. What flattens you must crush your internal organs, and so your internal organs would be crushed. Now crushed organs do not function, and if your internal organs are not functioning you will die. Thus it is clear that you would die.

2   I know that if it's 8:00 in New York, it's 5:00 in Los Angeles, and if you don't believe me I'll prove it. Look, suppose it is 8:00 in New York. Now there are three time zone changes going west from New York to Los Angeles, and at each the time shifts back an hour. So in Los Angeles it has to be 5:00.

3   If we continue to consume oil at the present rate, world supplies will be exhausted within 200 years. For suppose the current consumption rate continues. The world now consumes five billion barrels of oil a year. This means that in 200 years we will have burned or otherwise eliminated an additional trillion barrels of oil. But world oil reserves today do not exceed a trillion barrels. Hence in another 200 years, not a drop of oil will remain.

4   Suppose your cousin did stay at Greensboro last night. Then, since when she travels she always gets up at 6 A.M. sharp and is on the road by 7:30, she should have started from Greensboro by 7:30. Driving time between Greensboro and here is no more than three hours, and she wouldn't have stopped unless she had car trouble. So unless she were having trouble, she would have been here by 10:30.

5   If you are repeatedly unfaithful, you will not have a lasting satisfying relationship with your mate. That's simply a matter of logic. For suppose you are unfaithful, not just once, but again and again. Then

there are three possibilities: either your mate never finds out, or your mate finds out and puts up with your misbehavior, or your mate finds out and leaves you. If your mate never finds out, then he or she must be gullible, stupid, or easily manipulable. How can you have a satisfying relationship with a person like that? If he or she finds out and puts up with your cheating, then still there will be resentment boiling inside—the kind of resentment that prevents satisfying relationships. And finally, of course, if your mate finds out and leaves, then your relationship will not have been lasting.

6 Suppose that we obtain a sample of public opinion by hiring interviewers and sending them to street corners and shopping centers to interview the public. The typical interviewer is a white middle-class female. She is unlikely to interview many working-class males, blacks, or others who are unlike her. Even if we assign the interviewer quotas by race, age, and sex, she will tend to select the best-dressed and least threatening members of each group. The result will be a sample that systematically overrepresents some parts of the population (persons of middle-class appearance) and underrepresents others. (David S. Moore, *Statistics: Concepts and Controversies*)

7 Let's say you do make a million dollars. You still won't be happy. You're not happy now, and the more money you make, the more your troubles will multiply.

5.4   REDUCTIO AD ABSURDUM

Another valid argument form which uses a hypothetical assumption and requires a special diagram is **reductio ad absurdum**—or just plain **reductio** for short. The name is Latin for "reduction to absurdity." Reductio arguments are also sometimes called **indirect proofs.** They work, paradoxically enough, by assuming precisely the contrary of what they aim to prove. To establish a conclusion by reductio, we hypothetically assume the falsity of this conclusion and then deduce an absurdity. This shows that our hypothetical assumption is wrong, and hence that the conclusion is true after all. This procedure may at first appear backhanded and illicit. But it isn't. Reductio arguments are both valid (when all their component inferences are valid) and very powerful. Often reductio is the simplest way to establish a conclusion which would be very difficult to establish by other means.

Before examining reductio arguments more closely, however, we need to know precisely what an absurdity is. Some logicians count any false statement as an absurdity, but we're going to adopt a more precise definition, which is the one commonly used in formal logic. As I'll show at the end of this section, this definition imposes no essential limitations on our ability to deal with reductios, and it makes our analysis of them somewhat neater.

An absurdity, as we shall understand the term, is a **contradiction,** and a contradiction is any statement of the form *"p* and not-*p."* Here are some examples of contradictions:

Olaf is a lush, and Olaf is not a lush.
Moose is both at home and not at home.
Granite is a rock, and it's not a rock.

We have to insist pretty rigorously on this form *"p* and not-*p."* Just saying "opposite things" won't do, for the idea of opposites is too vague. Thus the following are *not* contradictions:

It is raining, and it is sunny.
I am happy, and I am sad.
Olaf is both male and female.

The important thing about contradictions, as opposed to statements like those above is that contradictions can't be true; their truth is logically impossible. Statements asserting "opposites," like "It is raining, and it is sunny," can sometimes be true. (I've seen it happen; maybe you have too.) But we can't even coherently conceive a contradiction.

To see why, you have to understand how the words "not" and "and" affect the truth and falsity of sentences containing them. Putting "not" in a true sentence makes it false. Putting "not" in a false sentence makes it true. This is illustrated by the following list of sentences:

Pizza is delicious.	(True)
Pizza is not delicious.	(False)
Pizza is not not delicious.	(True)
Pizza is not not not delicious.	(False)

I could continue, but you'd soon lose track of the "not"s and start yawning. (Eating pizza is far more stimulating than talking about it.) Anyway, the point is that things work the same way no matter how far you carry the series out. The behavior of "not" is invariable. It always changes truth to falsehood and falsehood to truth.

"And" also has a characteristic and invariable effect on truth and falsity. Its function is to join two or more sentences together to form a compound. (Sometimes it also joins words or phrases, but we're only interested in its sentence-joining function here.) The compound thus created is true if and only if all of its components are. Now if one of these components is *p* and the other is not-*p*, then obviously they can't both be true. If one is true, the other must be false, and vice versa. So any statement of the form "*p* and not-*p*" (i.e., any contradiction) has to be false. There's no way even to imagine it being true.

Having clarified the notion of an absurdity, we can now identify the clues which enable us to detect the presence of a reductio argument. Every completely stated reductio has (1) a hypothetical assumption denying the argument's final conclusion and (2) a chain of reasoning leading from this hypothetical assumption to a contradiction. As with conditional proofs, we will call this chain of reasoning the hypothetical argument. Here is a typical reductio:

①[There is no greatest number.] (For) suppose ②[there were a greatest number, *n*.] (Then) (since) ③[adding 1 to any number always yields a greater number,] ④[*n* + 1 is greater than *n*.] But (then it follows that) ⑤[*n* is not the greatest number.] (Hence) ⑥[*n* both is and is not the greatest number,] which is absurd.

The main conclusion is ①. To prove it, the author hypothetically assumes its denial, statement ②. Note that ② is prefixed by the hypothetical-assumption indicator "suppose" and is linked by a chain of reasoning to the contradiction, ⑥, which is marked by the phrase "which is absurd." Phrases of this sort are characteristic of reductios and may be taken as probable clues to their presence. The chain of reasoning which links ② to ⑥ is the hypothetical argument. The fact that ② implies a contradiction shows that ② is false and therefore that the final conclusion, ①, is true. The hypothetical argument should be diagramed as follows:

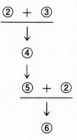

The hypothetical assumption, ②, appears twice in this diagram, in the manner discussed in Section 2.6. Multiple use of the hypothetical assumption is common in both reductios and conditional proofs. As you can verify, each inference in the diagram is valid.

This diagram, of course, does not represent the entire argument. We still have to add the final conclusion, ①. Is it inferred from ⑥? Hardly. That would make little sense. As in conditional proof, what justifies the final conclusion is the entire hypothetical argument—that is, the derivation of a contradiction from the denial of the conclusion. Therefore, as in conditional proof, we should use a box diagram:

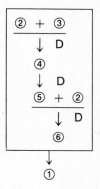

I've supplied evaluations for the inferences of the hypothetical argument.

There are only a few things left to do. Since ② is a hypothetical assumption, it does not count as a basic premise of the argument as a whole. So, as in conditional proof, we should cross it out. When a hypothetical assumption occurs more than once, as it does here, we cross out all the occurrences. This leaves only ③ as a basic premise of the whole argument.

As in conditional proof, if the hypothetical argument is valid, then so is the argument as a whole. To see this, consider just the hypothetical argument in isolation. Since this argument is not itself a reductio or similar form, premise ② functions within it, not as a hypothetical assumption, but as a genuine basic premise. Thus the basic premises of the hypothetical argument (as opposed to the argument as a whole) are ② and ③. Now if the hypothetical argument is valid, then by definition if its basic premises are true, its conclusion must be true. But its conclusion is a contradiction, which must be false. So if it is valid, not all its basic premises can be true; at least one must be false. Therefore if all the basic premises apart from the hypothetical assumption are true, then it must be the hypothetical assumption which is false. Hence if the basic premises of the argument as a whole (in this case just ③) are true, then the argument's final conclusion (in this case ①) must be true, for it is the denial of the hypothetical assumption. And by the definition of validity, this means that the argument as a whole is valid. Thus we can see that if the hypothetical argument is valid, so is the argument as a whole. (Again, I know this reasoning is hard to follow at first, but keep at it. It's like climbing a mountain in a fog. If you keep going, suddenly you reach a place where everything is bright and clear.) Here's the final argument diagram:

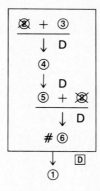

I've put a "D" in a box next to the final arrow to indicate that the entire argument is deductive. The only thing I haven't mentioned is the sign "#." This means "contradiction." It serves two purposes: to indicate which statement is the contradiction and to enable us to tell at a glance that this is the diagram of a reductio, not a conditional proof.

The argument, by the way, is sound. Mathematics, as I noted earlier, is one field in which sound arguments are plentiful. That is why so much of mathematics is known with certainty.

Mathematics, however, is not the only field in which reductios occur. Here's a fascinating example from philosophical theology. It purports to prove the nonexistence of an omnipotent being. God, as we saw in the discussion of the problem of evil in Section 3.6, is usually regarded as omnipotent. This argument, if sound, would establish with certainty that an omnipotent God does not exist:

①[There is no omnipotent being.] (For) suppose ②[there were.] (Then) ③[this being could move anything.] (Hence) ④[it could move absolutely immovable objects.] But ⑤[absolutely immovable objects cannot be moved by anything.] (Therefore), ⑥[this being could both move and not move immovable objects,] which is absurd.

Here again we have the characteristic features of a reductio. The final conclusion is ①. The hypothetical assumption, ②, which is marked by the premise indicator "for" and the hypothetical-assumption indicator "suppose," asserts that statement ① is false. "There were," of course, is short for "There were (or more grammatically, 'is') an omnipotent being." And there is a chain of reasoning leading from ② to the contradiction, ⑥. The diagram is as follows:

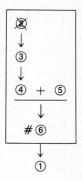

As you can see, there is only one basic premise, ⑤, and ⑤ is certainly true. Thus if the argument is valid, it is also sound. But is it valid? To find out, we must evaluate the hypothetical argument, and this requires testing each of its inferences. At first glance, they all seem convincing. Certainly the inferences from ② to ③ and from ④ and ⑤ to ⑥ are valid. But take a second look at the inference from ③ to ④. Here we can produce a counterexample. Imagine a possible world in which there is an omnipotent being and in which there are absolutely no immovable objects. In this world, ③ is true but ④ is false. That is, it would be false that this omnipotent being could move immovable objects, because there wouldn't *be* any immovable objects.[1] Indeed, when we think about it carefully, we see that there are no possible worlds in which ③ and ④ are both true. We can't imagine a world containing both a being which can move anything and immovable objects. If there are immovable objects in a world, then that world does not contain a being which can move anything. If there is a being which can move anything, then there are no immovable objects. Thus any possible world containing an omnipotent being provides a counterexample to the inference from ③ to ④. This shows that the inference from ③ to ④ is not merely invalid; it is most certainly fallacious. For among the possible worlds in which ③ is true, there are none in which ④ is true; and so, given ③, ④ is not only improbable, but totally impossible. Our hypothetical argument is therefore fallacious.

Now we know that if the hypothetical argument of a reductio is valid, then the entire argument is valid. But we have not yet discussed evaluation when the hypothetical argument is invalid. The situation here is again similar to conditional proof. If the hypothetical argument is fallacious, then it provides no good reason to believe the argument's final conclusion, and

---

[1] It should be noted that ④ is ambiguous. I intend it to mean, "There are absolutely immovable objects which it (the omnipotent being) could move." But there is a second reading on which it means, "It is possible for there to be absolutely immovable objects which it could move." A thorough analysis would take account of this ambiguity (see Section 7.6), but I have ignored it because the second reading involves subtleties which cannot be adequately explained in an introductory text.

so the whole thing is fallacious. Thus the argument under discussion is a fallacy. It does not prove that there is no omnipotent being. To complete the diagram, we record evaluations as follows:

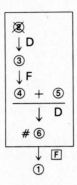

Curiously, the hypothetical argument of a reductio is never inductive, because it ends in a contradiction, and contradictions are false in all possible worlds. So if there are any worlds in which the basic premises are all true, then in each of these worlds the conclusion is false. Therefore in no case can the conclusion be true in the *majority* of worlds in which the basic premises are true, and hence in no case can the hypothetical argument be inductive. It may be inductive judging by rules 1–3 of Section 3.5, but these rules have exceptions, and in actual fact it will either be self-weakening and fallacious or deductive and fortuitously strong. Thus the argument as a whole will be either fallacious or deductive. There is no such thing as an inductive reductio.

Even more curiously, the only way in which the hypothetical argument of a reductio can be deductive is if there is no possible world in which all its basic premises are true. For its conclusion is a contradiction, false in all worlds; hence if there are any worlds in which all its basic premises are true, those worlds constitute counterexamples.

If you find the idea of a deductive argument based on premises which can't all be true in any world and leading to a conclusion which is false in every world uncomfortably confusing, ignore it for now. But you should realize that our definition of deductiveness allows such things. I'll discuss this oddity more thoroughly in Section 5.5, and after reading that section you ought to be able to make more sense of it. Remember—read nonlinearly!

Reductio arguments can be used to establish some remarkable conclusions. If I told you, for example, that you are incapable of liking just the people who don't like themselves, you'd almost certainly take me for a fool or a liar. You have free will; you can like or dislike whomever you please. And if you chose to do so, you could like just the people who don't like themselves—right? Wrong. It's impossible, as the following argument shows:

Suppose for the sake of argument that ①[you like exactly those people who don't like themselves.] (Then it follows that) ②[you don't like yourself.] (For) ③[if you did like yourself, you would like someone (namely you) who likes him- or herself.] But ④[if you don't like yourself, then you do like yourself,] (since) by hypothesis ①[you like just the people who don't like themselves.] (Therefore) ⑤[you both like and don't like yourself.] which is a contradiction. (Thus) ⑥[you can't like exactly the people who don't like themselves.]

Consider this argument carefully. It has all the earmarks of a reductio. There is a hypothetical assumption, ①, and a contradiction, ⑤, deduced from it. The final conclusion, ⑥, is the denial of ①. The role of ① is made clear by the hypothetical-assumption indicator "suppose for the sake of argument that" and is further emphasized in ①'s second occurrence by the phrase "by hypothesis." The contradiction is marked by the words "which is a contradiction." Notice too that ③ and ④ are conditionals and thus should not be broken up. Using the clues already mentioned and those provided by the inference indicators, you should be able to see that the flow chart of the argument is as follows:

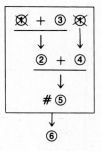

We now check for validity. Consider the inference from ① and ③ to ②. It is similar to modus tollens, for premise ① implies the denial of the consequent of the conditional premise, ③, and the intermediate conclusion ② is the denial of ③'s antecedent. So it is valid in essentially the same way that modus tollens is. (If you're uneasy about this, try the possible worlds test instead; you should be able to see that it is impossible for ① and ③ to be true while ② is false.)

The inference from ① to ④ is also valid. If you like exactly the people who don't like themselves, then certainly if you don't like yourself, you do like yourself (as crazy as that sounds), for then you would have to be among the people you like. Once again, you cannot coherently imagine that ① is true and ④ is false.

Finally, the inference from ② and ④ to the contradiction, ⑤, is valid as well. Half of the contradiction, "you don't like yourself," follows directly from ②. (In fact it just *is* ②.) The other half, "you do like yourself," follows from ② and ④ by modus ponens, which is invariably valid. So given ② and ④, ⑤ must be true.

Since each of its inferences is valid, the hypothetical argument is valid; hence the whole argument is valid. To indicate this, we should put a "D" next to each arrow of the hypothetical argument and a "D" in a box next to the final arrow.

Since the argument is valid, it will be sound if all its basic premises are true. But there is only one basic premise, ③, and it is obviously true. If you like yourself, then surely you like someone who likes him- or herself. From this basic premise together with ① we have validly derived the contradiction, ⑤. It is thus impossible for ① and ③ to be true and ⑤ false. But we know that ③ is true and ⑤ is false. So ①, the hypothetical assumption, must be false. Thus its denial, the final conclusion, ⑥, is true. You just can't like exactly the people who don't like themselves.

What is fascinating about this example is the way logic reveals an unexpected psychological limitation. Liking just the people who don't like themselves is something you simply cannot do, no matter how hard you try. (If you're still sceptical try it!) The sticking point, as the argument reveals, is yourself. It is perfectly possible for you to like just the people *apart from you* who don't like themselves. But if your goal is to like absolutely everyone who doesn't like him- or herself, and no one besides, then logic bars your way. For if you choose to like yourself, then you like someone who likes him- or herself and thus fail to achieve your goal. And if you choose not to like yourself, you still fail, because then there is someone (namely you) who doesn't like him- or herself and whom you have failed to like.

This example is no mere logician's trick. I chose it deliberately, because, though utterly simple by comparison, it is closely related to some of the most profound logical and mathematical proofs of this century. These proofs, the deepest of which are called Gödel's theorems (after their discoverer, Kurt Gödel), imply important limitations on the powers of computers and on the power of logic itself to prove mathematical truths, in much the same way as our example reveals limitations on whom you can like. These remarkable matters cannot be discussed further here, but I'll touch on them again in Section 10.6.

The reductios I have discussed so far have been fairly easy to recognize but often in practice one or more of a reductio's components is left implicit. Frequently it is the contradiction which is left unstated, so that we must supply it before making our diagram. Sometimes the hypothetical argument as stated ends merely in a conclusion which the author takes to be false, rather than proceeding to a contradiction. In mathematics, for example, the hypothetical arguments of reductios often end in falsehoods like "0 = 1." Frequently these are marked by the same phrases which typically occur with contradictions (e.g., "which is absurd" or "which is a contradiction"; mathematicians often employ a somewhat broader notion of contradiction than logicians do). We'll handle these cases by adding the denial of the purported falsehood as an implicit assumption. This is legitimate because the author obviously intends this assumption to be taken for granted. Then combining the purported falsehood and its implicit denial (in this case "0 ≠ 1") in a step of conjunction, we'll derive a genuine contradiction as an implicit conclusion (in this case "0 = 1 and 0 ≠ 1"). As usual, the implicit premise and conclusion should be labeled with letters and included in the diagram.

Sometimes only the contradiction is missing. In such cases the argument usually contains both a statement and its denial, so that the intended contradiction is obvious. In either case, adding the appropriate implicit statements always produces an argument which conforms to the pattern described in this section. Thus, as I noted at the outset, defining an absurdity as a contradiction imposes no essential limitation on our ability to analyze reductios.

Exercise 5.4 All of the following arguments are reductios, though some of them are incomplete as stated. Copy each, bracket and number statements, add missing statements, construct a diagram, and evaluate the reasoning.

1 Abortion is undeniably wrong. For suppose it weren't. Then, since murder is wrong, abortion is not murder. But clearly abortion is murder, for abortion is the killing of a human being and killing a human being is murder. Therefore, abortion is both murder and not murder, which of course is absurd.

2 Suppose the earth is hollow. If it were, it would collapse due to gravitational forces. But since it is not collapsing, it is not hollow. Hence it both is and is not hollow—a contradiction.

3 There can't be anything so small it can't be seen. Suppose there were. Now what can never be seen does not exist. Therefore, it would both exist and not exist, which is silly.

4 The result of adding 0 to any number n is n. For suppose this were not true. Then there would be some number m such that $0 + m \neq m$. Hence, subtracting m from both sides of this inequality, we get $0 \neq 0$, which is absurd.

5 Suppose there were no absolute truth. Then the statement "There is no absolute truth" would be absolutely true. Hence there would

be an absolute truth. Thus there would both be and not be an absolute truth, which is impossible. Therefore, there must be some absolute truth.

6   The universe has no boundary. For suppose that it has one. Now a boundary separates what is inside from what is outside. Therefore, the universe must have an outside. But since the universe by definition includes everything that exists, nothing (not even space) can be outside of it, and so it has no outside. It follows that the universe both has and does not have an outside, which is absurd. Therefore we must conclude that no boundary exists.

7   There will always be wars. Just think of what would happen if they stopped. The generals would have no place to play with their guns, and they'd get bored. And the young men would have no outlet for their thoughtless aggressions. They'd all be nervous wrecks. So they'd start a war again just to relieve the tension.

8   There is one and only one null class (i.e., a class with no members). For suppose this is not the case. Then either there is no null class or there is more than one. But there is at least one null class (the class of all unicorns is an example); therefore, there must be more than one. However, since all classes having the same members are identical and all null classes (being memberless) have the same members, it follows that each null class is identical with all the others, and hence that there is no more than one null class. But this contradicts our previous conclusion.

9   Suppose Muldoon did not have an accomplice in his prison escape. Now he knew exactly when the guards were changing, and he could not have known this unless he or an accomplice in communication with him was in the main compound at the changing of the guard. But we're assuming he had no accomplice. So on our hypothesis it follows that he was in the main compound as the guard changed. But he wasn't. He couldn't have gotten there until after his cell was unlocked, and his cell was unlocked only several minutes after the changing of the guard. Therefore, he must have had an accomplice.

10 There is no greatest prime number. For suppose there were a greatest prime p. Now consider the integer $n = (2 \cdot 3 \cdot 5 \ldots \cdot p) + 1$, formed by adding 1 to the product of all primes up to and including p. Clearly n is not evenly divisible by any of the primes up to and including p, since dividing by each of these primes always leaves a remainder of 1. But every integer is factorable into a number of primes which divide it evenly. Hence n must be evenly divisible by one or more primes greater than p. So a prime greater than p exists, which contradicts our hypothesis.

5.5   LOGICAL NECESSITY, CONTINGENCY, AND INCONSISTENCY

In Section 3.2 I introduced the distinction between logically possible and logically impossible situations. I did not mention then that there are two kinds of logically possible situations—those which hold in all possible worlds and those which hold only in some. Those which hold in all worlds are said to be **logically necessary.** The *non*existence of a four-sided triangle is, for example, a logically necessary situation. You can't imagine it not being the case. Statements describing logically necessary situations are also called logically necessary. Thus "No four-sided triangles exist" is a logically necessary statement. Such statements are also called **necessary truths.**

Situations which hold in some worlds but not in others are termed **contingent,** and statements describing them are **contingent statements.** Some contingent statements are true in the actual world, and some are actually false. The statement "You are reading this book," for example, is contingent and true. It is true but you can coherently imagine it otherwise. The statement "Germany developed nuclear weapons during World War II" is contingent and, fortunately, false.

There are also, as you know, situations which are logically impossible. The existence of a four-sided triangle is one. You can't coherently imagine it. Statements describing these situations (e.g., "Four-sided triangles exist") are termed **inconsistent.** Contradictions are a kind of inconsistency, but not the only kind. ("Four-sided triangles exist," for example, though inconsistent, is not a contradiction.)

The denial of an inconsistent statement is always logically necessary. Conversely, the denial of a logically necessary statement is always inconsistent. The denial of a contingent statement is always contingent.

Every statement is either logically necessary, contingent, or inconsistent, for every statement is true either in all worlds, only in some, or in none. Here are some further examples of each:

Necessary, and therefore true in the actual world:
    If roses are red, then roses are red.
    $2 + 2 = 4$
    Either there are some people or there aren't any at all.
    No moose is a nonmoose.
    It is not true that I am both dead and not dead.

Contingent and true in the actual world:
    Dogs are carnivores.
    Pumpkins ripen in the fall.

There are billions upon billions of galaxies.

Humans speak many different languages.

Gravity varies with the inverse square of distance.

Contingent and false in the actual world:

The earth is flat.

Unicorns exist.

Fidel Castro is President of the United States.

There is a mountain over 30,000 feet tall in Kansas.

Tarantula bites are always fatal.

Inconsistent, and therefore false in the actual world:

The earth is both flat and not flat.

My house is a round square.

2 + 2 = 3

Olaf is a husband who has never been married.

Nothing is green, but my plants are green.

The reason for including a discussion of logical necessity, contingency, and inconsistency in a chapter on deductive logic is that the two extremes—logical necessity and inconsistency—have some startling effects on strength of reasoning. They are, as you might already have noticed, the limiting cases of statement strength (see Section 3.6). That is, necessary truths, being true in all possible worlds, are the most inherently probable and hence the weakest kind of statement. And inconsistencies, being false in all worlds, are the least inherently probable and hence the strongest. (This may sound paradoxical, but think about it for a moment. In fact it is perfectly correct. When I utter an inconsistency, I make a very strong statement—so strong that it can't be true. When I utter a necessary truth, I make a very weak statement—so weak that it is true no matter what the world is like.) Now in Section 3.6 I mentioned the following principle: Strength of reasoning tends to vary in direct proportion to the strength of the basic premises and in inverse proportion to the strength of the conclusion. That would seem to imply, for example, that an argument with the strongest kind of premise, an inconsistency, ought to have the strongest kind of reasoning—namely, deductiveness—and similarly, that an argument with the weakest kind of conclusion, a necessary truth, ought also to be deductive. In fact, strange though it may seem, this is exactly what happens. The following principles are ironclad logical rules. They have no exceptions:

Any argument with an inconsistency among its basic premises is deductive.

Any argument whose conclusion is logically necessary is deductive.

Thus, for example, by the first rule the following argument is valid:

The moon is a beach ball.

I am blue and I am not blue.

∴ Olaf is a knave.

To see that this really is right, apply the test for validity. Is there any possible world in which the basic premises are true and the conclusion is false? Hardly! The second premise, being an inconsistency, is not true in any possible world. So of course there is no world in which both premises are true and the conclusion is false. The inference is undeniably valid. Moreover, this is obviously true of any argument with an inconsistency among its basic premises, since no matter what the conclusion is, there can be no counter-example.

This might appear to be a logical catastrophe, since it surely is profoundly ridiculous to infer an irrelevant conclusion like "Olaf is a knave" from premises of the sort given here. Actually, however, such inferences are utterly harmless. For no inference with an inconsistency among its premises can ever be sound, since the inconsistency itself is necessarily false. Therefore, although such inferences pass the test for validity, we never have to take them seriously; they always fail the test for soundness.

The other oddity I mentioned was that necessary truth in the conclusion also guarantees validity. Here's an example of that:

Aardvarks smile politely.

∴ If you shuffle the cards, then you shuffle the cards.

In this case there is no possible world in which the premise is true and the conclusion is false, because there is no possible world in which the conclusion is false. "If you shuffle the cards, then you shuffle the cards" is a necessary truth. It is true whether or not you shuffle the cards—indeed, whether or not you do anything. It's even true if you don't exist.

Unlike arguments with inconsistent premises, arguments with necessary conclusions can be sound. But again, though somewhat bizarre, this is harmless. It certainly will never enable us to prove a false conclusion. And though it seems strange at first that a necessary truth is validly implied by any premises whatsoever, all this means, really, is that a necessary truth is true no matter what we assume, which is just what we ought to expect.

Despite the fact that any argument with true premises and a logically necessary conclusion is sound, not all such arguments count as proofs for practical purposes. The purpose of a proof is to bring people to the realization that the conclusion is true. This is possible only if the argument starts from assumptions which are known to be true and proceeds by familiar patterns of reasoning, such as the valid forms discussed in Section 5.1. Consequently,

even if it were true that aardvarks smile politely, that fact would not constitute good evidence in any practical sense for the conclusion that if you
shuffle the cards, then you shuffle the cards. I'll have more to say about the
practical requirements of proof in the next section and in Chapter 9.

Besides the rules already discussed, the principle that strength of reasoning tends to vary in direct proportion to the strength of the basic premises
and in inverse proportion to the strength of the conclusion also implies that
arguments ending in inconsistencies or assuming logical truths will tend to
be weak. This is true in general, but there are exceptions. In the last section
I noted that the hypothetical argument of a reductio is never inductive and
is deductive only if there are no possible worlds in which its basic premises
are all true. More generally, any argument ending in an inconsistency is
fallacious, unless there is no world in which its basic premises all are true.
If there is no such world it is valid, since then it is impossible for its premises
all to be true and its conclusion false.

Similarly, an argument whose basic premises are logically necessary
cannot be valid unless its conclusion is also logically necessary, for otherwise it would be subject to counterexamples. It would, however, be inductive
if its conclusion were weak enough to be true in most possible worlds.

In proving logically necessary truths, reductios and conditional proofs
play a special role. This is made possible by the remarkable fact that sometimes they lack basic premises. You might have noticed that this was the
case with problem 5 of Exercise 5.4. Here's another example:

①[There is no such thing as a round square.] (For) suppose ②[there
were.]. (Then) (since) ③[this object is a square,] ④ [it is composed
of four straight lines.] But (since) ⑤[it is round,]⑥[it is not composed
of four straight lines.](Therefore), ⑦[it both is and is not composed of
four straight lines,] which is a contradiction.

This argument is a reductio with ① as the final conclusion, ② as the
hypothetical assumption, and ⑦ as the contradiction. As often is the case
with reductios, the hypothetical assumption is used twice, once to derive
③ and once to derive ⑤. The overall structure is this:

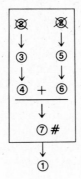

Since the hypothetical assumption does not count as a basic premise, the argument as a whole has no basic premises. Before exploring the consequences of this fact, let's check each inference for validity. Certainly the inferences from ② to ③ and from ② to ⑤ are valid. We can't imagine a world in which there is a round square which is not round or is not a square. (Indeed, we can't imagine a world in which there is a round square at all, so each inference is valid in virtue of the inconsistency of the premise, as well as in virtue of common sense.) The inferences from ③ to ④ and from ⑤ to ⑥ are valid, too. If something is a square (literally a square, not just "sort of square") then it must be composed of four straight lines. This is how a square is defined; it's impossible to imagine otherwise. Similarly, if something is round, it obviously cannot be composed of straight lines. That cannot be coherently imagined. Finally, the inference from ④ and ⑥ to ⑦ is valid. This can be seen in several ways. For one thing, it is an instance of conjunction, which is always valid. For another, it is easy to see that there is no possible world in which the premises are both true and hence that there can be no counterexample. And in any case, the validity of this inference is plainly evident to common sense. Since all the inferences are valid, we know that the hypothetical argument is valid.

But what of the argument as a whole? Here a strange problem arises. What does it mean to ask whether the whole argument is valid, given that it doesn't have any basic premises? A valid argument is an argument such that it is impossible for its basic premises to be true and its conclusion false. But how does this definition apply when there are no basic premises? The answer is simple, though perhaps a bit odd. When there are no basic premises, saying that it is impossible for the basic premises to be true and the conclusion false is the same thing as saying that it is impossible for the conclusion to be false. Thus an argument without basic premises is valid just in case its final conclusion is a necessary truth. That's just what validity means in this case.

Now I said earlier that a reductio is valid if its hypothetical argument is valid. But I didn't consider the case in which there are no basic premises. This case, however, is no exception. It should follow, then, that if the hypothetical argument of a reductio with no basic premises is valid, then the argument as a whole is valid, which is just to say that its conclusion is a logical truth. I will now prove that this is true. (Once again, bear with me; the reasoning is difficult, but give it a try!)

Any reductio without basic premises has just one assumption (the hypothetical assumption) in its hypothetical argument. Now suppose this hypothetical argument is valid. Then, since it ends in a contradiction, its assumption must be inconsistent, since otherwise there would be a counterexample. Consequently this hypothetical assumption is false in all possible worlds. Therefore its denial, the final conclusion, is true in all possible worlds (i.e., logically necessary). Hence by what I said in the next to the last paragraph, the argument as a whole is valid. Thus I have shown that if the hypothetical argument of a reductio without basic premises is valid, so is the argument as a whole. (And did you notice that I proved this by using conditional proof? Look back through this paragraph and see if you can recognize the argument's structure.)

By this reasoning, then, our sample argument is valid, and its final conclusion is logically necessary. And that is surely correct. We can't coherently imagine a round square. Hence in all coherently imaginable worlds it is true that there aren't any. The fact that this can be proved on no assumptions is quite natural, for it is true no matter what we assume the world is like.

Conditional proofs may also lack basic premises, and when they do, like reductios, they are valid if their hypothetical arguments are. To see this, suppose we have a conditional proof with a valid hypothetical argument and no basic premises. Once again, the only assumption of the hypothetical argument will be the hypothetical assumption. Since the hypothetical argument is valid, in any world in which the hypothetical assumption is true, the hypothetical argument's conclusion is true. This means that the conditional whose antecedent is the hypothetical assumption and whose consequent is the hypothetical argument's conclusion is true in every world. But this conditional is just the argument's final conclusion. So the argument's final conclusion is true in all possible worlds. And that is just to say, as I noted above, that the entire argument is valid.

This discussion has been rather complicated, but it can be summarized fairly simply. I have made two major points:

1 *When an argument has no basic premises, validity is the same thing as the logical necessity of the final conclusion.*

2 *If the hypothetical argument of a conditional proof or reductio with no basic premises is valid, then so is the argument as a whole.*

Combining these two points, we can draw the following conclusion:

3 *If the hypothetical argument of a conditional proof or reductio with no basic premises is valid, then the final conclusion of the argument as a whole is logically necessary.*

That's what I wanted you to see.

Exercise 5.5(a) Classify each of the following statements as logically necessary, contingent, or inconsistent.

1 The Great Pyramid is in Egypt.
2 The sky is green with purple polka dots.
3 All squares have four equal sides.

4   A barefoot boy with shoes on stood sitting in the grass.
5   Ophelia is neither a hijacker nor not a hijacker.
6   The ocean is wet.
7   The ocean is not wet.
8   Olaf spoke the truth when he said that he never talks.
9   Light travels at 3×10^{10} centimeters per second.
10   The Civil War ended in 1865.
11   Either I am going to Canada or I am not going to Canada.
12   Snerd, who is a lizard, is not a lizard.
13   The candy tasted both sweet and salty at the same time.
14   If you like everyone, then you like yourself.

Exercise 5.5(b)   Copy each of the following passages, bracket and number statements, add missing statements, construct a diagram, and evaluate the reasoning.

1   Olaf is both real and not real. Therefore, he is immensely puzzling to his cat, Fuzzball.
2   There can be no married bachelors. For suppose there were. Then they would be bachelors and hence unmarried. But they would also be married—a contradiction.
3   This argument is illogical. I dislike everything that is illogical. Therefore, I dislike this argument.
4   Since the world is a crazy mess over which we have no control, we can only conclude that what will be will be.
5   If Ophelia is either a man or a woman, and she's not a man, then she's female. For suppose that she is either a man or a woman, but not a man. Then she's a woman. Hence she's female.
6   Since $2 + 2 = 5$ and $5 = 7$, it follows that $2 + 2 = 8$. Therefore, $2 + 2 = 4$.
7   The sentence "This sentence is false" is not true. For suppose it were. Then it would have to be false, and so it would not be true. Hence it would be both true and not true—a contradiction.
8   The sentence "This sentence is false" is not false. For suppose it were. Then it would be true, and so it would not be false. Therefore, it would be both false and not false, which is absurd.

Note: Problems 7 and 8 together constitute one of the great paradoxes which have puzzled logicians since the time of the ancient Greeks. These paradoxes have played an important role in the history of logic. I'll return to them in Section 10.6.

5.6 BEGGING THE QUESTION

While we're on the subject of deductive oddities, it's worthwhile to mention **begging the question.** Begging the question is assuming what you're trying to prove. An argument begs the question if its conclusion is also one of its basic premises. Question-begging arguments are always deductive, because when the conclusion is a basic premise there certainly is no possible world in which the basic premises are all true and the conclusion is false.

Logic texts which employ very loose definitions of "fallacy" often treat begging the question as a fallacy. There is indeed something wrong with question-begging arguments, but it is not that they are fallacious. Their reasoning is impeccable. What is wrong is that they are useless as tools of persuasion or enlightenment. If the hearer does not already accept the conclusion, he or she cannot rationally be persuaded to accept it by a question-begging argument. This point can best be made with reference to a specific example:

①[The Bible is the word of God.] (For) ②[in Numbers 36:13 we read, "These are the commandments and the judgments which the Lord commanded. . . . "] And ③[what the scriptures say is surely true;] (for) could God's word ever be false or deceptive?

I have not bracketed or numbered the final question, for reasons which will become obvious shortly. Statement ① is the argument's conclusion. It is supported by an inference from ② and ③. And the "for" connecting ③ to the question which follows indicates that this question is meant to suggest further premises supporting ③. At least two premises are clearly intended:

Ⓐ God's word could never be false or deceptive.
Ⓑ The Bible (i.e., the scriptures) is (are) God's word.

Since these premises are clearly assumed, we should add them to the argument. But now notice that Ⓑ is just the conclusion, ①, so that the argument is structured as follows:

(Actually there may be several more implicit premises, but this is enough for our purposes.)

This argument begs the question. It is valid—and perhaps even sound (you can decide for yourself)—but it is worthless as a means of persuasion or proof. Presumably its author is a Christian or Jew who wishes to convince nonbelievers that the Bible is God's word. But the nonbeliever is precisely the person who doubts this. Therefore, he or she is certainly not going to be won over without trickery by an argument which assumes it. An argument can bring its audience to genuine new understanding only if it begins from assumptions they already accept and proceeds by reasoning they can follow to a conclusion whose truth is not already evident to them. (For further discussion of this point, see Chapter 9.) A question-begging argument cannot do this, and thus it never brings new understanding. It is therefore open to criticism on practical grounds, even if it is logically unobjectionable.

Begging the question is often called **circular reasoning,** because in a sense the argument runs in a circle. We can see this by rediagraming the previous argument as follows:

The argument is like a cat chasing its own tail. It goes nowhere and accomplishes nothing. This futile and groundless character can be seen in a somewhat different light by regarding the argument as a kind of dialogue between its author and a sceptical listener:

Author: The Bible is God's word.
Listener: What is your evidence?
Author: In Numbers 36:13 we read, "These are the commandments and the judgments which the Lord commanded. . . ." And what the scriptures say is surely true.
Listener: But how do you know that what the scriptures say is true?
Author: I know because God's word would never be deceptive, and the Bible is God's word.
Listener: Well, but, you see, that's just what I was trying to find out. How do you know that the Bible is God's word?
Author: I told you. In Numbers 36:13 we read. . . .

It is obvious that this discussion is going nowhere. It will just circle endlessly without anyone becoming the wiser.

A noteworthy feature of question-begging arguments is that since they are invariably deductive, normal ones containing nondeductive inferences are always fortuitously strong (see Section 3.8). In fact, begging the question is one of the commonest sources of fortuitous strength. To evaluate such arguments, you should treat the inferences as usual, but place a "D" in the box next to the argument as a whole, regardless of the quality of the inferences.

Question-begging is often camouflaged by wording the conclusion differently when it appears as a premise. This makes the circularity more difficult to recognize, but it doesn't change anything in principle. Here's an elementary example:

①[Laetrile is an effective cure for cancer,] ⓕⓞⓡ ①[it frequently stimulates complete recovery from this often fatal disease.]

I have given both statements the same number, because the second simply repeats the first. Saying that something frequently stimulates complete recovery from cancer is no different from saying that it is an effective cancer cure. The diagram of this argument is:

Or if we prefer:

Once again the futility of this sort of reasoning ought to be apparent. If someone doubts that Laetrile is an effective cure for cancer, then arguing from the premise that it frequently stimulates recovery from cancer will certainly not convince that person, for he or she will find the premise equally dubious. Even if this argument were sound (which it isn't), it wouldn't be of any practical value.

If an argument begs the question, it is useful to note this fact by writing "begs the question" next to its diagram. This will alert readers to the fact that the argument deserves criticism despite its validity.

Exercise 5.6 Some of the following arguments beg the question. Others illustrate other topics discussed in this chapter. Copy each, circle indicators, bracket and number statements, add missing statements, diagram and evaluate. If any inference in any of the arguments has one of the following forms, write the name of the form next to the arrow representing the inference:

Modus ponens   Disjunctive syllogism
Modus tollens   Simplification
Affirming the consequent   Conjunction
Denying the antecedent   Contraposition
Hypothetical syllogism   Constructive dilemma

1   Pornography is immoral, for the use of explicitly sexual material for erotic purposes transgresses ethical precepts.

2   If Fuzzball were dropped into Olaf's kennel, then he would be eaten by the angry dogs. And if he were eaten by the angry dogs, then he would no longer meow beneath my window at night and disturb my sleep. Therefore, if Fuzzball were dropped into Olaf's kennel, then he would no longer meow beneath my window at night and disturb my sleep.

3   It is clear that the moon is the size of a nickel, because it looks like it is the size of a nickel. And it *must* look like it is the size of a nickel, because that is just how big it is.

4   The very notion of a miracle is absurd, because proof of a miracle requires very strong evidence, but the only evidence we have is the testimony of fallible witnesses—and their testimony is worthless, because they believe such preposterous things.

5   Suppose that $1 + 1 = 3$. Then anything would be true. Therefore, if $1 + 1 = 3$, anything is true.

6   What better proof could be required that human beings survive death than the persistent phenomenon of mediumship? Through the medium's trance, we apprehend the voices of strange beings; and these beings are none other than the living departed!

7   Majority rule, without safeguards, could lead to some rather absurd situations. For example, if 51 percent rather mildly favor the confiscation of property of the other 49 percent of the society, the logic of unrestrained majoritarianism would so dictate. (R. Joseph Monsen, Jr., and Mark W. Cannon, *The Makers of Public Policy: American Power Groups and Their Ideologies*)

8   We must either chance the mountain pass or risk the dangers of the tunnels beneath the mountains. If we chance the pass, we'll be turned back by the impenetrable snowdrifts. But if we enter the tunnels, we will face the unknown evil that lurks in the darkness. Our journey must continue. Therefore, it falls to us to face the evil beneath the mountains.

9   If you capture my knight, you'll lose more than you gain. For suppose you do. That will leave your king open to check on the next move, and I would certainly take that opportunity. Okay, so then

your king is in check. Your only move at that point is to pull your king back. But doing so exposes your rook, which I can then capture at no immediate cost to me. Therefore, you would have lost a rook and I a knight. And since a rook is more valuable than a knight, you would have lost more than you gained, just as I said.

10 $\sqrt{2}$ is not a rational number (i.e., a number expressible by a fraction $\frac{x}{y}$, where x and y are integers). For suppose $\sqrt{2} = \frac{x}{y}$, where x and y are integers. Then it follows that $2 = \frac{x^2}{y^2}$ and hence that $x^2 = 2 \cdot y^2$. Now, like every integer, x and y can both be factored into prime numbers. And each of these prime factors occurs an even number of times in x^2 and y^2, since $x^2 = x \cdot x$ and $y^2 = y \cdot y$. But then in $2 \cdot y^2$ the prime factor 2 does not occur an even number of times. Hence $x^2 \neq 2 \cdot y^2$, and so we have a contradiction.

11 If God created the universe, there was a time when he commenced to create. Back of that commencement there must have been an eternity. In that eternity what was this God doing? He certainly did not think. There was nothing to think about. He did not remember. Nothing had ever happened. What did he do? Can you imagine anything more absurd than an infinite intelligence in infinite nothing wasting an eternity? (Robert G. Ingersoll, *Some Mistakes of Moses*)

6

Inductive Arguments

Evaluation of inductive arguments is usually more difficult and less precise than evaluation of deductive arguments. Primarily this is because, unlike validity, inductive strength is a matter of degree. By our definition, an inductive argument is an argument whose conclusion is true in most, but not all, of the possible worlds in which its premises are true. In other words, its conclusion is true in anywhere from just over 50 percent to just under 100 percent of these worlds. These percentages are to be interpreted in the frequency sense discussed in Section 3.3. They represent the frequency of occurrence of worlds in which the conclusion is true among all imaginable worlds in which the premises are true. You've already seen how difficult it is to estimate them accurately. But fortunately there are cases in which we can be precise. In this chapter we'll begin with such clear-cut cases and then proceed to arguments that are less precise, but also more powerful and more interesting.

6.1 STATISTICAL SYLLOGISM AND RELATED ARGUMENTS

Just as there are argument forms which are always deductive, so there are forms which, at least under certain conditions, are always inductive. Perhaps the most common is **statistical syllogism:**

> n percent of F are G
> x is F
> $\therefore$ x is G

As you'll soon see (if you don't see it already), this form is inductive so long as the number n is between 50 and 100. I've already discussed several instances of statistical syllogism, beginning with that now-too-familiar example:

> 95 percent of elves drink stout.
> Olaf is an elf.
> $\therefore$ Olaf drinks stout.

Here F stands for "elves," G stands for "stout drinkers," and the object x is Olaf. This theme has many variations. Here are a few:

1 Most F are G
  x is F
  $\therefore$ x is G

2 Nearly all F are G
  x is F
  $\therefore$ x is G

3 A small fraction of F are G
  x is F
  $\therefore$ x is not G

4 w, x, y, and z are the only F's
  Exactly three F's are G
  $\therefore$ x is G

5 There are exactly four F's
  Three of them are G
  x is F
  $\therefore$ x is G

6 There are over 3,000,000 F's
  Only two of them are G
  x is F
  $\therefore$ x is not G

Each of these forms is inductive.

Careful examination of some of these variations of statistical syllogism will provide an opportunity to understand the possible worlds analysis of induction more deeply. The simplest inductive forms from the standpoint of possible worlds are arguments like 4, in which the individuals having F are listed by name. Here's an example:

Mercury, Venus, Earth, and Mars are the only planets inside the asteroid belt.

Exactly three planets within the asteroid belt are lifeless.

∴ Venus is lifeless.

To evaluate this inference, we consider the range of possible worlds (a world, you must remember, is an entire universe, perhaps containing many planets) in which the premises are true. In each, one of the four planets supports life, while the others don't. But different planets may support life in different possible worlds. This range of worlds can therefore be divided into four classes, depending on which of the four planets is inhabited. That is, one class will contain all the worlds in which the premises are true and only Mercury is inhabited, another will contain all the worlds in which the premises are true and only Venus is inhabited, and so on. Now it might at first appear that the class of worlds in which only Earth is inhabited is the most numerous of the four, since Earth is the right distance from the sun and has the right atmosphere, climate, and chemical composition to support life. But that is the thinking of an earthbound imagination. We certainly needn't imagine things this way. Indeed, we can imagine these four planets at any distances from the sun we like, and we can think of them as having different atmospheres and climates. We can also imagine the sun to be bigger and hotter or smaller and cooler than it is. And we can imagine life forms which flourish in virtually any environment. Given this degree of freedom, it is obvious that we can conceive each of the other planets as having life in just as many ways as we can conceive Earth to be inhabited. Therefore, none of the four classes is more numerous than any of the others.

This means that as we allow our imaginations to wander at random through the worlds in which the premises are true, we should encounter members of each of the four classes with equal frequency: 25 percent of them are worlds in which only Mercury has life, 25 percent in which only Venus has life, 25 percent in which only Earth has life, and 25 percent in which only Mars has life.[1] It follows that among the worlds in which the premises are true, the frequency of worlds in which Venus is lifeless is 75 percent. Hence the conclusion is true in 75 percent of the worlds in which the premises are true, and so the argument is inductive. Classifying possible worlds as we did here reveals clearly why this is so.

Arguments which do not name specific individuals are harder to un-

---

[1] In classical treatments of induction the equal probability of these four cases is explained, not in terms of possible worlds, but by invoking the so-called **principle of indifference.** This rather vague rule of thumb says that in the absence of information to the contrary we should regard all possible cases relevant to the evaluation of an argument as equally probable. In some sense this is surely right—at least in application to arguments like the one considered here. But mere appeal to the principle does little to further our understanding. The possible worlds approach enables us to see more clearly why and in what sense the principle applies here.

derstand in detail, but the principle is the same. Consider, for example, this instance of form 5:

> There are exactly four planets inside the sun's asteroid belt.
> Exactly three of them are lifeless.
> Venus is a planet inside the sun's asteroid belt.
> ∴ Venus is lifeless.

Once again we survey the range of possible worlds in which the premises are true. This time, however, there is more variability. In all of these worlds there are four planets inside the sun's asteroid belt, one of which is Venus. But the other three are unspecified. They could be anything—the three mentioned in the last example, or any other planets, real or imagined. Nevertheless, there is order in this seeming chaos. To find it, we must first segregate the worlds in which the premises are true into classes based on the identities of these planets. All possible worlds with the same four planets inside the asteroid belt will belong to a single class. There will be infinitely many of these classes, since there is no end to the variety of planets we can imagine. Each class, however, consists of worlds structured just like the worlds of the previous example. That is, in all of the possible worlds of a given class, the same four planets (Venus among them) lie inside the asteroid belt, and one of them is inhabited. But which of the four is inhabited differs from world to world within a given class.

Because of this structural similarity, we can repeat the reasoning of the last example with respect to each class of worlds. We divide each class into four subclasses so that the same planet is inhabited in all the worlds of each subclass. By the reasoning of the last example, each of the four subclasses makes up 25 percent of the class to which it belongs. Now for each class, one and only one of its subclasses consists of worlds in which Venus is inhabited. Hence Venus is lifeless in 75 percent of the worlds in each class. And since this is true of every class, if we reunite all the classes into a single whole, the proportion of worlds in which Venus is lifeless will remain the same—75 percent. But this whole is just the range of worlds with which we began—that is, the range of worlds in which the premises of our argument are true. Hence the conclusion, "Venus is lifeless," is true in 75 percent of the worlds in which the premises are true. Once again the inductiveness of the argument is apparent.

Even more general arguments, where only percentages are mentioned, add yet another level of complexity. But the idea remains the same. Consider this straightforward statistical syllogism:

> Exactly 75 percent of planets inside the asteroid belt are lifeless.
> Venus is a planet inside the asteroid belt.
> ∴ Venus is lifeless.

Here we must imagine not only worlds in which three of the four planets inside the asteroid belt are lifeless, but also worlds in which six of eight planets are lifeless, or nine of twelve, or twelve of sixteen, and so on. Thus to see matters clearly, we need first to divide all the worlds in which the premises are true into classes based upon the number of planets inside the asteroid belt. This number will always be a multiple of four, since otherwise it's impossible for exactly 75 percent to be lifeless. (You can't, for example, take 75 percent of three planets.) Now the simplest of these classes is the one containing worlds in which there are exactly four planets (Venus among them) inside the asteroid belt. These are precisely the same worlds we looked at in the last example. By dividing them into further classes, as we did in the last example, we can see once again that 75 percent of them are worlds in which Venus is lifeless. Similar reasoning yields the same conclusion for each of our other classes. Thus, once again, when we bring all the classes back together, it is evident that 75 percent of the worlds in which the premises of our new argument are true are worlds in which Venus is lifeless.

The highest degree of generality is reached in arguments with the forms 1 and 2. Here the range of worlds in which the premises are true is even wider, and the details are correspondingly more complex, but I'll spare you an account of them. If you're interested, you can probably figure them out by generalizing once more on the discussion of the preceding example. My aim here has been primarily to convince you, if you remained unconvinced, that statistical syllogism really is inductive by the possible worlds test and to limber up your imagination in preparation for the discussions that follow. You should review this reasoning if any of it was unclear.

The general method used in all these cases was to divide the possible worlds in which the argument's premises are true into structurally similar (and hence equinumerous) classes. But the utility of this method is limited. It yields precise percentage figures for strength of reasoning only if the premises and conclusion are precisely stated and closely related to one another. Success in employing the method depends, too, on identification of the relevant structurally similar classes and on our ability to estimate the frequency of worlds in which the conclusion is true by letting our imaginations wander freely among the worlds of all these classes. With simple arguments, like statistical syllogism, proper application of the method is rather obvious. But with more complicated forms it becomes increasingly difficult and sometimes impossible to identify the relevant structurally similar classes. There may be no obvious way of dividing the worlds in which the premises are true into structurally similar classes, or there may be more than one. (For an example in which there is more than one, see the Appendix.) So, although this method is useful for deepening our understanding of simple forms of induction, for the most part we will continue to rely on less precise intuitive estimates of reasoning strength.

There is one more relative of statistical syllogism that is worth mention—the **probabilistic syllogism:**

> *F*'s are probably *G*'s
> *x* is *F*
> ∴ *x* is *G*

This sort of argument is also inductive, but it is highly ambiguous, because as I'll explain in Section 6.3, the word "probably" has multiple meanings. There is the further difficulty that on several of these meanings, to say that a statement is probable is to say that our world is a member of a class of worlds in most of which the statement is true. This means that the actual world is not the only world to consider in determining the truth of the first premise. Detailed analysis of arguments containing statements involving probability—or for that matter, possibility and necessity—is too involved to be adequately dealt with here. For our purposes it must suffice merely to note that probabilistic syllogism is an inductive form.

6.2   SUPPRESSED EVIDENCE

Inductive arguments are subject to a curious frailty that does not infect deduction; the strength of their reasoning can be altered by the addition of new premises. To see this, consider the following variant of statistical syllogism:

> Most bankers are wealthy.
> H. M. Smith is a banker.
> ∴ H. M. Smith is wealthy.

This argument is inductive, for the reasons discussed in the last section. But suppose now that we add the premises "H. M. Smith's bank has just folded" and "Almost all bankers whose banks have just folded are poor." The result is a rather confused argument—certainly not one that a reasonable person would offer to prove the conclusion—but that is not the point. The point is that this new argument is fallacious. Certainly the conclusion is not true in the majority of worlds in which the premises are true. The premises no longer make the conclusion even probable.

Adding premises can also strengthen nondeductive reasoning. One way to do this, as we saw in Section 4.1, is to conditionalize. But there are other ways as well. We could add, for example, "Mr. Smith is very old" and "All old bankers are wealthy." This makes the first premise of the original argument superfluous, but that's only a technicality. The overall effect is to make an inductive argument deductive.

Still other added premises may have no effect on the reasoning's strength. This is the case, for example, if an added premise is totally irrelevant to the conclusion. "Mr. Smith has a penchant for red bow ties" is a good example.

If this premise is added to the original argument, it remains inductive. The net effect is zero.

The sensitivity of inductive reasoning to new information adds a dimension of complexity not present in deduction. Deductive arguments are impervious to new information. No matter how many premises you add and no matter what they say, the argument remains deductive. The reason for this is simple. If an argument is deductive, there are absolutely no possible worlds in which its premises are true and its conclusion is false. Thus there are no worlds in which these premises *plus some new ones* are true and the conclusion false, because these would have to be worlds in which the original premises are true and the conclusion false, and there aren't any such worlds. Hence no matter what we add, there will never be a counterexample; the argument remains deductive.

There is a convenient way of visualizing this. Imagine all possible worlds as points contained within the area of a rectangle. (See Figure 1.) Then the worlds in which the argument's conclusion is true can be represented as the points contained in a circle within the rectangle. Worlds in which the conclusion is false are the points within the rectangle but outside the circle. If the argument is deductive, there are no worlds in which its basic premises

FIGURE 1   Effect of Adding Premises to a Deductive Argument

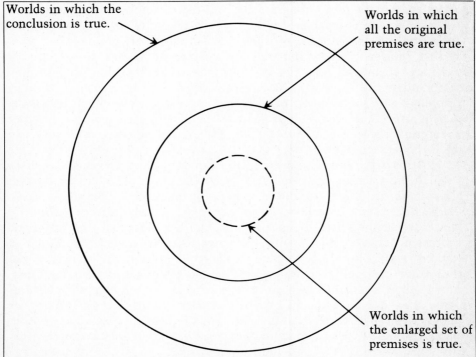

Worlds in which the conclusion is true.

Worlds in which all the original premises are true.

Worlds in which the enlarged set of premises is true.

are true and its conclusion false, so all worlds in which its basic premises are true are represented by points within the circle. We'll imagine them as gathered together in a smaller circle inside the original one. (The area outside this smaller circle then represents worlds in which one or more of the basic premises is false.)

Using this representation, the effect of adding premises to a deductive argument can be visualized as follows. Since the worlds in which the expanded set of premises are true are all worlds in which the original set was, they must all fall within the area of the smaller circle. We can think of them as the points within the dotted circle in Figure 1. The effect of adding premises is thus to shrink the class of worlds in which the premises are true—or at best, to leave it unchanged. After this addition, there are still no worlds in which the premises are true and the conclusion false. The argument remains deductive.

This is the case even if the added premises are inconsistencies or if they contradict the original ones. For if so, the class of worlds in which the premises are true shrinks to nothing. Even in this peculiar limiting case, as we saw in Section 5.5, the argument is still deductive.

But inductive arguments behave quite differently. To see this graphically, recall once again the argument with which this section began. The arrangement of worlds illustrative of this argument is shown in Figure 2. Once again the area of the rectangle represents all possible worlds, and the area of the large circle represents the worlds in which the conclusion (in this case "Smith is wealthy") is true. But if an argument is inductive, its conclusion is false in some of the worlds in which its premises are true. Thus the worlds in which the premises are true are represented in Figure 2 by the area of an oval, a part of which lies beyond the area encompassed by the conclusion. This part, shaded in the diagram, is the region of counter-examples—worlds in which the premises are true and the conclusion false. But it is smaller in area than the part of the oval inside the circle, in order to represent the fact that the conclusion is true in most of the worlds in which the premises are true.

Now, as before, adding new premises can only shrink the class of worlds in which the premises are true. But this can happen in three different ways, each represented by a small dotted oval in the diagram: (1) The added premises might contract this class in such a way that it falls entirely within the class of worlds in which the conclusion is true. In that case, the argument becomes deductive. This is what happened when we added "Mr. Smith is very old" and "All old bankers are wealthy." (2) Adding the premise could either leave the original class of worlds unchanged or shrink it so that most, but not all, of it remains within the class of worlds in which the conclusion is true. This is what happened when we added "Smith has a penchant for red bow ties." (3) Adding premises could shrink the class of worlds in which the premises are true so that at least half of it lies outside the class of worlds

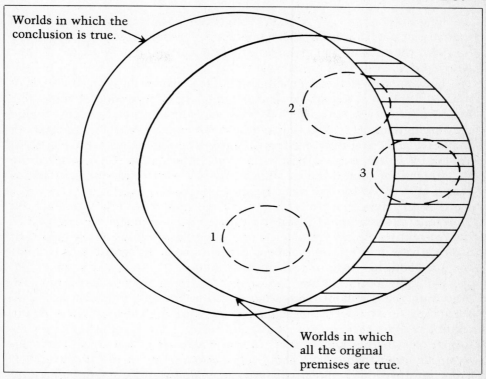

Worlds in which the
conclusion is true.

2

3

1

Worlds in which
all the original
premises are true.

FIGURE 2   Effect of Adding Premises to an Inductive Argument

in which the conclusion is true. If so, the argument becomes fallacious.
This is what happened when we added "Smith's bank has just folded" and
"Nearly all bankers whose banks have just folded are poor."

It is this last case which turns out to be particularly troublesome. Suppose we want to evaluate our original argument:

> Most bankers are wealthy.
> H. M. Smith is a banker.
> ∴ H. M. Smith is wealthy.

And suppose both of its premises are true. Now the reasoning is inductive;
hence the conclusion ought to be probable. But suppose, further, that Smith's
bank has just folded and that nearly all bankers whose banks have folded
are poor. On the basis of this additional evidence, the conclusion seems
improbable. What should we say?

One thing not to say is that the argument is fallacious. It can't be. It's inductive, as we saw earlier. The problem here is neither with the reasoning nor with the truth of the premises; it's that the argument does not tell the whole story.

In evaluating induction there is more to consider than just the truth of premises and the strength of the reasoning. Since induction is vulnerable to new information, we must consider as well any additional evidence which may strengthen or weaken the argument. To be fully reliable, therefore, an inductive argument must meet an additional requirement; it must contain among its assumptions all known relevant information. This is called the **requirement of total evidence.** What is wrong with the argument above is that it fails to satisfy this requirement.

The key terms of the requirement are "relevant" and "known." By "relevant information" I mean information which affects the strength of the reasoning. In our example, the pair of assumptions about the folding of Smith's bank was relevant; so was the pair about his wealth and age. But the one about his taste in bow ties was not.

By "known information" I mean information known to be true by those evaluating the argument. Thus what counts as known information will vary depending on our degree of acquaintance with the subject matter of the argument. Why this peculiar limitation? Why not demand *all* relevant information, whether known to us or not? There are two answers, one practical, the other theoretical. The practical answer is that to demand all relevant information is unrealistic. We can evaluate an argument based only on the relevant information we know. No more can be expected.

But practical limitations aside, wouldn't the ideal inductive argument be one which assumed all the relevant facts, not just the known ones? The answer, surprisingly, is no. This is where the theoretical consideration comes in. Assuming all relevant facts precludes induction. For the argument's conclusion will be either true or false. If it is true, the most relevant fact is the conclusion itself. Therefore, assuming all relevant evidence entails assuming the conclusion. But if we assume the conclusion, the argument becomes deductive. Of course, now it begs the question, but it has certainly ceased to be inductive. In contrast, if the conclusion is false, the most relevant fact is the conclusion's denial. But assuming the conclusion's denial makes the argument fallacious, for now the conclusion can be true in none of the worlds in which the premises are true.

Thus we can see that it is essential to induction that some truths relevant to the conclusion *not* be assumed. If every relevant truth is assumed, the argument becomes either deductive or fallacious. Induction flourishes only in a climate of partial ignorance. Accordingly, the requirement that inductive arguments assume only known information is justified, not only by its practicality, but also by the nature of induction itself.

The requirement of total evidence, then, is simply the demand that inductive arguments be as forthright and complete as they can be, given the limitations of our knowledge. When this demand is not met, criticism is in order, even if the reasoning is inductive and all the premises are true.

Failure to include all relevant information known to the evaluators of an argument is called **suppressing evidence.** Often it is the result of oversight or ignorance, but sometimes evidence is suppressed deliberately, with deceptive intent. Suppose, to recycle our example once more, that we wish to convince someone—a prospective creditor, say—of the solvency of our friend Mr. Smith. We know that his bank has just folded and that nearly anyone in his position would be broke, but we argue that because he is a banker by trade and most bankers are wealthy, Smith is wealthy. This is a deliberate deception, but it may involve neither lies (the premises are true and we may not really know about the conclusion) nor irrational reasoning. Our real breach of faith is the suppression of evidence.

Suppressed evidence should be dealt with in argument evaluation by adding a note to the argument diagram. For the argument just mentioned, for example, the note should read something like this:

Suppresses evidence that Smith's bank has folded and that most people whose banks have folded are not wealthy. If added, this evidence would render the reasoning fallacious. Argument is therefore deceptive and unreliable.

Suppressed statements should *not* be given numbers or letters and should *not* be added to the argument diagram. Don't confuse suppressed evidence with implicit premises. Implicit premises express the author's intent; suppressed evidence is often precisely what the author does not want us to assume.

Remember, too, that suppressed evidence is a matter of fact, not of imagination. You can't just make up a story casting doubt on the argument's conclusion and call it suppressed evidence. Suppressed evidence must be true in the actual world, and it must be known. Uncovering suppressed evidence is therefore not a matter of logic alone, but requires an acquaintance with the subject matter of the argument. In this respect it is like checking the truth of the premises. If you are aware of suppressed evidence which, if added, would make the argument irrational, then you should reject the argument on the basis of this evidence. But if the argument is inductive and has true assumptions and you know of no suppressed evidence, then the argument is the most reliable guide you have to the truth of its conclusion. You should consider this conclusion probable.

Exercise 6.2 Diagram and evaluate the following arguments, adding premises or revising wording where necessary. Add a note to your diagram discussing the truth of basic premises, the possibility of suppressed evidence, and the overall strength of the argument.

1 Since most people never experience a major earthquake, the chances are that you won't.

2 A fair die shows a one on only one sixth of its rolls. Therefore, if you toss a fair die once, it will not show a one.

3 Most movie stars never become President. Ronald Reagan was a movie star. Therefore, Ronald Reagan never became President.

4 Small cars usually get good gas mileage. Therefore, the cars driven at the Indianapolis 500 get good gas mileage, for they are relatively small.

5 Less than 50 percent of the population has type O positive blood. Therefore, you do not have type O positive blood.

6 Births of males are slightly more common than births of females. Therefore, if you have had or will have a child, your first child was or will be a boy.

7 In spite of the myth that divorce is a psychological cop out, . . . in reality it is considerably easier, legally and emotionally, to get married and stay married than it is to divorce. Marriage is therefore much more likely to be a cop out for young people who substitute artificial supports for genuine emotional maturity. (Susan Gettleman and Janet Markowitz, *The Courage to Divorce*)

8 [Sociobiologist Edward O. Wilson believes] that evolution may have built into mankind's genetic endowment traits that predispose individuals to bigotry and racism. Since xenophobia, the fear of strangers, would most likely have been an adaptive trait for primitive hunter-gatherers, a predisposition to fear outsiders was probably assimilated into man's gene pool. (Jeffrey Saver, "Edward O. Wilson: Father of a New Science," *Science Digest*, May 1982)

6.3 KINDS OF PROBABILITY

If you followed the discussion of the last section carefully, you may have been puzzled by an apparent paradox. Since an evidence-suppressing inductive argument is still genuinely inductive, if its basic premises are true, its conclusion should be probable. But in the last section I said that suppressed evidence can make the conclusion improbable. In that case, how can the argument be inductive?

The simple answer is that the conclusion remains probable *relative to the original premises* even if evidence is suppressed. It may be improbable, however, *relative to everything we know*. This simple answer is correct, but it's useful to understand the matter more deeply. To do that, we need a firm grasp of the various kinds of probability.

The sort of probability we have been mainly concerned with so far is the probability of a conclusion relative to a given set of premises. This is the kind of probability involved in the definition of an inductive argument, and it is called, appropriately enough, **inductive probability.** Inductive probability is a measure of strength of reasoning, and it is usually regarded as applying to arguments or inferences. The inductive probability of a deductive argument is 100 percent; for inductive arguments, it lies between 50 percent and 100 percent; and for fallacies, it is 50 percent or less.

Sometimes we are interested, not in the strength of an argument, but in the probability of a single statement. But here the notion of probability is ambiguous. Are we concerned with the probability of that statement in and of itself or with the probability of its being true given what we know? The probability of a statement in and of itself is called its **inherent probability, absolute probability,** or **logical probability** (all these terms are synonymous). The inherent probability of a logically necessary statement is 100 percent; that of an inconsistency is 0 percent; and that of a contingent statement is between 0 percent and 100 percent. It is impossible, however, to assign exact numerical values to contingent statements. Inherent probability can easily be defined in terms of possible worlds. The inherent probability of a statement is just the frequency among all possible worlds of the worlds in which it is true. As we saw in Section 3.6, it can also be defined as the inverse of statement strength. The stronger a statement is, the less inherently probable it is, and vice versa.

It is noteworthy that much of what is true in our world is inherently improbable. Only in an infinitesimal proportion of worlds, for example, were you born at the precise moment (whenever it was) that you were actually born. In fact, in most worlds you don't even exist. And this is only one of an endless variety of inherently improbable truths. The sum total of inherent improbabilities true in our world is staggering. We live in a universe whose inherent improbability is beyond our comprehension. Perhaps this is why many thinkers have felt an implacable astonishment that this particular universe should exist.

It is also worthy of note that negative statements tend to be inherently more probable than affirmative ones. It is inherently improbable, for example, that you have 3,129,732 hairs on your head. The denial of this statement has a much higher probability—in fact, it is inherently almost certain.

Despite its philosophical interest, inherent probability is of little practical value. Usually when we seek the probability of a statement, we want the best estimate of the statement's truth, based on everything we know. It is of little use to be told, for example, that it is inherently improbable that you have the plague, if all the evidence says that you do. Thus what interests us for most practical purposes is not inherent but **epistemic probability.** The epistemic probability of a statement (the term comes from the Greek word *episteme*, meaning "knowledge") is the frequency of worlds in which the statement is true among worlds in which all of what we know about the actual world is true. It can also be defined as the inductive probability of an inference consisting of the statement as conclusion and all known relevant evidence as premises. It follows that in an argument which meets the requirement of total evidence and assumes nothing not known, the inductive probability of the reasoning equals the epistemic probability of the conclusion. This probability is our best guess, based on everything we know, of the likelihood of the conclusion.

The epistemic probability of anything we know to be true is 100 percent. We all know, for example, that some people smoke cigars. Hence among the known relevant evidence for this statement is the statement itself. Therefore the argument deriving it from all known relevant evidence is deductive (indeed, question-begging). And so for us the epistemic probability of "some people smoke cigars" is 100 percent.

Similarly, the epistemic probability of any statement we know to be false is 0 percent. This is because the denial of any such statement is among the known relevant evidence. Contingent statements whose truth or falsity we do not know for sure have epistemic probabilities between 0 percent and 100 percent, depending on the strength of the evidence for or against them. If we have no evidence either way about a statement, its epistemic probability equals its inherent probability.

Normally, however, epistemic probabilities differ widely from inherent probabilities. It is inherently improbable, for example, that some people smoke cigars. Think of all the worlds in which there are no people, of all the worlds in which there are people but no cigars, and of all the worlds in which there are both cigars and people, but the people don't smoke them. Surely among all possible worlds the frequency of worlds in which there are cigar-smoking people is very small. Hence, while the epistemic probability of "Some people smoke cigars" is 100 percent, its inherent probability is considerably less than 50 percent.

Because epistemic probabilities depend on what we know, they are, unlike inherent probabilities, relative to person and time. For me the epistemic probability that my coffee cup sits here on the table beside me as I write is 100 percent. I see it there. But for you, who see neither me nor the cup and who perhaps suspect that I am lying, the epistemic probability of this statement is less than 100 percent. The only evidence you have is my word, and the word of others is never sufficient for certainty (see Section 7.1).

Weather forecasts, which contain estimates of the epistemic probability of rain, are a good example of the relativity of epistemic probability to time. A forecaster says on Wednesday that Saturday will be fair with only a 10 percent chance of rain. This figure of 10 percent is based on all relevant evidence available to the forecaster at the time. It is therefore an estimate of the epistemic probability of the statement "It will rain on Saturday." By Friday, as always seems to happen, new evidence has become available. A cold front, previously stationary, is now moving rapidly into the area. The epistemic probability of rain on Saturday rises to 90 percent.

Though epistemic probabilities may rise or fall with the acquisition of new information, inherent probabilities do not. Inherent probability is a fixed quantity, dependent only on the frequency of possible worlds in which a statement is true. This frequency does not vary from person to person or from time to time. Of course our estimates of inherent probabilities may change as we come to understand them better. But this does not mean that the probabilities themselves have changed, as epistemic probabilities do.

Epistemic probabilities are the most familiar sorts of probabilities in daily life. When a bookie gives odds on a sporting event, an economist estimates the probability of a recession, or a panel of experts judges the likelihood of a meltdown at a nuclear power plant, each is drawing on the full range of known relevant information to assess an epistemic probability. In logic, the chief role of epistemic probability is in estimating the likelihood of basic premises. When we say that a premise seems "implausible," "nearly certain," "doubtful," or "improbable," it is epistemic probability we have in mind.

The contrast between epistemic and inductive probabilities helps to clear up the paradox mentioned at the beginning of this section. In the most practical sense, the epistemic one, it is improbable that Mr. Smith is wealthy, given that his bank has folded—hence the strong impression that something has gone awry when we hear that given the premises "Smith is a banker" and "Most bankers are wealthy," the conclusion "Smith is wealthy" is probable. But there is no mystery once we understand that the probability here is inductive, not epistemic. It is a measure of strength of reasoning, not a measure of the reliability of the conclusion itself.

The same distinction dispels the oddity of other examples which may have puzzled you. In discussing the sinking of the *Titanic* in Section 1.2, for example, when I said that the improbable sometimes happens, your reaction might have been, "But the sinking of the *Titanic* is not improbable; it actually happened." If so, you were right, but you were thinking of the epistemic probability of the statement that the *Titanic* sunk on her maiden voyage, not the inductive probability of my argument that she didn't. I was concerned with the inductive probability.

Our discussion in this section has by no means covered all the kinds of probability. There is, for example, **statistical probability**—the limiting value of the frequency of a given event among a class of events. This is the concept most often used in mathematics. It is similar in some ways to inherent probability, but it concerns classes of events, rather than classes of possible worlds. For example, the statistical probability of heads in tossing a coin is 50 percent. This means that as more and more tosses occur, the frequency of heads among all the tosses, though it fluctuates, tends to get closer and closer to 50 percent. There are other concepts of probability as well, but enough is enough.

The following table summarizes the four kinds of probability discussed here:

KINDS OF PROBABILITY

Kind	Definition	Applies to
Inductive	Frequency of worlds in which conclusion is true among worlds in which premises are true.	Arguments and inferences
Inherent (absolute, logical)	Frequency of worlds in which statement is true among all possible worlds.	Statements
Epistemic	Frequency of worlds in which statement is true among worlds in which all of what we know about the actual world is true.	Statements
Statistical	Limit of frequency of occurrence of an event among a class of events.	Events

It should be noted that there are unresolved conceptual problems concerning all four kinds of probability, especially concerning the first three. This is not the place to pursue these problems, though I do discuss one particularly troublesome difficulty with inductive probability in the Appendix. If you'd like to know more, see the books listed in "Suggestions for Further Study."

Before leaving the topic of probability, it may be worthwhile to note an oddity that sometimes occurs when an argument's conclusion has a high inherent probability. We saw in Section 5.5 that arguments with logically necessary conclusions are always deductive, no matter what their premises are. Now logical necessity is just 100 percent inherent probability. So we might suspect that with a conclusion whose inherent probability was just under 100 percent, we'd still get a very strong—though perhaps not deductive—argument, regardless of the premises. This is often true. Consider for example the inherently probable statement "I will not go to a ball game on September 9, 1999." It is true in nearly all possible worlds—including all those in which I don't exist. So in a sense, it is "almost" necessary. Now let's see what happens when this statement becomes a conclusion:

Violets are blue.
∴ I will not go to a ball game on September 9, 1999.

It should be clear that in most of the worlds in which the premise is true, so is the conclusion. This is because the conclusion is true in most worlds in general; and the premise, being essentially irrelevant, is true in a class of worlds in which the truth or falsity of the conclusion occurs in roughly the same proportion as it occurs among worlds in general. Accordingly, however odd it may seem, this argument is inductive. But like arguments which are deductive only by virtue of logically necessary conclusions, this argument has little practical value. The conclusion is probable inherently, and that, not any relevant connection with the premise, is what makes the argument inductive. Hence, knowledge of the premise will not serve to enlighten anyone about the truth of the conclusion. It would therefore not be useful to argue this way, though logically there's nothing wrong with it.

Since a conclusion which is "almost necessary" tends to produce inductiveness, one might suspect by analogy that a premise which is "almost inconsistent" (i.e., inherently improbable) would tend to produce inductiveness as well. For a genuinely inconsistent premise always results in validity, just as a genuinely necessary conclusion does. But this suspicion proves false, unless the premise and conclusion are very closely related. Try a few examples and see if you can discover why.

> **Exercise 6.3** Estimate the epistemic probability (for you now) and the inherent probability of each of the following statements. You can't give exact figures, of course, unless the probabilities are 0 percent or 100 percent, but use such phrases as "very low" or "very high." Explain your estimates.
>
> 1 It will rain tomorrow.
> 2 Everyone always tells the truth.
> 3 Columbus came to America in 1492.
> 4 Columbus did not come to America in 1492.
> 5 You are taller than yourself.
> 6 You exist.
> 7 You don't exist.
> 8 Something exists.
> 9 $1 + 1 = 2$
> 10 You are thinking about this sentence.

6.4 STATISTICAL GENERALIZATION

In statistical syllogism we reason from an assumption about the composition of a class to a conclusion about one of its members. We assume, for example, that 95 percent of the class of elves drink stout and that Olaf is an elf, and we conclude that Olaf drinks stout. Often, however, we need to reason in the opposite direction—from individual members to the class as a whole. A polling organization infers the opinions of an entire population from interviews with a relatively small sample of individuals. A bigot jumps to conclusions about an entire race or culture on the basis of experience with a few of its members. A laboratory technician infers the relative proportions of cells in a patient's blood by counting the cells in a single drop. A quality-control expert samples products on an assembly line and concludes that 2 percent of all the products from that line are defective. In each case, a conclusion about a class of objects is drawn from data about a sample of its members.

Some of these inferences are rational; some are not. The difference depends primarily on how the sample is chosen. To illustrate the importance of the method of choice, let's consider this simple example:

> Eight of a sample of 10 frogs are green.
>
> ∴ About 80 percent of frogs are green.

This inference is fallacious, for the premise tells us nothing about the frogs not included in the sample. There could be billions of them, all green. Or trillions, all purple. Or quintillions, half green and half purple. In the first case, nearly all frogs would be green. In the second, almost none. In the third, about half. All three cases, and infinitely more that we could dream up, are counterexamples. Of course there are also worlds in which roughly 80 percent of the unsampled frogs are green. But these are clearly a minority. Only in these worlds and in worlds in which the frog population is not much more than 10 is the conclusion true. In most of the worlds in which the premise is true, the conclusion is false.

To make this inference rational, we need assurance that the sample is at least *likely* to reflect the population as a whole. One way to obtain this assurance is to guarantee that the sampling procedure gives each member of the population an equal chance of being chosen. Such a sampling procedure is said to be **random.**

To say that each member of the population has an equal chance of being chosen is to say that if samples were taken many times under the same conditions, each member of the population would be picked about the same number of times. This is the statistical concept of chance, or probability, mentioned briefly in the last section.

To see why randomness is important, let's compare the inference just discussed with the one that follows:

> Eight of 10 randomly sampled frogs are green.
>
> ∴ About 80 percent of all frogs are green.

The premise of this inference *does* say something about the unsampled frogs. It says that each was as likely to have been sampled as the ones that actually were. This means that all groups of 10 frogs had an equal chance of being picked. Now most of the possible ways of choosing a 10-member group from a population result in a sample which roughly reflects the population as a whole. If 97 percent of all frogs are green, for example, then most groups of ten will contain nine or ten green ones. If the population contains almost no green frogs, then most ten-membered groups will have none, or one, or maybe two. If half the frogs in the population are green, then most groups of ten will contain four or five or six; very few will consist entirely of green frogs or entirely of nongreen ones. Therefore, if the sampling procedure gives each group an equal chance of being chosen (as it does if it is random), then it is statistically likely to produce a sample which roughly reflects the population as a whole. Now most conceivable worlds in which we perform a procedure which is statistically likely to yield a roughly representative sample are worlds in which it does so. For these are worlds in which the procedure would *usually* yield roughly representative samples. Hence most possible worlds in which eight out of 10 randomly selected frogs are green are worlds in which roughly 80 percent of the frog population is green. So this second inference is inductive.

Knowing that the sampling procedure was random made all the difference here, for it enabled us to rule out a large class of counterexamples. Among counterexamples to the first inference are worlds in which the sample is chosen from a particular lake which contains more green frogs than usual, or worlds in which the frog collectors actively chose green frogs and rejected nongreen ones until, having found eight and no more, in frustration they threw two that were not green into the sample. In these worlds, and many more like them, some frogs are more likely to be sampled than others; hence the sample has little chance of being representative. It is because of possible worlds like these that the first inference is irrational. But they are not counterexamples to the second inference, because they are not worlds in which its premise is true.

The second inference is an instance of a form we'll call **statistical generalization:**

n percent of m randomly sampled F are G.

∴ About n percent of F are G.

In our example, n was 80, m was 10, and, serendipitously, "F" and "G" stood for "frogs" and "green," respectively. Statistical generalization is inductive, except when the number m gets too small—a problem we'll discuss shortly.

Without the word "randomly," this form is fallacious, as we saw earlier. In that case, we'll call it the **fallacy of possible bias.** Of course, in practice people do not always say that their sample was random, even if it was, so the wording is not as important as the facts of the case. In evaluating arguments, concentrate if you can on the facts and the author's intentions, and don't be too picky about wording.

One notorious case of bias occurred during the 1936 presidential campaign. The popular magazine *Literary Digest* sent out a huge number of

presidential preference questionnaires, of which over two million were returned. This was a very large sample. A substantial majority of the respondents picked Republican Alf Landon over incumbent Franklin Roosevelt, and
on this basis the magazine predicted a Landon victory.

Roosevelt won. The pollsters were shocked, but they shouldn't have
been, for their sampling technique was seriously defective. The sample, large
as it was, was not random. Not everyone had an equal chance of being
polled. The names of people to whom the questionnaires were sent were
chosen from telephone directories and auto registration lists. In 1936, in the
depths of the Great Depression, many families couldn't afford telephones
and cars. It was precisely among these poorer families that Roosevelt's support was strongest, and yet many of them had no chance of being sampled.

Because the sample was not random, either the pollsters' reasoning was
based on a false premise (if they assumed it was random) or they committed
the fallacy of possible bias (if they didn't). Either way, they had no good
evidence for their conclusion.

It should now be evident why some of the generalizations mentioned
at the beginning of this section are rational and some are not. Take the
bigot's inference, for example. Suppose this bigot lives in a neighborhood
in which there are a dozen or so Hispanics, most of them rowdy. From this,
he concludes that all Hispanics are rowdy. Now his sample is hardly random.
Only Hispanics living near him have any chance of being chosen. Thus he
has committed the fallacy of possible bias, and his reasoning is both short-
sighted and irrational.

Now there are other ways of reasoning from this sample, as we'll see
in later sections. So our indictment of his reasoning might be a bit premature.
But at least we've shown that he can't get his conclusion rationally by
statistical generalization.

Even with a random sample, statistical generalization may be fallacious
if the sample size, represented by the number m, is too small. This is easiest
to see in the most extreme cases—a sample with only one member. If we
sample only one frog, for example, there are only two possibilities: either
it's green or it's not. Either way, this sample is not very likely to reflect the
population at large. Let's suppose it's green. Then the reasoning would be
as follows.

One randomly chosen frog is green.
∴ About 100 percent of frogs are green.

This is obviously fallacious, even with the "fudge factor" provided by the
word "about" in the conclusion. This type of fallacy is called the **fallacy of
small sample.**

As the number m of objects in the sample increases, the reasoning
becomes increasingly stronger. Just when it becomes inductive is difficult
to say. It depends on how loosely we interpret the "about" in the conclusion.

If we're willing to allow a leeway of, say, 20 percent, then a sample of 10 will probably be adequate. But then if our conclusion is "About 80 percent of frogs are green," what we mean is that between 60 percent and 100 percent of frogs are green. Greater accuracy requires a larger sample. With random samples of a thousand or so, it is possible to obtain an accuracy of plus or minus a few percent. This is usually the sample size employed in major public-opinion surveys. Often the results of such surveys are reported this way:

> 67 percent of Americans say they favor tighter gun control, subject to a sampling error of plus or minus 4 percent.

What this means is that the pollsters have reasoned as follows:

> 67 percent of m (roughly 1000) randomly chosen Americans said they favor tighter gun control.
> ∴ Between 63 percent and 71 percent of all Americans would say they favor tighter gun control.

This is a typical statistical generalization. But where do they get the figure plus or minus 4 percent? Well, it's standard in the polling business, and in statistics generally, not to accept probabilities below 95 percent. This is an arbitrarily chosen figure, representing what statisticians have agreed to accept as reasonable certainty. Using statistical methods, it is possible to show that the inductive probability of the inference above is about 95 percent. If we narrow the figures mentioned in the conclusion—say, to 65 percent and 69 percent—the argument's inductive probability sinks below 95 percent. If we widen them—say, to 60 percent and 74 percent—the argument's inductive probability rises higher. But the statisticians chose plus or minus 4 percent, because 95 percent inductive probability is their criterion for reasonableness.

Any good statistics text explains the methods for calculating these figures (though not directly in terms of arguments and possible worlds), but we won't go into them here. It's enough that you recognize how the inductive probability of statistical generalization depends on both sample size and the strictness with which we interpret the term "about."

Notice that in contrast to statistical syllogism, the rationality of statistical generalization does not depend on the percentage figure n. So long as the sample size is adequate, the argument is inductive, regardless of whether n is 0 or 100 or anything in between. Actually, if you look at the mathematical details, the inductive probability of statistical generalization does vary slightly with the size of n, but the variation is small enough that in informal logic we can ignore it.

Like all inductive arguments, statistical generalizations must be evaluated, not only with respect to the strength of their reasoning, but also with respect to the truth of the premises and the possibility of suppressed evidence. One common source of falsehood, of course, is the claim of randomness. An author might think his or her sampling procedure is random when in fact it is not. This may have been the case with the *Literary Digest* poll.

Another potential source of falsehood, particularly in public-opinion polls, is the disparity between what people say and what they think. If, for example, a poll asks, "Would you like Congress to reduce defense spending?" and 54 percent of the respondents say yes, it would be a mistake to assume automatically that 54 percent of the sample actually want Congress to reduce defense spending. Some of the respondents may be lying. Others may not understand the question. Some may have no opinion, but answer yes or no because they don't want to sound uninformed. So it may be false that 54 percent, even of the sample, actually want defense cuts. All we really know is that 54 percent of the sample *say* they do. So strictly speaking, the only statistical induction justified by the poll is this:

54 percent of a random sample of *m* (whatever the sample size is) Americans say they want Congress to reduce defense spending.

∴ About 54 percent of all Americans would say they want Congress to reduce defense spending.

In practice, pollsters assume that inaccurate answers cancel each other out, that about as many people falsely answer no as falsely answer yes. But who knows? There is no foolproof test for finding out what a person really thinks. This assumption could be wrong.

This becomes a serious risk if the questions used in the survey are slanted or phrased in ways that influence the answer. Most people like the word "defense." If you say "military" instead, you're likely to get more answers in favor of cuts, because "military" conjures up images of guns and bombs, which for most people have negative associations. If you say "war" instead of "military," the percentages will go even higher. So which set of answers reflects what people *really* think? It's a difficult problem.

Finally, there is the problem of suppressed evidence. Theoretically, we should seldom have to worry about this with statistical generalization. If the sample is large enough and the sampling procedure is genuinely random, then the only thing that can go wrong is that we choose an unrepresentative sample purely by chance. This, as we saw, is unlikely. But because in practice there is often doubt about the phrasing of the premise or the randomness of the sample, there is room for additional error. Therefore, contrary evidence from other sources should not be ignored. If, for example, one poll finds that 54 percent say they favor military spending cuts, but several other random polls obtain much lower percentages, then a statistical generalization based on the first poll alone suppresses the evidence of the others. Such an inference is dubious, even if its inductive probability is high and there is every reason to think that its premise is true.

Exercise 6.4 Diagram and evaluate each of the following arguments. Add a note to each diagram explaining why you judged the reasoning as you did and discussing possible sources of falsehood and suppressed evidence.

1 I talked at random to three of the students in Miss Thistlebottom's English class yesterday, and all of them said they didn't like her. Therefore, Miss Thistlebottom is a very unpopular teacher.

2 Only 1 percent of the several hundred 1984 automobiles randomly selected from the Detroit assembly plant had major defects. So the percentage of seriously defective 1984 cars produced by this plant is fairly low.

3 Contrary to what they always tell you, tossed coins do come up heads more often than tails. I was tossing coins last night and got five heads in a row!

4 Convicted drunken drivers have been treated very leniently in this country recently. Leafing through the court records for the past 10 years, I found case after case in which they received minimal sentences. In only a tiny fraction of the cases were stiff fines or jail sentences imposed.

5 Voters are angry about the economy. A recent randomly conducted CBS/*New York Times* survey of 1572 registered voters revealed that 73 percent believe their economic circumstances to be worse now than five years ago.

6 Only one of the nine planets in our solar system is inhabited. Therefore, it seems reasonable to think that the proportion of inhabited planets in the universe at large is relatively small.

7 The orchard is badly infested. We picked a bushel of apples from there this morning, and over half of them had worms.

8 Asked, "Do you think people respond more positively when you're wearing makeup and prettier clothes?" 94 percent of the respondents to *Glamour* magazine's February 1982 survey said yes. This shows the importance women place on appearance. (Note: these results were published in the April 1982 issue of *Glamour*. The survey technique was to have readers fill in questionnaires contained in the magazine, cut them out, and send them in. Sample size was not reported.)

9 Americans came to believe the national fortunes were in decline. That was the famous "malaise" Jimmy Carter cited on July 15 of last year when he addressed the nation after weeks of musing at Camp David. The gloomy feeling persisted, however. A Gallup poll at the beginning of this year found Americans less optimistic about the future than the people of any other major country excepting

Great Britain and India. Fifty-six percent of those surveyed in the United States believed this year would be worse than last year. (Joseph Kraft, "The Changing American Dream: Reflections at a Time for Choosing," *House & Garden*, November 1980)

6.5   THE PRINCIPLE OF THE UNIFORMITY OF NATURE

The uses of statistical generalization are severely limited by the need for the sample to be random. Often we want to generalize in circumstances where a random sample is impossible. Suppose, for example, we want to show that the speed of light in a vacuum is always 3×10^{10} centimeters per second. (This is roughly the correct figure.) Now there are devices for measuring the speed of light, and we'll assume they work as advertised. So it would seem that all we'd need to do is take a random sample of light beams, measure their velocities (which should all approximate the figure above), and derive our conclusion by statistical generalization. But it's not that easy. If we're talking about all the light in the universe, we mean all the light that ever has shone and ever will shine, and all the light that is shining in regions of space too distant for us to observe. At best we can test only light beams near the surface of our planet during the brief span of time since the invention of the measuring devices. Most of the light in the universe has no chance of being observed by us. Our sample will not be random. We could perhaps have taken a random sample of light near earth in the past century or so. That would allow us to generalize to the population of light beams near earth during this span of time. But it would not allow us to generalize to all the light beams in the universe. It is perfectly conceivable that light beams have quite different velocities in distant reaches of time and space.

If this example seems excessively unrealistic, consider the similar quandary of the life insurance statistician who wants to determine the percentage of deaths due to accidents in the American home. Now mortality statistics are readily available, and it is perfectly feasible to randomly sample information on deaths for, say, the past 20 years. Indeed, with the help of a computer, one could probably compile data on all deaths in the past 20 years. But the people the statistician really wants to know about are those who are now paying life insurance premiums. There is no way to collect mortality data on these people, for the simple reason that they are not yet dead. Therefore, there is no way now to obtain a random sample of mortality data for any population which includes them. We can use statistical generalization to get figures for the class of people who have died in the last 20 years, but we cannot rely on it alone to make predictions about the future. What guarantees that the future will resemble the past?

Let's consider one more example. You leap off a diving board, secure in the knowledge that you'll plunge safely into the water. Your evidence? Well, it always happened that way before. But your premise only concerns past jumps. The conclusion concerns future ones. Therefore, the sample is biased, since no future jumps had a chance to be included in it. How do you know that this time won't be different?

The central problem in all these cases is to infer a conclusion about phenomena in unobservable expanses of time or space from premises about things we can observe. It's a problem which cannot be solved by statistical generalization alone, because if some of the phenomena in a population are unobservable, no random sample of that population is possible. An entirely new principle of reasoning is needed. To see this more clearly, let's take a closer look at the diving board inference:

> Every time I've jumped off a diving board, I've plunged safely into the water.
> I'm about to jump again.
> ∴ I'll plunge safely into the water again.

The inference is from the observed past to the yet to be observed future. You can see at once that it's not deductive. (You might slip and hit your head, or the pool might be empty.) But we'd like to think that it is at least inductive. If not, it might be wise to avoid diving boards.

As it stands, however, it's completely fallacious. You must remember that possible worlds can be very disconcerting places. Absolutely anything might happen next. You might leap into the air and vanish. You might die of old age before you hit the water. The pool might vanish. The water might turn to carbon steel. You might fall halfway to the water, stop, and hang suspended in the air, or turn into a hideous bat and flutter madly away, . . . well, you get the point. Given the range of logical possibilities, it is not even probable (inductively probable, relative to the premises, that is) that you'll make it safely into the water. Similar considerations reveal the apparent irrationality of the inferences about the speed of light and the percentage of accidental deaths.

Does this mean that we can infer nothing about what happens at other times or places from our knowledge of the here and now? Of course not! All three inferences are perfectly rational, but they're incomplete. Implicit in each of them—and in many other inductive arguments as well—is the assumption that our world exhibits a certain constancy or uniformity. This assumption is known as **the principle of the uniformity of nature.** It is also called the **principle of induction.**

This principle is difficult to formulate precisely. There have been many attempts, none of them entirely satisfactory, and I have no special wisdom to offer on the subject. The problem is that the principle occurs in many different contexts, and wording which is appropriate for one is not appropriate for others. Indeed, there may be no single principle of the uniformity of nature, but rather a series of interrelated principles, all functioning similarly, to which we give a single name. Here are some typical formulations:

Like causes produce like effects.

The future is likely to resemble the past.

The laws of nature are constant.

Most regularities present in observed regions of time and space extend as well to unobserved regions.

For our purposes in this section, the last and most general of these is best. Notice that it says *"most* regularities." If it said "all" it would be false, because there are observed regularities which do not extend into the distance, the past, or the future. Bertrand Russell provides a case in point:

> Domestic animals expect food when they see the person who usually feeds them. We know that all these rather crude expectations of uniformity are liable to be misleading. The man who has fed the chicken every day throughout its life at last wrings its neck instead, showing that more refined views as to the uniformity of nature would have been useful to the chicken.[2]

But all things considered, our universe is remarkably uniform. Divers do plunge safely into the water (at least most of the time). Accidental-death statistics may vary somewhat from one generation to the next, but they do so slowly and rather predictably, not suddenly and without explanation. The speed of light *is* constant throughout the universe, and so are the law of gravity and all other physical laws, so far as anyone can tell. Even the most important aspects of human behavior are constant. Everywhere people eat, sleep, talk, reproduce, bicker, and mourn the dead. Everyone dies. No one turns into a bat. No one simply vanishes. These are the sorts of regularities the principle of the uniformity of nature proclaims. Evidently this principle or something very like it is true.

Still, the notion of a regularity is problematic. It's very difficult to define precisely. Roughly, we can say that a regularity is a consistently and frequently repeated pattern. If a baby cries twice in a row when we show it a teddy bear, that is not a regularity. But if it does so every time it sees the teddy bear, and it sees the teddy bear a lot, then that is a regularity. This, however, is just an example. If we try to get much more general or precise, we'll quickly find ourselves in deep water. The American philosopher Nelson Goodman has shown that if we take certain bizarre "regularities" seriously, then the principle of the uniformity of nature can be cast into serious doubt.[3] This is the so-called **new riddle of induction** (the old riddle is the problem of induction, which I'll discuss briefly at the end of this section).

---

[2]*The Problems of Philosophy*, Oxford University Press, Oxford, 1959, p. 63.

[3]*Fact, Fiction and Forecast*, Hackett Publishing Company, Indianapolis, 1977.

But such philosophical doubts are of little practical interest, and we won't bother with them here. Our formulation of the principle is rough, but serviceable.

You should keep in mind that the principle of the uniformity of nature is an assumption about our world. It is not logically necessary. We can imagine chaotic worlds in which the laws of nature change every inch and every second, and which are filled with horrors and abominations even worse than those recently discussed. But we have the good fortune not to live in such a universe.

When we add the principle to the inference about diving, the rationality of this inference becomes apparent:

> Every time I've jumped off a diving board, I've plunged safely into the water.
>
> I'm about to jump again.
>
> Most regularities present in observed regions of time and space extend as well to unobserved regions.
>
> ∴ I'll plunge safely into the water again.

The correlation of jump with safe plunge is a regularity in an observed region of time (the near past). The impending jump is an event in the yet to be observed future. It is now easy to see that this argument is inductive—indeed, a close cousin of statistical syllogism.

The other two inferences are likewise inductive:

> Over the past 20 years 0.4 percent of deaths in the United States were due to accidents in the home.
>
> Most regularities present in observed regions of time and space extend as well to unobserved regions.
>
> ∴ About 0.4 percent of Americans now living will die as a result of accidents in the home.

> Light observed near the earth's surface during the past century or so always traveled at 3×10^{10} centimeters per second.
>
> Most regularities present in observed regions of time and space extend as well to unobserved regions.
>
> ∴ All light travels at 3×10^{10} centimeters per second.

In the first, the percentage of deaths due to accidents is a regularity observed over the past 20 years. This regularity is being extrapolated to an unobserved region of time (the span during which those now living will die). In the second, the speed of light near the earth's surface is a regularity observed in a certain region of space and time (earth, the past century or so), and it is being extrapolated to the whole expanse and history of the universe. Again, both inferences resemble statistical syllogism, and both are inductive.

All three arguments are similar in conception, but they do not share a common form. Arguments employing the principle of the uniformity of nature take many forms. The only thing common to them all is that they extrapolate beyond the expanse of space and time open to our observations. Virtually every argument which makes such an extrapolation assumes the principle; in particular, it is the basis of all rational inferences from past and present to the future. Despite, or perhaps because of, its widespread use, the principle is rarely stated explicitly. We seem to take it completely for granted.

The strength of reasoning employing the principle of the uniformity of nature depends on two considerations: the extent to which the regularity has been observed and the extent to which it is being extrapolated. Regularities observed frequently under a variety of conditions make for stronger reasoning than regularities observed less frequently or under only limited conditions. To see why, consider the familiar fact that when you drop something it falls to the earth. For most of human history, this was regarded as a universal regularity. But we now know that it does not hold, for example, in orbiting spacecraft. This does not mean that the behavior of massive bodies is irregular. It simply means that until recently we hadn't observed them under conditions sufficiently varied to make the nature of the regularity fully clear. When observations are made under fairly limited conditions, there are many more possibilities for this sort of mistake to occur than if the conditions are widely varied. So the reasoning is weaker.

The second consideration is how far the extrapolation extends. Timid extrapolations produce better arguments than bold ones. If we concluded from our observations of objects near the earth's surface only that massive objects dropped *near the earth's surface* always fall (that is, if we extrapolated through time but not through space) we'd be right. But the bolder extrapolation through all of space is inaccurate. Similarly, if we extrapolate only a week into the future, we're more likely to be right than if we extrapolate a year. There are more possibilities for error in a bolder extrapolation.

Let's consider the strength of the reasoning in each of the inferences we've discussed here. The diver's argument is very strong. Although the extent of the observed regularity is not great (a limited set of conditions during the diver's lifetime), the extent of the extrapolation is minimal—only the next moment in time.

The statistician's reasoning is also fairly strong. Here a well-established regularity is extrapolated from one generation to the next.

The physicist's extrapolation, however, is extraordinarily bold. A regularity (the speed of light) observed sporadically under fairly limited conditions near the earth's surface over a century or so is being extrapolated to the entire breadth and history of the universe. The reasoning here is therefore considerably weaker than in the other two cases.

These, however, are not the only considerations relevant to the strengths of the three arguments. As with all inductive reasoning, we also need to check for suppressed evidence. Here again the diver's argument gets high marks. Unless we have reason to think that the diver is drunk or otherwise disabled or that the diving board is defective or something else of that sort— and we don't—there is no contrary evidence. Our own experiences confirm the diver's expectations; diving is usually safe. Of course, as with any inductive argument, something could still go wrong, even if the premises are true and contrary evidence is lacking. But this is unlikely.

The statistician's argument is touchier. Contrary evidence could come from several sources. Perhaps consumer-protection programs are making the home considerably safer. If so, that's suppressed evidence against the argument. Or perhaps there's reason to think that we'll all die soon in a nuclear holocaust. That would also be contrary evidence. Since we know that many factors can significantly influence the percentage of deaths due to accidents in the home, all these factors would have to be weighed in order to meet the requirement of total evidence. The argument therefore seems rather weak and incomplete, despite the fact that it is strongly inductive and may well have true premises.

Not so for the physicist's argument. To my knowledge there is absolutely no contrary evidence here. Thus the argument is fairly substantial, despite the relative weakness of its reasoning.

When you encounter an argument which implicitly assumes the principle of the uniformity of nature, give the principle a letter and add it to your diagram as you would any other assumption. In evaluating the argument, however, you needn't make a special effort to verify its truth. You should take its truth for granted.

In fact, you have to. You couldn't verify it, even if you tried. Not even a spaceship or a time machine would help, for the principle concerns unobserved regions of time and space. In order to verify what it says about them, you'd have to observe them, in which case they would no longer be unobserved and hence no longer relevant to the truth of the principle. This startling difficulty is known as the **problem of induction.** It has been an embarrassment to logicians, ever since the philosopher David Hume unearthed it in the middle of the eighteenth century. However, despite the apparent impossibility of verifying the principle of the uniformity of nature, one can hardly doubt its truth. Inductive arguments based on it usually do yield correct conclusions. And in practice it is indispensable.

Exercise 6.5   Each of the following arguments implicitly assumes the principle of the uniformity of nature. Diagram and evaluate each as usual, adding implicit statements where necessary. Then add a note explaining your evaluation and discussing the possibility of suppressed evidence.

1   Most of the Hispanics in my neighborhood are rowdy. Therefore, most Hispanics are rowdy.

2   Nearly every effective weapon ever created has eventually seen widespread use in warfare, and thermonuclear devices are the most effective weapons mankind has produced.

3   Though many people have passed the threshold of death, none has ever returned to tell about it. It is unlikely, then, that anyone ever will.

4   Again and again the course of American history has been a continual swinging back and forth between periods of liberalism and periods of conservatism. It seems likely that this pattern will continue.

5   Cave paintings made by primitive people today all seem to have some religious or ritual significance. Therefore, it seems likely that the cave paintings of our remote ancestors served similar purposes.

6   In the present, and in the probable near future, therefore, deterrence is playing and is likely to continue to play a less dominant role in U.S. foreign policy—a happy development, we believe, as previous policy depended too heavily upon deterrence efforts. (Alexander L. George and Richard Smoke, *Deterrence in American Foreign Policy: Theory and Practice*)

7   You want to know if I think it's a good idea to take your cat camping? In a word, no. . . . [M]y long association with cats leads me to believe they are not generally good travellers and do much better left in familiar surroundings or even in a good boarding kennel. The stories of cats lost en route are legion. Their uncanny ability to escape almost any kind of restraint makes them poor risks for camping. (Jean Burden, "Pets: When Rover Goes Camping," *Woman's Day*, May 19, 1981)

8   The real challenge to Social Security lies in the future. The proportion of the U.S. population 65 years old and older has been growing (from 9.2 percent in 1960 to 11.2 percent last year) and will continue to grow (to an estimated 12.2 percent in the year 2000). Retired people and their spouses are living longer: in 1950 the average life expectancy at 65 was another 13 years for men and 15 years for women, whereas in 1980 it reached 15 years for men and 20 years for women. (Eli Ginzberg, "The Social Security System," *Scientific American*, January 1982)

9   In all the great ages of the past, people have believed themselves very close to possession of the ultimate truth about the universe. In each age, they have pointed to their technological and intellectual achievements as evidence of this. But the thought of each past age, as we now know, was riddled with falsehood, superstition, and

half-truths. Likewise, today we see our technological wizardry as evidence of a thorough comprehension of reality. Is it not likely, however, that much of what seems so certain now will later prove to be mistaken?

10 U.S. imperialism has violated the agreements reached at the first Geneva Conference by obstructing the unification of Viet Nam, openly carrying out armed aggression against southern Viet Nam and engaging in so-called special warfare for many years. It has also violated the agreements of the second Geneva Conference by its flagrant intervention in Laos in an attempt to rekindle the civil war there. Apart from those who are deliberately deceiving the people or are utterly naïve, no one will believe that a treaty will make U.S. imperialism lay down its butcher's knife and suddenly become a Buddha, or behave itself a little better. (Mao Zedong, 1963)

6.6 INDUCTION BY ANALOGY

Statistical generalization and induction via the principle of the uniformity of nature both require a substantial number of observations—in the first case to insure an adequate sample and in the second to establish a regularity. But it is also possible to reason inductively from a few observations—or even just one, if the circumstances are right. The following story provides an illustration:

An explorer on an expedition through a South American jungle is startled by a huge red and black insect hovering near his head. Curious, having never seen such a creature before, he snatches it from the air. For a moment it struggles in his hand; then he feels a fiery sting. He throws the insect to the ground and squashes it with his boot.

Sometime later in the same region, he and a companion are buzzed by a similar insect. Annoyed, his companion swats at it. "Don't!" the explorer shouts. "That little _____ has a sting that hurts like hell!"

What is remarkable about this example is that the explorer has jumped to a conclusion based on a single previously observed instance, and yet his inference seems quite rational. Would you swat at the bug?

What accounts for the strength of this reasoning? The salient fact is the similarity of the two insects. Things that seem a lot alike usually are a lot alike, and on that basis it seems probable that the second insect is as noxious as the first. The reasoning here may be summarized as follows:

The first insect could sting painfully.

The second insect was seen to be closely similar to the first.

Objects observed to be closely similar are usually similar in most unobserved respects.

∴ The second insect can sting painfully.

The strength of this inference hinges, not on the number or regularity of observed cases, but on the degree of similarity between the cases observed. The third assumption, which was implicit in the explorer's original reasoning, can be regarded as a variant of the principle of the uniformity of nature. It asserts that our world is uniform in the sense that observed similarities are fairly reliable indicators of underlying unobserved similarities. We'll call it the **principle of analogy,** because it is concerned with likenesses, or analogies, among things. Like previously discussed uniformity principles, it is true but not logically necessary. We can imagine, for example, worlds in which most objects are "camouflaged," so that overt similarities are consistently misleading. But our world is not one of these.

The form of the explorer's argument is called **induction by analogy.** It may be schematized as follows:

x is F.

y is observed to be closely similar to x in many respects (other than F).

Objects or events closely similar in observed respects are usually similar in most unobserved respects.

∴ y is F.

In our example, x is the first insect, y is the second, and F stands for "able to sting painfully."

As I noted, the strength of this form depends primarily on the extent of the observed similarity between x and y. The greater the similarity the stronger the reasoning. If the similarity is slight, then the form is fallacious, but it's impossible to say how slight is too slight. You just have to rely on common sense.

Induction by analogy is especially sensitive to suppressed evidence. Usually contrary evidence takes the form of a **relevant disanalogy,** as in the following example:

Shaving cream is palpably similar in color, texture, moistness, and body to whipped cream. Whipped cream is delicious on pumpkin pie. Therefore, shaving cream is delicious on pumpkin pie.

Here x is whipped cream, y is shaving cream, and F stands for "delicious on pumpkin pie." Now whipped cream and shaving cream are rather closely similar with respect to many observable properties, so it's hard to fault the assumptions. But the argument ignores a most important item of contrary evidence. Even if you've never tasted shaving cream, you are no doubt aware that its ingredients are a far cry from the wholesome cream and sugar in genuine whipped cream. And you are aware, too, that taste is more closely linked to ingredients than to color, texture, moistness, or body. This contrary evidence is a relevant disanalogy. Whipped cream and shaving cream differ radically in precisely the respect most relevant to taste. Though the argument has true premises and may well be inductive, this disanalogy renders it worthless.

Incidentally, I suspect that more than one erring toddler has been seduced by this argument, thereby discovering the hard way that the fruits of inductive reasoning from inadequate evidence may be bitter indeed.

Perhaps the most famous instance of induction by analogy is the **argument from design** for the existence of God. It is based on an analogy between the universe and a machine. The reasoning runs something like this:

> A well-designed machine is a dynamic, orderly whole in which each part has a purpose and in which all parts work together harmoniously. The universe exhibits these same characteristics. In the balances of nature, in the motions of the stars and planets, in the rhythms and cycles of life, we find the unity, harmony, and purpose characteristic of a well-designed machine. But a machine is the product of an intelligent and thoughtful creator. Therefore, the universe, too, was fashioned by a thoughtful and creative intelligence.

In terms of our schema, x is a machine, y is the universe, and F stands for "created by a thoughtful intelligence."

Many thinkers have found this argument compelling, but two considerations weigh heavily against it. One concerns the strength of the analogy. Just how similar are the universe and a machine? Surely not as similar as the two insects of our first example. Similar enough to make the argument inductive? It's hard to say. But it seems clear that it is not strongly inductive.

The second negative consideration is a relevant disanalogy. Opponents of the argument have insisted that it's as easy to find disorder and senselessness in the universe as it is to find harmony and purpose. Floods, earthquakes, wars, and other disasters choose their victims at random, afflicting the good and the bad alike, to no evident purpose. Predators, diseases, and parasites make life miserable and short for hosts of helpless creatures. Crime, ignorance, and evil abound. Here is evidence of disorder, disharmony, and purposelessness that is uncharacteristic of a well-designed machine. And such disorder is certainly relevant to the question of intelligent design. So in the light of the contrary evidence and the thinness of the original analogy, the argument as a whole is disappointingly weak.

It is not easy to draw a clear line between induction by analogy and induction based on the versions of the principle of the uniformity of nature discussed in Section 6.5. As the number of observed instances of x increases and we rely less on the similarity between x and y than on regularities among instances of x, induction by analogy becomes more and more like the forms discussed in that section. But it is not really important to make fine distinctions with respect to form. The important thing is to understand the general principles at work in all these arguments and to be able to apply them to specific cases.

One final word of warning: don't suppose that every analogy is an argument. There are many practical and literary uses of analogy which have nothing to do with giving evidence for a conclusion. When, for example, Shakespeare writes:

> We are such stuff
> As dreams are made of, and our little life
> Is rounded with a sleep.

he's drawing an analogy between life and dreams. But it's a poetic analogy, meant to express an attitude toward life, not an argument. Logic has nothing to say here.

Exercise 6.6 Each of the following arguments involves induction by analogy. Diagram and evaluate each, adding implicit statements where necessary. Supplement each diagram with a note explaining your evaluation and discussing the possibility of suppressed evidence.

1 Katherine's car gets excellent mileage, needs few repairs, and handles well on the road. The one I'm about to buy is the same make, model, and year. Therefore, I can expect the same from it.

2 Everyone agrees that Hitler's persecution of the Jews was immoral. The Israelis' persecution of the Palestinians is therefore immoral as well.

3 I should have a good crop of spinach this spring. I planted, fertilized, watered, and hoed it just as I did last year, and the weather this spring has been similar.

4 You must be on drugs. You're acting just like you did that time you took LSD.

5 You agree that it's wrong to shoplift. So stealing from your employer is wrong, too. One is just like the other.

6   ... tanmātras or basic sensations can be regarded as divided or separated in a manner analogous to a spectrum, leading us to agree to the proposition that ultimately they will merge into one white light of pure consciousness, such oneness not implying any loss but only a complete lack of separateness. This implies an inner completion in and at the back of the mind. (Ernest Wood, *Yoga*)

7   Obviously there is no way that the Air Force or anyone else can prove that alien spacecraft are not visiting us. Is there a tooth fairy? No amount of cases in which a grownup is caught pushing a quarter under a child's pillow will add up to irrefutable negative evidence. Always there is a small residue of cases in which grownups are not caught, and the morning appearance of money remains mysterious. No matter how many sightings of UFOs are shown to have natural explanations, there is always a residue—how could it be otherwise?—of cases for which information is insufficient for judgment. (Martin Gardner, "Close Encounters of the Third Kind," in *Science: Good, Bad and Bogus*)

8   Sex is a natural human need like food and drink. It is true that men can survive without it, whereas they cannot survive without food and drink, but from a psychological standpoint the desire for sex is precisely analogous to the desire for food and drink. It is enormously enhanced by abstinence, and temporarily allayed by satisfaction. While it is urgent, it shuts out all the rest of the world from the mental purview. All other interests fade for the moment, and actions may be performed which will subsequently appear insane to the man who has been guilty of them. Moreover, as in the case of food and drink, the desire is enormously stimulated by prohibition. (Bertrand Russell, "The Place of Sex Among Human Values")

9   The first of these [suppositions about the effects of mass media violence] is that to see vicarious violence on film or television will 'discharge' the aggressive energy of the individual. This is called *catharsis.* . . . [T]o argue that media violence is cathartic is tantamount to suggesting that witnessing people eating when one is hungry will make one feel less hungry. No empirical studies have investigated this but it would be surprising to find that 'vicarious' eating reduced hunger. (Dennis Howitt and Guy Cumberbatch, *Mass Media Violence and Society*)

10   ... I have discovered, for example, that when I have an infected tooth I feel considerable pain and that I tend to express this feeling in certain characteristic ways. And I have found that these connections hold independently of other circumstances such as the place where I happen to be, the way in which I am dressed, the state of the weather, the nature of my political opinions, and so

forth. . . . So when I observe that some other person is similarly afflicted and that he acts in a similar way, I may infer that a similar feeling is also present. . . . (A. J. Ayer, *The Problem of Knowledge*)

6.7 CORRELATION

One of the most important applications of the principle of the uniformity of nature is in proving that one thing is correlated with another. It is important to distinguish correlation from cause. Two phenomena are **correlated** if an occurrence of or change in one is always accompanied by or tends to be accompanied by an occurrence of or change in the other. Night and day are correlated with the rising and setting of the sun, heavy exercise is correlated with rapid heartbeat, and there is a correlation in the chiming of two properly adjusted grandfather clocks. Cause is a specific kind of correlation which results from the involvement of one phenomenon in the production of another. The correlation between exercise and heartbeat is causal; exercise produces alterations in body chemistry, which in turn hasten the beating of the heart. But the correlated chiming of the clocks is not causal, at least not in the same way. Neither clock produces the chiming of the other. The correlation between night and day and the rising and setting of the sun is a more difficult case. Sunrise, for example, doesn't really cause the new day. The correlation is essentially a matter of definition. The beginning of the day is *defined* as the time when the sun rises. This is a conceptual, not a causal correlation. Let's not worry about causes for now. We'll return to them in Section 6.8. In this section we'll consider the nature and variety of correlations in general.

One of the simplest forms of correlation is the **necessary condition.** Saying that x is a necessary condition for y means that whenever y occurs, x occurs. Fuel is a necessary condition for fire; the meeting of sperm and egg is necessary for human reproduction; sunlight is necessary for the growth of trees; intelligence is necessary for understanding; four-sidedness is necessary for squareness; the typhoid bacillus is necessary for typhoid fever. Some necessary conditions are causal; some are not. The typhoid bacillus, for example, causes typhoid fever, but four-sidedness is not a cause of squareness.

It is important to see that in this context the term "necessary" does not mean "logically necessary." One thing's being a necessary condition for another is a fact about our world; it need not hold true in others. The statement that fuel is a necessary condition for fire means that whenever fire occurs, fuel is also present. This is true in our world, but not in all possible worlds. We can, for example, imagine worlds in which fires flare up in empty space.

Some necessary conditions, however, are logically necessary as well. Condition x is a **logically necessary condition** for y if x occurs in every possible situation in which y occurs—that is, we can't coherently conceive

x without y. Four-sidedness, for example is both necessary and logically necessary for squareness. A square without four sides is inconceivable.

Here we'll be concerned primarily with **contingently necessary conditions**—that is, necessary but not logically necessary conditions. Logically necessary conditions are most efficiently handled by deductive techniques, and in this chapter our topic is induction.

Statements about necessary conditions make very strong claims. To say that fuel is a necessary condition for fire, for example, is to say that in all of the universe there has never been and never will be a fire in the absence of fuel. If there ever was or will be, this claim would be false. Such a statement obviously concerns a regularity extending to unobservable reaches of space and time, and so its justification requires the principle of the uniformity of nature. Typically, the sort of argument used to establish a necessary condition looks like this:

> In observed regions of space and time, y occurs frequently and is always accompanied by x.
>
> Most regularities present in observed regions of time and space extend as well to unobserved regions.
>
> ∴ x is a necessary condition for y.

If x is fuel and y is fire, this is an inductive argument with true premises. (The second premise is the version of the principle of the uniformity of nature discussed in Section 6.5.) There is no known evidence to the contrary. Hence this argument provides good evidence that fuel is necessary for fire.

The converse, or "mirror image," of a necessary condition is a **sufficient condition.** Condition x is sufficient for y if whenever x occurs, y occurs. Motherhood is a sufficient condition for parenthood; laughing is a sufficient condition for life; being an integer is sufficient for being a number; complete incineration is sufficient for death; having the higher score at the final buzzer of a basketball game is sufficient for winning; mixing the proper proportions of gin and dry vermouth in a glass and adding an olive is sufficient for the creation of a martini.

Like necessary conditions, sufficient conditions may be either causal or noncausal. Incinerating someone is sufficient to cause his or her death. But, though laughing is sufficient for life, it does not cause life.

Moreover, like necessary conditions, sufficient conditions may be either contingently sufficient or sufficient by logical necessity. Incineration, for example, is contingently sufficient for death. In our world, any living creature that gets incinerated dies. But this is not always true in the eerie worlds of our imagination. We can imagine the ashes, still alive somehow, slowly congealing back into their original form. Motherhood, by contrast, is a logically sufficient condition for parenthood. The idea of a mother who is not a parent is incoherent.

I said that a sufficient condition is the "mirror image" of a necessary condition. This is true in the following sense: *x* is sufficient for *y* just in case *y* is necessary for *x*. Thus, knowing that incineration is sufficient for death, we may conclude that death is necessary in cases of incineration. Or knowing that fuel is necessary for fire, we may conclude that the presence of fire is sufficient for the presence of fuel. (Check this by thinking about some of the other examples.) Such inferences are deductive, and in general the following forms are valid:

> *x* is sufficient for *y*
> ∴ *y* is necessary for *x*

> *x* is necessary for *y*
> ∴ *y* is sufficient for *x*

Because of this "mirror image" relationship, arguments used to establish contingently sufficient conditions are simple variants of those used to establish contingently necessary conditions. (Logically sufficient conditions, like logically necessary ones, are best handled deductively and will not be discussed here.) Here is a typical form:

> In observed regions of space and time, *x* occurs frequently and is always accompanied by *y*.
> Most regularities present in observed regions of time and space extend as well to unobserved regions.
> ∴ *x* is a sufficient condition for *y*.

Compare this to the form for establishing necessary conditions. If *x* is complete incineration and *y* is death, we have an argument justifying the assertion that complete incineration is a sufficient condition for death. It is a good inductive argument. The premises are true, and there is no contrary evidence.

One of the closest kinds of correlation occurs when one condition is both **necessary and sufficient** for another. This means that the two conditions always occur together; neither is ever present alone. The moon's passage in front of the sun is necessary and sufficient for a solar eclipse; divisibility without remainder by two is necessary and sufficient for evenness; the existence of a massive body is necessary and sufficient for the presence of a gravitational field; being a member of the largest species of mammal is necessary and sufficient for being a blue whale; having a brother or sister is necessary and sufficient for being someone's sibling. Usually the best way to prove that one condition is both necessary and sufficient for another is to give two arguments, one showing that it is necessary and the other showing that it is sufficient.

Many phenomena are related by **partial correlations,** or **statistical cor-**

relations. Two conditions are statistically correlated if an occurrence of or change in one tends to be accompanied by an occurrence of or change in the other. Hunger, for example, is statistically correlated with eating. People tend to eat when they're hungry, but they don't always do so, and sometimes they eat when they're not hungry. So hunger is neither necessary nor sufficient for eating, but the two conditions are statistically correlated. Here are some other examples of partial correlations: industrialization and pollution, poverty and disease, rain and low barometric pressure, alcoholism and depression. Arguments to establish partial correlations are essentially no different from the sorts of arguments just discussed. We find a tendency for two phenomena to occur together among observed cases and extrapolate to unobserved cases by the principle of the uniformity of nature.

The following table summarizes the types of correlations discussed so far:

TYPES OF CORRELATIONS OF DISCRETE EVENTS

Correlation	Definition	Example
x is contingently necessary for y	Whenever y occurs, x occurs	x = fuel y = fire
x is logically necessary for y	In every possible situation in which y occurs, x occurs	x = four-sidedness y = squareness
x is contingently sufficient for y	Whenever x occurs, y occurs	x = complete incineration y = death
x is logically sufficient for y	In every possible situation in which x occurs, y occurs	x = motherhood y = parenthood
x is contingently necessary and sufficient for y	Neither x nor y occurs without the other	x = being a member of the largest species of mammal y = being a blue whale
x is logically necessary and sufficient for y	There is no possible situation in which either x or y occurs without the other	x = having a brother or sister y = being someone's sibling
x is (contingently) statistically correlated with y	x and y tend to occur together	x = hunger y = eating

I have not mentioned logically necessary statistical correlations because, although they do occur in number theory and certain other branches of mathematics, they are difficult to describe concisely and, anyway, need not concern us here.

The table above is headed "Types of Correlations of Discrete Events"; the phrase "discrete events" emphasizes the fact that so far I have been considering phenomena as all-or-nothing occurrences and ignoring the fact that they often are matters of degree. This way of conceiving things is fine if we're dealing with genuinely discrete events—like total incineration, death, the meeting of sperm and egg, and the conception of a human being. Such phenomena really are all-or-nothing affairs. There's no such thing as being "a little bit dead" or "sort of pregnant." But other phenomena—such as hunger, barometric pressure, poverty, sunlight, plant growth, and so on—come in degrees. Although we can consider them simply with respect to their presence and absence, as I have been doing here, it is often more useful to regard them as variable quantities, perhaps measured on a numerical scale.

Correlations among variable quantities, like correlations among discrete events, can be either statistical or absolute. Government spending and the inflation rate, for example, are variable quantities which are statistically correlated. Increases in government spending tend to fuel inflation, but so many other variables also influence inflation that there is no apparent precise relation between the two. In fact, sometimes the inflation rate actually decreases with increased government spending.

However, many correlations between variable quantities are precise and absolute. There is, for example, the correlation between the variables of time and distance expressed by the law of falling bodies:

$$d = \frac{1}{2} gt^2$$

Here d is the distance an object falls through a vacuum over a given time t, and g represents acceleration due to gravity, which near the earth's surface is about 9.8 meters/second^2. Thus, one second after being released an object has fallen a distance of:

$$\frac{1}{2} \times 9.8 \text{ meters/second}^2 \times (1 \text{ second})^2 = 4.9 \text{ meters}$$

Similarly, two seconds after its release, it has fallen:

$$\frac{1}{2} \times 9.8 \text{ meters/second}^2 \times (2 \text{ seconds})^2 = 19.6 \text{ meters}$$

and so on. This is a precise, absolute correlation, not a statistical one.

Like correlations among discrete phenomena, correlations among variable quantities can be either contingent or logically necessary. The laws of mathematics, for example, usually express logically necessary correlations, such as the correlation between the area A of a rectangle and its base b and height h:

$$A = bh$$

Like the law of falling bodies, this formula expresses an absolute correlation, but unlike the law of falling bodies, it is impossible to coherently imagine this formula to be false.

Logically necessary correlations among variable quantities, like those among discrete events, are most efficiently handled by deductive techniques. (You may be familiar with such techniques in mathematics.) Establishing contingent correlations, however, requires extrapolation from observed regularities by means of the principle of the uniformity of nature. But often, especially with statistical correlations, even detecting regularities in the observed data can be very difficult. Here a variety of sophisticated statistical procedures, including regression analysis, come into play. These procedures are beyond the scope of this book, but you should realize that many of them employ the principle of the uniformity of nature in much the same way as in the examples we have considered.

Exercise 6.7 The table below lists pairs of conditions x and y. Assuming x and y to be discrete conditions, not variable quantities, tell what sort of correlation, if any, exists between the two and whether it is contingent or logically necessary.

x	y
Being a plant	Being a tree
Being a tree	Being a plant
Being a tree	Being a tree
Being bigger than an atom	Being visible to the unaided human eye
Crowds	Noise
Having at least a million dollars	Being a millionaire
Rain	Heavy overcast
Sunspots	Plagues
Being an even number	Being a whole number
Application of force	Acceleration
Electrochemical or electrical stimulation of muscles	Human walking
Being an unprotected person situated at ground zero of a nuclear explosion	Being vaporized

6.8   CAUSATION

Assertions of the form "x causes y" are of two different kinds, depending on the identities of x and y: (1) x and y may be general types of events, like heavy exercise and rapid heartbeat, or (2) y might be a single, unique event, like the fall of Rome, and x a single, unique circumstance or set of circumstances thought to have produced it. In the first case the assertion concerns a **general cause,** in the second a **specific cause.** Arguments to establish specific causes are different from arguments to establish general ones. In this section we'll discuss both, beginning with general causes.

If x and y are general types of events, we'll say that x **causes** y if an occurrence of x always produces, is needed to produce, or tends to produce an occurrence of y. If x always produces y, then x is a **causally sufficient condition** for y. Complete incineration, for example, is causally sufficient for death. If x is needed to produce y, then x is a **causally necessary condition** for y. Fuel is causally necessary for fire. If x tends to produce y (i.e., produces y under certain conditions), then x is a **partial cause,** or **contributory cause,** of y. Smoking is a contributory cause of lung cancer. General causes, then, are either causally sufficient conditions, causally necessary conditions, or contributory causes. These three kinds of causes are the causal forms of the three types of contingent correlation between discrete events discussed in the last section—sufficient conditions, necessary conditions, and partial correlations, respectively.

The most common mistake in dealing with causes is to infer them directly from correlations:

x is correlated with y

∴ x causes y

As will soon be apparent, any inference of this sort, regardless of the nature of the correlation or the cause, is fallacious. Such reasoning is known as the **false cause fallacy,** or **post hoc fallacy.** I stated the inference in this general way because most people use the term "cause" without specifying which of the three types of cause they are talking about, and many people are equally unspecific about correlations. But even in specific versions, like:

x is a necessary condition of y

∴ x is a causally necessary condition of y

the inference is fallacious.

To see this, let's consider a typical example. Suppose we are medical researchers who notice that a certain nervous disorder is always accompanied by abnormally high concentrations of a certain chemical—call it "C"—in the blood. We have found, in other words, that high levels of C are a necessary condition of the disease. However, if we immediately try to infer that excess C is causally necessary for the disease (i.e., needed to produce it), at least three classes of counterexamples interfere. First, it may be the disease which produces the excess C. Perhaps the disorder affects certain glands, causing them to secrete abnormal quantities of C. Then excess C would still be a necessary condition of the disease but not causally necessary for it. Second, the correlation between the disease and excessive C may be produced by some third factor. Stress, for example, might independently give rise to both. Again this would enable the premise to be true and the conclusion false. Finally, there may be no causal connection between the two conditions at all. We can imagine, for example, that the correlation is pure coincidence. Given the range of counterexamples here, it should be clear that the inference is irrational.

These same three classes of counterexamples intrude whenever we attempt to infer cause from correlation. Generally, in fact, whenever a correlation exists between two conditions x and y, there are four classes of possibilities:

1   The correlation results from x's role in the production of y.

2   The correlation results from y's role in the production of x.

3   The correlation results from the production of both x and y by some additional factor or factors.

4   There are no causal links at all between x and y; the correlation is noncausal.

In the case we were considering, excessive C was x and the disease was y. What we wanted to infer was 1, that the correlation results from C's role in the production of the disease. But we were prevented from reaching this conclusion by the three classes of counterexamples which stem from possibilities 2–4.

It should be clear, then, that any attempt to infer cause from correlation alone is logically worthless. We always need more information than that. To show, for example, that excess C is causally necessary for the disease, we must show, not just that it always accompanies the disease, but that it is needed to produce it. In negative terms, this means that preventing an excessive accumulation of C would invariably prevent the disease. Indeed, this is what is most significant about causally necessary conditions; by controlling them we can forestall the phenomena for which they are necessary. They are the keys to prevention.

This is not true of necessary conditions in general. If, for example, the disease always produced excess C, then although excess C would be a necessary condition of the disease, it would not be causally necessary. In that case, we could not prevent the disease by preventing a buildup of C; rather, in order to prevent a buildup of C, we'd have to find some independent way of preventing the disease. That would require finding a genuinely causally necessary condition.

If causally necessary conditions are the keys to prevention, causally sufficient conditions are the keys to production. Remember that the statement "*x* is causally sufficient for *y*" means that *x* always produces *y*. Therefore, if *x* is causally sufficient for *y* and we can control *x*, then we can produce *y* at will. To see how causally sufficient conditions differ from sufficient conditions in general, consider the case of thunder and lightning. Thunder is sufficient for lightning; whenever thunder occurs, lightning does as well (though it may not always be seen). But it's not causally sufficient. Thunder does not produce lightning. The causation flows the other way. It's the lightning discharge which produces the thunder. We'd be guilty of a ridiculous sort of backwards logic if we tried to produce thunder first in the hope that somehow through our efforts lightning would ensue.

But now turn this case on its head. Lightning *is* causally sufficient for thunder. If we could produce lightning—real lightning, I mean, not just little sparks in the laboratory—then we could be sure of producing thunder as well.

Control of partial causes, by contrast, assures us of neither prevention nor production, but merely gives us some chance of influencing one or the other. Avoiding smoking, for example, does not always prevent lung cancer, but it does decrease the risk. Likewise, smoking three packs a day doesn't guarantee cancer production, but it's a bad idea if you value your health.

In general, then, what assertions of cause contain that assertions of mere correlations lack is information about which condition influences the other. Thus, to prove causation we need to determine what is involved in the production of what. We also need to extrapolate. The assertion "*x* is causally necessary for *y*," for example, is a claim about the universe at large; it goes well beyond the boundaries of observation. Therefore, establishing it requires the principle of the uniformity of nature. Typically, we'd argue as follows:

> *x* is always needed to produce *y* in observed cases.
>
> Most regularities present in observed regions of time and space extend as well to unobserved regions.
>
> ∴ *x* is causally necessary for *y*.

This is easy enough in principle, but in practice there's a catch: How do we know that the first premise is true?

There is no simple or universal answer. Perhaps we can verify it simply by becoming more closely acquainted with the processes in question. But the most generally useful method is to perform controlled experiments. Suppose once again that we're trying to show that excess C is a causally necessary condition for the disease. To do so, we need to establish the premise:

Excess C is always needed to produce the disease in observed cases.

Our conclusion will then follow by the reasoning just discussed. But what sort of experiment can confirm this premise?

The basic trick is to manipulate C levels artificially, while keeping all other conditions the same. Given the complexity of the human body, this probably couldn't be done. But let's take the liberty of idealizing for a while.

Now one way to proceed would be to choose two groups of people who are prone to excessive C levels (this avoids the ethical problem of injecting C into normal people). We then keep the C levels of the first group artificially low. They will be called the experimental group. The other group, called the control group, is rigorously subjected to the same conditions, except that we allow their C levels to soar. Now we watch. Both groups must be large enough and the time span of the experiment long enough to insure that the disease develops in a considerable number of the subjects.

Suppose, however, that it develops only among members of the control group. Then we can reason as follows. Something needed to produce the disease must have been present in the control group but not in the experimental group. But the experiment was constructed so that the only thing present in the control group but not in the experimental group was excess C. Therefore, among the subjects we observed, excess C was always needed to produce the disease. This is just the premise we needed, and we can now conclude that excess C is a causally necessary condition of the disease.

However, if some of the members of the experimental group got sick as well, then we were wrong. Excess C is not causally necessary for the disease; indeed, if we were able to keep their C levels low even after they got sick, excess C is not even a necessary condition.

In imagining this experiment, we idealized by assuming that we could lower C levels without affecting anything else and that we could choose two groups which were identical in all other respects. In practice, as I noted, such tight control is seldom, if ever, possible. When it isn't, we have to make sure that what is needed to produce the condition we are studying is not an extraneous condition that we have failed to control. This makes the actual reasoning for premises of causal arguments much more complicated than we have imagined it here. But the complications differ from case to case, and circumventing them requires specialized knowledge, so I will not discuss them here.

Successful arguments for causally sufficient conditions or partial causes are little different from the argument just considered. In each case, we establish causal involvement among observed cases, usually by controlled experiment, and then extrapolate with the aid of the principle of the uniformity of nature. I won't discuss details; you can probably fill them in if you want. They quickly become second nature to any working scientist. What I want you to get from this discussion is not a wholesale introduction to experimental science (that would require a book in itself), but an appreciation of the delicacy and complexity of good causal reasoning. Many people infer causation at the drop of a hat. I want you to see that it's not that simple.

To emphasize this point, let's consider one last example of really bad causal reasoning:

> Optimism never pays. Every time I start thinking that my life is getting better, something terrible happens.

Here the conclusion that optimism doesn't pay is inferred by way of an unstated intermediate conclusion—namely that optimism causes terrible things to happen. We won't worry about the final inference. But let's consider the first one carefully:

> Every time I start thinking that my life is getting better, something terrible happens.
> ∴ Optimism (i.e., thinking that my life is getting better) causes terrible things to happen.

The errors here are legion. Presumably the kind of cause the author has in mind is a causally sufficient condition. In other words, the conclusion is supposed to mean that optimism always produces terrible things.

But the argument is not even strong enough to establish a sufficient condition, much less a causally sufficient one. The author's observations concern only him- or herself, but are extrapolated to everyone at all times (at least there is no stated limitation on the conclusion). Thus even the reasoning of an inference such as this one would be weak:

> Every time I start thinking that my life is getting better, something terrible happens.
> Most regularities present in observed regions of time and space extend as well to unobserved regions.
> ∴ Optimism is a sufficient condition for the occurrence of terrible things.

The conditions under which the observations are made are not varied enough to support such a bold generalization very strongly. But that's by no means the worst of it, for there is obvious contrary evidence. There are people whose optimism is not always accompanied by tragedy, and that evidence is enough to destroy the inference completely, for it shows that the conclusion is false.

Now the author's inference is even bolder than this one. Since optimism isn't even a sufficient condition for terrible things, it surely is not causally sufficient. Hence this contrary evidence destroys the author's inference as well. But even if it didn't, that inference would be worthless. It's fallacious—even worse than a false cause fallacy—because the premise does not even assert a correlation. It merely notes a curious pattern in the scattered observations of a single individual.

Finally, if this were a real case I'd bet that the premise was false. There are plenty of psychological reasons why it should seem that optimism is always accompanied by tragedy, even if it isn't. (I'll have more to say about this kind of falsehood in Section 8.1.) But I really shouldn't go on like this, kicking a dog that's already long dead. I think you see the point. Causation requires caution.

So far, the arguments we've discussed in this section have all involved inferring a causal connection between two general conditions, both of which are already familiar. It is also possible to infer unknown conditions or events from their causal effects. Such arguments can be divided into two types, depending on whether we're seeking the cause of a single, unique event or of a general class of events.

Here are some cases which call for the first sort of argument: A house burned down. What was the cause? A gunman went berserk. What drove him to madness? The plants in your window turned yellow and died. What did you do wrong?

And here are some cases in which we'd need to infer general causes from general events: Magnets consistently attract iron. Why? Certain biological traits are passed from one generation to the next. How is this accomplished? Stars cluster into pinwheel-shaped masses called galaxies. What causes them to do this?

The second sort of case requires creation of a general scientific theory. I'll discuss scientific theories in Section 6.9. For the remainder of this section, we'll be concerned with the inference of specific unobserved causes from specific observed effects.

In this context, the word "cause" will have a different meaning from that in our recent discussion of general causes. It will mean, roughly, the specific condition or set of conditions which in this instance produced the observed effects.

Inferring a specific cause from its effects is a matter of considering all the facts of the case and envisioning the possible ways they could have come about. These possibilities are then weighed in the light of all our relevant knowledge. If the sum of the evidence overwhelmingly supports one over all the others, then that one is the probable cause.

Unfortunately, however, the knowledge required for this weighing of possibilities is often so extensive that it cannot be conveniently diagramed, and so evaluation of such arguments may be quite difficult. Let's consider a typical case:

> In the winter of 1953, a flying saucer was reported to have circled around a B-36 bomber and blinked a light as though signaling. Investigators from ATIC [Aerospace Technical Intelligence Center] determined the following facts:
>
> At 1:13 A.M. on February 6, 1953, the pilot of a B-36 plane bound for Spokane, Washington, was near Rosalia when he sighted a round white light below him, circling and rising at a speed estimated at 150 to 200 knots as it proceeded on a southeast course. The B-36 made a sharp descending turn toward the light, which was in view for a period of three to five minutes, but the pilot could not identify it.
>
> At 1 A.M., thirteen minutes before the sighting, the United States Weather Bureau station at Fairchild Air Force Base had released a pribal balloon. Winds aloft at altitudes of 7,000 to 10,000 feet were from the northwest with a speed of about fifty knots. Computations showed that the existing winds would have carried the balloon to the southeast, and it would have been over Rosalia, which is 12.5 nautical miles southeast of Fairchild Air Force Base, in about fifteen minutes. The plane sighted the unknown near Rosalia thirteen minutes after the launching. The balloon carried white running lights which accounted for the blinking described, and the circling climb of the UFO is typical of a balloon's course. Thus all the evidence supports ATIC's conclusion that the UFO was a weather balloon.[4]

This argument consists of a statement of the facts, followed by a conclusion: the UFO (unidentified flying object) was a weather balloon. The facts include the observed effect (the pilot's sighting), plus some auxiliary data, and the conclusion concerns the no longer observable cause. If the argument were diagramed as it stands, it would appear as a single inference with all the facts linked together as premises.

The first thing to notice is that this inference is far from deductive. We can imagine endlessly many worlds in which all the reported facts are true and yet the UFO is not a balloon. It could indeed be an alien spaceship, as the pilot apparently thought. Or it might be an ordinary electric light flying magically through the air, or a giant firefly, or the eye of Satan, or a secret Russian weapon. It might also have been a hallucination. Given this range of alternatives, the argument as stated is fallacious. But its authors seem confident of their conclusion. Why? Are they wrong?

I don't think so. Most of these counterexamples are preposterous, and the authors would surely have known it. They are counting on us to supply the premises needed to rule them out. In other words, they are tacitly assuming a tremendous quantity of background information.

[4]Donald H. Menzel and Lyle G. Boyd, *The World of Flying Saucers: A Scientific Examination of a Major Myth of the Space Age*, Doubleday & Company, Inc., Garden City, New York, 1963, p. 46.

First of all, they've assumed that the UFO wasn't anything fantastic or supernatural. It wasn't a magical lightbulb, a giant firefly, or a flying devil's eye, because the actual world does not contain such delightful nonsense. That's common knowledge, and the authors take it for granted. Perhaps, however, it would be more accurate to express their assumption as follows: "It is *nearly* certain that the UFO wasn't anything fantastic or supernatural." After all, we have no absolute proof that such things don't exist—only a lot of very strong inductive evidence. Nothing we've ever found flying around the night sky has been utterly fantastic. That's a well-established regularity with no contrary evidence, and so by the principle of the uniformity of nature we conclude that nothing ever is. And this is only one line of reasoning to establish that conclusion. There are others as well.

But alien spacecraft, Russian weapons, and hallucinations are not utterly fantastic. What rules them out? Here again the authors are assuming more than they say. It is obvious that such things are either rare or nonexistent under the reported conditions. The Russians may make secret weapons, but they're not so reckless as to fly them over the continental United States. Hallucinations lasting three to five minutes are rare; besides, a bomber pilot ought to know when he's having one. Alien spacecraft, even if they exist (a big if) and even if they visit the earth (a very, very big if) do not appear often, since extensive investigations have failed to turn up any solid evidence of them. It is safe to say, then, that precious few if any of the lights we see at night are flying saucers.

But perhaps it would be more illuminating to state all this in a positive way. It's not just the rarity or nonexistence of the phenomena just mentioned that makes these romantic explanations improbable, but also the prevalence of more mundane sources of light in the night sky. In fact, virtually all lights flying under conditions even remotely like those reported are the lights of conventional aircraft or balloons. The authors know this and take it, too, for granted. This positive assumption, then, narrows the range of likely possibilities down to two—aircraft and balloons. And the fact that a lighted balloon was in the area tips the scale heavily in favor of the second of these. Therefore, the balloon is by far the most probable cause.

Does this mean that the argument is inductive? Not necessarily. What it means is that among worlds in which the argument's premises (including all the implicit background information) are true, the most common type are worlds in which the conclusion is true. Worlds in which the UFO is something else—a helicopter, a Russian weapon, or a giant firefly—are far less frequent. But this does not automatically mean that the conclusion is true in *most* of the worlds in which the premises are true. For there are many small classes of counterexamples, and added together they may total more than 50 percent. It is therefore difficult to tell whether this argument is inductive. But most of the alternatives are so improbable given what we know, and the evidence in favor of the authors' conclusion is so strong, that I'd say it probably is.

Evaluation of the argument's reasoning involved consideration of a number of implicit assumptions, among them:

It is nearly certain that the UFO wasn't anything fantastic or supernatural.

Hallucinations seldom last three to five minutes.

Virtually all lights flying under conditions even remotely like those reported are the lights of conventional aircraft or balloons.

And these, of course, are just a sample. Obviously the authors didn't have these premises in mind in precisely the way in which I worded them; in fact, they may not have had anything precise in mind. But they certainly were drawing on the sorts of knowledge which these premises express. Therefore we must take this knowledge into account in order to understand and evaluate the argument fairly. But because this knowledge is so extensive and so fluid (even in the minds of the authors), our diagraming technique is virtually useless here. There's too much to add, it can't be done accurately, and even if it could it would be too much trouble. Therefore, we are forced to fall back on vague overall impressions, rather like a pilot whose instruments fail in a fog.

Still, this is no reason not to be careful and methodical. We're faced with what is at best an inductive argument. Therefore, there are three things to check: quality of reasoning, truth of the basic premises, and the possibility of suppressed evidence. I've already discussed the quality of the reasoning. It seems to be inductive, though I'm not absolutely sure. Let's suppose the basic premises are true. Again, I'm not sure, but I won't pursue the matter here because it has little to do with logic. That leaves suppressed evidence.

How might contrary evidence affect this argument? Well suppose, for example, we discover that a helicopter was in the area at the time of the sighting and that it followed a path similar to that of the balloon. Then the conclusion that the UFO was the helicopter would be just as probable as the conclusion that it was the balloon. Since there are other less likely possibilities as well, neither conclusion will be true in most of the worlds in which the premises are true. So adding this new information would make the argument fallacious. Therefore, although it may be inductive as intended, it would fail to meet the requirement of total evidence and would thus be unreliable.

Now of course we don't actually have reason to believe that a helicopter was in the area. So this is not a real case of suppressed evidence. But as I was thinking about this argument I discovered, much to my surprise, that some genuinely relevant evidence is suppressed. The UFO reportedly rose at a rate of 150 to 200 knots. That's about 172 to 230 miles per hour. Those figures sounded too high to me, and so I called the weather bureau. They said that the climbing rate of a pribal balloon 15 minutes after launch is about 7 miles per hour. The authors didn't mention that, but being experts on such matters, they surely knew it. Evidently it is evidence they consciously suppressed.

So now what should we think? As disturbed as I am by the authors' omission, I'm still inclined to believe their conclusion. The figure of 150 to 200 knots was the pilot's estimate. Visual estimates of the speed and distance of an unknown object in the air at night—even by experienced pilots—are seldom accurate. The authors knew this (they mention it elsewhere), and so apparently they assumed that the pilot had made a mistake. It's a shame they didn't say so, but I think they are right. The evidence that the object was a balloon is so strong and the probability of error in the pilot's estimate is so high that the authors' conclusion still seems the most probable.

However, if I had some reservations about the argument before, I have even more now. I'd be hard pressed in the light of this new evidence to say that the conclusion is epistemically probable. The argument may well be inductive, but it suppresses relevant, though weak, contrary evidence. If the conclusion remains epistemically probable, it's only by the skin of its teeth.

Most attempts to infer unobserved causes from observed effects require extensive background information, as we see in this example. When the unobserved causes are quite different from anything previously known, we need not only extensive background information, but creative guesswork, followed by repeated and rigorous experimentation. This is the method of theoretical science. It is the topic of this chapter's next and final section.

Exercise 6.8(a)   Listed below are pairs of conditions x and y. For each pair, describe the relation between them. Is it a mere correlation? If so, what kind? Is it causal? Then what kind of causal relation is it? Assume x and y to be discrete phenomena, not variables, and general, not specific, events.

x	y
Joke-telling	Laughter
Force	Change in motion
Heating ice above 0°C	Melting it
Striking a match	Lighting it
Obtaining nourishment	Living more than a year
Attending school	Learning calculus
Irritation of a cat	Hissing of the cat
Sugar	Tooth decay
Today's being Tuesday	Tomorrow's being Wednesday
Fire	Oxygen
Oxygen	Fire
Fire	Smoke
Smoke	Fire
Striking a chicken's egg with a heavy direct blow of a sledge hammer	Breaking said egg

Exercise 6.8(b) The following arguments all concern general causes. Diagram and evaluate each, and add a note answering the following questions: What kind of cause is being discussed? What sorts of counterexamples, if any, affect the argument? What sorts of contrary evidence might there be? How strong is the argument overall?

1. Prior to every great war there has been an increase in defense spending among the participants. Therefore, increased defense spending is a cause of major wars.

2. We were consistently able to liquify metallic lutetium under a variety of conditions by heating it to a temperature of 1652°C. Therefore, heating metallic lutetium to 1652° causes it to melt.

3. A marine biologist investigating a skin disease in fish discovers that all fish afflicted with the disease have a certain crustacean parasite beneath their scales, whereas most healthy fish do not. She concludes that the parasite causes the disease.

4. There is a strong statistical correlation between high scores on college entrance examinations and high grade-point averages in college. Therefore, if you want to get good grades in college, score high on the college entrance exams.

5. The ancient Chinese, who believed that solar eclipses were caused by a dragon devouring the sun, used to beat gongs and set off fireworks during an eclipse to frighten the dragon away. Remarkably, each time they did this, the eclipse came to an end. This incredible correlation shows that their technique actually produced the desired result.

6. Since there is a strong correlation between personality type and astrological sign, the influence of the stars on human events is indisputable.

7. Studies have shown that abused children are much more likely to become abusive parents than are children who have not been subjected to violence. Thus abusive parents are a cause of child abuse in the succeeding generation.

8. A deep sexual inhibition seems to develop between people who live in close domestic contact for the first six years of their lives, regardless of their familial relations. Of 2,700 marriages recorded on Israeli kibbutzim, for example, *none* has involved members of the same communally raised peer group. (Jeffrey Saver, "Edward O. Wilson: Father of a New Science," *Science Digest*, May 1982)

9. Has the sale of all-savers certificates helped the ailing savings and loan industry? Although it is still too early to spot any conclusive trends, the consensus seems to be that, while sales are less than expected, they are helping to reduce deficits at savings and loan

institutions. For October 1981, the first month all-savers were offered for sale, the U.S. League of Savings Associations reported S&Ls experienced a net savings gain of $4.3 billion. This compares to a $2.0 billion net savings gain for September and a $1.3 billion net savings gain for August. ("All Savers and You: Are They a Good Buy?" *Consumers' Research,* January 1982)

10   Recent studies have shown that high school marriages have become an important factor in the drop-out trend—youngsters leaving school before graduation, with all the later consequences of ruined careers. A statewide study in Iowa showed that 80 per cent of the girls who married in high school dropped out and only 8 per cent of them eventually came back. Of the boys, 43 per cent who married left school, and only 9 per cent of them returned to the classroom. (Grace and Fred Hechinger, *Teen-age Tyranny*)

11   The following passage describes an experiment performed by researchers Beverly Rubik and Elizabeth Rauscher on faith healer Olga Worrall:

[T]he researchers had given bacteria a "whopping" dose of phenol, an antiseptic. Olga briefly held her hands near microscope slides on which the bacteria had been placed. In over 30 previous experiments Rubik had found that the phenol would paralyze all the bacteria within two minutes. In the control sample, which Olga did not treat, all the bacteria were again paralyzed, but on Olga's slides 7 per cent of the bacteria were still swimming around 12 minutes after the phenol had been administered.

[Concluded Rauscher]: "I'd say it appeared that Olga was able to overcome the effects of the chemicals." (Lygeri Koromvokis, "Faith Healers in the Laboratory," *Science Digest,* May 1982)

Exercise 6.8(c)   The arguments below are attempts to infer a specific unknown cause from specific observed effects. Discuss the strength of each, using my discussion of the UFO argument as a model.

1   Why the dramatic rise in the incidence of herpes? Sexual freedom is obviously implicated. . . . Not only are more people indulging in sex, they are also more active—starting younger, marrying later, divorcing more often. (*Time,* August 2, 1982)

2   In the 1960s and 1970s the divorce rate in America skyrocketed. How can we account for this? The facts are fairly clear. It was during the 1960s that the birth control pill first achieved widespread distribution. The convenience and reliability of the pill gave women far greater sexual freedom than before. In this climate of enhanced freedom, both men and women became more openly promiscuous,

and many marriages collapsed under the resultant pressure. America's unprecedented divorce rate during this period was therefore due to the introduction of the pill.

3   One morning I got into my car and turned on the ignition. Nothing happened. Puzzled, I tried again. Still nothing. I opened the engine compartment. Everything seemed to be in order. Then I lifted up the back seat to inspect the battery (the car was an old Volkswagen). It was gone! Completely gone! At that moment I remembered noticing that the door had been ajar when I entered the car. And I recalled closing it but not locking it the night before. Looking closer, I found several burnt matches on the floor of the car. These had evidently been used to illuminate what I now realized was the cause of my troubles: the theft of my car's battery by person or persons unknown.

4   On August 9, 1979, 63 employees of a polyvinyl chloride (PVC) fabricating plant developed acute upper and lower respiratory irritation, headache, nausea, and fainting following exposure to fumes from an overheated PVC extruding machine. All affected personnel had been in an area west of the machine, where fumes from the machine could easily have drifted, given the nature of the plant's ventilating system. The earliest cases occurred closest to the machine, and incidence decreased with distance westward. Overheated PVC releases gaseous hydrochloric acid (HCl) and carbon monoxide (CO), which are known to cause symptoms similar to those reported. Plant managers attributed the outbreak to mass hysteria, but investigators from the National Institute for Occupational Safety and Health concluded that it was due to exposure to toxic HCl and CO emitted by the extruding machine.[5]

5   Some scientists have suggested that it [the Tunguska Event, a huge explosion in Central Siberia on June 30, 1908] was caused by a piece of antimatter, annihilated on contact with the ordinary matter of the Earth, disappearing in a flash of gamma rays. But the absence of radioactivity at the impact site gives no support to this explanation. Others postulate that a mini black hole passed through the Earth in Siberia and out the other side. But the records of atmospheric shock waves show no hint of an object booming out of the North Atlantic later that day. Perhaps it was a spaceship of some unimaginably advanced extraterrestrial civilization in desperate mechanical trouble, crashing in a remote region of an obscure planet. But at the site of the impact there is no trace of such a ship. Each of these ideas has been proposed, some of them more or less seriously. Not one of them is strongly supported by the evidence. The key point of the

[5]This incident was reported in the *British Journal of Industrial Medicine*, vol. 39, 1982, pp. 239–243.

Tunguska Event is that there was a tremendous explosion, a great shock wave, an enormous forest fire, and yet there is no impact crater at the site. There seems to be only one explanation consistent with all the facts: In 1908 a piece of a comet hit the Earth. (Carl Sagan, *Cosmos*)

6.9   SCIENTIFIC THEORIES

The most creative and intricate inductive reasoning of all occurs in the development of scientific theories. A **scientific theory** is an account of an entire class of phenomena inferred from their observable effects. Frequently these theoretical phenomena are themselves totally unobservable—x-rays, subatomic particles, unconscious desires, the ancestors of man. Our only clues to their nature and existence are the effects they have or the traces they leave in regions of time and space accessible to our senses. But we cannot infer their existence or nature simply by extrapolating familiar regularities, for theoretical phenomena are genuine novelties, not just extensions of the familiar beyond the boundaries of observation.

It is important not to confuse scientific theories with scientific laws. The laws of science are merely expressions of correlations, many of which are established by extrapolating observable regularities. Take Boyle's gas law, for example. This law, embodied in the formula:

$$p \, v = p'v'$$

expresses a correlation among four variable quantities for gases in closed containers at constant temperature. The variables p and v are an initial pressure and volume, and p' and v' are some subsequent pressure and volume. This law can be verified by making repeated measurements at various pressures and volumes and then extrapolating the results to the universe at large via the principle of the uniformity of nature.

No theory can be established so easily. The theory which accounts for Boyle's law, for example, is the molecular theory of gases. It explains the observable correlation expressed in the law as an effect of the unobservable behavior of the profusion of tiny molecules which make up the gas. Our knowledge of these molecules was not obtained merely by extrapolating observations of already familiar phenomena. Rather, it developed through a complex, dynamic process of scientific reasoning. It is this process that I want to focus on here.

For expository purposes, we can divide the theoretical process into two stages: (1) hypothesis formation and (2) testing and revision. Hypothesis formation is the creation of a tentative account of the unobserved phenomena for the purpose of guiding research. This tentative account is then put to work in the stage of testing and revision. Observable consequences are deduced from it, and these are either confirmed or disconfirmed by careful observation. If any are disconfirmed, the hypothesis is revised or replaced. If all are confirmed, it may eventually become epistemically probable.

The stage of hypothesis formation begins when data accumulated by previous efforts fall into patterns which suggest a common underlying explanation. This spurs formation of a **tentative hypothesis,** a kind of story about the unobserved phenomena responsible for these patterns. This hypothesis is not deduced or even inferred inductively from the established facts. At this stage the facts are too sketchy. Too many possible worlds are compatible with what is known. Rather, the theorist imaginatively explores the range of possible phenomena which could account for the known facts and ventures a detailed guess, based on all the information available, as to which of these possible phenomena are actual. This guess is the tentative hypothesis.

Though the tentative hypothesis is forged to fit the facts, other considerations are also involved in shaping it. Foremost among these are testability, breadth, and simplicity.

A tentative hypothesis is a **testable hypothesis** to the extent that it makes some difference to experience. Suppose, for example, that someone hypothesizes that the cause of winning in games of chance is an immaterial substance called luck. Luck resides in the person of the winning gambler, but it has no solidity, color, mass, energy, or any other physically detectable property. You can't even feel it inside of you. But, says the hypothesis, it is real nonetheless. Obviously, this hypothesis is completely untestable. Nothing we could experience would be different if it were true from what we could experience if it were false. With respect to everything we could observe, a world in which this substance existed would be exactly like one in which it didn't.

Why should we reject untestable hypotheses? It has sometimes been suggested that the reason is that they are meaningless, but this hardly seems true. What I said in the previous paragraph was meaningful enough. You understood it. The real problem with untestable hypotheses is that their epistemic probability always remains vanishingly small. Under no conditions do they ever become probable. To see this, consider the range of worlds compatible with everything we know at present (i.e., the worlds in which all of our current knowledge is true). Among these, some (but only a minute fraction) are worlds in which this substance called luck exists and somehow causes wins in gambling. The alternative possibilities are endless: wins in gambling are caused by the will of God, by a variety of natural phenomena, by the mental telepathy of aliens from Sirius, by nothing at all, by any combination of the above—and much more. Hence the luck hypothesis is for us at this moment epistemically improbable. Among worlds in which all of what we know is true, only a trifling portion are worlds in which this hypothesis is true. Moreover, since the hypothesis is untestable, nothing can ever happen to increase its epistemic probability. No new evidence in its favor will ever emerge. Hence it has no chance of ever being proved—or even shown to be probable. It's a dead end; to pursue it would be a waste of time.

Incidentally, it is worth noting that the denial of an untestable hypothesis, while also untestable, is and will remain epistemically probable. In most of the worlds in which our current knowledge is true, it is not the case that an unobservable substance called luck causes gamblers to win. Hence the statement that winning is not caused by such a substance is epistemically probable. And since nothing we can experience can add to or subtract from the evidence for this negative statement, it will always remain highly probable.

The second criterion for shaping tentative hypotheses is **breadth.** A broad hypothesis is one that accounts for a wide range of observable phenomena. A hypothesis which is both broad and testable is fruitful; it suggests many new lines of investigation. If true, it is likely to have widespread applications. And if false, it should soon clash with observation and thereby quickly give way to a better hypothesis. All these traits are desirable.

The final criterion is **simplicity.** Some have said that simple hypotheses are preferable because the universe is fundamentally simple, but that may be disputed. The real reason is practical. It must be kept in mind that the tentative hypothesis is not the final truth, but only a conjecture formulated to guide investigation. Revision is to be expected. Therefore, it is more efficient to begin with a simple hypothesis and then revise or complicate it as the evidence requires than to get tangled in complications from the start. The path to the truth is generally easier and straighter from a simple hypothesis than from an arcane and elaborate one.

Often in science a number of competing hypotheses are offered to explain the same phenomena. If all these hypotheses fit the facts equally well, then the criteria of testability, breadth, and simplicity help to determine which of them will be the most useful guide to further research.

Once we have settled on a hypothesis, the second stage of theorizing—testing and revision—begins. This stage has two goals, which are approached simultaneously: to disprove the hypothesis if it is false (so that it can be revised or replaced by a better one) and to gather enough evidence to make it epistemically probable if it is true. Though these two goals are inseparable in practice, they are logically distinct, and we will consider them separately.

Let's consider first the goal of disproving the hypothesis if it is false. Active pursuit of disproof is one of the hallmarks of honest science, as opposed to pseudosciences like astrology, spiritualism, or pop psychology, whose practitioners seldom subject their hypotheses to rigorous tests. The thoughtful investigator is aware that tentative hypotheses, no matter how convincing they seem, are usually wrong, and that the purpose of theorizing is not to prove what you feel is right, but to discover the truth. Disproof, then, is to be welcomed, for it sets the stage for the development of better hypotheses. It is only by repeated testing, rejection, and revision that scientific theorizing approaches truth.

Since theoretical hypotheses generally concern phenomena which are not directly observable, they can't be disproved by direct observation. But if they are testable, their truth makes some difference to experience. It is this difference by which the theorist seeks to disprove them. Using the hypothesis as a premise, together with other items of previously established knowledge, the theorist deduces an observational consequence or prediction. This consequence or prediction is then tested. If it turns out to be false, then, since the reasoning was deductive, at least one of the assumptions must be false. Hence if the assumptions embodying the previously established knowledge are true, the false assumption must be the hypothesis. You will recognize here the familiar form of reductio.

The careful theorist deduces as many observational consequences as possible and checks each one, thereby maximizing the chances of disproving the hypothesis. If none of them turn out to be false, then the theorist has failed to attain the goal of disproof. But in the process, as we shall see shortly, the second goal may have been attained; the hypothesis may have become epistemically probable.

In practice, however, even if some of the observational consequences do turn out to be false, that may not suffice to disprove the hypothesis with certainty. For some of the background information needed to deduce these consequences may not be certain, and in that case there may be some doubt about whether it is the hypothesis or this background information which is false. However, if the epistemic probability of the background information is high, then it is also highly probable that the false assumption is the hypothesis. So the rational attitude is still to reject the hypothesis and if possible formulate a better one.

This rational attitude contrasts sharply with the attitude of the dogmatist or pseudoscientist, who is more interested in clinging to a favorite hypothesis than in knowing the truth. When the dogmatist's hypothesis leads to false predictions, he or she seizes on the uncertainty of background assumptions, no matter how probable they are, and denies them instead of denying the hypothesis.

To illustrate this dogmatic strategy, let's consider a fanciful example. Suppose that a certain unusual species of insect suddenly infests your neighborhood. Your neighbor, a lonely and demented soul, contrives a hypothesis to account for this fact. These insects are not real insects, he says, but clever devices sent here by extraterrestrials to gather information for an impending invasion.

You try to convince him of the (epistemic) improbability of this bizarre hypothesis, but to no avail. Finally, in desperation, you decide to put it to the test. You reason as follows:

Look, suppose these insects really are alien devices. Now a spying device would not look like a real bug if you cut it open. It wouldn't have guts and things. There would be electrical components and transmitters and whatnot—or at least something noticeably unusual. Therefore, if we cut one open, we ought to find something out of the ordinary.

Here the hypothesis is combined with elements of background information to deduce an observable consequence—namely that the bugs ought to contain something noticeably strange.

Now, like a good scientist, you test this consequence. You get out a set of old dissecting instruments left over from a biology class, capture one of the unfortunate creatures, and proceed to dismantle it. All you find is guts—plain, ordinary guts. You show your neighbor. "Look. There's nothing unusual here. Just guts. So you were wrong."

"No," he says quietly, "You are wrong. It just goes to show how diabolically clever these aliens are. Just imagine! They knew that somebody would get suspicious, so they put guts in these devices just to throw us off the track."

Instead of accepting your conclusion, this person has rejected the background assumption that alien spying devices would contain something noticeably unusual. It is, after all, not absolutely certain—though it seems highly probable indeed. Your argument is pretty good, although not utterly conclusive, and the rational thing to do would be to reject the hypothesis. But your neighbor is being dogmatic. He'll cling to his delusion no matter what evidence you muster.

His attitude illustrates the essence of dogmatism: total insensitivity to probabilities. The dogmatist blithely ignores the weight of the evidence and thinks that because his or her hypothesis has not been conclusively disproved it must be right. Carried to extremes, dogmatism is genuine madness. But even in milder forms it contributes immensely to human blindness and stupidity. One needs only to think of the dogmatic attitude of the medieval church or of the Nazis' dogmatic hypothesis that Germany's ills were the result of a vast Jewish conspiracy to see that this is true.

Each time a dogmatist denies an item of background evidence, he or she explains this denial by adding a new wrinkle to his or her hypothesis. Thus when the dogmatic neighbor denied the assumption that alien spying devices would contain something noticeably unusual, he elaborated his hypothesis by assuming that the aliens purposefully supplied their devices with guts to confound the suspicious. This new wrinkle may be thought of as an additional hypothesis. Notice that it is assumed only to block disconfirmation of the original one. The neighbor had no reason to believe it, apart from his stubborn insistence on the original. Any idea introduced only to block disconfirmation of a previous hypothesis and lacking supporting evidence itself is called an **ad hoc hypothesis.** Ad hoc hypotheses are symptomatic of dogmatism.

To summarize: good scientific theorizing actively seeks to disprove hypotheses by deducing observational consequences, putting them to the test, and rejecting the hypotheses if they prove false; dogmatism, in contrast, formulates an initial hypothesis and clings to it, no matter how much evidence accumulates against it.

But what if all attempts to disconfirm the hypothesis fail? What if all the observational consequences we deduce turn out to be true? Then the second goal of testing and revision—acquiring enough evidence to make the hypothesis epistemically probable—may be within our grasp.

Of course, confirmation of an observational consequence does not prove a hypothesis. Deducing a true conclusion from a premise in no way shows the premise to be true. However, each time we make a new observation confirming one of the consequences of a hypothesis, new evidence in favor of the hypothesis is added to our store of knowledge, and the epistemic probability of the hypothesis increases. If enough confirmatory observations are made, the epistemic probability of the hypothesis eventually approaches (though virtually never reaches) 100 percent.

For an illustration of this important effect, let's return to the molecular theory of gases. One observational consequence of this theory is that small particles suspended in gases should exhibit tiny random movements—the so-called Brownian motion. The reasoning is roughly as follows:

> Gases are composed of many small, light, fairly densely concentrated particles in quick random motion.
>
> Fairly densely concentrated particles in quick random motion frequently strike other particles placed in their midst in a random fashion.
>
> Any free particle struck by a quickly moving particle of roughly comparable mass will exhibit a significant recoil in the direction opposite to the collision.
>
> ∴ Particles of small mass freely suspended in a gas exhibit frequent and significant random changes of motion.

The first premise is the molecular hypothesis—or at least a part of it. The other two are items of background knowledge. The conclusion is an observable consequence. The inference is deductive.

Now if the conclusion were false, we'd have to reject one of the assumptions, as in the previous example. But in fact it's true. Smoke or dust particles suspended in a gas are perceptibly jiggled and buffeted, as microscopic examination reveals. Of course observation of the jiggling doesn't prove the molecular theory. Other hypotheses could explain it as well. But by ruling out possibilities that previously we would have had to consider, it raises the epistemic probability of the hypothesis.

To see this clearly, recall once more that the epistemic probability of a statement is the frequency of worlds in which it is true among worlds in which all of what we know is true. All hypotheses are epistemically improbable at first. There are too many worlds compatible with the few facts available to us in the stage of hypothesis formation. Before the molecular theory of gases was extensively confirmed, for example, it was compatible with everything we knew that gases were not composed of moving molecules—that, for example, they were continuous fluids, or that they were composed of relatively stationary particles, or that they consisted of rotating particles in a fluid medium, or any of a number of other alternatives. So among all the worlds in which all of what we knew was true, the worlds in which the molecular hypothesis was true were a small minority, as Figure 3 illustrates. But since observational confirmation of hypothetical consequences increases our store of knowledge, it narrows the range of worlds in which all of what we know is true. Observation of the motions of small particles suspended in gases rules out worlds in which this motion would not occur—worlds, for example, in which gases are relatively motionless fluids or aggregates of particles, containing no forces which would jiggle particles suspended within them. These worlds are no longer worlds in which all of what we know is true. But notice that no worlds in which the hypothesis is true have been ruled out. Thus the frequency of worlds in which the hypothesis is true among worlds in which all of what we know is true is greater than it was before. Confirmation of the observational consequence has raised the epistemic probability of the hypothesis.

Such an increase in epistemic probability occurs each time a new observational consequence of the hypothesis is confirmed. After confirmation of many consequences, assuming that none have been disconfirmed, the epistemic probability of the hypothesis becomes very high. Exactly how high it is at any moment, however, is impossible to say. As with the arguments for specific causes discussed in the last section, the evidence for theoretical hypotheses is too broad and fluid to evaluate precisely. We must, as before, rely on overall impressions. This can be done by considering all known information relevant to the hypothesis (including whatever evidence has been gathered through observational tests) and getting a feel for the range of worlds in which it all is true. The frequency among these worlds of worlds in which the hypothesis is true is the epistemic probability of the hypothesis.

The entire process of scientific theorizing—framing a tentative hypothesis, deducing observational consequences, testing, revising the hypothesis, and eventually confirming enough consequences of some version of the hypothesis to make it epistemically probable—is called the **hypothetico-deductive method.** It is the logical core of theoretical science and perhaps

Worlds compatible
with our knowledge
before observation
of Brownian motion

Worlds compatible
with our knowledge
after observation
of Brownian motion

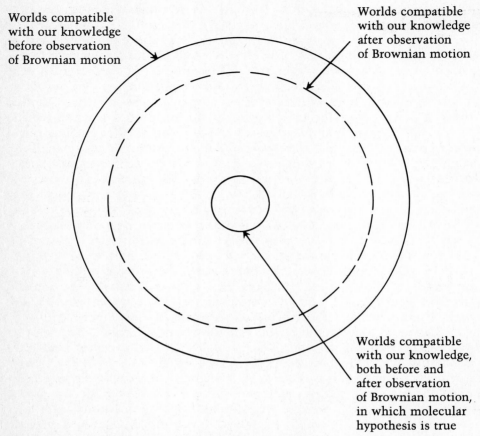

Worlds compatible
with our knowledge,
both before and
after observation
of Brownian motion,
in which molecular
hypothesis is true

FIGURE 3   Effect of Observation of Brownian Motion on Epistemic Probability of Molecular Theory of Gases

the most powerful and sophisticated form of inductive reasoning. Only by means of the hypothetico-deductive method can we successfully reason from observed effects to the wholly novel unobserved phenomena underlying them—phenomena which may themselves remain forever beyond our observational grasp.

Exercise 6.9(a)   Imagine yourself confronted by the neighbor who believes that insects are alien spying devices. What tests in addition to dissection might you perform to confirm or disconfirm this hypothesis? Can you think of a test which would conclusively disprove it? If not, discuss the sorts of ad hoc hypotheses the neighbor might invent to discredit the various tests you could perform.

Exercise 6.9(b) Each of the following passages suggests a hypothesis concerning a novel unobserved cause of observed effects. For each: (A) Discuss to what degree the suggested hypothesis satisfies the three criteria of testability, breadth, and simplicity. (B) To the best of your ability, estimate the epistemic probability of the hypothesis, based on all your current knowledge and the evidence (if any) presented in the passage. Explain the evidence you used and defend your estimate. (C) What sorts of observational consequences might be deduced from the suggested hypothesis in order to test it? What background information would be needed to carry out these deductions? What sorts of tests could be performed to confirm or disconfirm the observational consequences? (D) What alternative hypotheses might also account for the data? Are any of them better than the suggested hypothesis? Why or why not?

1   A test was run in one hospital which tended to show that babies, when left without attention, ran fevers. When given attention the fevers immediately abated. The test, while not observed personally by the author, seems to have been conducted with proper controls according to report. If this is true, it postulates a mechanism in the human being which uses illness for affection on a genetic basis. (L. Ron Hubbard, *Dianetics: The Modern Science of Mental Health*)

2   As a boy, I used to snigger at the prayer concluding the Roman Catholic Mass: "Protect us from Satan, who prowls the world, seeking the ruin of souls." The thought of a mischievous red imp, with arrowhead tail, hairy legs, pointy horns and a handy pitchfork seemed quite droll. Now, as an old man, I find the Devil no longer funny. In a beseiged world wallowing in evil, the prowling Devil seems very real indeed. (Donald A. Windsor, letter to the editor, *Newsweek*, September 13, 1982)

    (Hint: the suggested hypothesis is that the Devil is the cause of the world's evil.)

3   It seems certain that some level of intellectual processing continues even during sleep. Mathematicians working on difficult problems frequently report going to bed frustrated, unable to find a solution, but then waking up the next morning with the solution clearly in mind. Apparently some portion of the mind remains at work while we sleep.

4   Have you ever noticed that no experience is ever exactly as you anticipated it? Consider, for example, the fact that when you go on a vacation, no matter how vividly the place you visit has been described to you, and even regardless of whether you've seen photographs of it, it always looks different from what you imagined. How can this be? Why is anticipation *always* inaccurate? May we dare

to infer that there exists a mysterious force which alters the world in response to our expectations, a force which guarantees that our experiences will be novel? This is certainly what the facts suggest.

5   The Cherokees had a legend to account for the phases of the moon. There was once, so the story goes, a young brave who was very handsome but took no interest in the women of the village. He kept to himself, and each night he stood quietly on a high hill and gazed at the moon. One night he found himself lifted far into the sky until he came up to the moon. He saw that she was a beautiful maiden, more radiant than any on earth, and he fell in love with her. The moon loved him as well, for she had seen him watching from the hill and she knew that he was noble and pure. For a long time they were happy together, but at last the young man grew restless and curious about his people back on earth. The moon begged him not to go, but he did not heed her, though he promised to return quickly. Once home, however, he forgot the moon and his promise. As the time grew longer, the moon's heart was saddened; and overcome by loneliness, she began to wane. It seemed that she would die and her light would go out completely. But one summer evening her lover looked into the western sky and saw a thin crescent shining with a dim light. The memory of his love returned to him. He went back to her, and his love made her round and whole again. But she was mortally weakened, so that she could not remain whole. And even now her waning continues, though always she is restored again by love.

7

Fallacies

Since virtually any two or more unrelated statements can be combined to form a fallacious inference, the variety of fallacies is endless. Nevertheless, certain fallacious patterns occur again and again in practical reasoning. Many of these have been named and cataloged by logicians. In this chapter, we'll study some of the most prominent.

7.1 APPEALS TO THE ACTIONS OR OPINIONS OF OTHERS

All of us depend on other people for clues about how to act and what to believe. If we have evidence that these others are reliable, then this dependence can be rational. But if not, it is likely to be fallacious.

The opinions of people who are eminent, popular, and respected have a special appeal, and often we use them as evidence. Here's an example:

How do we know that reality is not statistical in nature, even at the subatomic level? Well, because no less eminent a scientist than Albert Einstein said so.[1]

The question, of course, is a veiled conclusion: reality is not statistical in nature, even at the subatomic level. But it has no logical connection with the premise. Among imaginable worlds in which the premise is true, there are at least as many in which the conclusion is false as there are in which it is true. The inference is therefore fallacious.

If you doubt this, you are probably making the implicit assumption that eminent scientists are usually right, especially about matters of science. This assumption may well be true in our world, but nothing compels us to imagine it so. There are many possible worlds in which eminent scientists are all habitual liars. Keep your imagination nimble!

Nevertheless, if this was your reaction, you had a point. Perhaps the author was assuming the same thing you were. Adding this assumption would make the inference inductive and would account as well for its persuasiveness. The argument would then be:

1　The eminent scientist Albert Einstein said that reality is not statistical in nature, even at the subatomic level.

2　Eminent scientists are generally right about matters of science.

∴ 3　Reality is not statistical in nature, even at the subatomic level.

The first premise is true, and the second seems at least reasonable. Should we therefore accept the conclusion?

Not without some further checking. We saw in Section 6.2 that inductive arguments are trustworthy only if they meet the requirement of total evidence. In this one some evidence has been suppressed. Virtually all the data available to modern physicists runs counter to Einstein's claim, and nearly all physicists now believe that in this matter Einstein was mistaken.

A number of lessons can be drawn from this example. First, the argument as originally stated was plainly fallacious. In fact, almost any argument of the form:

Authority x affirms that p

∴ p

is fallacious and remains so even if we add a long list of the authority's qualifications. The fallacy involved here is called **appeal to authority.**

---

[1]Einstein did say this, though he expressed it **more elegantly:** "God does not play dice with the universe."

We have observed, however, that appeals to authority can be regarded as implicitly inductive by adding the assumption that the authority is reliable concerning the matter at issue. Whether we should add such a premise in evaluating the inference depends on what we can glean of the author's intentions by applying the criteria discussed in Section 4.1. In this case it seems probable that the author intended the implicit premise "Eminent scientists are generally right about matters of science" to be taken for granted. Therefore, we should add this premise and evaluate the reasoning as inductive. But though the premises are true, the argument is still weak because of the suppressed contrary evidence. Thus the complete evaluation essed as follows:

① + ②   Premises seem to be true, but argument is weak because
　↓ I　　　of suppressed evidence of contrary findings.
③

Evaluating weak arguments is a tricky business. It's often impossible to tell whether or not a premise really is intended. Even the author may not be sure. In relatively clear cases, like the last example, we should of course add the premise. The weakness will then be seen to lie either in suppressed evidence or in the falsehood of one of the premises. But if there is reasonable doubt about the author's intentions, the best thing to do is to add nothing. We'll then regard the weakness as due to simple fallacy.

Exactly where we draw the line is not vitally important. There will often be some confusion about whether to add a premise and hence about whether to attribute the argument's weakness to suppressed evidence, falsehood, or fallacy. But we should not let this confusion discourage us, for though we may be unsure about the location of the weakness, generally there will be no uncertainty about its existence. If the argument is genuinely weak, it will appear so any way we look at it. Hence for evaluating the argument's total strength, one standpoint is as good as another. I've suggested that we treat doubtful cases as fallacies, because that policy is simplest and because it prevents us from reading unintended thoughts into the author's words. But there is still room for disagreement about what counts as "doubtful." (You may well disagree with my judgment in some of the cases discussed in this chapter.) This doesn't really matter, so long as there is a fair and reasonable consensus on the argument's overall strength at the end. If everyone is careful, there usually is.

It's a different story, of course, if there are true premises whose addition produces a strong argument. In that case, if there is any reason to think that the author intended these premises, then the principle of charity demands that we add them.

This often happens with appeals to authority. Many authorities are genuinely reliable, so that adding the assumption of their reliability significantly strengthens the argument. This is especially true of established authorities in those professions—most notably science and journalism—whose workers are specifically trained to verify their professional pronouncements. These authorities are subject to constant scrutiny by their colleagues and by any member of the public who wishes to check their sources or observations. Those who lie or fake data do so at the risk of their careers. Therefore it is reasonable to assume that reputable scientists, journalists, and other professionals usually speak truthfully, at least in their professional pronouncements. Adding this assumption makes many appeals to authority good inductive inferences. In fact a great portion of our knowledge is obtained precisely by inferences of this sort. There simply is not time for us to verify everything for ourselves.

Still, the use of inductive appeals to authority requires extreme care. Like all inductive arguments, they are always vulnerable to contrary evidence. Even a generally reliable authority speaking within his or her field is suspect if there is evidence of pressure, bribery, collusion, vested or emotional interest, fraud, or negligence. And arguments from authority lose their force completely when equally qualified and trustworthy experts disagree. For then any argument based on the reliability of one side suppresses evidence of the reliability of the other, so that it's impossible to get a good argument either way. In such cases, the only way to determine the truth is to take the trouble to investigate the facts for yourself.

Arguments from authority also lose their force if the authority's pronouncements lie outside the field in which he or she is reliable. And when the "authority" is not especially noted for concern with the truth even within his or her field of expertise, we should be doubly suspicious. This is often the case, for example, in advertisements featuring endorsements by entertainers or sports figures. Such ads are apparently persuasive, for they stimulate demand. But their persuasiveness is due to the charm and charisma of personality, not to logic. There is seldom reason to believe that the celebrity knows or even cares much about the product in question. Probably in most cases the main thing he or she knows and cares about is a not inconsiderable royalty.

Sometimes it is not glamor, charisma, or authority that sways us, but popularity. We all exhibit some degree of what Nietzsche unflatteringly calls the "herd instinct." We feel more secure when we act and believe as others act and believe. Occasionally this tendency seems to manifest itself in argument, as in the following example:

> Human beings certainly have some sort of extrasensory perception. For belief in extrasensory powers occurs in many societies all around the world.

This kind of argument is called **appeal to popularity.** It has two forms, a factual one and a prescriptive one:

Factual Version	Prescriptive Version
Believing that p is popular	Doing x is popular
$\therefore$ p	$\therefore$ x is permissible (or should be done)

Both are generally fallacious. Our example is an instance of the factual version, in which the statement p is "Human beings have some sort of extrasensory perception."

The appeal of appeal to popularity comes from a feeling that large numbers of people all doing or believing the same thing are unlikely to be wrong. But logic does not support this feeling. Consider the possible worlds in which the premise of our sample argument is true. In each of these worlds either all the people who believe in ESP are wrong and the conclusion is false, or they all are right and the conclusion is true. (Since they all believe the same thing in the worlds in which the premise is true, it can't be that some are right and some are wrong, for this would be contradictory and hence not a coherently imaginable situation.) It is as easy to imagine them all wrong as all right; the proportion of imaginable situations in which they are right is no higher than that in which they are wrong. Thus the inference is clearly fallacious.

The similarity between this case and appeal to authority suggests augmenting the argument with the assumption that beliefs which occur in many societies around the world are seldom wrong. But this premise is dubious, even in the actual world. Instances of widespread false belief abound. Great portions of the earth's population have at one time or another affirmed that the earth is flat, that tomatoes are fatally poisonous, that heavy objects fall faster than light ones, that there is nothing wrong with slavery, that the stars are little bits of fire, that certain charms bring good luck, that there are innumerable anthropomorphic gods, that the sky is a solid inverted dome, that consciousness is located in the heart, that plants have souls . . . the list goes on and on. Science and civilization have managed to disabuse us of many of these false beliefs, but widespread falsehood remains. In fact in some ways it has become more insidious.

The effects of modern propaganda are a case in point. Hitler managed to delude much of the German nation into thinking that they were a superior race. We know the result of that. Simultaneously, Japan waged a war motivated in part by the preposterous proposition that its emperor was a god. Citizens of the Soviet Union today have a much distorted impression of western societies. And westerners often have surprisingly distorted conceptions of what is going on in the rest of the world. Many of these distortions are fueled by propaganda from a variety of sources, both governmental and private.

And propaganda is not the only source of popular falsehood. Rumor, superstition, religious and nationalistic fervor, bigotry, media manipulation, self-deception, and fear still create widespread false belief even apart from the direct persuasiveness of propaganda.

Thus assumptions about the reliability of large groups of people—particularly on obscure or controversial matters—are frequently false. Without such assumptions, appeals to popularity are certainly fallacious. And even with them they are seldom strong.

This is obviously the case with our sample argument. For the assumption needed to make it inductive—namely, that beliefs which occur in many societies around the world are usually correct—is questionable at best. In fact, when you think about it, this assumption seems so questionable that you might begin to wonder whether the author really intended it. Given this doubt, it seems to me reasonable to omit the premise and treat the inference as a simple fallacy. But it would also be reasonable to add it and then attribute the argument's weakness to the premise. In that case, we would also have to consider the question of suppressed evidence. Either way, the argument as a whole is extremely weak.

Appeals to popularity, like appeals to authority, are standard fare in advertising. We're all familiar with such phrases as "largest-selling model in its class." There are two implications here. The first is that since everyone else is buying this product, you should too. That's a prescriptive version of the fallacy. And the second is that since so many people buy the product, they must think it is good; hence it is good. That's a factual version. Neither version provides any rational assurance. The popularity of a product is often less an indicator of its quality than of the effectiveness of the advertising which promotes it.

Television ads which show throngs of vibrant citizens moved to ecstasy, song, and even riot by soft drinks or insurance policies also express a prescriptive appeal to popularity, but in pictures rather than words.

Sometimes in a conflict of adversaries appeal is made, not to the popularity of an action, but to the fact that "the other guy does it too." This sort of inference, which is heard everywhere from kindergarten playgrounds to the state departments of so-called advanced nations, is perhaps the most foolish and irrational form of appeal to the behavior of others. It is commonly called the fallacy of **two wrongs make a right,** or in Latin **tu quoque** (you too). The reasoning can be schematized as follows:

They are doing *x.*
∴ There is nothing wrong with us doing *x.*

In most instances, this is blatantly fallacious. Counterexamples abound. Moreover, if there were a hidden assumption, it would have to be something like "It's okay for us to do whatever they do," which is so obviously false that no one who was thinking clearly could seriously assume it. Almost always, therefore, inferences of this form are simple fallacies, committed thoughtlessly in the heat of emotion.

Sometimes the rejoinder "Well, they do it too!" is hardly even an argument but something more like a diversion to draw attention away from the speaker's own wrongdoing. Public officials charged with corruption frequently use this tactic. But often it serves both functions.

The lines separating the three types of fallacies discussed in this section are not sharply drawn. Where the speaker's adversaries are numerous, the two wrongs fallacy becomes indistinguishable from the prescriptive form of appeal to popularity. If the speaker cites a number of authorities, the line between appeal to authority and appeal to popularity can blur. And if the speaker's adversary is an authority, it might be difficult to decide between appeal to authority and two wrongs. Don't worry too much about these borderline cases. What is important is not how we label the case, but how well we understand it.

7.2 ARGUMENTS AGAINST THE PERSON

In the last section we saw how fallacy arises from our tendency to act and believe as others do. Another seemingly inexhaustible source of fallacy is prejudice against those whom we despise. Instead of irrationally regarding others as fountainheads of truth, we may irrationally regard them as diabolical purveyors of falsehood. Here's an example:

> The Marquis de Sade held that only by fulfilling our desires to their uttermost can we fully understand them. But de Sade was a depraved voluptuary, so vile that from his name the word "sadist" is derived.

The implied conclusion is that de Sade was wrong; it is not true that only by fulfilling our desires to their uttermost can we fully understand them. The general structure of the argument is this:

Person x affirms that p

Person x has negative characteristic F

∴ Not-p

In our example, the person x is de Sade, the statement p is "Only by fulfilling our desires to their uttermost can we fully understand them," and the negative characteristic F is the property of being a vile and depraved voluptuary.

Arguments of this form are called **arguments against the person,** or more traditionally, arguments **ad hominem** (Latin for "to the man"). Unless the negative characteristics mentioned in the argument include a propensity to speak falsely on the matters mentioned in p, the inference is generally fallacious. We can readily imagine that the things said here about de Sade are true (in fact, they are) but that he is right nevertheless. There is no logical connection between moral, social, political, or personal depravity and the utterance of falsehoods. (We can even imagine worlds in which the most repugnant people are the most truthful.)

Arguments against the person are tempting because we are loath to attribute knowledge or honesty to those whom we despise. But this is a purely irrational prejudice. Even habitual liars tell the truth most of the time. Otherwise, it would be too easy to see through their deceptions. All we'd have to do is translate all their negative statements into positive ones and all their positive statements into negative ones, and we'd generally have the truth. But things are never that easy. Therefore, adding a premise that says:

Any person with negative characteristic *F* usually speaks falsely.

will not strengthen the argument, because it is almost certainly false. Moreover, its falsehood is so obvious that it is unlikely that any author would intend it to be taken for granted. Therefore, most arguments against the person are simply fallacies. The de Sade argument is no exception.

The negative characteristics mentioned in arguments against the person may be of two types. They may constitute either a direct attack on the person, as in the de Sade example, or an indirect insinuation that the person is prejudiced by special circumstances. In the first case we have what is known as an **abusive ad hominem.** In the second case, it is said to be a **circumstantial ad hominem.** Here is an example of this second type:

I always shudder when I hear demands by this country's minorities for increased government spending for the poor. You can tell that something is wrong with these demands as soon as you consider where the money will go—right into the hands of those who are crying the loudest for it.

In effect, the inference is this:

This country's minorities are demanding increased spending for the poor.

These people would be enriched by this spending.

∴ Their demands are wrong.

The "person" *x* in this case is the minority groups. The statement *p* is that the government ought to increase spending for the poor. And the "negative characteristic" *F* is the enrichment of these groups. The argument is not an attack on the minority groups *per se*, but an insinuation that their circumstance of potential gain refutes what they have to say about the matter. If there is a hidden assumption here, it is that:

People who support an action from which they will benefit are usually wrong in their support.

As with previous examples, this assumption is so obviously wrong that it is difficult to believe that the author really intended it. While it is true that people often seek undeserved gain, it is hardly true that their demands are *usually* wrong. Legitimate demands are probably as common as illegitimate ones. We may rightfully be sceptical of demands made by people who stand to benefit from their fulfillment, and we certainly should scrutinize such demands carefully. But it is illogical to conclude automatically that they are wrong. Circumstantial ad hominems, like abusive ones, are generally fallacious.

7.3   THE AESTHETIC FALLACY

Just as there is no logical connection between what others say or believe and the truth, so too there is no logical connection between what we ourselves feel or believe and the truth. We are fallible. Yet the following sort of reasoning is common:

The Bears are going to win tomorrow. I can just feel it!

This argument has the form:

I feel that p
∴ p

This is very similar to an appeal to authority without a hidden premise and tends to be fallacious for essentially the same reason. We can generally imagine at least as many ways in which what we feel could be wrong as in which it could be right. We'll call this sort of inference the **aesthetic fallacy,** from the Greek word *aisthesis*, which means "feeling" or "perception."

Such inferences are often made with some implicit assumption about the reliability of the author's feelings, perhaps something like:

My feelings about such matters are usually reliable.

Adding the assumption makes the inference inductive but often fails to strengthen the argument, because in many cases the assumption is false.

Human feelings are often totally *un*reliable. Who does not, for example, know at least one couple who at first felt with utmost sincerity that their love would last forever, but wound up shortly thereafter on the divorce docket? Or to take a different example, consider the fact that show business is haunted by thousands of inveterate failures who wake up every day thinking, "Today I'll get my big break." Curiously, we all seem to think that *our* feelings are different. *Our* feelings are so clear, so right. We are not blind fools, like these others. But that, precisely, is the seduction of the aesthetic fallacy and the reason why it snares its victims again and again.

Conviction, intensity, passion—none of these are touchstones of truth. Often, in fact, our convictions are strongest where our evidence is thinnest. Perhaps it is even a law of psychology: when we want to believe something but suspect it to be false, we suppress our suspicion and fill ourselves with emotion instead. Under these conditions feeling tends to vary in inverse proportion to truth.

Sometimes, however, our feelings are reliable indicators of truth. People who get migraine headaches, for example, can often sense their imminence. Such a person may reason as follows:

I feel that I'm about to get a migraine.

∴ I'm about to get one.

Here the implicit premise, "My feelings about such matters are usually reliable," may well be true. And if so, this is a perfectly good inductive argument—provided, of course, that no contrary evidence has been suppressed.

The aesthetic fallacy has a number of intriguing relatives. Consider this one, for example:

I see Ophelia practicing karate.

∴ Ophelia is practicing karate.

This is like the previous cases, except that instead of "feel," the argument says "see." How good is the reasoning? Well, the following case seems to be a counterexample: suppose the speaker is hallucinating. Then it could be true that he or she sees Ophelia practicing karate and yet that Ophelia is doing nothing of the sort. Ophelia may not even exist.

But is this an accurate description of the case? If the speaker was hallucinating, then in one sense it seems wrong to say that he or she was seeing the event. Perhaps this isn't a counterexample after all; perhaps it's a possible situation in which both premise and conclusion are false.

Our puzzlement here can be reduced to a single question: if someone hallucinates or misperceives a scene, does he or she truly see it? If so, then we do have a counterexample and the inference is invalid. If not, then seeing requires the truth of what is seen, and so the inference is valid.

This is a problem which in one guise or another has troubled philosophers for a long time. One plausible solution is that our puzzlement arises from a verbal ambiguity; the word "see" has two meanings. On the first, it is what is called a **success verb.** On this meaning, something counts as an act of seeing only if it successfully reveals the truth. Hallucinations and other misperceptions, then, are not really seeing but only "seeming to see." If this is the meaning of the word "see" in the argument, then the inference is deductive. If the speaker actually saw Ophelia practicing karate, then that is what Ophelia must have been doing. But there is apparently another meaning of "see" in which we can truly be said to see what we hallucinate or misperceive. This, perhaps, is the sense of "see" we use when we say, "I saw my dead grandfather last night in a dream." Here seeing is compatible with falsehood. My dead grandfather wasn't really there. So in this sense of "see" our sample inference is invalid. It can be true that I see Ophelia practicing karate and yet false that she's doing so.

Accordingly, whether the argument is valid or not depends on which meaning of "see" is intended. If "see" is meant as a success verb, it is valid. We'd want to verify, however, that the speaker really was seeing (i.e., that the premise was true). If "see" is not meant as a success verb, the argument is invalid, and we'll need to consider the possibility of an implicit premise. (See Section 7.6 for a discussion of how to deal with multiplicity of meaning in evaluating arguments.)

There are many expressions which, like "see," can be used both as success verbs and otherwise. These include "hear," "taste," "smell," "apprehend," "sense," "perceive," and sometimes even "feel" (especially in reference to the sense of touch). We need to be very cautious in evaluating arguments containing these terms.

"Feel," when predicated on emotions or convictions, as in the first example of this section, is generally not a success verb. Neither are such terms as "believe," "think," "hope," "suppose," "guess," and so on. One can do all these things falsely. All of them can occur in fallacies similar to the aesthetic fallacy.

One term, however, which is invariably a success verb is "know." To know means to succeed in apprehending the truth. One cannot know falsely. Therefore, all inferences of the following form are valid:

Person x knows that p

∴ p

But such inferences are of little practical value, since the premise is usually more doubtful and difficult to prove than the conclusion. The same is true of inferences containing the other success verbs mentioned above.

Inferences based on perception are fundamental to most of our knowledge—maybe to all of it. The sights, sounds, and tactile sensations I feel at this moment, for example, are what allow me to conclude correctly (I hope) that I am typing on a typewriter. But the nature of these inferences is not thoroughly understood, and their reliability has been a source of philosophical controversy for centuries. These are deep issues—too deep, I'm afraid, to fathom here.

7.4 THE ARGUMENT FROM IGNORANCE

One of the first points made in Chapter 1 was that refuting an argument does not show its conclusion to be false. All it shows is that this particular argument does not prove the conclusion. Concerning the conclusion itself, it leaves us none the wiser. The same is true even if we refute all known arguments for the conclusion. So long as there is no independent reason for thinking the conclusion false, its truth or falsity remains unknown. Thus, at least so long as their conclusions are not inherently probable, the following patterns of reasoning are fallacious:

> There is no proof that p There is no proof that not-p
> ∴ Not-p ∴ p

These are the two forms of the **argument from ignorance.** In each case we assume our ignorance of a certain statement and then conclude that its denial must be true. I discussed an example of the second form at the beginning of Section 4.2:

> There is no proof that the Senator didn't take the money.
> ∴ She took it.

This is clearly fallacious. Among all the imaginable situations in which the premise is true, the conclusion is true in only a small proportion.

Instances of the first form, however, are often more problematic. Notice that I said that the two forms are fallacious *so long as their conclusions are not inherently probable.* This qualification is necessary because as I noted in Section 6.3, an inherently probable conclusion can make an argument inductive, regardless of the relevance of the premises. I also noted that negative statements tend to be inherently probable. Since arguments of the first form have negative conclusions, it follows that they tend to be inductive—not because of any support which the premise gives to the conclusion, but because of the conclusion's inherent probability. This makes them bad arguments in a practical sense, since the premise sheds no new light on the conclusion. Moreover, in practice they are frequently undercut by contrary evidence. But still they are often inductive. Here's an example:

> Even though scientists have been investigating the matter for well over a century, no one has ever traced an unbroken line of ancestry from

man back to his allegedly apelike forebears. Therefore such a line of ancestry does not exist.

In this example the statement *p* is "There exists an unbroken line of ancestry from man back to his allegedly apelike forebears." The conclusion, which is the denial of this statement, is inherently probable. Among all the worlds we can imagine, only a small proportion are worlds in which we descended directly from simian ancestors. Even among the worlds in which we exist, there are millions of other conceivable sources of our origin. Likewise, among possible worlds in which the premise is true—that is, in which science, after over a century of investigation, has failed to trace such a line of descent—the majority are worlds in which no such line of descent exists. So the argument is inductive, though only because of the inherent probability of the conclusion. But as you can see, it is not very illuminating. Since the premise makes no significant contribution to the probability of the conclusion, it adds virtually nothing to the grounds we already have for believing the conclusion—namely, its inherent probability.

Moreover, important contrary evidence is suppressed. The fossil record, while it does not preserve an unbroken line of descent, does reveal portions of such a line and thus strongly suggests its existence. Similar evolutionary developments have been observed in other living creatures. Furthermore, it is unrealistic to expect that we could trace our ancestry completely. Most of us can't trace our family trees much past great-grandparents. Given this suppressed evidence (which I've merely outlined; we'd need an anthropologist to fill in the details), it is quite probable that an unbroken line of descent does exist, despite our inability to trace it completely. So in spite of its inductiveness, the argument is weak, because it violates the requirement of total evidence.

Not only the argument from ignorance, but also the other forms discussed in this chapter, may become inductive or even deductive if their conclusions are inherently probable or logically necessary. (If this still puzzles you, review sections 5.5 and 6.3.) Thus it is important to treat each case individually and not to assume that all arguments of any of these forms are fallacious.

7.5   FALLACIES OF COMPOSITION AND DIVISION

Two fallacies common in reasoning about parts and wholes are the fallacies of composition and division. In a certain sense, each is the converse of the other. The fallacy of composition may occur when we reason that a property belonging to the parts is possessed by the whole. And the fallacy of division may occur when we reason that a property belonging to the whole is also possessed by the parts. Each form has two versions, which may be schematized as follows:

FALLACY OF COMPOSITION

Particular Version	*General Version*
y has property F y is a part of x ∴ x has property F	The parts of x have property F ∴ x has property F

FALLACY OF DIVISION

Particular Version	*General Version*
x has property F y is a part of x ∴ y has property F	x has property F ∴ The parts of x have property F

Many instances of these forms are just silly, like the following example of the general version of the fallacy of composition:

> The atoms which comprise this bull elephant are so small they can't be seen.
> ∴ This bull elephant is so small it can't be seen.

In this case, the object x is a bull elephant, the parts are its atoms, and the property F is the property of being so small as to be invisible. Anyone who argues this way about bull elephants is a candidate for a rude awakening.

The following example of the particular version of the fallacy of division is equally preposterous:

> *Homo sapiens* has flourished on the earth for hundreds of thousands of years.
> Jason McBee, age $2\frac{1}{2}$, is a member of *Homo sapiens*.
> ∴ Jason McBee, age $2\frac{1}{2}$, has flourished on the earth for hundreds of thousands of years.

Here the object y is Jason McBee, age $2\frac{1}{2}$. The whole, x, is the species *Homo sapiens*. And the property F is the property of flourishing on the earth for hundreds of thousands of years. I'm sure that both Jason and his parents would be puzzled by the conclusion. It is easy to construct equally ridiculous examples of the other forms of this fallacy.

There are, however, more subtle cases. Here's an example of the general version of the fallacy of composition that's a classic. It was committed by the ancient Greek philosopher Aristotle, who being one of the founders of logic, should have known better:

> Seeing that eye and hand and foot and every one of our members has some obvious function, must we not believe that in like manner a human being has a function over and above these particular functions?

More simply, the idea is that since a person's parts have the property of serving some function, the whole person must have this property as well. But it's easy to imagine situations in which the parts of a person all have some particular function and yet the person as a whole has either no function or so many that it doesn't make sense to speak of *the* function of that person. Though less absurd than the previous examples, this one is no less fallacious.

Our next example is also rather subtle. It's a modern instance of the general version of the fallacy of division:

> Smithson Company Insurance. With over 75 years experience in helping people. So our agents can serve you better.

The intent of this inference is cloudy, but in part it seems to be that since the whole company has 75 years of experience in helping people, the agents do too—or at least that they share to some degree in the company's experience. This may be true. Perhaps the company's experience is passed on to agents through an excellent training program. But it doesn't follow rationally. We can imagine that the premises are true and yet that the agents are all incompetents who were just hired yesterday. Or they might have been with the company for a long time and still not have benefited from its experience. There are many kinds of counterexamples.

The argument could perhaps be salvaged by adding the assumption that the more experience a company has, the better able its agents are to serve the public. But that hardly seems true. (Very good agents often found new companies, and old, inefficient agents may linger in experienced companies.) We may therefore doubt that the author seriously intended to assert it. I'm inclined to regard this argument as just plain old sloppy reasoning—a simple fallacy.

There are other problems with this argument as well. For one thing, it is ungrammatical. The first two "sentences" are merely fragments. Such fragments are fashionable in advertising and broadcasting. They are supposed to convey an impression of confident frankness—and they do, but often at the expense of clear thought.

Another problem is the use of the term "better" in the conclusion. Better than what? A blithering cretin? A potato? The word "better" used without mention of a comparison class is virtually meaningless. Of course, what is intended here is probably something more like "better than other agents" or "better than they could if they were working for less experienced companies." But that is still intolerably vague. What other agents? Which companies? The argument gives us no hint. Thus even if there were no other problems with this inference, its vagueness alone would threaten its rationality. We'll return to this problem in Section 7.7.

7.6 FALLACIES OF AMBIGUITY

Some words have two or more meanings; that is, they are **ambiguous.** When these words occur in an argument, they splinter it into an array of arguments. As you might suspect, evaluation then becomes quite tricky. Let's begin with a simple and artificial example:

> Only man creates art.
> No woman is a man.
> ∴ No woman creates art.

Is this argument valid or not? It depends on what is meant by "man." "Man" can mean either "human" or "adult male human." Since this word occurs twice in the argument, any one of four arguments could be intended here:

1 Only humans create art.
   No woman is human.
   ∴ No woman creates art.

2 Only adult male humans create art.
   No woman is an adult male human.
   ∴ No woman creates art.

3 Only humans create art.
   No woman is an adult male human.
   ∴ No woman creates art.

4 Only adult male humans create art.
   No woman is human.
   ∴ No woman creates art.

In the first two, the meaning of "man" is interpreted consistently. That is, it means the same thing in both occurrences. In the second two, its meaning shifts as we move from the first premise to the second. The first two and the fourth are valid. The third is fallacious. But only the third has the true premises. So none of them are sound.

How can we evaluate this mess? As always, we need to respect the author's intentions. If one of the arguments were sound, the charitable thing would be to regard that as the author's intention. But nothing is sound here. Notice, however, that versions 1, 2, and 4 all contain premises so blatantly false that no sane person would assert them, except in jest. Hence, unless the author is joking (which in this case is a real possibility), 3 is most likely the intended meaning. Since 3 is fallacious, we should evaluate the argument as a fallacy.

This type of fallacy is called a **fallacy of equivocation.** It occurs when an argument contains an ambiguous word or phrase whose intended meaning shifts from one occurrence to another. Often such an argument has an inductive or deductive form, which makes it appear rational; and in fact it would be rational if the ambiguous word were interpreted consistently. But the shift in meaning disrupts the formal relations among premises and conclusion, and fallacy is the result. Because of their deceptive appearance, fallacies of equivocation readily beguile unwary listeners who fail to sense the meaning shift. This problem is compounded by the fact that the argument has unintended interpretations, as well as the intended one, and all these may be confused in the listener's mind. These complexities could easily lead us to despair. But a little patience and some care in making distinctions can clear the matter up completely.

There are several things to keep in mind. First, any argument containing an ambiguous word will have more than one interpretation. Exactly how many depends on the number of occurrences of the word and the number of meanings it has. Probably only one of these is the intended interpretation, and that interpretation is the one we wish to evaluate. This interpretation may be consistent—that is, the ambiguous word's meaning might not shift at all—in which case the argument may be rational and perhaps even sound, despite the ambiguity. But if there is a shift in meaning, the resulting fallacy is a fallacy of equivocation.

We discover the intended interpretation in the same way that we discover authors' intentions generally—by using all the clues available to us, both in the wording of the argument and in our general knowledge of the author. Charity plays a role, too. If one interpretation is significantly stronger than the others, then unless we have reason to doubt that the author intended it, we should assume that it is the intended interpretation. If we simply can't make out the author's intention at all, then the only thing to do is evaluate all the interpretations. If they are all extremely weak, as in the last example, then even without knowing what the author meant, we will have successfully refuted the argument.

In diagraming an argument containing an ambiguity, it is best to explain the ambiguity in a brief note next to the diagram. With its statements numbered consecutively, our previous argument would be diagramed as follows:

$$\frac{① + ②}{↓ \quad F}$$
$$③$$

Fallacy of equivocation. Premises are true, but "man" means "human" in ① and "adult male human" in ②. All other interpretations have false premises and seem highly implausible.

Several diagrams and notes may be required if you can't decide which interpretation is intended.

Not all equivocations are as silly as the last one. The next example contains a more subtle equivocation:

> It was stupid. We were fighting for Freedom, but Freedom was just a word.

The conclusion here is that "it"—the fighting, presumably—was stupid. This conclusion is derived by means of an implicit assumption:

> Fighting for words is stupid.

Thus, the argument as a whole is:

> We were fighting for freedom.
> Freedom was just a word.
> Fighting for words is stupid.
> ∴ The fighting was stupid.

The ambiguity lies in the word "freedom," which here could mean one of two things: liberty (i.e., absence of political oppression) or the English word spelled f-r-e-e-d-o-m, which designates the condition. Technically speaking, if it has this second meaning, it should be set off by quotation marks, since that is the correct way to designate the word, as opposed to the political condition. But many people ignore this convention, a practice which results in ambiguities. These are called **use-mention ambiguities,** because they confuse talking with a word (using it) with talking about it (mentioning it). The word "freedom" in our example is used if it designates liberty, but only mentioned if it designates itself. In the latter case it should be surrounded by quotation marks. This ambiguity results in four possible interpretations of the argument:

1. We were fighting for the political condition of liberty.
The political condition of liberty was just a word.
Fighting for words is stupid.
∴ The fighting was stupid.

2. We were fighting for the word "freedom."
The word "freedom" was just a word.
Fighting for words is stupid.
∴ The fighting was stupid.

3. We were fighting for the political condition of liberty.
The word "freedom" was just a word.
Fighting for words was stupid.
∴ The fighting was stupid.

4. We were fighting for the word "freedom."
The political condition of liberty was just a word.
Fighting for words was stupid.
∴ The fighting was stupid.

Only the first two are valid; 3 and 4 are fallacious. We can rule out 1 and 4 as intended interpretations, because each contains the preposterously false assertion "The political condition of liberty was just a word." Taken literally, this would imply, for example, that the only difference between a political prisoner and a person living free is that the latter somehow possesses the English word spelled f-r-e-e-d-o-m. Surely the author didn't intend to say that. This leaves interpretations 2 and 3. Interpretation 2 is also unlikely to be intended because it contains the equally outlandish assertion "We were fighting for the word 'freedom'." It's hard to imagine what that could even mean. The only version whose premises make any literal sense at all is 3. But 3 contains a meaning shift which renders it fallacious. So it seems best to regard this inference as a fallacy of equivocation.

It should be noted, however, that this argument has a level of metaphorical meaning which our analysis did not capture. In saying that freedom was just a word, the author probably meant to suggest that the goal of the fighting, which had been labeled as "freedom," was so ill-defined that all one could grasp concretely was the label, the word itself. If so, the author was talking about neither freedom nor "freedom," but some vacuous idea dreamed up, perhaps, in the minds of the generals or politicians. But even if this is so, what the author says is still literally false. This vacuous idea is not itself a word. The argument still is not sound.

We might push this analysis further in the hope of squeezing a metaphorical truth from the argument. But we've gone far enough already. The logic of metaphor is a topic beyond the scope of this book. What I wanted you to see was only that there is no literal way in which the argument can soundly establish its conclusion. Whether it succeeds as a metaphor, I'll leave to you to judge.

Use-mention ambiguity can be very perplexing. You should suspect it whenever anyone's inferences move from words to things or vice versa. Almost always it spawns fallacy.

A different sort of ambiguity is involved in that delightful old riddle about the tree falling in the forest when no one is there to hear. Does it make a sound or not? Well, of course, that depends on what you mean by "sound." "Sound" can mean either a certain compressive vibration of the air (this is the way physicists use the term) or an auditory sensation. Auditory sensations are usually caused by physical sound, but not always. When we have a ringing in our ears or when we hear voices in a dream, we have auditory sensations caused, not by vibrations of the air, but by the internal condition of our nervous system. Physical sound can be present without a hearer (it is, after all, nothing but the motions of air molecules). But auditory sensation cannot. Thus in the absence of a hearer, the falling tree makes only a physical sound, not an auditory sensation. In one sense it makes a sound. In the other it does not.

This ambiguity can be used to construct a paradoxical (i.e., puzzling) argument, as follows:

1 A tree falling in a forest with no one there to hear causes compressive vibrations of the air.

2 These vibrations are sounds.

∴ 3   A tree falling in a forest with no one there to hear makes sounds. 1,2

∴ 4 If no one is present to hear, there can be no sound.

∴ 5 A tree falling in a forest with no one there to hear makes no sound. 4

∴ 6 A tree falling in a forest with no one there to hear both does and does not make sounds. 3,5

The premises all seem true. The reasoning looks deductive. And yet the conclusion is a contradiction! A sound argument ending in a contradiction? This is an impossibility indeed!

But of course you've seen through my ruse. The premises *are* all true as I have intended them. "Sound" means "physical sound" in 2 and 3, and "auditory sensation" in 4 and 5. The first two inferences are deductive. But there is a shift in meaning as we move from 3 and 5 to 6. This inference only appears deductive. Actually, it is a fallacy of equivocation. I don't know which meaning I intended "sound" to have in 6. But it doesn't matter. This contradiction in no way follows from the intended premises.

Another interesting sort of ambiguity is the ambiguity of "is." This innocuous-seeming little word can mean either "is identical with," as in the sentence "St. Nicholas is Santa Claus," or "has the property of being," as in the sentence "The sky is blue." The first sense of "is" is called the **"is" of identity.** The second is called the **"is" of predication.** Usually you can tell them apart by asking the question, Could I replace "is" with the phrase "is identical with" without changing the meaning? If the answer is yes, then it's the "is" of identity. If it's no, then it's the "is" of predication.

Notice that we couldn't replace the "is" in "The sky is blue" with "is identical with." The sky is not identical with blue. That hardly makes sense. Rather, the sky has the property of being blue.

Statements consisting of two terms linked by the "is" of identity are called **identity statements.** Identity statements play a special role in logic. Given an identity statement (say, "The GOP is the Republican Party"), if either of the two terms (in this case, "the GOP" and "the Republican Party") occurs in another statement, we may validly substitute the other term for it. For example:

The GOP is likely to make substantial gains in November.

The GOP is the Republican Party.

∴ The Republican Party is likely to make substantial gains in November.

is a valid inference. The idea governing such inferences is called the **principle of substitutivity of identity,** or simply **identity substitution.** You are already familiar with it in mathematics, where the "is" of identity is symbolized by the equals sign. But it applies in other contexts as well. Inferences employing identity substitution are always valid. (It has been argued that some inferences concerning possibility or mental attitudes are exceptions, but this is a technical controversy which will not concern us here.)

It is, however, a clear fallacy to substitute terms joined by the "is" of predication. For example:

> My new suit is blue.
> The sky is blue.
> ∴ My new suit is the sky.

Here the terms "the sky" and "blue" are linked by the "is" of predication, but when we replace "blue" in the first premise by "the sky," as if they designated identicals, we get a fallacious inference. The intent here seems to be to interpret "is" as the "is" of predication in the premises and the "is" of identity in the conclusion. (No other interpretation makes much sense.) But the fallacy is caused not so much by this meaning shift as by the application of identity substitution to premises which do not really assert an identity. We'll count this as an equivocation, though it has a degree of complexity not exhibited by the equivocations discussed earlier.

Some ambiguities arise, not because a particular word has two meanings, but because of the way a sentence is constructed. These ambiguities are called **amphibolies.** One of the most frequent sources of amphiboly is the **dangling modifier,** a phrase whose position in the sentence makes its referent unclear. Here's an example:

> Roasted to a succulent medium rare, we all enjoyed the delicious steaks.

Exactly what, or whom, was roasted here? The placement of the modifier, "roasted to a succulent medium rare," allows it to be interpreted as referring either to the steaks or to the diners. This amphiboly could have been avoided by proper placement of the modifier:

> We all enjoyed the steaks, which were roasted to a succulent medium rare.

Dangling modifiers and other kinds of amphiboly sometimes find their way into arguments, and when they do fallacy is often the result.

Bertrand Russell relates an amusing example. Upon seeing a friend's yacht, a man remarked, "I thought your yacht was bigger than it is." "Only an idiot would think something is bigger than it is," replied the owner, who was apparently somewhat insulted. What the owner was implying, of course, was this:

> You thought my yacht was bigger than it is.
> Only an idiot would think something is bigger than it is.
> ∴ You are an idiot.

Fortunately for the owner's friend, this reasoning is marred by amphiboly. The sentence "You thought my yacht was bigger than it is" has two meanings:

> 1 The size you thought my yacht to be is greater than its actual size.
> 2 You thought my yacht's actual size is greater than its actual size.

The second premise is similarly amphibolous. Note that in both cases the duality of meaning does not stem from any ambiguous word. It is, rather, a result of the sentence structure as a whole. Moreover, neither sentence contains a dangling modifier. The amphiboly here is of a different sort entirely. The only interpretation which makes the premises true is this one:

> The size you thought my yacht to be is greater than its actual size.
> Only an idiot would think that a thing's actual size is greater than its actual size.
> ∴ You are an idiot.

This is probably the intended interpretation. But it is fallacious, as you can readily see, because of the shift in meaning from the first premise to the second. (Note that with meaning 2 of the first premise it would be deductive.) It is therefore an example of the **fallacy of amphiboly.** The fallacy of amphiboly differs from the fallacy of equivocation in that the meaning shift occurs at the level of sentences rather than in a single word or phrase.

But even if this is not the intended interpretation of the argument— and a case could be made, I suppose, for regarding 2 as the intended interpretation of the first premise—we can be certain that the argument is unsound, because all other interpretations have false premises. You can verify this for yourself.

Ambiguity can result not only from ambiguous words and sentence structure, but also from the stress we place on certain expressions in pronouncing them. As simple a phrase as "Don't hurt me!" can take on various shades of meaning, depending on which word we emphasize. Emphasis on "don't" seems to presuppose that the offending party has already been warned not to hurt the speaker. Emphasis on "hurt" suggests an invitation to do something to the speaker, but something not involving pain. And emphasis on "me" carries implicit approval of hurting someone else. Such shifts in emphasis can generate fallacies, particularly in spoken argument. Imagine, for example, the following conversation:

Olaf: *"Don't* hurt me!"
Ophelia: "Okay, then I'll hurt Fuzzball."

Here Olaf has placed the emphasis on "don't," which suggests that he has already warned Ophelia not to hurt him. But then Ophelia interprets his command "Don't hurt me!" as if the emphasis were on "me," implying permission to hurt something else, which is not at all what he intended. Ophelia's fallacious reasoning, then, is something like this:

Olaf says, "Don't hurt me!"
∴ He is giving me permission to hurt something else.
∴ It's okay for me to hurt something else.
∴ It's okay for me to hurt Fuzzball.

The first inference is a **fallacy of accent** if Ophelia intends to put the emphasis on "don't," which is what Olaf intended. However, if Ophelia intends to put the emphasis on "me," then the first premise does in a peculiar sense imply the second, but it is false. Olaf didn't say it that way. The second inference is a fallacious appeal to authority. And the third is a fallacy for which we have no name. Ophelia has reasoned pretty carelessly here!

I said that if Ophelia did intend the emphasis to be on "me" in the first premise, then *in a peculiar sense* the first premise would imply the second. This is not a logical implication, however. We can easily imagine the first premise true and the second false. It is, rather, just something suggested by the tone of the words. Ordinary conversation carries many such suggestions, but their study is more a matter of linguistics than of logic. Since it is they which are usually responsible for fallacies of accent, we'll consider these fallacies no further.

7.7 FALLACIES OF VAGUENESS

Ambiguity must be carefully distinguished from **vagueness.** While ambiguity is the possession of two or more distinct meanings, vagueness is the possession of a meaning which is indistinct. Vague expressions convey some hint of an idea, but no more, so that we are not quite sure what has been said.

One example of this, which came up at the end of Section 7.5, was the use of comparative terms like "better" without mention of a comparison class. Comparatives used in this way are very common sources of vagueness, particularly in advertising. Phrases like the following are all too familiar:

Faster, longer lasting relief

More value for your money

For skin that looks and feels *younger*

Working *harder* to serve you *better*

Smoother, silkier hair

The comparatives are italicized. There is nothing inherently vague about comparatives. The statement "Our product gives faster, longer-lasting relief than any other brand" is, for example, quite clear and meaningful. But if the phrase "than any other brand" is omitted, then it says practically nothing. In many ads, such phrases are deliberately omitted. The result may be deception and fallacy. Suppose, for example, that an advertisement says:

You get more for less at Dollars and Sense.

What the ad writers want you to think, of course, is that you can get more for less at Dollars and Sense than at any other store. But that is not what they said. Even if you could pay less elsewhere, you couldn't accuse Dollars and Sense of false advertising. For what they said is not false; it's so vague that it's virtually meaningless.

Advertisements often imply the unstated conclusion that you should patronize the business or buy the product advertised. The slogan above suggests the following argument:

You get more for less at Dollars and Sense.

You should shop where you get the best value for your money.

∴ You should shop at Dollars and Sense.

The second premise, which like the conclusion is implicit, is relatively unobjectionable. But given the vagueness of the first premise, the conclusion does not follow. There are many possible worlds in which the second premise is true and in which the first is true as well—in the sense, say, that you get more for less at Dollars and Sense *than at the most expensive stores*—but in which the conclusion is false. Inferences like this one which are fallacious because of vagueness are called **fallacies of vagueness.** They are quite common and result in some deplorably sloppy thinking.

Comparatives are not the only sources of vagueness. One particularly guilty expression is the small, unobtrusive phase "up to." This phrase passes through the mind so quickly that it escapes practically everyone's attention.

But it can completely nullify an otherwise logical inference. There is, for example, a certain nasal spray which, claims the manufacturer, "lasts up to 12 full hours." If from this claim you draw the conclusion that by using it you will get 12 hours of relief, you have committed a fallacy. "Up to 12 hours" means "12 hours or less." It's compatible with what the manufacturer says that the relief, at least in some cases, lasts only a few minutes. Moreover, it makes no difference that the manufacturer describes these as "full" hours. That's only to throw you further off the track. Similarly, it would be naive to infer that you are going to realize great savings at a sale where "you can save up to 50 percent." Some items may be reduced that much, but most probably aren't.

Astrological forecasts are a gold mine of vagueness. In fact, that's precisely why they seem so often to fit the facts. For example, if your horoscope for a certain day says, "Mercury creates positive romantic influences this evening," it has said virtually nothing. Even if you spend a lousy, lonely evening in front of the television, the astrologer could still say, "well, the *influences* were there." Hence to reason like this:

Mercury creates positive romantic influences this evening.

∴ My evening will be romantic.

is to commit a fallacy. Even if the premise were true, what it says is so vague that nothing substantial follows with any degree of probability. And of course there's still the question of the truth of the premise.

Plural common nouns, like "people," "kids," "rocks," and "railroad tracks," are frequent sources of vagueness, especially when standing alone as the subject or direct object of a sentence. Consider, for example, the sentence, "People like Mr. Merryweather." Does it mean that *all* people like Mr. Merryweather? That *most* do? That only *some* do? It's really indeterminate. Thus it would be fallacious to argue, for example, as follows:

People like Mr. Merryweather.

Mrs. Merryweather is a person.

∴ Mrs. Merryweather likes Mr. Merryweather.

The term "people" is so vague that the inference is not even inductive.

Fallacies of vagueness can result from vagueness in the conclusion as well as in the premises. Consider this example:

The greatness of Karl Marx is evidenced by his decisive influence on some of the most powerful leaders of our century—Lenin, Stalin, and Mao Zedong.

The inference, of course, is this:

> Karl Marx decisively influenced some of the most powerful leaders of our century—Lenin, Stalin, and Mao Zedong.
> ∴ Karl Marx was great.

The main problem here is the vagueness of the term "great." The concept of greatness is so unclear that it is simply indeterminate whether having a decisive influence on powerful leaders qualifies even as probable evidence of greatness. (And the notion of "decisive influence" itself compounds the vagueness.) Thus we can only class this inference as a fallacy.

Though fallacies of vagueness are quite common, it is a serious mistake to think that every argument containing a vague expression is fallacious. A fallacy of vagueness occurs only when the vagueness of an expression directly affects the strength of the inference. Even the most extraordinarily vague terms can occur in perfectly valid arguments:

> If Olaf tends to be sort of nasty, then he isn't really very nice.
> Olaf tends to be sort of nasty.
> ∴ He isn't really very nice.

Whatever is meant by these premises (and it's certainly nothing clear), if the premises are true, the conclusion must be true as well.

So use your judgment carefully in identifying fallacies of vagueness. If you can pinpoint a specific vague expression or set of expressions which is obviously responsible for an inference's irrationality, then treat the inference as a fallacy of vagueness. But use this label with caution.

7.8   SLIPPERY-SLOPE FALLACIES

Nearly every word is vague to some extent. Consider, for example, the adjective "bald." We count a person as bald if he or she has no hair or just a little hair around the edges, and as not bald if he or she has a full head of hair. But what about people in between? At what point do we draw the line? The term is not defined sharply enough to decide. The fact is that we don't draw a line. There is a fringe of indeterminacy between baldness and non-baldness, and many people fit somewhere in this fringe. Such people are **borderline cases** of baldness. They are neither clearly bald nor clearly not bald. The vaguer a term is, the more borderline cases it has.

In much of our reasoning, this fringe of indeterminacy plays no role. Thus, for example, though it contains the vague term "bald," the following inference is perfectly valid:

All tadpoles are bald.

No gorilla is bald.

∴ No gorilla is a tadpole.

The cases mentioned here are all clear-cut cases of baldness or nonbaldness. No borderline cases enter into the reasoning.

But occasionally borderline cases are exploited to produce irrational confusion. One way of doing this is illustrated in the following example:

> A man without any hair or only a small amount of hair around the edges is certainly bald. Now if this man had just one more hair, he'd still be bald, since one hair would make so little difference. The same is true if he had another, and another still, and so on. Therefore, no matter how much hair a man has, he's still bald.

The argument is, of course, fallacious, but the fallacy is not easy to pin down. The author has begun with a typical case of baldness and argued that it is not significantly different from a slightly less typical case, and that this in turn is not significantly different from a still less typical case, and so on, until we pass into the fringe of indeterminacy and ultimately beyond into typical cases of nonbaldness. What makes the fallacy difficult to pinpoint is that there is no precise point at which we can say, "Enough! You've just passed out of the realm of baldness," for the borders of the realm of baldness are indistinct. The author is exploiting this indistinctness, hoping that we'll slide right through it into the region of men who are definitely not bald without knowing how to stop. His argument is like an icy incline; once we lose our footing on it, we seem doomed inexorably to slip all the way down to the conclusion. Logicians call it a **slippery slope.** Slippery-slope arguments have the following form:

x_1 is a typical case of F.

x_1 is not significantly different from x_2.

x_2 is not significantly different from x_3.

.

.

.

x_n is not significantly different from x_{n+1}.

∴ x_{n+1} has the property F.

With respect to the bald man argument, x_1 is the hairless or nearly hairless man and F is the property of baldness. The succeeding cases $x_2, x_3, \ldots, x_n,$

x_{n+1} are men, each of whom has one more hair than the last. By the time we get to x_{n+1}, we may pass out of the realm of baldness altogether. Thus, the premises can well be true and the conclusion false. Therefore, this argument form is invalid, and it becomes increasingly weaker as the number n of intermediate cases increases. If n is very large or if each individual difference is great, it is likely to be fallacious. A lot of insignificant differences or a few slightly significant ones can add up to a very significant gap. There is, after all, certainly a significant difference between a typical case of baldness and a typical case of nonbaldness, despite the fact that they are connected by a thread of intermediate cases. "It's only a matter of degree," the author of a slippery slope will say with a crafty grin. But this ignores the fact that matters of degree can make substantial qualitative differences. The typical bald man, for example, must shield his scalp on a sunny day to prevent sunburn. The typical nonbald person needn't worry about this. The difference between them may be a matter of degree, but it's not *only* a matter of degree. It makes qualitative differences in their lives.

Slippery slopes are common in moral controversy. It is sometimes argued, for example, that all abortion is murder, because killing an adult is murder, and an adult is not significantly different from a child, a child from a newborn infant, a newborn infant from an infant in the womb, an infant in the womb from a fetus, and a fetus from a fertilized egg. Here the typical case x_1 is the killing of an adult, and the property F is murder. The successive cases $x_2, x_3, \ldots, x_n, x_{..5_{n+1}}$ are killing at various stages of growth and development, beginning with childhood and moving backwards to the fertilized egg. It is the vagueness of the concept murder which causes trouble in this case. The slippery slope takes us into borderline cases of murder, and perhaps beyond. Like the bald man argument, this one is invalid, and probably fallacious, because of the number and diversity of cases involved. Despite the fact that it's a "matter of degree" from the first case to the last, we can imagine ways in which this difference of degree might result in a significant qualitative difference. One such difference, for example, might involve brain activity. Death is usually defined as the moment when brain activity ceases. And, of course, it is not possible to murder someone who is already dead. A newly fertilized egg, like a dead person, has no brain activity, because it has no brain. And this might well make it sufficiently different from an adult to make the concept of murder inapplicable in this case as well.

I'm not trying to settle the abortion issue here. There are important similarities as well as important differences between abortion and murder of an adult. Both, for example, end a potential for human development. But I do want to make it clear why slippery-slope arguments like the one just discussed fail to provide a conclusive solution. They fail because they are invalid and usually fallacious.

Exercise 7 For each of the following arguments, bracket and number statements, add or rewrite statements if necessary, and diagram and evaluate as usual. If the argument exhibits any of the forms discussed in this chapter, write the name of the form next to the arrow representing the inference which exemplifies it. More complete notes and additional diagrams may be necessary for ambiguous arguments.

1   There's nothing wrong with cheating on your taxes. Everyone does it.

2   I've been cheated! This was supposed to be a pound cake, but it only weighs 10 ounces!

3   Aw, Mom! All the other kids have mopeds. Why can't I have one too?

4   First kid: There is too a Santa Claus!
    Second kid: How do you know?
    First kid: My mom says so.

5   He's been cheating on his wife. Everyone knows it.

6   I had to hit her. She hit me first!

7   The defendant was in the alley behind the liquor store. The witness saw him there.

8   Everything that is human within us cries out that nuclear proliferation must cease.

9   What value can there be in Christian ideals if Christians themselves can't live up to them?

10 Even some scientists and engineers reject the theory of evolution. So why should I accept it?

11 The sculpture was composed entirely of transparent panes and blocks of Plexiglas. It was, therefore, thoroughly transparent.

12 It was Friedrich Nietzsche who stridently announced to the modern world that God is dead. And it was Nietzsche, too, who in 1889 collapsed in a fit of gibbering madness from which he was never to recover.

13 Nothing is better than sex. Logic is better than nothing. Therefore, logic is better than sex.

14 The new lighter skirts and blouses are the coming thing. Don't exclude them from your fall wardrobe.

15 When all is said and done, the final refutation of Puritanism lies in the Puritans themselves—particularly in their singular lack of humor.

16 This car gets excellent mileage. They say it goes 25 percent farther on a tank of gas.

17 Special Forces units are made up of well-equipped, handpicked soldiers who are superbly trained and extremely efficient in combat

situations. Consequently, they are devastatingly effective fighting teams.

18 Since $2 + 2 = 4$ and $4 \times 4 = 16$, we may infer that $(2 + 2) \times (2 + 2) = 16$.

19 Historically, it has been the Soviets' explicit intention to impose their iron dictatorship over the entire world. There is no evidence that this intention has changed.

20 Of course the Civil War was good for the South. It was good for the entire nation.

21 Every man will be a poet if he can; otherwise a philosopher or a man of science. This proves the superiority of the poet. (Henry David Thoreau, *Journals*)

22 "I'm sure that nobody walks much faster than I do."
"He can't do that," said the King, "or else he'd have been here first." (Lewis Carroll, *Through the Looking Glass*)

23 Mark Twain is Samuel Clemens. Mark Twain wrote *Huckleberry Finn*. Therefore, Samuel Clemens wrote *Huckleberry Finn*.

24 Since the end of the draft, a lot of young people are discovering a good place to invest their time. The Army. They've come, over 250,000 strong. . . . Join the people who've joined the Army. (U.S. Army recruitment ad)

25 It has never been shown that the increasing levels of atmospheric carbon dioxide produced by the burning of fossil fuels have caused any alteration in the world's climate. Therefore, contrary to the claims of many environmentalists, such fears are illusory.

26 It's a fact. Concentrated Pine-Sol cleans grease better than *any* leading liquid cleaner! Katie the Cleaning Lady proves it on TV. (Pine-Sol ad, *Woman's Day*, May 19, 1981)

27 Impress friends and influence people. Seagram's V.O. Bottled in Canada. Preferred throughout the world. (Seagrams V.O. ad, *House Beautiful*, April 1979)

28 It would not be impossible to prove with sufficient repetition and psychological understanding of the people concerned that a square is in fact a circle. What after all are a square and a circle? They are mere words and words can be moulded until they clothe ideas in disguise. (Adolf Hitler, *Mein Kampf*)

29 The phenomenon of diabolic possession, the mere possibility of which materialists and modernists in recent years have for the most part stoutly denied, has, nevertheless, been believed by all peoples and at all periods of the earth's history. In truth he who accepts the spiritual world is bound to realize all about him the age-long struggle for empery of discarnate evil ceaselessly contending with

a thousand cunning sleights and a myriad vizardings against the eternal unconquerable powers of good. (Montague Summers, *The History of Witchcraft and Demonology*)

30 Consort® is the hairspray designed to meet stylists' demands.
   Designed by professionals for professionals.
   Designed to hold yet feel clean, not sticky. Look natural, not stiff. As if you hadn't used a spray at all.
   That's why it's the number one professional hairspray in America and in the world. That's why stylists recommend Consort Hair Spray. It's the professional's choice. Make it yours. (Consort Hair Spray ad, *Newsweek*, September 27, 1982)

31 In fact, recently we have come to the realization that there is no such thing as insanity. It is true that the "mentally ill" exhibit bizarre behaviors and beliefs. But these are hardly different from the behaviors and beliefs of normal members of less advanced cultures. It is only a matter of time and technical sophistication which separates us from these so-called "primitives." In this way the insight has dawned that the so-called "mentally ill" are essentially as sane as the rest of us.

32 Friends, tonight we have heard Councilman Schneider propose a 20 percent increase in property taxes. I say that that in itself is good reason to conclude that this tax is both unnecessary and unwarranted. For Councilman Schneider's greed and corruption have been a thorn in the side of this community since the day he took office. The Sunshine Corporation, of which he is a high-ranking employee, has persistently demonstrated its avarice through fraudulent contracts, phony stock manipulations, and a diverse assortment of illegal business practices, too numerous to mention here.

33 It is a relatively simple matter simultaneously to determine both the position and the velocity of a macroscopic object with extraordinary accuracy. It should, therefore, at least in principle, be possible simultaneously to determine the positions and velocities of the microparticles which comprise it.

34 Nature is governed by fixed and immutable laws, and there is no law that is not the work of a legislator. Therefore, nature itself is governed by a sublime and powerful legislator, and it is he whom we know by the name of "God."

35 Throughout history, presidents senators and representatives, seizing upon short-run political or popular opposition, have attempted to negotiate unpopular constitutional decisions through the action of mere legislative majorities: by impeaching Justices, by packing the Court or by curtailing its jurisdiction. Always in the past, despite their discontent with particular decisions, the American peo-

ple and the Congress have rejected the backdoor assaults upon the Constitution as dangerously unprincipled.

They should be rejected again today. (Archibald Cox, "Don't Overrule the Court," *Newsweek*, September 28, 1981)

36 Though normally we do not think of sounds as having shapes, in a certain peculiar and rather mysterious sense, they do. Musical tones, for example, may be either sharp or flat.

37 "I am not possessed," said Jesus . . . . "In very truth I tell you, if anyone obeys my teaching he shall never know what it is to die."

The Jews said, "Now we are certain that you are possessed. Abraham is dead; the prophets are dead; and yet you say, "If anyone obeys my teaching he shall not know what it is to die." Are you greater than our father Abraham, who is dead? The prophets are dead too. What do you claim to be?" (*John* 8:49–51)

38 . . . the American government is not entitled to talk about terrorism since it practices the highest degree of terrorism in the world. . . . As long as the big powers continue to manufacture atomic weapons, it means that they are continuing to terrorize the world; also the deployment of military bases on other countries' territories; also deploying naval fleets around the world. This is one reason why the U.S. is a top terrorist force in the world. (Libyan dictator Muammar Gaddafi in response to U.S. charges that he was promoting world terrorism, quoted in *Time*, June 1981)

39 At this point, when everyone could see that Thrasymachus' definition of justice had been turned inside out, instead of making any reply, he said:

Socrates, have you a nurse?

Why do you ask such a question as that? I said. Wouldn't it be better to answer mine?

Because she lets you go about sniffling like a child whose nose wants wiping. (Plato, *Republic*)

40 The Inquisition must have been justified and beneficial, if whole peoples invoked and defended it, if men of the loftiest souls founded and created it severally and impartially, and its very adversaries applied it on their own account, pyre answering to pyre. (Benedetto Croce, *Philosophy of the Practical*)

41 There is nothing objective about matters of taste. The question of whether horseradish tastes good, for example, is purely subjective and depends entirely upon individual preferences. Questions of morality are little different in this regard, as is shown by the radical diversity of moral viewpoints. Further, questions of morality are hardly distinguishable from questions of practicality. There is, for example, little difference between the question of whether it is

right to go to war and the question of whether this war is practical. Finally, matters of practice are essentially no different from what are called "matters of fact." Whether or not a war is practical depends upon such "facts" as the strength of our army. Thus we are led inevitably to the conclusion that everything, including even alleged matters of fact, is purely a matter of subjective opinion, and hence that objectivity is an illusion.

42   From the point of view of the biochemical determinist, bacteria do not think. Rather, they respond to stimuli in the environment, using known chemical principles. . . . Following this line of reasoning, fungi do not think, protozoans do not think, and mimosa do not think. But if this is true, where does thought as a distinguishable feature arise in evolution? The most consistent materialists say that it never arises. Annelids do not think, planaria do not think, and invertebrates do not think. They respond to signals with a response/output whose usefulness is tested by evolution. This line of reasoning leads inexorably to the conclusion that Supreme Court justices also do not think, but simply respond to stimuli in a manner that has passed the evolutionary filter for survival.

Mentalists—believers in the existence of mind—would argue from the continuity of behavior to an opposite conclusion. Since we are able to move step by step from Supreme Court justices, who we know can think, down the evolutionary ladder to successively simpler forms, then some sort of psychic activity must be ascribed even to the lowliest organism, bacteria.

We are left with the dilemma of having to accept one of two conclusions: either bacteria think or Supreme Court justices do not. The only way out is to assume that at some level of organization between microbe and man, thought arose as a new phenomenon. (Harold S. Morowitz, "Do Bacteria Think?" *Psychology Today*, February 1981)

8

Falsehood, Deception, and Emotion

The subject of this chapter is primarily **rhetoric,** not logic. Rhetoric is the art of persuasion. It is concerned with influencing people's beliefs without regard for truth. But a chapter on rhetoric is not out of place in a logic book, because a thorough understanding of arguments requires sensitivity to their rhetorical aspects.

The arguments and nonarguments we'll study here are of interest, not because they are fallacies (many are not), but because they are defective or misleading in other ways. Some of them have false, evasive, or meaningless premises. Others only seem to be arguments; when you look at them closely, they contain no reasoning at all.

8.1   VARIETIES OF FALSEHOOD

Falsehood is a matter of cold facts. What we can imagine has nothing to do with it. It is important to keep this in mind in the following discussion. Possibility is no longer relevant; we're talking solely about the actual world.

To show that a premise is false, we need to find an exception—that is, an actual situation or fact contrary to what the premise says. Specific statements, like "Boston is south of New York," concern only one actual situation, and if they are false there is only one exception which shows it. (You are, I hope, aware of the actual fact which constitutes the exception here.) General statements, like "Everyone east of the Mississippi is greedy," concern many separate situations and are false if even one of them is not as described. If everyone east of the Mississippi is greedy, except for generous little Tommy T. of Hoboken, New Jersey, then the statement that everyone east of the Mississippi is greedy is still plainly false.

General statements are probably the most common source of falsehood in argument. The accusations people hurl at one another while bickering are often full of such falsehoods:

"You're a slob. Everywhere you go you leave a filthy mess."

"Oh yeah? Well you're a nag. You can never keep your mouth shut for just one second!"

"You see? It's always like this! You never listen to me; you never care what I think; you treat me like dirt!"

"I treat you like dirt? You haven't said a kind word to me in years! You just go around with that constant ugly scowl on your face and do nothing but complain!"

You are no doubt familiar with such convivial discussions. Each line spoken here is an argument, and some of them are logically quite good (especially if you make allowances for the colorful language and add an implicit premise or two). But if this were a real conversation, I'd bet good money that all of the generalizations which serve as premises would be false.

Expressions of national, racial, regional, or religious bigotry are often false generalities not much more sophisticated than these. From a logical point of view they are easy to refute; one exception suffices. But their psychological hold on people can be very tenacious. Accuracy commands less attention than sweeping rhetoric, especially in a climate charged with emotion. The rational voice is easily overwhelmed amid loud proclamations of broad and simple delusions. Those who take the care to describe the world as it is are easily dismissed as "quibblers." Sometimes this charge of quibbling is justified; the existence of one or two exceptions may not matter much. But often it's a way of maintaining an intentional blindness to the facts. If, for example, we pointed out the falsehoods in the conversation above to the disputants, they would probably both accuse us of quibbling. That is because each wants to remain blind to any hint of goodness in the other. Perhaps this blindness gives them some pleasure. But I doubt that in the long run it enhances the quality of their lives.

Some generalizations, while not obviously false, obviously cannot be known to be true. These, of course, should never be trusted as premises in an argument. Suppose, for example, that a magazine announces, "Women are happier now than 20 years ago." What this means, of course, is that women *on the average* are happier, so single exceptions won't suffice to disprove it. But there's no way to prove it either. Who could look into the human heart and tell? At most, it might be shown that women on the average *say* they're happier. But even this would require statistical generalization from a pair of careful random surveys, and we saw in Section 6.4 how difficult it is to conduct such surveys accurately. (We might also wonder which women the statement was referring to; surely no one took a random sample of all the women in the world!) It might be true that women are happier, but there's not a mortal soul who knows it. This statement has no place as an assumption in any serious argument.

Demagogues and politicians are frequently apt to utter the unknowable. "It is the destiny of our great nation to bring hope to all the people of the world." How often have you heard things like this? How could anyone know that they are true?

Philosophy, psychology, and literary criticism are also fertile hunting grounds for examples: "The author's deeply suppressed hatred of his sister is revealed in the portrayal of the two main female characters." Well, maybe, but how could anyone really know?

Where access to information is limited or controlled, one often finds the most blatant mode of falsehood, the big lie. The big lie is an egregious falsehood reiterated with such insistence that people eventually start to believe it. Here's how it works, in the words of one of the masters of the technique, Adolf Hitler:

> . . . the people . . . fall victim more easily to a big lie than to a small one, since they themselves occasionally lie in small matters but they would be ashamed to tell great lies. Such a falsehood will not enter their minds, and they will also not be able to imagine others asserting the great boldness of the most infamous representation. And even with the explanation of the matter they long hesitate and vacillate and accept at least some ground as true; consequently, from the most bold lie, something will remain . . . *(Mein Kampf)*

The big lie is the stock-in-trade of despots, petty manipulators, and con artists. The idea, as Hitler explains, is to play on our tendency to find some truth in what people say. This tendency is perfectly rational, since lies of great boldness are rare. But for that very reason they are seductive; we don't expect them. Their power, of course, is multiplied considerably if their victims uncritically respect the authority of the liar.

History abounds with examples of the big lie. Tyrants from the pharaohs of Egypt and the emperors of Rome down to Hirohito in World War II have claimed to be gods or descendants of gods in order to enhance their status in the eyes of their subjects. (Some even appear to have deceived themselves with these lies.) Warring nations have often described their enemies as bloodthirsty monsters who torture captives, worship devils, or even eat human flesh. Unfortunately, such accusations are sometimes true, but frequently they are pure fabrications, consciously crafted to inspire hatred.

The big lie is difficult to combat logically, especially if contrary information is not readily available. Fortunately, it tends to be self-destructive. First a trickle and eventually a torrent of contrary evidence emerges, and the victims' faith collapses. Unless, like the con artist, the liar can move on to new territory, he or she will find few people gullible enough to swallow further falsehoods.

A more subtle mode of falsehood, safer because it is more difficult to refute conclusively, is false interpretation. I have heard it said, for example, on the basis of the eighth chapter of Revelation that the Bible forecasts a nuclear war. Here are some of the relevant verses:

> Then the seven angels that held the seven trumpets prepared to blow them.
>
> The first blew his trumpet; and there came hail and fire mingled with blood, and this was hurled upon the earth. A third of the earth was burnt, a third of the trees were burnt, all the green grass was burnt.
>
> The second angel blew his trumpet; and what looked like a great blazing mountain was hurled into the sea. A third of the sea was turned to blood, a third of the living creatures in it died, and a third of the ships in it foundered.
>
> The third angel blew his trumpet; and a great star shot from the sky, flaming like a torch; and it fell on a third of the rivers and the springs. The name of the star was Wormwood; and a third of the water turned to wormwood, and men in great numbers died of the water because it had been poisoned.

It is true that to the modern mind, haunted by visions of nuclear cataclysm, these images provoke obvious associations: the atomic blast raining fiery debris upon the earth, the scorching of soil and vegetation, ballistic missiles falling from the sky, water poisoned by radioactive fallout. But these are just *our* associations. No other age has read the passages this way. Literally, the Bible says nothing about a nuclear war, not in these passages or anywhere else. There is no mention of missiles, only of falling stars. There is no talk of radioactive fallout; the word is "wormwood," which designates a bitter herb. It is easy to read our own hopes and fears into words which were never meant to express them. But that shouldn't lead us to think that these words say something which in fact they do not.

Another form of false interpretation is misquotation, or quotation out of context. The classic case is the misuse of movie, book, and theater reviews in advertising. The quotation, " . . . stunning . . . lively plot . . . ," followed by the name of a respected critic, appears on the jacket of a new novel. This sounds like a sterling recommendation, until you discover that what the critic really said was, "The author's stunning ineptitude reduces what could have been a lively plot to sheer tedium." You never know what's hiding behind those little dots until you look.

Here's a similar but more subtle case, interesting because of its implicit appeal to authority. Inside the cover of a 1977 printing of L. Ron Hubbard's *Dianetics: The Modern Science of Mental Health* there appears the following quotation:

> "History has become a race between Dianetics and catastrophe. Dianetics will win if enough people are challenged, in time, to understand it."—Frederick L. Schuman, *New York Times Book Review*, August 6, 1950.

The casual reader would take this as a glowing endorsement by a reviewer for a highly respected publication. The quotation in fact is accurate, but it comes from a letter to the editor, not a review. Schuman, the letter's author, was replying to a negative review of the book by psychologist Rollo May, which had appeared in an earlier issue of the *Times Book Review*. Judging by his letter, Schuman was an avid follower of Hubbard (the founder of Scientology) and by no means a spokesman for the *Times*. The quotation misleads by giving the reader the false impression that Dianetics was endorsed by the *Times*, whereas in fact the *Times'* reviewer had roundly criticized it. This deception was accomplished, not by making a false statement, but by relying on the reader to make certain faulty inferences. It is not always necessary to lie in order to deceive.

8.2   STRAW MAN ARGUMENTS

When an argument misrepresents an opponent's views in order to make them easier to criticize, it is called a **straw man argument.** The idea behind the name is that instead of doing battle with a real opponent, you set up a straw man—a ridiculous view which your opponent does not hold—and then triumphantly demolish it. The argument may or may not be logically strong, but in either case it should be faulted for falsehood and irrelevance.

Straw men are common in political disputes. In a 1982 letter soliciting funds for liberal Democratic candidates, Senator Edward Kennedy wrote: "General Haig himself [the Secretary of State] has spoken of firing a 'nuclear warning shot' during a European crisis. And the President [Ronald Reagan] has endorsed the idea of a 'limited nuclear war.'" The implication was that Reagan's Republican administration was promoting nuclear war and hence that people ought to elect Democrats.

Let's not worry about Kennedy's reasoning. The point is that he set up a straw man. Haig had indeed spoken of the possibility of firing a nuclear warning shot. But it does not follow that he favored such a course or that he would suggest it without careful consideration of the alternatives. The statement about Reagan is even more misleading. Reagan had discussed the possibility of a limited nuclear war and indicated that the United States ought to be prepared for it. But he surely never *endorsed*—that is, supported or approved—the idea. Kennedy's assertion that he did is simply false.

But maybe Kennedy did not mean precisely what he said. Perhaps he meant only to charge Reagan with endorsing preparedness to fight a limited nuclear war or with endorsing the idea that such a war could be kept limited and still be won. (Both these things are a far cry from endorsing the idea of war itself.) Still, what he literally said was false, and he has, though perhaps unintentionally, set up a straw man. Whether a mere slip of the pen or an intentional inaccuracy, this sort of misrepresentation can lead to serious misunderstanding.

Straw man arguments result from an attitude opposed to the spirit of charity discussed in Section 4.1. Either their authors don't take the trouble to state an opponent's position accurately, or they deliberately distort it. This can only foster confusion and needless strife.

8.3   FALSE DILEMMAS

One kind of statement in which it is easy to conceal falsehood is the **disjunction.** A disjunction is any statement of the form "*p* or *q*," where *p* and *q* are component sentences. It focuses our attention on two alternatives and asserts that these are the only two, but often there are others which remain unmentioned. If so, the disjunction is false. Someone might say, for example:

Either McDougal is living in Toronto, or he's living elsewhere.

This seems like an obvious, perhaps even a logically necessary, truth. But it's not, for it fails to take account of a third alternative: McDougal may be dead. Because disjunctions can be false in rather subtle ways, they should be scrutinized carefully when they occur in arguments.

This is all the more important when disjunctions occur, as they often do, in deductive reasoning. (Disjunctive syllogism and constructive dilemma are the most common forms which employ them, but there are many others.) The deductiveness lends an air of certainty to the argument and can make reasoning based on a false disjunction extremely persuasive. Arguments with false disjunctive premises are called **false dilemmas.**

One of my favorite examples occurred during a television interview with a participant in a cow-chip throwing contest. (You know what cow chips are, don't you?) The interviewer asked the obvious. "Why would anyone want to throw cow chips?" "Well," the contestant replied in a thoughtful country drawl, "It's better than standin' around holdin' 'em."

If we may interpolate, the contestant's reasoning appears to be as follows:

Either you stand around holding a cow chip or you throw it.
Throwing it is better than standing around holding it.
∴ You'd better throw it.

This is a classic false dilemma.

There are, of course, more serious cases. Consider this one:

Grades provide incentive to no one. Those who are self-motivated would learn without grades, and those who don't care won't learn even with them.

Adding the missing premises, we get this:

Either people are self-motivated or they don't care.
Those who are self-motivated would learn without grades.
Those who don't care won't learn even with them.
Grades provide no incentive to those who would learn without them.
Grades provide no incentive to those who won't learn even with them.
∴ Grades provide incentive to no one.

Several of the implicit premises are questionable, but it's the initial disjunction which really undermines the argument. There are many people who do care and yet need some extra incentive. The disjunction ignores this fact and is therefore false.

8.4 DOMINO ARGUMENTS

When you set up a line of dominos and knock the first one down, the whole line falls—if you've set them up correctly. There is an argument form which works similarly:

If p_1, then p_2
If p_2, then p_3
If p_3, then p_4
.
.
.
If p_n, then p_{n+1}
∴ If p_1, then p_{n+1}

This is just an extended form of hypothetical syllogism (see Section 5.1). It is always valid. If the premises are true, it is sound. But if even one is false then the argument fails, like a cascade of dominos stopped halfway down the line. That's why it's called a **domino argument.**

Historically, the name is derived from the so-called domino theory— an argument really, not a theory—in support of U.S. involvement in the Vietnam war. The argument went roughly like this:

> If we pull out of Vietnam, then the communists will take over in South Vietnam.
>
> If they take over in South Vietnam, they'll take over in Cambodia, Laos, and Thailand.
>
> If they take over in Cambodia, Laos, and Thailand, then they'll overrun all of Southeast Asia.
>
> If they overrun all of Southeast Asia, then eventually they will threaten India, Indonesia, the Philippines, and even Australia.
>
> ∴ If we pull out of Vietnam, then the communists will eventually threaten India, Indonesia, the Philippines, and even Australia.

In this case the dominos stopped at the second premise. The communists did take over in Laos and Cambodia, but not in Thailand. And at the time of this writing, they pose no serious threat to the countries mentioned in the conclusion. (Several of these countries suffer from serious domestic turmoil, but that's another matter.) So the second premise and probably some of the others were false.

I should mention that the argument above is my reconstructed version. Various forms of the argument were given by a variety of public officials, and no two were exactly alike.

Some textbooks fail to distinguish domino arguments from slippery slopes. But despite a superficial similarity, they are quite different. Slippery slope (see Section 7.8) is an invalid form which trades on vagueness. Domino arguments are valid and have nothing to do with vagueness. Their fault, if it exists, lies in the falsehood of their premises.

Domino arguments consist of a single inference. If we consecutively number the five statements of the argument above, for example, its diagram is this:

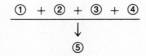

Many people are tempted to diagram such an argument this way:

But this is clearly wrong. Conditionals ①–③ are not given as evidence for their successors. Rather, all of ①–④ are given together as evidence for the conclusion, ⑤.

Another problem with domino arguments is that the conditionals are not always expressed as such. Here's an example:

> If you start censoring pornographic films, where will you draw the line? Soon there will be censorship of really sensitive treatments of sexual matters. And censorship of other serious topics will follow. The inevitable conclusion is the complete loss of freedom of speech.

There are several ways of looking at this argument. It might, for example, be regarded as a conditional proof. But the easiest way is probably to think of it as a domino argument:

> If you start censoring pornographic films, then soon there will be censorship of really sensitive treatments of sexual matters.
>
> If there is censorship of really sensitive treatments of sexual matters, then censorship of other serious topics will follow.
>
> If there is censorship of other serious topics, then there will be a complete loss of freedom of speech.
>
> ∴ If you start censoring pornographic films, then there will be a complete loss of freedom of speech.

Serious doubts can be raised about each of the conditional premises, so despite its validity this argument is not very convincing. Viewed as a conditional proof it is equally weak, but its weakness is differently conceived. Try it and see.

8.5 GOBBLEDYGOOK

Whether the motive is self-indulgence, pomp, or a desire not to be clearly understood, some people use words so airy and sentences so scatterbrained that reading them is like swimming through a sea of balloons. Some technical writing requires specialized terms, and that's fine, but there's no excuse for jargon like this:

> *Learning is a self-activity.* The accumulation of knowledge, skills, and attitudes is an experience that occurs within the learner and is really activated by the learner. While we as trainers can set the stage and do much to orchestrate a climate conducive to learning, it is an internal process. One of the richest resources for learning is the learners themselves, and the learning process may be different for each of them. For this reason, human resource developers must recognize and respect the individuality of the trainees. (Les Donaldson and Edward E. Scannell, *Human Resource Development: The New Trainer's Guide*)

This is an argument, and what it says is essentially this:

> Learning occurs within the learner, and the learner does it, though trainers can help. Learners themselves provide much that is needed for learning, and each may learn differently. Therefore, trainers must recognize and respect the individuality of trainees.

Reduced to this humbler form, the argument is easier to understand. But it is also easier to criticize. Its triteness and vagueness become painfully apparent. Its implicit assumptions are more obvious too: that the learner's contribution to learning demands respect for the learner, that learning differences require trainers to recognize the individuality of trainees. We should examine these hidden assumptions carefully before accepting the argument. In this case, they seem rather reasonable, and perhaps we'd ultimately accept them.

But notice how difficult it would be for the average reader to spot any hidden assumptions in the first version. Just understanding it takes considerable effort. When we finally succeed, we're liable to be so enchanted by the accomplishment that we forget criticism and take the conclusion for granted. That's one reason why gobbledygook like this is so prevalent; it's an effective way of getting people to agree without thinking critically about what is being said. Criticism takes too much effort. Gobbledygook turns people into sheep.

Obviously, not everyone who writes this way is cynically seeking uncritical agreement. Maybe some people do it because they think it sounds sophisticated, others because it's commonplace among their associates. But, whatever the motive, the net effect is to hinder communication. This is no way to talk if you sincerely want to be understood.

The trouble with gobbledygook, then, is not that it is false (it's as easy to garble truth as it is to garble falsehood) but that it produces a mental fog. And fog is the perfect environment for deception.

Nowhere is foggy wording exploited more vigorously than in the public organs of a government at war. People want to believe that their side is right and that it is winning; so even if neither is true, they are easily deluded into believing both—so long as they can be prevented from thinking clearly. Was there a retreat? Call it a "strategic redeployment of forces." Were peasants slaughtered in their villages? Call it a "pacification program." Are we supporting revolutionaries? Call them "freedom-fighters." Are we opposing revolutionaries? Then call them "terrorists."

The passage by Lenin in Exercise 4.3 provides a good example of linguistic befuddlement in a government facing crisis. Notice that when Lenin speaks of his opponents he calls them, not "people" or "men and women," but "elements of disintegration," as if they were some inorganic rot or decay from which society needed to be "cleansed." Such language allows people to maintain an ambiguous state of mind about things which if clearly described would arouse horror: secret police, torture, firing squads, concentration camps, and so on.

Expressions created to disguise ugly realities are called **euphemisms.** Perhaps the most appalling example is Hitler's term for the murder of the Jews: *die endgültige Lösung,* the final solution.

Most euphemisms are less sinister, yet each in its own way dulls thought. Death is not death, but "passing away," sex shows are called "adult entertainment," used cars are described as "preowned," and sleeping pills are euphemistically labeled "sleep aids."

Just as destructive of thought are expressions which lack any discernible meaning: "now generation banking," "preferred housing" (preferred by whom?), "exclusive design," "special beauty formula," . . . leaf through any newspaper or magazine and you'll find dozens more.

And there are also just needless complications, words and phrases which add bulk but no substance: "rain activity" instead of "rain," "subsequent to" instead of "after," "crisis situation" instead of "crisis," "I can relate to that" instead of "I understand," "at this point in time" instead of "now."

All these ways of talking fill our minds with garbage that impedes critical thinking. Hence they are always grounds for alertness and suspicion. Failure to see them for what they are makes us dull and manipulable. It's easy to pull wool over the eyes of a sheep.

8.6   EMOTION

Gobbledygook is one thing; emotion is another. There is nothing inherently wrong with using emotional language in an argument. Some situations call for emotion, and we'd be less than human if we responded with cold objectivity. But emotional language is no substitute for reason. If we are swayed by emotion alone and fail to think, then we are being irrational. And that kind of irrationality is foolish and often dangerous.

The rabble-rousing politician, the fire-and-brimstone preacher, and the fast-talking salesperson are familiar figures whose emotional machinations need little comment. They seldom offer a real argument, and when they do it usually comes equipped with such an array of emotional claptrap that it's difficult to discern. The emotions are the real message. These people don't want you to think carefully.

On a more personal level, there are those domineering people who play on your pity, your fears, or your pride to bend you to their will. Again, emotions, not arguments, are their chief weapons. But I'm telling you nothing new.

What might be worth a little more attention, because it is more subtle and because it usefully illustrates the contrast between emotional persuasion and argument, is the use of emotion in advertising. Consider, for example, the costly and apparently successful campaign to promote Virginia Slims cigarettes. (The campaign is still under way at the time of this writing.) The ads, prominently displayed in magazines and on billboards, typically consist of a sequence of brownish, aged-looking photographs depicting turn-of-the-century women burdened in various ways by drudgery and subjugation and set off against a glossy full-color picture of a flashy, modern female model. The model holds a cigarette. The text varies from layout to layout, but it always ends with the motto: "You've come a long way, baby."

The point is how cleverly these ads appeal to emotion while bypassing reason. There is no argument here, only a loose collection of images and ideas. Their purpose is to play on both the resentments and the aspirations of women. The goal is to manipulate behavior. The creators of these ads realized that many women resent the way they are treated by many men. And they saw that this resentment could be harnessed to their purposes by suggesting that one of the forms of male domination is disapproval of smoking. Once this idea is successfully implanted, smoking becomes an act of defiance, a symbolic assertion of one's rights. The cigarette is now a weapon in the war of the sexes. The woman grows attached to it like a soldier to his gun.

But that's only one side of this campaign's emotional appeal. The other is the appeal to women's aspirations. The model wears a look of easy confidence. Her clothing is fashionable and expensive, yet worn with a casual grace. She is mature. She is sexy. She is enjoying herself. In other words, she is the ideal American woman—or at least what is popularly perceived as such. And she is smoking Virginia Slims. The makers of these ads obviously know that we emulate our ideals and that most people do so without thinking.

Everything about these ads has a purpose. Even the name seems carefully chosen for its connotations—the sexual irony of the word "Virginia" (virgin) and the obvious positive associations of "slim." But nowhere is there an attempt to stimulate thought. No reasons are given for smoking Virginia Slims or even for preferring them over other brands. There is no argument. The persuasion is entirely emotional. The admakers don't want us to think. If we did, their emotional sorcery probably wouldn't work.

There is much more to say about emotional persuasion than this one example indicates. I could, for example, have achieved a more balanced presentation by discussing the "macho appeal" of cigarettes for men. I could also have discussed emotional appeals in other forms of advertising, in the news business, and in various kinds of propaganda. But this is a logic book, and I don't want to wander too far afield. It helps, though, to step outside of logic occasionally, if only to mark its boundaries more clearly.

8.7   DEFINITIONS, GOOD AND BAD

One rhetorical device which is frequently used to manipulate emotions is the **persuasive definition.** The idea is to redefine a word that has strong emotional associations, either positive or negative, so that these associations are transferred to the objects or conditions mentioned in the new definition. Suppose, for example, that we are trying to convert a group of young business executives to a certain religion. One word which will have very strong positive associations for this group is "success." So at the end of an emotional speech we might say:

> True success is not measured in dollars. It is not a matter of property or prestige. True success is a condition of the soul; it means being right with God.

Whatever the merits of the definition expressed in the last sentence, it is not what business people commonly mean by "success." The word has been redefined and its positive associations transferred to the religious condition of "being right with God." This is a persuasive definition.

In themselves, persuasive definitions are neither good nor bad. The new usages they suggest may be better than the old ones. And the transfer of emotion may be all for the best. But from a logical point of view they can be troublesome, because if taken seriously they generate ambiguity. "Success" now has two meanings for this group. Which will be intended in future arguments? We'll have to be careful if confusion is not to result.

This raises the broader question of what makes a definition good or bad. The answer depends on our purposes. In a sense, we can define any term any way we want. I can, for example, decide to use the term "cat" to designate every kind of unpleasant animal. So for me mosquitoes, flies, rats, and tapeworms will all be "cats." There's nothing to stop me from using the word this way, but it would be stupid, because of the confusion that would result. People unfamiliar with my usage wouldn't understand me and people who were familiar with it would constantly have to translate from my language to theirs.

Efficient communication is possible only when we all give the same meanings to the same terms. If people took the anarchic attitude of the previous paragraph, speech would be reduced to self-indulgent gibberish. So if our purpose is communication, we need to rely primarily on the public meanings which words already have. Private definitions are pointless.

In contrast, definitions which assign words their customary public meaning are both unobjectionable and true. If we say, for example, that a blimp is a nonrigid or semirigid airship, then we have expressed the common meaning of "blimp." Our statement is true. And it would be perfectly legitimate as an assumption in an argument. If fact, it is more than true; it is logically necessary. Since we keep the meanings of our terms constant in describing the various possible worlds (recall the discussion of Section 3.4), it is true in any world (even in worlds in which blimps don't exist) that a blimp is a nonrigid or semirigid airship.

Traditionally, definitions have been regarded as giving logically necessary and sufficient conditions (see Section 6.7) for the condition being defined. In the case of the term "blimp," this means that in every possible world, a blimp is present if and only if a nonrigid or semirigid airship is present. But definition by logically necessary and sufficient conditions is an ideal seldom achieved in practice. Even most dictionary definitions fall seriously short. The term "horse," for example, is defined in *Webster's New Twentieth Century Dictionary* as follows:

> a large, strong animal, *Equus caballus*, with four legs, solid hoofs, and flowing mane and tail, long ago domesticated for drawing or carrying loads, carrying riders, etc.

The conditions described here do not apply to all horses, even in the actual world. Some are sick and weak, not strong. Not all of them have four legs (some have lost legs or been born with too few or too many). Not all horses have flowing manes and tails. Some are still wild.

Thus, not only does this definition not give logically necessary and sufficient conditions for being a horse; if the term "horse" is used with its common meaning, the statement that horses are the things which meet this definition is false. There are numerous exceptions. (To make matters worse, there is some confusion here between individual horses and the horse as a species, but let's ignore this.) Since dictionary definitions are meant to express the common meanings of terms, not to recommend new meanings, the term "horse" is indeed intended to have its common meaning here. Hence the definition genuinely is false.

Suppose a certain woman were to decide to adopt this definition. In that case, what she meant by "horse" would be different from what we mean. If we brought her a horse whose mane and tail had been sheared off, she would say, "It is not a horse." That would be a true statement in her private language, but she is no longer speaking English. In English it is false.

Definitions in which a term is intended to have its common meaning are called **lexical definitions.** Lexical definitions which are subject to exceptions are false. If our purposes include accuracy and truth, they are bad definitions. Webster's definition of "horse" would be a bad definition to use in an argument—especially an argument in which the exceptions to it mattered. Some definitions, however, are intended to alter common meanings or originate new ones, and these definitions must be judged by other criteria. Definitions which make intentional innovations in meaning are called **stipulative definitions.** Persuasive definitions are one kind of stipulative definition.

Stipulative definitions are never false. In making them, we stipulate that they are true—indeed, logically necessary. They are, in effect, recommendations to change our language. But as we saw earlier, stipulative definitions can be troublesome sources of ambiguity and confusion. So to decide whether a stipulative definition is good or bad, we need to weigh its usefulness against the bewilderment it causes.

One kind of stipulative definition is almost always unobjectionable. If English lacks a word for a concept we need to express, then it may be extremely useful to coin a new word and stipulate its definition. No ambiguity can result, since the new word has no meaning to begin with. "Quark" is a good example. When physicists discovered that subatomic particles seemed to be composed of even more basic particles for which they had no name, they adopted the nonsense word "quark" and stipulated that it was to designate these previously unnamed particles. The result was a very useful bit of new terminology.

Stipulative definition may also prove valuable when it involves sharpening the meaning of an existing term. This is called a **precising definition.** Precising definitions are common in mathematics and the sciences. In elementary geometry, for example, a line is regarded as the path of a moving point, infinitely extended, perfectly straight, and without breadth. This is more precise than our ordinary definition of "line," and in advanced mathematics the definition gets even sharper. Some confusion results from these stipulations (as you may recall from your earliest geometry classes), but "line" in geometry is so closely related to "line" in ordinary usage that the resulting confusion is usually minor and can be cleared up fairly easily. On the whole, the definition is useful.

Stipulative definitions become objectionable only when they create more trouble than they're worth. Using the term "cat" to mean "unpleasant animal" is an example. To be more realistic, consider the case of an office employee caught using company supplies for private purposes. "I wasn't stealing," he pleads. "Stealing is taking something on the sly. I wasn't trying to hide what I was doing." This, of course, is an argument, and it's based on a rather peculiar definition of "stealing." If the term is intended to have its common meaning (i.e., if the definition is supposed to be lexical), then the definition is false and the argument is unsound. But if the culprit insists that his definition is stipulative, then he is right. His argument *is* sound. The only problem is that it doesn't prove what he thinks it does. It proves only that he wasn't engaged in what he calls "stealing." He was stealing nevertheless. His stipulation created confusion, probably more in his own mind than in anyone else's—confusion which led to serious trouble. It was for that reason a very bad definition.

Exercise 8   Some of the following selections are arguments. Some are not. Diagram and evaluate each of the arguments as usual, rewriting and adding statements if necessary. For each selection, write a brief note discussing such matters as truth, meaning, and rhetorical effectiveness.

1   You never leave me alone. You're always telling me that I need to lose weight.

2   Either you're for us or against us, and so far you haven't been for us.

3   Come to where the flavor is. Marlboro.

4   Cruelty is undeserved suffering. But the violent criminal deserves to suffer. Therefore to cause him suffering is not cruel.

5   The real aim of those who advocate prayer in public schools is to establish a single state religion. That is contrary to everything this country stands for. And so we must do everything we can to stop them.

6   Current stockpiles of ordnance for all major antitank weapons systems are already sufficiently formidable to repulse any remotely plausible injection of Soviet armored units into the European theater of operations. Continued stockpiling of such ordnance therefore represents an expenditure of funds unwarranted by the current tactical situation.

7   Free-spirited and emphatically feminine—that is the magic of Cabochard. (Cabochard perfume ad, *Vogue*, December 1980)

8   If you marry now, soon you'll be having kids. Then it will be the whole suburban trap—house, car, steady job. Your life will become stale and mediocre, and you'll lose your spirit.

9   Caption beneath photo of a bottle of Tanqueray gin next to a jade statuette: "Why go halfway around the world to find a masterpiece, when you can acquire one right around the corner. Tanqueray Gin. A singular experience." (Tanqueray gin ad, *New York Times Magazine*, April 25, 1982)

10   Either we disarm or we destroy ourselves. It's that simple.

11   Scoundrel. A major new disturbance. From Revlon. (Scoundrel perfume ad, *Vogue,* February 1981)

12   I can't help being depressed. When I'm home I'm bored, because it's lonely and there's nothing to do. And if I got a job, I'd hate it, and that would be depressing too.

13   Because patriotism means doing the will of one's country as expressed in the decisions of its leaders, when a nation's leaders call citizens to their country's defense, all those motivated by patriotism will heed the call. The rest, then, are unpatriotic and hence unworthy of citizenship.

14   I'm telling you, we *can* have a good relationship now. If you could only get into my head, you could really relate to what I am saying. I've had some real heavy experiences, but I'm back in touch with myself. I'm finally getting it together. I mean I've learned how to deal creatively with my hangups, you know? It'll be more real this time, I promise.

15   Let us call the "self" the system of contacts at any moment. As such, the self is flexibly various, for it varies with the dominant organic needs and the pressing environmental stimuli; it is the system of responses; it diminishes in sleep when there is less need to respond. (Frederick Perls, Ralph E. Hefferline, and Paul Goodman, *Gestalt Therapy: Excitement and Growth in the Human Personality*)

16   The basic state of sight shows itself in a peculiar tendency-of-Being which belongs to everydayness—the tendency towards 'seeing'. We designate this tendency by the term "curiosity".... In this kind of seeing, that which is an issue for care does not lie in grasping something and being knowingly in its truth; it lies rather in its possibilities of abandoning itself to the world. Therefore, curiosity is characterized by a specific way of *not tarrying* alongside what is closest. (Martin Heidegger, *Being and Time*)

17   Dogmatists the world over believe that although the truth is known to them, others will be led into false beliefs provided they are allowed to hear the arguments on both sides. This is a view which leads to one or another of two misfortunes: either one set of dogmatists conquers the world and prohibits all new ideas, or, what is worse, rival dogmatists conquer different regions and preach the gospel of hate against each other.... The first makes civilization static, the second tends to destroy it completely. (Bertrand Russell, "The Functions of a Teacher")

18   Shades brazenly bright, or sultry and smoky-voiced, these are the smash-hit nail shades Cutex calls Shady Lady.

All are very much of the moment. Because suddenly dolled-up is right. And really dressing, with all the finishing touches, feels like fun.

You can see why we say the nails to wear now are lacquered to the hilt in shades as unafraid as Shady Lady. (Cutex Shady Lady ad, *Self*, August 1981)

19 For the average teacher, diagnostic validity is related to an instrument's ability to be translated into practical classroom realities. In effect, valid diagnostic instruments describe aspects of children's behavior which can be directly observed and quantified. They further provide information which is useful to the teacher; that is, information which suggests constructive courses of action for behavior modification, instruction, and parent involvement.

For this reason, individual instruments are more likely to be valid than those involving mass test administrations. The former allows the test examiner to observe the behavior of the child during test administration; the latter does not. (Edward J. Kelly, *Parent-Teacher Interaction: A Special Educational Perspective*)

20 Perhaps there *is* something physiological about the interest in guns, say the cultists, and we ought to be more tolerant and understanding about this need. It is a matter of human nature, they claim, invoking once again the instinct theory of human aggression. And what is this primal force that explains people's intractable resistance to firearms control? It is man's innate desire to take aim, they tell us, the apparently instinctive desire to shoot at a target, be it a numbered chart or a live animal. . . . All of this makes one wonder how the ancient prefirearms people got along. (Robert Brent Toplin, *Unchallenged Violence: An American Ordeal*)
(Hint: the implied conclusion is that the "cultists" are wrong in saying that there is a specific instinctual need to shoot guns. Note the author's use of the term "cultists" to refer to opponents of gun control.)

21 Any set of human activities affecting exchange relations is of crucial importance. Regarded from this perspective, marketing is [sic] the body of thought and action addressed to exchanges, becomes a major motor force in society and in social change in particular. Marketing, then, is concerned with understanding the various factors that help bring about social exchange and with using this understanding to stimulate selected social exchanges. (Sidney J. Levy and Gerald Zaltman, *Marketing, Society and Conflict*)

22 . . . I shall use 'alienation' in this study in the special sense of powerless/meaninglessness, a subjective feeling of helplessness in the face of an all-pervasive social control, and an apparently endless social complexity. . . . From this viewpoint, it is precisely the rad-

ical activist who is *not* alienated, since he has grasped (rightly or wrongly) at least part of his situation, and is trying to take control of his own destiny. In other words, we can view radical ideologies as avenues of *escape* from alienation. (David Bouchier, *Idealism and Revolution: New Ideologies of Liberation in Britain and the United States*)

23 The liberals' "positive" domestic policies always bring the federal government into the role of subsidizing and controlling the economic activities of the people; and that is the known highway to the total, tyrannical socialist state. (Dan Smoot, *The Invisible Government*)

24 *Philonous:* This point is then agreed between us, that *sensible things are those only which are immediately perceived by sense.* You will further inform me, whether we immediately perceive by sight anything beside light, and colors, and figures: or by hearing anything but sounds: by the palate, anything beside tastes: by the smell, besides odors: or by the touch, more than tangible qualities.
Hylas: We do not.
Philonous: It seems, therefore, that if you take away all sensible qualities, there remains nothing sensible.
Hylas: I grant it.
Philonous: Sensible things therefore are nothing else but so many sensible qualities, or combinations of sensible qualities. (George Berkeley, *Three Dialogues between Hylas and Philonous*)

9

Argument Construction

Until now we've concentrated on analyzing the arguments of others. In this chapter we shift perspective. Here the question is, How can we ourselves produce effective arguments? Before we can answer this question, however, we need to consider another, Effective for what?

9.1 THE NATURE OF INSIGHT

Arguments have many uses, some good, some evil. One pernicious use, as the last couple of chapters illustrate, is the dissemination of falsehood and confusion, generally for the purpose of manipulating others. If that's your interest, then you will consider an argument effective to the extent that it brings people under your power—regardless of its relation to the truth. If so, here's where we part company. I'm not writing this chapter for you.

Another rather sinister use of argument is the rationalization of prejudice. Sometimes when one of our ill-supported beliefs is challenged, we parry by inventing a spurious argument on the spot. Though the argument may represent neither our beliefs nor the truth, with a little bluff and bluster we can often intimidate others, and even ourselves, sufficiently to silence the challenge. Here logic functions as a psychological defense to protect beliefs from embarrassing questions. It is a means of maintaining the *status quo* for people with broad egos and narrow minds. Needless to say, I don't think much of this tactic either, and I'll say no more about it.

What I want to discuss in this chapter are two more beneficial uses of reasoning: communication of insight and examination of one's own beliefs. We'll begin with the first. We have insight into something when we not only know that it's true, but also see why it's true. Communication of insight thus involves more than mere communication of facts. I communicated a fact to you in Section 3.6 when I claimed that you can't like just the people who don't like themselves. What I told you was true, but unless you were already familiar with this sort of paradox you probably couldn't see why it was true. You had knowledge of a fact, but no insight. It wasn't until Section 5.4 that I actually proved this fact. And, if you followed the argument there, you may recall that something remarkable happened. At some point a light dawned; you saw—not literally, of course, but you understood—why this peculiar fact has to be true. The "seeing" is insight. And that's what I was trying to communicate. (If this example didn't make sense to you before, now might be a good time to think through it again. It is, I think, potentially the most striking source of insight in this book.)

Insight, like propaganda, is persuasive. To successfully communicate an insight to someone is almost always to convince that person of its truth. But propaganda persuades by confusing people and entangling them in powerful emotions. In contrast, the persuasiveness of insight lies in its clear revelation of truth. The old adage "seeing is believing" applies as much to insight as it does to ordinary sight. Bringing people to insight is seldom useful if you want them to do your will. But it is useful if you want them to accept the truth. And that is my main answer to the question asked above—effective for what? In this chapter we'll consider the construction of arguments effective for communication of insight into the truth.

As we'll see, however, the attempt to construct such arguments has a disquieting side effect: it forces us to examine the foundations of our own beliefs. In doing so, we risk the potentially disruptive revelation that some of our deepest beliefs are rationally groundless. We risk, in other words, an encounter with the depths of our own ignorance. Such an encounter, I believe, is worth the genuine anxiety it may provoke, for it fosters a beneficial sense of humility. If you believe yourself or your cause to be infallible, it's much easier to demand that others conform to your beliefs—and to afflict them with guilt, oppress them, or kill them if they resist—than it is if you grasp the fact that you could be wrong.

The main topic of this chapter, however, is communication of insight.

I'll discuss self-examination only as a beneficial by-product of this communication.

The knack of communicating insight is to present your audience with a series of true premises which they both understand and accept, and to lead them from these premises to your conclusion by a series of rational and intelligible inferences. It is important to begin with premises your audience accepts, because if they reject the basis of your reasoning, the only thing communicated will be a difference of opinion. The real power of the process, though, lies in the cumulative inevitability of the inferences. By dividing the progression of thought from premises to conclusion into a series of clear, perhaps even trivial, inferences, we enable others to grasp this progression one small step at a time. No deep insight is generated by any single step, but the effect of the entire series can be profound. Perhaps the best illustration of this fact lies in geometry, where from a small group of assumptions (called axioms or postulates) it is possible by a lengthy and cumulative process of deduction to obtain insight into some astonishing and unexpected truths.

As a general rule, then, communication of deep insight requires many inferences—though, of course, proliferation of inferences is no guarantee either of insight or of depth. At least two other conditions must be met: the audience must know that the assumptions are true, and the argument as a whole must be rational—and preferably deductive. But even these requirements are insufficient. For unless the argument is clear and well organized, it will be too obscure to communicate effectively. Therefore clarity and organization are also essential. But we'll postpone discussion of these additional requirements until later sections.

9.2   FORMULATING THE CONCLUSION

Our immediate task, then, is to construct an argument with these properties: It begins with assumptions which our audience knows to be true and proceeds by small, rational, intelligible steps of reasoning to the conclusion we wish to establish. To illustrate the difficulties involved in developing such an argument, I'm going to construct one myself, which will serve as an example in the discussion.

The first step is to choose a conclusion—a proposition whose truth you would like to demonstrate to others. One conclusion which I would like very much to establish is this:

It is better to know the truth than to remain in ignorance.

This is something I believe strongly. In fact, it's one of the convictions underlying the writing of this book. But it's also a very vague and broad idea. Before I can hope to prove it, or anything like it, I need to subject it to a rigorous and critical examination, with the aim of formulating it more precisely.

The best way to do this is to look for exceptions—actual situations which clearly show that it is false. This might appear self-defeating, since my aim is to prove the conclusion, not to refute it. But in fact it may save a great deal of time and effort. The point of this examination is to survey the obstacles standing in the way of proof before attempting the proof itself. If careful criticism reveals no genuine exceptions to the conclusion, then the way is clear to begin the proof. But if apparent exceptions arise, they must be eliminated first. Perhaps these apparent exceptions are mere misunderstandings. If so, they can probably be dealt with by clarifying the wording. But if they are genuine, so that the conclusion is false, then of course proof is impossible and the only remedy is to revise the conclusion substantially. In either case, however, looking for exceptions saves time and effort. Either you'll anticipate surmountable problems and thus begin to deal with them at an early stage, or you'll see that the problems are insurmountable and so refrain from a futile quest for the impossible.

A critical look at my proposed conclusion brings me to this latter realization. My conclusion is much too broad and can easily be shown to be false. There are situations in which knowing the truth is worse than remaining in ignorance. In wartime, people who possess dangerous military secrets are sometimes tortured or put to death because of what they know. Surely, in some cases at least, it would be better for them if they had remained in ignorance. There are many situations, too, in which knowing the truth is neither better nor worse than remaining in ignorance. Much of our knowledge is trivial and useless. I was once required to memorize the names of all 88 counties in Ohio. And I am certain that, having that knowledge, I was not one whit better off than if I had remained in ignorance. My proposed conclusion is therefore simply false. If I had jumped in and tried to prove it immediately, I'd have been wasting my time. For sooner or later exceptions like these would begin to emerge—probably as objections to my premises—and I'd have to start all over again anyway.

Yet I don't think the idea was completely wrongheaded. My proposed conclusion was overstated, but I think it contained a kernel of truth. I'll just need to formulate it more precisely. What I should have said was something more like this:

> Knowing about things that really matter to us is usually better than remaining in ignorance.

This is not quite as elegant, but it seems closer to the truth. I added the phrase "about things that really matter to us" to rule out useless knowledge of trivia, and I added "usually" in recognition of those relatively rare cases—

like knowing a dangerous military secret—in which knowledge results in definite harm to the knower. Thus stated, the conclusion seems much more likely to be provable.

It is difficult to overemphasize the importance of critical examination of the conclusion. Moving blindly ahead with rigidly preconceived ideas will ultimately get you nowhere. Worse, it may tempt you to employ deception, of yourself or others or both, to rationalize a conclusion which could not be established by honest means. This advice applies, not only at the initial stage of formulating the conclusion, but throughout the entire construction process. Though I now have a conclusion which seems workable, I shouldn't shrink from revising it again later if that is what the nature of the case demands. At this point, however, no need for further revisions is apparent, and so I'll proceed with the formulation of premises.

9.3 FINDING COMMON GROUND: THE SOCRATIC METHOD

To communicate insight effectively, an argument must be tailored to its audience. Mere soundness is not enough. The argument must lead its audience from truths they already know by rational inferences they can comprehend to the conclusion you wish them to grasp. That is why books on tensor calculus or partial differential equations, though full of sound arguments of great clarity and precision, fail to illuminate most of us. We are familiar with neither their assumptions nor their modes of inference, and so we obtain no insight. It is for similar reasons that arguments which beg the question, though frequently sound, are unilluminating (see Section 5.6). Since these arguments assume their conclusions, those who accept the conclusion already will learn nothing new, and those who do not will certainly reject it as a premise.

Thus communication of insight requires finding true assumptions that both you and your audience share. Such shared assumptions are called **common ground.** Common ground is relative to both your knowledge and the knowledge of your audience. If you are a mathematician writing for other mathematicians, then you will have a vast wealth of mathematical knowledge as common ground. If, however, you are a parent trying to bring a fifth-grader to the realization that she ought to do her homework, then your common ground is more limited—and you'll have to keep the inferences relatively simple.

The audience for my sample argument in this chapter is you, the reader. I know nothing about you except that since you are reading this book, you are intelligent and probably have at least a high school education. Therefore I can assume as common ground only premises which nearly every intelligent high school graduate knows or can easily verify to be true.

Perhaps the most frequent mistake in dealing with such a general audience is to underestimate its diversity. While there is much knowledge that we all share—for example, that there are seven days in a week, that we must have nourishment to stay alive, that automobile exhaust contains carbon monoxide, that Columbus came to the New World in 1492—there are many issues about which there is no consensus. Most prominent among these are issues of morality, philosophy, religion, and public policy. There is widespread disagreement, for example, about the best way to handle the economy, the moral and legal status of a fetus, the authority of religious texts, obligation in warfare, and so on. Most assumptions about these matters are not common ground for a general audience.

It is a mistake, however, to assume that there is no agreement on moral, religious, or pragmatic issues. Virtually everyone agrees that torturing children for the fun of it is wrong. That's common ground. So is the fact that religious faith gives many people a deep and satisfying sense of meaning. We are nearly all aware that it does. And so, too, is the assertion that we ought to avoid immolating this planet with nuclear weapons. There are, of course, a few mavericks who deny such propositions. But for practical purposes we can ignore them in an argument addressed to the general public. (Of course, it's a different matter if we're arguing with these mavericks themselves; then we *are* committed to finding common ground with them.)

To qualify as common ground, a statement need not be generally known by its audience, but it must be something that they can readily verify. It is reasonable, for instance, in an argument to the general public, to employ statistics gathered in scientific studies, facts of history, reliable accounts of current events, and so on, even if these are not generally known, so long as there are ways of verifying them and tracing them back to their sources. Such means of verification include libraries, textbooks, newspapers, scientific journals, and so forth. Anyone not convinced of an assumption can then check the evidence personally and pursue it to its source if necessary. If such verifiability is lacking, however, doubt will remain, and it will be impossible to make your audience see clearly that your conclusion is true.

Having determined the extent of the knowledge which you and your audience share, the next step is to find within this common ground assumptions adequate to establish the conclusion. The most efficient way to do this is to work backwards from conclusion to premises and from these premises to further premises until either common ground is attained or you see that it is unattainable. If you attain common ground, then you have the argument you want. If you can't, then the only remaining options are to revise the conclusion or to give up.

The process of working backwards from conclusions to premises involves continual reiteration of the question "What is my evidence for this?" The question will usually bring to mind a series of premises, but in most cases these premises will not be common ground. After stating them, the first thing to do is to check them for exceptions, just as we did with the conclusion, and replace or revise them if they are false. When you are satisfied that your premises are true and that they rationally support your conclusion, then you need to repeat the question "What is my evidence for this?" for those that are not common ground. This will bring to mind premises for the premises, and these in turn need to be examined for exceptions and replaced or revised if necessary. Repetition of this process is what generates the argument.

We'll call this iterative process the **Socratic method,** because of its similarity to the technique of repeated questioning which Socrates practiced on his fellow Athenians. The point of Socrates' method was to probe his opponents' beliefs to discover if they were supported by good reasons. The point here is the same. We subject our own beliefs to a kind of internal Socratic interrogation in order to uncover the reasons behind them.

The danger in this, as real today as it was in Socrates' time, is that we may ultimately find that our beliefs rest on nothing. Socrates was very skilled at showing his adversaries precisely this, and his skill often aroused their wrath. In fact, his insistence on reasons angered his contemporaries so much that they finally put him to death.

The story of Socrates is history, but it is also a powerful parable of the human mind. It is easier to silence the questioning Socrates within ourselves than to risk facing what he might reveal. To employ the Socratic method is to awaken the Socratic spirit within us, and this cannot be done without considerable honesty, energy, and courage. Socrates was—and still is—a dangerous man.

Let's apply the Socratic method to the conclusion I have proposed— that knowing about things that really matter to us is usually better than remaining in ignorance. What's my evidence? As a first approximation, I'd say that knowledge gives us power to influence our environment and anticipate its effect on us. Now we're much likelier to be happy if we can influence and anticipate events, and that is what makes knowledge better than ignorance—at least if it's knowledge about things that matter. These thoughts suggest the following premises:

1   Knowing about things that really matter to us usually gives us more power to influence our environment and anticipate its effects than remaining in ignorance does.
2   We are likelier to be happy if we can influence and anticipate events than if not.

And to get to my conclusion from these premises, I'm evidently also going to need the assumption:

3   The likelier something is to make us happy, the better it is.

Now are these propositions true? I'm not by any means confident that they are. Though 1 seems fairly safe, serious doubts can be raised about 2 and 3. Consider 2, for example. Is the human race really happier with its vastly increased ability to influence and anticipate events in modern times? Do we really have the wisdom to use our power to make ourselves happier? Perhaps so, but I have my doubts, and the more I think about it the less confident I am that I could prove this. And 3, too, is doubtful. It is well known that drugs can induce artificial euphoria, but does that mean they are good? What if a drug could be developed that would keep us happy all the time? I seriously doubt that that would be an improvement. These apparent exceptions to 2 and 3 seem fairly formidable. That's discouraging, but it is to be expected. No one formulates a really effective argument on the first try.

I could try to revise 2 and 3 to accommodate these objections, but the more I think about it, the more I'm beginning to suspect that happiness and the power to change things are not really the point. I think I'd want to say that knowledge is better than ignorance, even if it leaves us sadder, simply because it provides opportunity to go through life with open eyes—to face reality—and I think there's something admirable in that. So instead of revising 2 and 3 I'm going to propose a completely new inference:

1　Knowledge provides opportunity to face reality, and ignorance prevents it.

2　It is more admirable to face reality—at least about things that really matter to us—than not to face it.

3　What enables us to do what is admirable is usually better than what prevents this.

∴　4　Knowing about things that really matter to us is usually better than remaining in ignorance.

Now once again I need to ask whether my premises are true. Premises 1 and 3, though vague, are perhaps defensible. And the inference, though not quite deductive, could probably be shored up. But my real worry is 2. Certainly some people would deny it, and so it is not common ground. But that's not the problem. I still think it's true, and if I could deduce it from common ground, everything would be fine. The problem is that I can't think of any clear reasons for believing it. Apparently I just take it on faith, and the Socratic method has brought me to the realization that this faith has no rational foundation.

Does this mean that I should reject this belief? Certainly not. I haven't shown that it is false; I know of no exceptions. I've merely discovered that I can't prove it. To deny it would be to commit the fallacy of ignorance. But I can't honestly claim to know that it's true, either. I *feel* that it's true, but to conclude that I'm right would be to commit the aesthetic fallacy. Honesty permits me only to say that I believe but I don't know. It may even be that there is no truth about such matters, though I don't really know that either.

For each of us, there are many propositions like this that we accept without good evidence. Typically, these are propositions that we learned from parents or other authorities, that we have adopted to gain social acceptance, or that we hold on the basis of emotion. Because we dislike the doubt and insecurity that arise with the realization that some of these beliefs are rationally groundless, we tend to deceive ourselves into thinking that we really do have good reasons for them. When threatened with the loss of this illusion, we may become irritable and defensive—hence the hostility toward the Socratic spirit, both historically and within ourselves.

But there is, I think, a more constructive response. For Socratic interrogation is also an opportunity to examine fundamental beliefs and determine our attitude toward them, if not rationally, at least consciously and freely. Often, in the absence of good reasons, the logical attitude is to suspend judgment. But frequently life demands more of a commitment than that. Though, for example, I do not know whether facing reality is ultimately worthwhile, I will by the very act of living either try to face reality or shun the attempt. This choice of action is tantamount to acceptance or rejection of the belief, and it is unavoidable. The only real question is whether I will make the choice thoughtlessly—"programmed," as it were, by authorities, peers, or whim—or freely and deliberately. The Socratic method, by making me aware of my choice, provides an opportunity to make it freely. In doing so, I sense my fallibility, but I also recognize my responsibility. It is now fully *my* choice, and I must forever abandon the excuse that this belief and the actions which flow from it are the responsibility of others. That realization is in my opinion a great benefit of the Socratic method. But I won't attempt to prove that opinion here.

I am, after all, in the middle of trying to prove something else. And, having digressed, I need to take stock. The result of my inability to prove 2 is that again I've reached a dead end. I cannot hope to bring a general audience to insight with an argument based on this premise, because it is not common ground and I know of no way of deducing it from common ground—or, indeed, from any premises that don't simply beg the question. The avenues of rational persuasion are closed to me. If I were an artist or a novelist, I might use my artistic skill to infect others with my faith in 2. I might even in this way bring them to a kind of insight. But I can't do it logically, and that's what we're concerned with here.

So once again I must begin anew. By now it's starting to dawn on me that my intended conclusion—that knowing about things that really matter to us is usually better than remaining in ignorance—is still too strong. My belief in that conclusion depends fundamentally on the idea that facing reality is somehow admirable, an idea that I cannot rationally defend. So if I'm going to prove anything at all, it will have to be something weaker. Perhaps I could make more headway if I eliminated the moral tone of my conclusion and tried to show, not that knowledge is *better* than ignorance, but at least that it's *more useful*. But, of course, some knowledge really isn't useful, either because it is trivial or because it concerns things which we are powerless to change. Therefore, if I am going to take this line, I would do well to restrict my conclusion to knowledge of practical situations—that is, situations in which we have various alternatives of action whose outcomes differ in ways that matter to us. My conclusions, then, would be something like this:

> Knowledge about practical situations is more useful in those situations than remaining in ignorance.

Now this formulation, though a far cry from what I started with, is certainly specific and seems quite obviously true. But still, as with any conclusion, we need to check it carefully for exceptions. If we do, we will see that it is not as obvious as it first appeared.

Here is one sort of exception: a woman's husband is having an illicit love affair. Perhaps, if she acted, she could stop the affair, and so it is a practical situation. But it could be more useful to her—say, if her primary goal were preservation of the marriage—to remain in ignorance. If she never found out, perhaps the affair would pass and be forgotten. And if she did find out, perhaps the resulting tension and mistrust would destroy the marriage. Admittedly, many extramarital affairs begin with trouble in the marriage itself, so that often it is best to discover the affair and deal with this trouble in the open. But there are exceptions, and sometimes the affair, if not discovered, eventually ends, leaving the marriage intact. In these cases, though many of us might prefer to know the truth anyway, to a person whose main concern was preservation of the marriage, it might be more useful not to know the truth. And so, at least for some people, this would be a practical situation about which it would be more useful to remain in ignorance than to know the truth.

Such situations are, however, pretty rare. Therefore, we can preserve the truth of the proposed conclusion by means of a device we used earlier. Again, we'll simply insert the word "usually":

> Knowledge about practical situations is usually more useful in those situations than remaining in ignorance.

This conclusion, at last, seems unobjectionable. But now it is so obviously true that it hardly seems worth proving. Practically everyone would accept it. It is probably common ground as it stands.

Yet acceptance is not insight. Though nearly everyone may believe that this is true, probably fewer can see why it is true, and fewer still could offer a good argument for it. So there is some point, after all, in constructing such an argument. The point is to make some of the reasons for this conclusion clear and perhaps to offer some insight into why it is true.

Having said this, however, I ought to confess a sense of disappointment, which perhaps you share. I would much rather prove a broader and more controversial conclusion, one to which my reasoning would bring insight like a sudden radiance. But in logic, clarity and truth are preferable to drama, and I see no legitimate way of reaching such a dramatic conclusion on the topic I have chosen. So I'll press on with this more mundane conclusion.

Once again I apply the Socratic method. What is my evidence for this conclusion? Well, rather trivially, the reason why knowledge about practical situations is useful is that it helps us in those situations to achieve our goals. My inference, then, is something like this:

> Knowledge of a practical situation usually enables us to achieve our goals in that situation more effectively than remaining in ignorance does.
>
> The more effectively something enables us to achieve our goals, the more useful it is.
>
> ∴ Knowledge about practical situations is usually more useful in those situations than remaining in ignorance.

The second premise here is definitely common ground. It is clear that the more effectively something helps us to achieve our goals, the more useful it is, because that's just what "useful" means—enabling the achievement of goals.

The first premise is also pretty obvious, but let's pursue its justification further. Why does knowledge about practical situations usually enable us to achieve our goals better than ignorance does? The answer, I think, lies in the fact that it gives us greater control. My inference, then, is this:

> Knowledge of practical situations gives us more control over their outcomes than remaining in ignorance does.
>
> The better we are able to control the outcomes of practical situations, the more effectively we can achieve our goals in those situations.
>
> ∴ Knowledge of a practical situation usually enables us to achieve our goals in that situation more effectively than remaining in ignorance does.

Here both premises seem true enough, but neither has the transparency and certainty desirable in a basic premise. Therefore I'll apply the Socratic method, in turn, to each. What is my evidence for believing that knowledge or practical situations gives us greater control? Well, knowledge about practical situations enables us to predict with greater accuracy which outcome will follow from a given action, and the more accurately we can make such predictions, the better we can tailor our actions to produce the outcome we desire. More explicitly:

> Knowledge of a practical situation enables us to predict the outcomes of the actions we could take in that situation more accurately than remaining in ignorance does.

> The more accurately we can predict the outcomes of the actions we could take in a practical situation, the more control we have over those outcomes.

> ∴ Knowledge of practical situations gives us more control over their outcomes than remaining in ignorance does.

I am fairly satisfied with both premises here. The first one states that knowledge about practical situations helps us to predict their outcomes—at least better than remaining in ignorance does. That seems true enough. If I know that the battery in my car is weak, then I am able to predict with a fairly high degree of probability that if I do nothing there will soon come a day when my car will not start. But if I had remained in ignorance about the battery's condition, then I could not so easily have anticipated this outcome. Practical examples like this abound, and you could easily think of dozens more. Perhaps my expression of the premise is a bit too vague, and perhaps with some thought we could spot exceptions. But probably only small adjustments are needed. We'll make such adjustments in the next section. For now this premise is passable.

The same goes for the second premise. If we know what actions will produce various outcomes and we are able to take those actions (as we are in a practical situation), then we are in better control than if we lack this predictive ability. For example, if I know that eating fried onion rings will upset my stomach, then I can choose either to upset or not to upset my stomach by eating them. But if I could not predict the outcome of my action, then I would lack control. Of course, I never have complete control of my stomach. But being able to predict the outcome of eating onion rings provides more control than I would have otherwise. Consideration of examples like this makes the truth of the second premise fairly clear. It's probably not far from common ground. Let's accept it for now.

Only one line of reasoning remains incomplete (as you know if you are reading nonlinearly): the line leading to the second premise of the inference preceding the one just discussed. In other words, I still need to provide evidence that the better we are able to control the outcomes of practical situations, the more effectively we are able to achieve our goals in those situations. What is my evidence here? Well, since a practical situation is one whose outcome makes some difference to us, in such a situation we prefer some outcomes to others. It would follow, then, that certain of these possible outcomes are goals for us, while others are to be avoided. Hence ability to control the outcome of a practical situation is in effect ability to achieve our goals in that situation, which is what I want to prove. This line of thought suggests the following argument:

> A practical situation is a situation in which we have various possible alternatives of action, whose outcomes make some difference to us.
>
> When things make some difference to us, we prefer some to others.
>
> ∴ A practical situation is a situation in which we prefer some possible outcomes of our actions to others.
>
> The possible outcomes which we prefer in a situation are goals for us in that situation.
>
> ∴ Some of the possible outcomes of a practical situation are goals for us in that situation.
>
> ∴ The better we are able to control the outcomes of practical situations, the more effectively we can achieve our goals in those situations.

The final conclusion here is the premise which I am trying to support. The support which I provide is itself a complex argument, consisting of three inferences and utilizing three basic premises. The first of these basic premises is common ground, for it is merely a definition of what I mean by "practical situation." Definitions, as we saw in Section 8.7, are unobjectionable, so long as they do not ascribe to a term a meaning which conflicts with current usage, thereby generating troublesome ambiguity.

But there is no danger of ambiguity here. The term "practical situation" has only a vague meaning in common usage, and nothing in my definition conflicts with that vague meaning. I have merely sharpened it so that it will work more precisely for me. If you still feel uneasy about this, look at it this way: the term "practical situation" as it appears in my argument is nothing more than an abbreviation for the longer phrase "situation in which we have various possible alternatives of action, whose outcomes make some difference to us." Anyone who mistrusts my usage may simply substitute this longer phrase for the shorter one wherever it occurs in the argument, thus making my meaning fully clear. The only reason I have not done so is that it would make the premises too long and cumbersome. Using an abbreviatory definition avoids this complexity. And once again, since my definition does not actually conflict with common usage, there is no threat of harmful ambiguity. As a general rule, such abbreviatory definitions should be regarded as common ground (since their harmlessness can easily be verified by the reader) unless they induce ambiguity. So the first premise is acceptable as it stands.

The second premise is totally obvious, for when we say that things "make some difference to us," what we mean is that we prefer some of these things to others. If we have no preferences among a group of events, then it makes no difference to us which occurs. This premise is common ground.

The third premise is nonbasic, and so we needn't worry about whether it is common ground, but the fourth is basic again. Is it common ground? Well, there may be some dispute about the use of the word "goal" here. It doesn't quite fit. But the idea seems true enough. Since we're planning to take care of fine details of wording in the next section, let's not worry about it just yet.

We now have compiled a rough but serviceable argument. All of its basic premises seem close to common ground, and though we've not been too careful in checking the inferences for rationality, all of them seem fairly reasonable. Assembling them in annotated standard form, we get this:

	1	A practical situation is a situation in which we have various possible alternatives of action, whose outcomes make some difference to us.
	2	When things make some difference to us, we prefer some to others.
∴	3	A practical situation is a situation in which we prefer some possible outcomes of our actions to others. 1,2
	4	The possible outcomes which we prefer in a situation are goals for us in that situation.
∴	5	Some of the possible outcomes of a practical situation are goals for us in that situation. 3,4
∴	6	The better we are able to control the outcomes of practical situations, the more effectively we can achieve our goals in those situations. 5
	7	Knowledge of a practical situation enables us to predict the outcomes of the actions we could take in that situation more accurately than remaining in ignorance does.
	8	The more accurately we can predict the outcomes of the actions we could take in a practical situation, the more control we have over those outcomes.
∴	9	Knowledge of practical situations gives us more control over their outcomes than remaining in ignorance does. 7,8
∴	10	Knowledge of a practical situation usually enables us to achieve our goals in that situation more effectively than remaining in ignorance does. 6,9
	11	The more effectively something enables us to achieve our goals, the more useful it is.

∴ 12 Knowledge about practical situations is usually more useful in those situations than remaining in ignorance.   10,11

This looks impressive, but our work is by no means finished. Some of the basic premises are still vague or dubious, some of the inferences are unclear, and the whole thing is excessively wordy and complicated. But normally this is the sort of argument which the Socratic method yields. Thus, after the Socratic method has done its work, there comes a stage of polishing, adjusting, and sharpening the argument to clarity.

9.4   CLARITY

Communication of insight requires precision. Vague or ambiguous statements, weak inferences, and dubious premises all hinder communication. But so does excessive precision. Too many distinctions and too many details distract and confuse. Thus, the ideal of communication lies somewhere between abject sloppiness and byzantine exactitude. This ideal is clarity.

Good reasoning, then, is a compromise. It transmits essential thoughts with careful rigor but ruthlessly rejects inessential detail. This is a delicate balance, and no one achieves it on the first try. It takes a good bit of tinkering to bring an argument to clarity.

The rough argument of the last section errs on the side of complexity. It takes too many words to say too little. It needs some coldhearted editing. Now one of the things that bothered me as I was composing it was the use of the word "goal" in premise 4. Goals are not always the *possible* outcomes we prefer; rather, they are any outcomes we strive for, whether possible or not. So 4 is not strictly true. It must be replaced or eliminated. One way to accomplish this would be to replace all occurrences of the term "goal" in the argument by the more accurate term "possible outcomes we prefer." This revision has the advantage, not only of clarifying our meaning, but also of eliminating the need for the inference from 3 and 4 to 5. The purpose of this inference was to take us from talk of possible outcomes we value most to talk of goals. But under our new strategy this step is unnecessary; statements 4 and 5 can be omitted. This solves the problem of the falsehood of 4 and in the same stroke achieves a welcome simplification. If switching from "goals" to "possible outcomes we prefer" creates no problems with other premises—and as you can verify, it does not—then this switch is a notable improvement.

We can simplify the argument still further by altering the definition of "practical situation" slightly. Notice that 1 and 3 say roughly the same thing. Why not define "practical situation" by the terms used in 3, rather than as in 1? The inference from 1 and 2 to 3 then becomes superfluous, and we can begin with 3 alone.

This simplification, together with the previous one, shortens the argument considerably. Renumbering to compensate for omissions, the result is as follows:

1 (formerly 3)   A practical situation is a situation in which we prefer some possible outcomes of our actions to others.

∴ 2 (formerly 6)   The better we are able to control the outcomes of practical situations, the more effectively we can attain the possible outcomes we prefer in those situations.   1

3 (formerly 7)   Knowledge of a practical situation enables us to predict the outcomes of the actions we could take in that situation more accurately than remaining in ignorance does.

4 (formerly 8)   The more accurately we can predict the outcomes of actions we could take in a practical situation, the more control we have over those outcomes.

∴ 5 (formerly 9)   Knowledge of practical situations gives us more control over their outcomes than remaining in ignorance does.   3,4

∴ 6 (formerly 10)   Knowledge of a practical situation usually enables us to attain the possible outcomes we prefer in that situation more effectively than remaining in ignorance does.   2,5

7 (formerly 11)   The more effectively something enables us to attain the possible outcomes we prefer in a situation, the more useful it is in that situation.

∴ 8 (formerly 12)   Knowledge about practical situations is usually more useful in those situations than remaining in ignorance.   6,7

Compare this version with the initial version at the end of Section 9.3 to make sure you understand the reasons for the changes. Simplification of this sort is often possible, and usually beneficial, in argument construction.

The argument is now more compact, but hardly more compelling. There are still a number of trouble spots. One is the vagueness of the term "possible" as it occurs in 1 and elsewhere. I certainly don't mean "logically possible," though that is one reading of what I have said. For since we can imagine ourselves in any situation having the power to change everything to suit our whims, in every situation there are *logically possible* alternatives of action, some of whose outcomes we value more than others. Thus if I meant "logically possible" in 1, every situation would be a practical situation. But that's not what I meant. The sorts of possible outcomes I was talking about are those which are *realistically attainable* (i.e., actually within our ability to produce). To avoid confusion, I need to say this explicitly, and thus to reword all those premises in which the term "possible" occurs.

A second trouble spot is the inference from 1 to 2. It is invalid, as the following counterexample shows: Imagine a situation in which we acquire the ability to predict which actions lead to undesirable outcomes, but not which ones lead to the outcomes we value. We now have more control than we had before we could predict anything, but we are no more effectively able to achieve the outcomes we value most. Thus 2 is false in this situation, though 1 may well be true. Indeed, this counterexample suggests that there may be exceptions to 2 itself.

What is the remedy? Well, apparently we need to talk, not about outcomes in general, as in 2, but specifically about the ability to attain the outcomes we value most. Such a change would eliminate 2 and require a careful revision of all those other statements—3, 4, and 5—which talk about outcomes in general. The idea is to get to 6 directly by establishing that knowledge helps us attain the outcomes we value most, rather than to go at it indirectly by first establishing, as in 5, that it gives us control over outcomes in general. This entails a major reorganization of the first part of the argument.

Keeping in mind that we also need to replace the term "possible" with more accurate wording, let's attempt another reformulation:

    1 (formerly 1) A practical situation is a situation in which we prefer some realistically attainable outcomes of our actions to others.

    2 If we prefer some realistically attainable outcomes of our actions to others, then the more accurately we can predict which actions lead to outcomes we prefer, the more effectively we can attain these outcomes.

∴ 3 In a practical situation, the more accurately we can predict which actions lead to realistic outcomes we prefer, the more effectively we can attain these outcomes.   1,2

    4 Knowledge of practical situations enables us to predict which actions lead to realistic outcomes we prefer more accurately than remaining in ignorance does.

∴ 5 (formerly 6) Knowledge of a practical situation usually enables us to attain the realistic outcomes we prefer in that situation more effectively than remaining in ignorance does.   3,4

    6 (formerly 7) The more effectively something enables us to attain the realistic outcomes we prefer in a situation, the more useful it is in that situation.

∴ 7 (formerly 8) Knowledge about practical situations is usually more useful in those situations than remaining in ignorance.   5,6

The first part of the argument has undergone a radical reorganization, and though most of the new premises have counterparts in the previous version, they now stand in different logical relations to one another; the inference structure is no longer the same. Keeping in mind that the point of this reorganization is to establish 5 (formerly 6) by more reliable inferences than we had before, compare this version with the last one, reread the discussion, and try to get a clear idea of why I made the changes in this way.

By now the argument bears little resemblance to the initial version of Section 9.3. You may be starting to wonder why we ever bothered with the Socratic method in the first place. Couldn't we just have begun with the argument we now have? Perhaps, if we were omniscient. But we are short-sighted and inefficient creatures. I could not have invented the argument in its present form all at once. I had to feel my way through the various exceptions and counterexamples and make innumerable errors and false starts before I became familiar with the conceptual territory I was exploring. That, of course, is a nuisance, but for creatures of finite intelligence it's unavoidable. (In fact, the process of constructing this argument was even more complex than my discussion here suggests; I am really only sum-marizing its highlights.)

There remains a bit more nuisance to be endured, but we are nearing the finish. I can think of only two further substantial objections to the argument. The first is quite simple. Premise 4 is false. The problem is that not just any knowledge of practical situations facilitates prediction. If our knowledge is superficial or irrelevant in some way, then it will be of no help at all. But the remedy is also simple. For 4 would become true, and obviously so, if instead of just "knowledge" I said "thorough knowledge." There's a bit more to it than this, however, since once I have made this change in 4, the rest of the argument will not follow unless I make a similar change in subsequent statements, including the conclusion. That makes the conclusion even weaker than it was, but it's the price we must pay for the truth of 4. I suggest we pay it.

There is one final objection. Where did the term "usually" come from in 5? It is not in any of the previous premises, and 5 seems to follow from 3 and 4 even if we omit it. So what is its purpose? As you may recall, we added this term to our final conclusion and to a prototype of 5 clear back in Section 9.3 in response to certain objections. These objections concerned situations—like that of the betrayed lover or the discoverer of a dangerous secret—in which knowing itself somehow prevented a desired outcome. These situations, we said, are rare, but not unheard of, and so we modified our conclusion and the prototype of 5 to take account of them. But as we added further premises, these cases were forgotten, and we stopped allowing for them. Now at last they've come back to haunt us. For they infect our reasoning with falsehood clear up to premise 2. Premise 2 is false because sometimes—as in the cases just mentioned—what gives us predictive ability in a situation, namely knowledge, is the very thing which prevents a valued outcome. (The betrayed spouse's knowledge of the betrayal, for example, may prevent continuation of the marriage.) In such cases, though we may be able to predict the results of our actions more accurately, we are less effective at producing the outcome we desire.

Now since, as we just noted, this sort of case is rare, we could solve the problem simply by inserting "usually" into premise 2 and the intermediate conclusion, 3, which follows from it. Then, since 3 and 4 lead to 5, the presence of "usually" in 3 would account for its appearance in 5 as well. But this strategy has a distinct disadvantage. "Usually" is terribly vague, and its presence introduces more obscurity than insight. "Why just usually?" the reader will wonder. Since my purpose is to generate insight, I ought to explain. Therefore, instead of just adding "usually" to 2 and 3, I suggest that we qualify these premises with the phrase "—unless what enables us to predict them (i.e., the favored outcomes) somehow prevents their attainment." That should inform the reader of the sorts of exceptions I have in mind. Once I have offered this explanation, I can then reintroduce "usually" as a kind of shorthand. This will require an extra premise or two, as we'll see momentarily, but the gain in clarity is worth it.

I have now proposed two additional changes: the insertion of the term "thorough" in 4 and subsequent statements, and the inclusion of the phrase "—unless what enables us to predict them somehow prevents their attainment" in several premises in order to correct 2 and account for the appearance of "usually" in 5. The result, renumbered and rewritten, is as follows:

1   (formerly 1)   A practical situation is a situation in which we prefer some realistically attainable outcomes of our actions to others.

2   (formerly 2)   If we prefer some realistically attainable outcomes of our actions to others, then the more accurately we can predict which actions lead to outcomes we prefer, the more effectively we can attain these outcomes—unless what enables us to predict them somehow prevents their attainment.

∴ 3   (formerly 3)   In a practical situation, the more accurately we can predict which actions lead to realistic outcomes we prefer, the more effectively we can attain these outcomes—unless what enables us to predict them somehow prevents their attainment.   1,2

4   (formerly 4)   Thorough knowledge of practical situations enables us to predict which actions lead to realistic outcomes we prefer more accurately than remaining in ignorance does.

∴ 5   (new intermediate conclusion)   Thorough knowledge of practical situations enables us to attain the realistic outcomes we prefer in those situations more effectively than remaining in ignorance does—unless that knowledge somehow prevents their attainment.   3,4

6   (new basic premise)   Thorough knowledge of practical situations rarely prevents attainment of the realistic outcomes we prefer in those situations.

∴ 7   (formerly 5)   Thorough knowledge of practical situations usually enables us to attain the realistic outcomes we prefer in those situations more effectively than remaining in ignorance does.   5,6

8 (formerly 6)   The more effectively something enables us to attain the realistic outcomes we prefer in a situation, the more useful it is in that situation.

∴ 9 (formerly 7)   Thorough knowledge of practical situations is usually more useful in those situations than remaining in ignorance.   7,8

This, at last, is a good argument. Each of the inferences is deductive, and each basic premise is probably common ground for my readers. The argument is not easy to follow, and that is regrettable, but with care most readers could understand it, and I see no way to simplify it further without sacrificing essential detail. Thus, I think it is a fair compromise between sloppiness and excess precision. It is clear.

How well does it communicate insight? Well, as I noted before, it will strike no one as a rush of dawning light. The conclusion is too obvious for that. But insight is not always so spectacular. Most people, I think, would assent automatically to the flat and simple proposition that knowledge is more useful than ignorance. This argument gives some insight into why that proposition requires qualification. It also helps us to see that the utility of knowledge is based largely on its predictive power and hints at the role of this predictive power in action. These are not profound thoughts, but they are worth thinking. The argument communicates some degree of insight.

The focus of the last few sections, however, has not been the argument itself, but the complex process of its creation. As arguments go, this one is pretty dull. The creative process, however, is anything but dull. In fact, when pursued honestly, it can produce discoveries which are both perilous and exciting. I myself learned a great deal in constructing this argument— a lot more than the final product reveals. I learned, for example, that one of the beliefs that motivated this book—that knowledge is better than ignorance—is not something I can rationally prove, but is based on faith. I choose to maintain that faith, but I do so now with an enhanced appreciation of my fallibility. I could be wrong.

The discussion of this section was tedious, but I hope you stuck with it. Crafting a good argument requires painstaking attention to detail, so that some tedium is unavoidable. I'll make no apologies for that.

I must ultimately admit, however, that my argument is a poor illustration of the power of rational persuasion. Though it sheds some light on its conclusion, it will not *persuade* anyone, because practically everyone accepts the conclusion already. Why, then, didn't I construct a better example? I could have. There are examples of genuinely persuasive arguments throughout this book, all constructed by essentially the same method described here. But I decided not to, because that would have left the unrealistic impression that the Socratic method generates deep, persuasive arguments as a matter of course. It doesn't. In fact, the usual outcome is, as my argument illustrates, something of a letdown. The method *can* yield profound arguments, and of course these are what we aim for, but even for logicians they are the exception rather than the rule. Thus, though my argument is a poor example of rational persuasion, it does illustrate another point, one which I think is even more important. The point is that often when we set out to persuade others by honest reason, we fall short—and in the process come to appreciate how little we ourselves actually know.

9.5   ORGANIZATION

Only a logician would present an argument as a series of numbered propositions. Though this mode of formulation is indispensable in argument construction and evaluation (it helps us to see exactly what the argument lacks and to keep its structure firmly in mind), it is not the most efficient way to present an argument to readers. The reasons for this are rooted in the facts of human psychology.

The mind can encompass only a small amount of information at a time. A reader working through an argument in annotated standard form first encounters some basic premises and then is drawn into the inferences. Unless the argument is very simple, the reader, struggling with the inferences themselves, quickly loses sight of the starting point and becomes disoriented and confused. He or she comes back to the basic premises and starts over, or perhaps looks ahead to the conclusion to find out where the whole thing is going. If the argument is clear and the reader is persistent, eventually this back-and-forth perusal pays off in understanding. But it is wasteful and time-consuming.

This waste can be minimized by perspicuous organization.

What a reader needs to know most at the beginning of an argument is where the argument will end. That is, he or she needs to know what the conclusion is. Without this knowledge, readers can seldom grasp the purpose of what they are reading and almost never know what to look for next. While there is drama in drawing unsuspecting readers through strange twists of reasoning and clobbering them with a startling conclusion at the end, too often there is also smugness and self-indulgence, and seldom is there efficient communication of insight. Even if the argument is sound, readers are likely to suspect that they have been tricked.

It is generally best, therefore, to put your cards on the table at once—that is, to begin by announcing your conclusion. If the argument is brief and simple, you can then present it immediately. But if it is too complex to grasp all at once, then you can facilitate communication by summarizing the reasoning beforehand. This helps readers to get their bearings before having to wrestle with the argument's fine points. My sample argument contains nine statements, and its inferences are rather complex. So a summary would be helpful. After introducing the conclusion, I might say this:

This is because practical knowledge, by enabling us to predict the outcomes of our actions, enables us to choose those actions which best accomplish what we want.

This is vague in comparison with the argument, but it gives readers an idea of what to expect.

If the argument is extremely complex, insight can be enhanced by dividing it into subproofs, called **lemmas.** Then, in addition to a summary at the beginning which announces the organization of the lemmas, it helps to begin each lemma with its own summary and a reminder of its place in the argument. In even more complex arguments, lemmas may be broken down into sublemmas, and so on, and in these cases even more levels of summaries and reminders may be necessary. But you are unlikely to construct such an argument unless you become a logician or mathematician, and so we won't bother with examples. My argument is short enough that a single introductory summary will do.

Another way to enhance comprehensibility is to eliminate unnecessary repetition. Arguments in standard form exhibit considerable reiteration of words and phrases, and this has a mind-numbing, almost hypnotic, effect on the reader. Repetition can profitably be reduced, not only by omission of statements as discussed in Chapter 4, but also by the use of pronouns and other devices which enable us to refer to previous expressions without explicitly repeating them.

The addition of appropriate inference indicators (see Section 1.3) and other transitional words and phrases (Section 2.1) also helps to make the presentation smooth and clear.

Short sentences are a further aid to clarity. Don't ensnare your readers in a bramble of verbiage. Some of the sentences in my argument, especially 2, are monstrosities. In the final version, I'll try to break them up into simpler units.

Finally, whenever a statement is very general or abstract, it is useful to provide clarifying examples. We understand the particular and concrete far more readily than the general and abstract, and specific examples help to focus the reader's mind on the kinds of cases to which a general statement applies. This focus makes the general statement easier to comprehend. Thus, for example, when in my argument I mention those exceptional situations in which the source of our predictive ability (knowledge) somehow prevents a preferred outcome, it will be useful to mention the specific cases I was thinking about (e.g., the case of the betrayed spouse).

With these pointers in mind, I'm going to rewrite my argument in a form more useful for public presentation. Compare this final version to the one near the end of Section 9.4, and note the reasons for the omissions, revisions, and additions. It would also be instructive to diagram this final version and supply missing premises according to the procedure discussed in Chapter 4. Since in this case you have full knowledge of the author's intentions, that shouldn't be too difficult.

Here's the final product:

Though much knowledge is useless, either because it is trivial or because of our powerlessness to employ it, thorough knowledge of practical situations is usually more useful in those situations than remaining in ignorance. This is because practical knowledge, by enabling us to predict the outcomes of our actions, enables us to choose those actions which best accomplish what we want. Let's consider this in more detail.

By the term "practical situation," I mean any situation in which we prefer some realistically attainable outcomes of our actions to others. In such a situation, the more accurately we can predict which actions lead to outcomes we prefer, the more effectively we can attain these outcomes. This is so, at any rate, unless what enables us to predict these outcomes somehow prevents their attainment. Now thorough knowledge of practical situations obviously enables us to predict the results of our actions in these situations more accurately than remaining in ignorance does. Moreover, such knowledge rarely prevents attainment of preferred outcomes. (There are exceptions; a betrayed spouse, for example, may react so adversely to knowledge of the betrayal that survival of the marriage, perhaps still a valued outcome, becomes impossible. But exceptions like this are rare.) Therefore, thorough knowledge of practical situations usually enables us to attain the realistic outcomes we prefer more effectively than remaining in ignorance does. Thus it is generally more useful in those situations than remaining in ignorance.

Exercise 9

1   Choose a conclusion which interests you and construct an argument for it, using the methods described in this chapter. (Don't hesitate to modify the conclusion if necessary.) Assume as your audience intelligent readers with at least a high school education. Present the argument both in annotated standard form and as a fully organized prose passage. Diagram and evaluate the prose version. You might also make some notes on the construction process itself and provide a record of the various stages by which the argument evolved.

2 Find an editorial or letter to the editor in a current newspaper or magazine and discuss how well or how poorly it communicates insight. How could it have been improved?

3 Criticize the organization and clarity of some of the lengthy passages of reasoning in Exercise 4.3. What could the authors have done to increase a reader's comprehension of these passages?

10

Introduction to Formal Logic

Until now we have approached arguments informally, case by case. This chapter introduces the more abstract and rigorous perspective of formal logic. Formal logic, as its name implies, is the study of argument forms, as opposed to individual arguments. This new perspective offers important advantages.

First, as we noted in Section 5.1, it enables us to deal with whole classes of arguments at once. If we know, for example, that modus ponens is a valid form, then whenever we encounter an argument of this form we can recognize its validity immediately. There is no need to perform the imaginative test for each new example.

Second, the formal approach focuses attention on certain crucial structural features of arguments. The forms discussed in Section 5.1, for example, are not pure combinations of statement variables. They all contain a residue of English. And their validity or invalidity is obviously linked very intimately with this residue. Typical among these residual expressions are:

Not

And

Or

If . . . then

By emphasizing these expressions, the formal perspective points the way toward a deeper understanding of validity.

But perhaps the most substantial advantage of formal logic is precision. The imaginative tests we have used so far are adequate for most everyday purposes, but their success depends to some degree on the breadth of the user's imagination, and they are not perfectly precise. In contrast, form is a very precise idea. If we could understand the link between form and validity, then we might develop accurate tests for validity based purely on form and thereby circumvent the need for imagination altogether. This work was begun in a modest and unsystematic way in Chapter 5, by cataloging some common deductive forms. In this chapter we will carry it on in greater depth and generality.

Unfortunately, as we'll see, formal techniques have serious drawbacks; they work only for limited classes of arguments and only after these arguments have been translated into unambiguous symbolic notation. Nevertheless, these techniques are a considerable advance over unaided imagination, and they profoundly deepen our understanding of validity.

We will examine only one formal method, the truth-table test, which works for only one class of arguments, those whose validity depends on the expressions listed above. You should keep in mind that there are many forms of reasoning whose strength has nothing to do with these expressions. Other formal methods have been developed for some of them; but for many, satisfactory formal treatment is still a very distant hope. That's one reason why informal logic is still in business.

10.1 NEGATION, CONJUNCTION, AND DISJUNCTION

To understand how the expressions listed above contribute to validity, we must understand their **semantics.** Semantics, roughly, is the study of meaning; more particularly, it is the study of the contribution various expressions make to the truth or falsity of statements in which they occur. You should already be familiar with the semantics of the word "not" from the discussion in Section 5.4. The effect of inserting "not" into a statement is to make it true if it was false and false if it was true. Let's adopt some terminology which enables us to say this more concisely. We'll call the truth or falsity of a sentence its **truth value.** Thus, the truth value of a true sentence is "true," and the truth value of a false sentence is "false." The semantic contribution of "not," then, is to reverse truth value.

Unlike "not," the other three expressions—"and," "or," "if . . . then"—are never inserted into a single sentence. Each links two sentences into a compound. In each case, the truth value of the compound depends solely on the truth values of the two components. Thus, as with "not," we can determine the truth value of the newly formed expression just by knowing the truth value(s) of the component(s). Any expression which works this way is called a **truth functional operator.** This chapter, then, is a study of the logic of four important truth functional operators. We'll discuss the first three—"not," "and," and "or"—in this section. "If . . . then" poses special difficulties and will be reserved for Section 10.2. Before we discuss the semantics of these operators, however, it will be useful to become familiar with some additional terminology and symbolism.

Sentences formed by inserting "not" into a statement are called **negations.** Those formed by joining two statements with "and" are called **conjunctions.** Their two components are **conjuncts.** Similarly, sentences formed by joining two statements with "or" are called **disjunctions,** and their components are **disjuncts.** You already know the terminology for compounds created by "if . . . then." Such compounds are conditionals. The statement following the "if" is the **antecedent,** and the statement following the "then" is the **consequent.**

Logicians have devised special symbols to represent the truth functional operators. These are as follows:

Not	~
And	&
Or	$\vee$
If . . . then	$\supset$

Sometimes "—" or " ⌐ " is used for "not," "·" for "and," and "→" for "if . . . then," but we will stick to the notation listed above. Notice that the two-word expression "if . . . then" is represented by a single symbol. This is to emphasize its formal and semantic similarities to "and" and "or." Thus, "If p then q" is symbolized as $p \supset q$. The insertion of "not" in a sentence is symbolized simply by writing "~" in front of the sentence.

Our discussion of the semantics of all the truth functional operators will be based on the following assumption:

In every possible world, each statement is either true or false, but not both.

This does not mean that a statement can't be true in one world and false in another, but only that in every world it has exactly one of the two truth values. This assumption is called the **principle of bivalence,** and sentences which conform to it are said to be **bivalent.**

The purpose of assuming bivalence is to simplify our discussion. Strictly speaking, this assumption is false. Though no sentence is ever both true and false in any possible world, there are some which are neither. (For an example, see problems 7 and 8 of Exercise 5.5(b) and the discussion in Section 10.6.) There may also be statements which lack truth value because of vagueness. The following discussion simply does not apply to arguments containing such statements. But this is a minor restriction, since virtually all statements of genuine practical interest can be treated as bivalent. There are formal techniques for dealing with nonbivalent statements, but they involve complications which at this stage are best avoided.

Given the principle of bivalence and our newly established symbol for "not," we can conveniently summarize the semantical effect of adding "not" to a sentence p as follows:

p	$\sim p$
T	F
F	T

This summary is called a **truth table.** Under the entry for p are listed two possibilities: p is true or p is false. The entries for $\sim p$ indicate the truth value of $\sim p$ in each of these possible circumstances. Each horizontal row of truth values stands for a class of possible worlds. The first row represents the worlds in which p is true. In those worlds we see that $\sim p$ is false. The second row represents the worlds in which p is false. The table tells us that in those worlds $\sim p$ is true. Since we're assuming bivalence, there are no worlds in which p is truth-valueless or something other than true or false. Hence the table indicates the truth value of $\sim p$ in every possible world.

It is easy to formulate a similar table for "and." We saw in Section 5.4 that compounds formed by "and" are true if both conjuncts are true, and false otherwise. Thus the table is:

p	q	$p \,\&\, q$
T	T	T
T	F	F
F	T	F
F	F	F

Since two statements are joined to produce $p \,\&\, q$, there are four classes of possible worlds to consider: those in which p and q are both true, those in which p is true and q is false, those in which p is false and q is true, and those in which both p and q are false. These are represented, respectively, by the four horizontal rows of truth values. The vertical column under p & q gives us the truth value of p & q in each of these four classes of possible worlds.

Now what about the truth table for "or"? Let's consider a specific example:

Patti is president of her sorority, or she's president of student council.

If Patti is president of neither organization, then of course this statement is false. If she is president of one, but not the other, it's true. But what if she's president of both? Under these conditions the statement seems true to some people, but false to others.

Why the disagreement? The problem is that "or" is ambiguous. On one reading it means "either . . . or . . . *but not both.*" On this reading, which is called the **exclusive sense** of "or," if both disjuncts are true the whole disjunction is false. On the other reading, which is called the **inclusive sense,** if both disjuncts are true so is the whole disjunction. This reading is sometimes expressed by the hybrid term "and/or." The two meanings are entirely distinct. In fact, in Latin they are expressed by two different words: *aut* for the exclusive sense, and *vel* for the inclusive one. It is unfortunate that English has only one word for both.

To avoid confusion, the symbol "$\lor$" is used only for the inclusive sense of "or." (Indeed, it was chosen because it is the first letter of *vel.*) The appropriate truth table for "$\lor$" is as follows:

p	q	$p \lor q$
T	T	T
T	F	T
F	T	T
F	F	F

To get the truth table for "*p aut q,*" the exclusive sense of "or," we simply replace the first T under $p \lor q$ by an F. The exclusive sense of "or" is sometimes represented by the symbol "$\underline{\lor}$" but later in this section we'll discuss a way of expressing it using the symbols we already have.

We now have a clear understanding of the semantics of the first three truth functional operators. Our purpose in acquiring this understanding is to illuminate the relation between form and validity. But before we can do this, we need to understand how the truth functional operators interact with one another when two or more are present in a single sentence. Consider, for example, the sentence:

I will not go with you, and I will not stay home.

The basic components of this sentence are "I will go with you" and "I will stay home." Into each a "not" has been inserted, and then they have been conjoined by "and." If we symbolize "I will go with you" by p and "I will stay home" by q, the form of this sentence is $\sim p$ & $\sim q$. This complex sentence can now be represented on a truth table so that we can see explicitly how its truth value depends on the truth values of its basic components. Since there are two of these, the truth table will have four lines. The first step in constructing it is to write the truth values for $\sim p$ and for $\sim q$ into the table as follows:

p	q	$\sim p$ & $\sim q$	
T	T	F	F
T	F	F	T
F	T	T	F
F	F	T	T

Once again, horizontal rows represent distinct classes of possible worlds. In the first two of these classes (represented by the first two horizontal rows) $\sim p$ is false, because p is true. Likewise, in the third and fourth classes, $\sim p$ is true, because p is false. Similarly, $\sim q$ is false in the first and third classes, because there q is true, and $\sim q$ is true in the second and fourth classes, because there q is false.

Now that we know the truth values of the conjuncts in all possible circumstances, we can calculate truth values for the whole conjunction in accordance with the truth table for "&." This table tells us that a conjunction is true just in case both conjuncts are true. Therefore, since the only class of worlds in which both conjuncts are true is the fourth one, only in the worlds of this fourth class will $\sim p$ & $\sim q$ be true. In all the others it is false. We record this fact by writing the appropriate truth values under the symbol "&" and circling them to indicate that they are the truth values for the whole formula:

p	q	$\sim p$	&	$\sim q$
T	T	F	F	F
T	F	F	F	T
F	T	T	F	F
F	F	T	T	T

This truth table shows at a glance that the only worlds in which $\sim p$ & $\sim q$ is true are the worlds in which both p and q are false. In all other worlds $\sim p$ & $\sim q$ is false.

To prevent ambiguity, complex sentence forms frequently require brackets similar to those used in arithmetic. In arithmetic, the formula "3 × 2 + 4" can be read two different ways—either as "(3 × 2) + 4," in which case it stands for 10, or as "3 × (2 + 4)," in which case it stands for 18. Likewise, the sentence form $p \lor q \,\&\, r$ is ambiguous. It could be either the disjunction of p with $(q \,\&\, r)$ —i.e., $p \lor (q \,\&\, r)$—or the conjunction of $(p \lor q)$ with r— i.e., $(p \lor q) \,\&\, r$. To see the difference, let p be "The princess will dine," q be "The queen will dine," and r be "Rats will gnaw on the scraps." Then the first formula says "Either the princess will dine, or the queen will dine and rats will gnaw on the scraps," and the second says "Either the princess or the queen will dine, and rats will gnaw on the scraps." These are not the same statement. The first leaves open the question of whether rats will gnaw on the scraps if the princess dines. The second asserts that the rats will gnaw on the scraps regardless of whether it is the queen or the princess who dines. The brackets are essential to differentiate the two statements.

The negation symbol, like the negative sign in mathematics, is presumed to apply to the shortest complete formula which follows it. The extent of its application is controlled by the use of brackets. Thus, for example, in the formula $(\sim p \,\&\, q) \lor r$, only p is negated; in $\sim(p \,\&\, q) \lor r$, $(p \,\&\, q)$ is negated; and in $\sim((p \,\&\, q) \lor r)$, $((p \,\&\, q) \lor r)$ is negated.

The formula or formulas to which an operator applies, together with that operator itself, is called the **scope** of the operator. Thus, for example, in the formula $\sim((p \lor q) \,\&\, r)$, the scope of "$\sim$" is the whole formula, the scope of "$\lor$" is $p \lor q$, and the scope of "$\&$" is $(p \lor q) \,\&\, r$. Or to take a quite different example, in the formula $(p \,\&\, \sim q) \lor \sim(r \,\&\, s)$ the scope of the first "$\&$" is $p \,\&\, \sim q$, the scope of the first "$\sim$" is $\sim q$, the scope of the "$\lor$" is the whole formula, the scope of the second "$\sim$" is $\sim(r \,\&\, s)$, and the scope of the second "$\&$" is $r \,\&\, s$.

Every properly constructed formula has one and only one operator whose scope is the formula itself. This is called the **main operator.** Thus, for example, the main operator of $\sim((p \lor q) \,\&\, r)$ is "$\sim$." The main operator is important, because in the truth table of a complex formula, the column listing the truth values for the whole formula (i.e., the column which should be circled) always occurs under the main operator.

The size and complexity of a truth table increases with the number of basic variables in the formula we wish to examine. With a single variable, only two horizontal rows are required, for there are only two possibilities: either the sentence represented by that variable is true, or it's false. With two variables, as we saw, four rows are required. And in general, if the number of variables is n, the number of rows is 2^n.

No matter how many rows a truth table has, there is a simple procedure for setting them up. First, list all the variables of the formula you are testing in the upper left corner of the table. Their order is irrelevant, but alphabetical listing is standard. Next, where n is the number of these variables, list beneath the rightmost variable a column of 2^n alternating T's and F's, beginning with T. Then, under the next variable to the left, if any remains, write another column of T's and F's, starting once again with T, but alternating every two symbols. Repeat this procedure, moving constantly to the left and doubling the alternation each time, until you have exhausted all the variables. If, for example, we are working with the three variables p, q, and r, the table should look like this:

p	q	r	
T	T	T	
T	T	F	
T	F	T	
T	F	F	
F	T	T	
F	T	F	
F	F	T	
F	F	F	

Now, after writing the formula to be tested at the top of the table and to the right of the listing of variables, we are ready to begin calculating its truth values. Suppose that the formula is $(\sim p \mathbin{\&} q) \lor r$. We begin by copying the column for each variable under the occurrences of that variable in the formula. If a variable is negated, we can save effort by simply reversing the T's and F's in the column and placing this reversed column under the negation sign. Thus we have:

p	q	r	$(\sim p$	$\mathbin{\&} q)$	$\lor r$
T	T	T	F	T	T
T	T	F	F	T	F
T	F	T	F	F	T
T	F	F	F	F	F
F	T	T	T	T	T
F	T	F	T	T	F
F	F	T	T	F	T
F	F	F	T	F	F

Then, beginning with operators having smallest scope, we calculate the truth values of subformulas, using the truth tables for the connectives they contain. Apart from "$\sim$," which we have already accounted for by reversing T's and F's, the operator with smallest scope in the formula above is "$\&$." Using the truth table for "$\&$," we fill in the truth values for $\sim p \mathbin{\&} q$ as follows:

p	q	r	(~p	&	q)	∨	r
T	T	T	F	F	T		T
T	T	F	F	F	T		F
T	F	T	F	F	F		T
T	F	F	F	F	F		F
F	T	T	T	T	T		T
F	T	F	T	T	T		F
F	F	T	T	F	F		T
F	F	F	T	F	F		F

Only one more step is required to complete the table. The formula's main operator is "∨." It connects the disjuncts (~p & q) and r. We have listed the truth values for (~p & q) under the "&" and those for r under r. Now all we have to do is to apply the disjunction table to these values to calculate the truth values for the whole formula. These are listed under the "∨" and circled, as follows:

p	q	r	(~p	&	q)	∨	r
T	T	T	F	F	T	(T)	T
T	T	F	F	F	T	F	F
T	F	T	F	F	F	T	T
T	F	F	F	F	F	F	F
F	T	T	T	T	T	T	T
F	T	F	T	T	T	T	F
F	F	T	T	F	F	T	T
F	F	F	T	F	F	(F)	F

The table indicates the formula (~p & q) ∨ r is false in all worlds in which p and q are true and r is false, or in which p is true and q and r are false, or in which all three are false. In all other worlds it is true.

Let's do one more example just to make sure the procedure is clear. This time our formula will be ~((p & q) ∨ r). Notice that it differs from the previous formula only in the scope of the negation. Once again we fill in truth values under variables:

p	q	r	~((p	&	q)	∨	r)
T	T	T	T		T		T
T	T	F	T		T		F
T	F	T	T		F		T
T	F	F	T		F		F
F	T	T	F		T		T
F	T	F	F		T		F
F	F	T	F		F		T
F	F	F	F		F		F

Since none of the variables are negated (the "~" negates the whole formula), we don't reverse any truth values at this first stage. Next, we fill in the column for the operator of smallest scope, which in this case is "&":

p	q	r	~((p	&	q)	∨	r)
T	T	T	T	T	T		T
T	T	F	T	T	T		F
T	F	T	T	F	F		T
T	F	F	T	F	F		F
F	T	T	F	F	T		T
F	T	F	F	F	T		F
F	F	T	F	F	F		T
F	F	F	F	F	F		F

Then, using the values for the disjuncts (p & q) and r, we calculate the values for the disjunction (p & q) ∨ r and list them under "∨":

p	q	r	~((p	&	q)	∨	r)
T	T	T	T	T	T	T	T
T	T	F	T	T	T	T	F
T	F	T	T	F	F	T	T
T	F	F	T	F	F	F	F
F	T	T	F	F	T	T	T
F	T	F	F	F	T	F	F
F	F	T	F	F	F	T	T
F	F	F	F	F	F	F	F

Now the truth values for ~((p & q) ∨ r) will be simply the reverse of those for (p & q) ∨ r. Hence we take the values listed under "∨" and reverse them. These are recorded under the main operator "~" and circled to show that they are the values for the whole formula:

p	q	r	~(	(p	&	q)	∨	r)
T	T	T	(F)	T	T	T	T	T
T	T	F	F	T	T	T	T	F
T	F	T	F	T	F	F	T	T
T	F	F	T	T	F	F	F	F
F	T	T	F	F	F	T	T	T
F	T	F	T	F	F	T	F	F
F	F	T	F	F	F	F	T	T
F	F	F	(T)	F	F	F	F	F

The truth is now complete. Comparison with the previous example provides a good illustration of the importance of bracket placement.

The truth table method enables us to determine the truth value of a complex sentence in any possible world, given the truth values of its basic components in that world. In Section 10.5 we'll see how this helps us to test the validity of arguments. But before we go any further, we need to clarify the relation between English sentences and symbolic notation.

To construct a truth table for a statement, we must fully understand the statement's structure. That's the purpose of translating it into logical symbols. The symbolic translation of an English sentence is called the sentence's **logical form.** Often the logical form of a sentence is obvious, but sometimes there are complications.

If a disjunction is present, we must determine whether it is intended as inclusive or exclusive. The exclusive disjunction of p and q is best symbolized as $(p \lor q) \And \sim(p \And q)$. (Check to see that the truth table of this formula correctly expresses exclusive disjunction.) Thus its logical form is quite different from that of inclusive disjunction.

Not only do some English expressions, like disjunctions, have several different meanings; often several different expressions have the same meaning. We saw in Section 5.2 how many different ways English has of expressing the conditional. There are also various ways of expressing the other operators. "Or" can occur either with or without the term "either." Negation can be expressed by a number of phrases and prefixes—for example, "it is false that," "it is not the case that," "non-," "un-," "in-," and "im-." Conjunction, too, is expressible in a variety of ways. These include "but," "yet," "although," "nevertheless"—indeed almost any of the compound-forming transitional expressions discussed in Section 2.1. Some of these words have an emotive meaning in addition to their logical one, expressing surprise or contrast, for example, but their effect on truth value is precisely that of "and." Our policy in diagraming arguments has generally been to break conjunctions into their components; but as I noted near the end of Section 5.1, it is often useful not to do this when the conjunction plays a central role in the reasoning. In the examples of this chapter it does, and so here we will treat conjunctions as single compound sentences, rather than splitting them up.

Sometimes grammatical form is an unreliable guide to logical form. The sentences "The princess and the queen are excellent runners" and "Hydrogen and oxygen are an explosive combination," while grammatically quite similar, are logically distinct. Letting p stand for "The princess is an excellent runner" and q for "The queen is an excellent runner," the first sentence is best symbolized as $p \And q$. This symbolization reflects the sentence's internal structure without distorting its meaning. But there is no analogous way of translating the second sentence. If we try to break it into conjuncts, the results—"Hydrogen is an explosive combination" and "Oxygen is an explosive combination"—make no sense. Therefore, the only way to symbolize this sentence is with a single variable, say r.

When deciding how to symbolize a sentence, you should try to bring out as much logical structure as possible. The more structure we can see, the better we understand the sentence. It is possible to symbolize any sentence—even the most complex—by a single variable. But this is pointless, because it obscures features which may be crucial to understanding. Where logical structure exists, the symbolization should express it.

Some English locutions, such as "neither . . . nor," have several equally acceptable symbolic translations. "Neither p nor q" can be written symbolically either as the negation of a disjunction, $\sim(p \vee q)$, or as a conjunction of negations, $\sim p$ & $\sim q$. They have the same truth table, as you can verify for yourself.

There are no precise rules for translation from English into symbols. English is so rich and ambiguous that only sensitive and careful attention to meanings can assure accurate translation. Perhaps the best way to learn is simply by example. Here is a list of some English sentences together with their translations into symbolic notation:

Sentence	Symbol Scheme	Translation
The sky is blue.	p = The sky is blue.	p
The sky and the sea are blue.	p = The sky is blue. q = The sea is blue.	p & q
The sky is blue, but the sea is not.	Same.	p & $\sim q$
Neither the sky nor the sea is blue.	Same.	$\sim p$ & $\sim q$, or $\sim(p \vee q)$
Everything is blue.	p = Everything is blue.	p
She is either in London or in Paris.	p = She is in London. q = She is in Paris.	$p \vee q$, or $(p \vee q)$ & $\sim(p$ & $q)$ if this is exclusive disjunction.
Either I'll keep working or I'll go home and go to bed.	p = I'll keep working. q = I'll go home. r = I'll go to bed.	$p \vee (q$ & $r)$, or $(p \vee (q$ & $r))$ & $\sim(p$ & $(q$ & $r)$ if it's exclusive.
Though I like you, I don't love you.	p = I like you. q = I love you.	p & $\sim q$
It's not the case that I'm not smiling.	p = I'm smiling.	$\sim\sim p$
I'm not both male and female.	p = I'm male. q = I'm female.	$\sim(p$ & $q)$
Either I'm nonfemale or I'm not pregnant.	p = I'm female. q = I'm pregnant.	$\sim p \vee \sim q$

Exercise 10.1(a) Construct a truth table for each of the symbolic formulas listed in the table above.

Exercise 10.1(b)   Translate each of the sentences below into symbolic notation, using the following symbol scheme:

p = Pamela is going.
q = Quinton is going.
r = Rob is going.

Then construct the formula's truth table. All disjunctions are presumed to be inclusive.

1   Pamela and Quinton are going, and so is Rob.
2   Either Pamela is going, or she's not.
3   Neither Pamela nor Quinton is going, but Rob is.
4   It's not true that neither Pamela nor Quinton is going.
5   Pamela is both going and not going.
6   Pamela is not going; however, Quinton and Rob are.
7   It is not true that it is not the case that Rob is not going.
8   It is not the case that Pamela is going and Rob is not.
9   Either Pamela is not going, or Rob is going.
10   Either Pamela and Rob are going, or Pamela and Quinton are going.

10.2   CONDITIONALS

In the last section we noted that English disjunctions are ambiguous, and we banished this ambiguity from our symbolic notation by stipulating that "$\lor$" stands only for inclusive disjunction. English conditionals are also ambiguous, but more perplexingly so. For one thing, there are not just two meanings for the conditional, but many. (Exactly how many is a matter of some dispute.) For another, only one of these is a genuine truth functional operator. That is, only one is such that its truth value depends solely on the truth values of its antecedent and consequent.

We shall discuss two meanings of the conditional—strict and material. **A strict conditional** is true if its consequent is true in all the possible worlds in which its antecedent is true. Otherwise it is false. In other words, a strict conditional is true just in case the inference consisting of its antecedent as premise and consequent as conclusion is valid. It follows that strict conditionals are not truth functional operators. For just as the validity of an inference does not depend solely on the truth values of its premises and conclusion, so the truth value of a strict conditional does not depend solely on the truth values of its antecedent and consequent. Knowing that the antecedent and consequent are both true, for example, tells us nothing about whether the conditional is true. It depends on whether the antecedent validly implies the conclusion. This means that a strict conditional cannot be represented on a truth table. A truth table shows how the truth value of a formula in a given world depends on the truth values of its components *in that same world*. But the truth value of a strict conditional in a given world depends, not on the truth values of its components *in that world*, but on the truth value of its consequent in all the worlds in which its antecedent is true. In fact, a strict conditional has the same truth value in every possible world. It is either logically necessary or inconsistent.

But since strict conditionals cannot be represented on truth tables, we will discuss them no further here. Their behavior is quite well understood, but its study belongs to more advanced levels of logic.

The only conditional which is a truth functional operator is the **material conditional.** In the material sense, "If p then q" is synonymous with "It is not the case that p and not q." Thus, for example, if I say, "If you're in this, so am I" in the material sense, what I mean is "It's not the case that you're in this and I'm not." Under what circumstances will my statement be true? Obviously, the way to find out is to let p stand for "You're in this" and q for "I'm in this" and then do the truth table for $\sim(p \;\&\; \sim q)$. Here it is:

p	q	$\sim$	$(p$	$\&$	$\sim q)$
T	T	T	T	F	F
T	F	F	T	T	T
F	T	T	F	F	F
F	F	T	F	F	T

Now we're going to use the symbol "$\supset$" to represent the material conditional. Thus the truth table for $p \supset q$ will be the same as the truth table for $\sim(p \;\&\; \sim q)$, as follows:

p	q	$p \supset q$
T	T	T
T	F	F
F	T	T
F	F	T

This is the only meaning of "If p, then q" which is representable in our notation.

The material conditional is a rather reasonable sort of conditional in some ways, but a very peculiar one in others. It is false if its antecedent is true and its consequent is false, which is just what we'd expect. Certainly, for example, the sentence "If the princess will dine, then so will the queen" is false if the princess dines and the queen doesn't.

But the cases represented by the other lines of its truth table are all a bit surprising. The material conditional is true whenever both its antecedent and consequent are true. This contrasts sharply with the strict conditional. Considered materially, the conditional "If Panama is near the equator, then its climate is warm" is true, for both its antecedent and consequent are true. But considered strictly it is false, because the argument

Panama is near the equator.
∴ Its climate is warm.

is invalid. Here the material conditional is perhaps a bit closer to ordinary usage than the strict one. But sometimes when its antecedent and consequent are both true the material conditional acts very strangely. Consider the conditional "If Panama is near the equator, then Caesar conquered Gaul." Here both the antecedent and consequent are true and so, considered materially, the conditional is true. But most people would regard this statement as false, because Caesar had nothing to do with Panama. This does not mean that there is something wrong with the material conditional. All it shows is that most people interpret the "if . . . then" in this sentence as having a meaning different from the material conditional. Perhaps they interpret it as a strict conditional, but there are other possible meanings as well. The nature of the conditional involved in statements such as this is a matter of lively dispute in contemporary logic.

Perhaps the greatest oddity of the material conditional is that it is always true if its antecedent is false. In some cases this accords with common sense, but in others it is bizarre. We'd normally consider the conditional "If it is 1492, then this is the year Columbus came to America" to be true. And so it is, according to the truth table for the material conditional, since both its antecedent and consequent are false. But both components of "If there are flying saucers in my attic, then Attila the Hun was a philanthropist" are also false, and we'd hardly consider this conditional true, except perhaps in jest. Yet in the material sense it is true.

Examples like this make it clear that the material conditional is not very much like the conditionals we're acccustomed to. It is, frankly, a logicians' artifice. Yet despite its oddity, it is extremely simple, precise, and useful. Indeed, it is the simplest and most precise of all conditionals, which makes it especially useful for logical and mathematical work.

Conditionals in ordinary language, however, are seldom, if ever, intended in the material sense. Thus translating an English conditional by "⊃" usually distorts its meaning. Nevertheless, even if the translation fails to capture the intended meaning, it is still one possible reading of the sentence, and for logical purposes the distortion is actually rather small. In this chapter we will translate all English conditionals by "⊃." The resultant distortions can perhaps be justified by the enhanced understanding we will gain of the material conditional and by the fact that any other policy would introduce more complexities than we could manage at this stage.

Having the symbol "⊃" enables us to formalize many statements which would otherwise be difficult to translate (though really we could do without this symbol altogether, since the material conditional is also expressible in terms of "&" and "~"). All of the ways in which English permits us to express conditionals (see Section 5.2) now become amenable to formal treatment. Here are some typical translations:

Sentence	Symbol Scheme	Translation
I will go only if you do.	p = I will go. q = You will go.	$p \supset q$
I will go if you do.	Same.	$q \supset p$
Only if you go will I go.	Same.	$p \supset q$
If I finish my work and my car is running, I'll come visit you.	p = I finish my work. q = My car is running. r = I'll come visit you.	$(p \, \& \, q) \supset r$
If it's a virus, then it's neither alive nor dead.	p = It's a virus. q = It's alive. r = It's dead.	$p \supset (\sim q \, \& \, \sim r)$, or $p \supset \sim(q \lor r)$
If I'm wrong, then I'm wrong.	p = I'm wrong.	$p \supset p$
I can't live without her.	p = I can live. q = She is with me.	$\sim q \supset \sim p$
I can't live with her or without her.	Same.	$(q \supset \sim p) \, \&$ $(\sim q \supset \sim p)$, or $(q \lor$ $\sim q) \supset \sim p$
If he set the fire, then if he did so intentionally, he's an arsonist.	p = He set the fire. q = He did so intentionally. r = He's an arsonist.	$p \supset (q \supset r)$
It's not the case that if you don't lose you win.	p = You lose. q = You win.	$\sim(\sim p \supset q)$
If you didn't lose and you didn't win, then either you didn't play or the game was a draw.	p = You lost. q = You won. r = You played. s = The game was a draw.	$(\sim p \, \& \, \sim q) \supset (\sim r \lor s)$

Notice again how the logical form of a sentence may differ radically from its grammatical form, and notice too that there may be several equally satisfactory ways of translating a single sentence into logical symbols. Both facts are strikingly illustrated by the sentence "I can't live with her or without her." Remember, translation is not a mechanical activity; it requires a careful touch and a clear sensitivity to nuances of meaning.

> **Exercise 10.2(a)**   Construct a truth table for each of the symbolic formulas listed in the table above.

> **Exercise 10.2(b)**   Translate each of the following sentences into symbolic notation, using the symbol scheme given in Exercise 10.1(b). Then construct the formula's truth table.

1   Pamela is going, provided that Quinton goes.
2   If Pamela is going, then she's not not going.
3   If Pamela goes, then if Quinton goes, Rob won't go.
4   Rob will go only if neither Quinton nor Pamela does.
5   Quinton will go only if neither Rob nor Pamela does.
6   Pamela won't go without both Rob and Quinton.
7   If either Pamela or Quinton goes, Rob won't.
8   If Pamela and Quinton go, then Pamela goes.
9   It's not the case that if Quinton goes, Quinton goes.
10   If either Pamela doesn't go or Quinton does, then it's not the case that Pamela is going and Quinton isn't.

10.3   BICONDITIONALS

In Section 5.2 we cast a passing glance at the expression "if and only if." This expression, which is often abbreviated to "iff," is called the **biconditional.** The reason for the name is that, as we saw in Section 5.2, the biconditional can be regarded as a conjunction of two conditionals. If these are interpreted as material conditionals, the expression "p if and only if q" can be symbolized as $(p \supset q) \;\&\; (q \supset p)$. This expression is called the **material biconditional.** Its truth table is:

p	q	$(p$	$\supset$	$q)$	$\&$	$(q$	$\supset$	$p)$
T	T	T	T	T	T	T	T	T
T	F	T	F	F	F	F	T	T
F	T	F	T	T	F	T	F	F
F	F	F	T	F	T	F	T	F

From this truth table it is evident that "*p* if and only if *q*" is true when, and only when, *p* and *q* have the same truth value.

Just as we have a special symbol for the material conditional, though we could do without it, so too it is convenient to have a special symbol for the material biconditional. We shall adopt the symbol "≡," though "↔" is also used. The truth table for "≡" is, obviously:

p	*q*	*p* ≡ q
T	T	T
T	F	F
F	T	F
F	F	T

The biconditional is uncommon in ordinary language, and so the material biconditional tends not to violate our preconceptions as much as the material conditional does. Biconditionals used in logic, mathematics, and the sciences are usually intended to be read materially, though **strict biconditionals** (biconditionals whose two conditional conjuncts are strict conditionals) are often used in definitions, especially when these are philosophical in nature. Strict biconditionals express logically necessary and sufficient conditions (see Section 6.7), in the sense that the statement "*x* is logically necessary and sufficient for *y*" means that "*x* occurs if and only if *y* occurs," where "if and only if" is a strict biconditional. But strict biconditionals, like strict conditionals, cannot be represented on truth tables, and I will say no more about them here.

There aren't too many ways of saying "if and only if" in English. I've already mentioned "is necessary and sufficient for." This can be used to express the material biconditional, so long as the word "logically" is not included. The expression "is equivalent to" works similarly. Grammatically, both expressions link phrases, rather than sentences, as in the statement "Getting the highest score is equivalent to winning." We may simply regard this as saying that one gets the highest score if and only if one wins. The phrase "when and only when" is another way of saying "if and only if."

Sometimes the word "unless" can be symbolized by means of the biconditional and negation. If someone says, for example, "We'll play unless it rains," probably what is meant is that we'll play if it doesn't rain and only if it doesn't rain. Using *p* for "We'll play" and *q* for "It rains," this can be symbolized as $p \equiv \sim q$. But "unless" is ambiguous. In making this statement the speaker might not really want to say that we won't play if it does rain, but only that we will play if it doesn't. In that case only one conjunct of the biconditional is meant, and the symbolization is $\sim q \supset p$.

This simple conditional meaning of "unless" is probably the one intended in a statement like "The patient will die unless she gets a transfusion." Letting *p* be "The patient will die" and *q* be "She gets a transfusion," we should symbolize this sentence as ~*q* ⊃ *p*. The converse, *p* ⊃ ~*q*, is probably not intended. In other words, the speaker probably does not wish to assert that the patient will die *only if* she doesn't get a transfusion, for she might die even if she gets one.

Here are some examples of translation involving the biconditional:

Sentence	Symbol Scheme	Translation
He eats when and only when he's hungry.	*p* = He eats. *q* = He's hungry.	*p* ≡ *q*
I'll jump unless you apologize.	*p* = I'll jump. *q* = You apologize.	~*q* ⊃ *p*, or perhaps *p* ≡ ~*q*
Olaf is a bachelor if and only if he's an unmarried man.	*p* = Olaf is a bachelor. *q* = Olaf is married. *r* = Olaf is a man.	*p* ≡ (~*q* & *r*)
She's a knave if and only if she's not a knave.	*p* = She's a knave.	*p* ≡ ~*p*
Her being a knave is both necessary and sufficient for her not being a nonknave.	*p* = She's a knave.	*p* ≡ ~~*p*
Iodine is an element if and only if it isn't a compound.	*p* = Iodine is an element. *q* = It's a compound.	*p* ≡ ~*q*
You are a parent if and only if you are a mother or a father.	*p* = You are a parent. *q* = You are a mother. *r* = You are a father.	*p* ≡ (*q* ∨ *r*)
If *x* is an even number, then *x* is prime if and only if *x* = 2.	*p* = *x* is an even number *q* = *x* is prime *r* = *x* = 2	*p* ⊃ (*q* ≡ *r*)

Exercise 10.3(a)   Construct a truth table for each of the symbolic formulas listed in the table above.

Exercise 10.3(b)   Translate the sentences below into symbolic notation, using the following symbol scheme:

p = Logic is painful.
q = You ask questions.
r = You find out what's right.

Then construct the formula's truth table.

1   Logic is painful unless you ask questions.
2   If it's true that you ask questions if and only if you find out what's right, then logic is not painful.
3   You ask questions and find out what's right if and only if you neither ask questions nor find out what's right.
4   Logic is painful if and only if you don't ask questions or don't find out what's right.
5   Logic is not painful if and only if you ask questions and find out what's right.

10.4   NECESSITY, CONTINGENCY, AND INCONSISTENCY REVISITED

If you did the exercises for the previous three sections, you probably noticed something peculiar about certain formulas. Some of them are true in all possible situations, and some of them are false in all possible situations. The expression $p \supset p$ is an example of the former; $p \equiv {\sim}p$ is an example of the latter:

p		p	$\supset$	p		p		p	$\equiv$	${\sim}p$
T		T	T	T		T		T	F	F
F		F	T	F		F		F	F	T

By now you probably realize what this means: a sentence form with all T's in its truth table under its main operator is logically necessary (true in all possible worlds), and one with all F's is inconsistent (false in all worlds).

What may not be so apparent is the significance of these facts. Always before, we had to rely on imagination and intuitive understanding to determine whether a given statement was logically necessary or inconsistent. There was always room for subjective disagreement and error. But truth tables enable us to test for necessity and inconsistency by a simple calculation. The subjectivity is eliminated. To be sure, they are applicable only to a small class of sentences and to these only after they have been translated unambiguously into symbolic notation. But still this is a notable advance.

Truth tables, however, are more than just a calculational trick; they provide genuine insight into necessity and inconsistency. The truth table shows, for example, why there can be no world in which $p \equiv {\sim}p$ is true.

We cannot conceive a world, for instance, in which Olaf is drunk if and only if he's not drunk, because the very idea of such a world is incoherent; and this idea is incoherent because of the semantical properties of the biconditional and negation.

Since statements whose logical forms exhibit all T's in their truth tables are logically necessary and since those which exhibit all F's are inconsistent, it might seem to follow that those which exhibit a mixture of T's and F's are contingent. This is not always so. The sentence "Everything is itself," for example, is logically necessary, but there is no way to represent its necessity on a truth table. It contains no truth functional operators. The best we can do is to represent it as a single variable, say p, in which case its truth table is:

p	p
T	T
F	F

So truth tables are unreliable as a test for contingency. They reveal logical necessity and inconsistency only if it is generated by truth functional operators. The necessity of "Everything is itself" is due to the semantical properties of the expressions "Everything" and "is" (which are not truth functional operators), and these properties are not detected by the truth table. Both expressions, however, are thoroughly understood by logicians; and if we were to pursue formal logic much beyond this chapter, they would be among the first items we would discuss.

To summarize: Truth tables accurately detect logical necessity and inconsistency insofar as they result from the semantical properties of truth functional operators. If the truth table of a formula shows all T's, then all sentences of that form are necessary truths. If it shows all F's, then all sentences of that form are inconsistent. But if it shows a mix of T's and F's, then all we can say is that sentences of that form are contingent unless non-truth-functional elements of their structure make them necessary or inconsistent.

Exercise 10.4(a)   Check back over the truth tables for all the exercises in previous sections of this chapter, and determine which of the formulas represented in the tables are logically necessary and which are inconsistent.

Exercise 10.4(b)   Construct a truth table for each of the following formulas, and determine which are logically necessary and which are inconsistent.

1 $p \lor \sim p$
2 $p \lor \sim q$
3 $p \supset \sim p$
4 $\sim p \ \& \ \sim\sim p$
5 $\sim(p \lor q) \ \& \ p$
6 $(p \ \& \ (p \supset q)) \ \& \ \sim p$
7 $p \ \& \ p$
8 $p \equiv (p \ \& \ p)$
9 $p \lor p$
10 $(p \lor p) \supset p$

10.5   THE TRUTH-TABLE TEST FOR VALIDITY

We have been studying the semantics of the truth functional operators in order to develop a formal test for validity. In this section our work finally yields results. Let's review once again what a truth table signifies. A truth table separates possible worlds into classes according to the truth values of the statements represented by the variables. Each such class is represented by a horizontal line of the table, and every possible world falls into one and only one of these classes. The column under the formula's main operator gives us the truth value of the formula in each class of possible worlds.

Now suppose that instead of a single formula, we put a whole argument form on the table. Since the table would tell us the truth value of each of the listed formulas in every possible world, we could tell simply by inspection of the table whether there was any possible world in which the premises were true and the conclusion false. If not, then we would know that the argument form was deductive. Let's try this with a simple argument form, modus ponens:

$p \supset q$

p

$\therefore q$

Listing both premises and the conclusion on the same truth table, we get:

p	q	$p \supset q$	p	$\therefore q$
T	T	T	T	T
T	F	F	T	F
F	T	T	F	T
F	F	T	F	F

The truth table segregates possible worlds into four classes: those in which both p and q are true, those in which p is true and q is false, those in which p is false and q is true, and those in which both p and q are false. Now to tell whether the argument is valid, we simply scan across the rows to see if there are any classes of worlds in which both premises are true and the conclusion is false. The only class in which both premises are true is the first one, the one in which both p and q are true. But in these worlds the conclusion is true as well. Hence there are no possible worlds in which both premises are true and the conclusion is false. Modus ponens is unquestionably valid.

Here at last is a way of determining validity independently of the subjective vagaries of imagination. One needn't envision possible worlds to perform this test. (Indeed, it was developed before logicians thought very much about possible worlds.) All you have to know is how to arrange the T's and F's and what to look for once you've put them there. A computer, which has no imagination at all, can do this quite efficiently. Moreover, the truth-table test is a source of insight into validity. It enables us to see precisely how the validity of an argument form arises from the semantics of its truth functional operators.

Some argument forms, as we saw in Section 5.1, are invalid. This means simply that not all arguments having these forms are valid. Some may be, but in each case their validity depends on something besides the semantics of the truth functional operators comprising the form. Truth tables detect invalidity as well as validity of argument forms. Consider, for example, the invalid form denying the antecedent:

$p \supset q$

$\sim p$

$\therefore \sim q$

Its truth table is:

p	q	$p \supset q$	$\sim p$	$\therefore \sim q$
T	T	T	F	F
T	F	F	F	T
F	T	T	T	F
F	F	T	T	T

Here we see that there can be worlds in which the premises are both true and the conclusion is false—specifically, worlds in which p is false and q is true. It is among these worlds that we can find counterexamples to the argument. Let's see how this works in a specific case. In Exercise 3.4, problem 7, we find the following argument:

If we had received messages from deep space, we could be confident that alien civilizations exist on other planets.

We have received no such messages.

∴ We cannot be confident of the existence of alien civilizations.

If we allow *p* to stand for "We have received messages from deep space" and *q* for "We can be confident that alien civilizations exist," it is obvious that the form of this argument is denying the antecedent. The truth table informs us that, at least if we read the conditional materially, we'll find counterexamples among worlds in which *p* is false and *q* is true. So to construct a counterexample, all we have to do is envision a world in which we have not received messages from deep space, but in which we can be confident that alien civilizations exist. There are many such worlds, as you probably already know from doing the exercise in Chapter 3. In some, for example, we have gone to the alien planets and seen them for ourselves. In others, their spaceships have come here (though they have transmitted no messages to us). In still others, we are confident of the existence of alien civilizations on purely statistical grounds. (There may be so many planets in the universe, that it is quite likely that civilization has evolved on some of them. Indeed, this seems to be the case in the actual universe.) In all of the worlds just described, *p* is false and *q* is true. All constitute counter-examples to the argument. Their formulation is made easier and more comprehensible by our understanding of the truth table.

Let's now consider a more complicated example. Here is an unfamiliar argument form—one which, so far as I know, has no name:

$p \supset (q \ \& \ r)$

$p \lor r$

$\sim q$

∴ *r*

Since three variables are involved, the truth table requires eight lines:

p	*q*	*r*	*p*	$\supset$	(*q*	&	*r*)	*p* $\lor$ *r*	$\sim q$	∴ *r*
T	T	T	T	T	T	T	T	T	F	T
T	T	F	T	F	T	F	F	T	F	F
T	F	T	T	F	F	F	T	T	T	T
T	F	F	T	F	F	F	F	T	T	F
F	T	T	F	T	T	T	T	T	F	T
F	T	F	F	T	T	F	F	F	F	F
F	F	T	F	T	F	F	T	T	T	T
F	F	F	F	T	F	F	F	F	T	F

Inspection of the table reveals that there is only one class of worlds in which all three premises are true: the worlds in which p and q are false and r is true. But in these worlds the conclusion r is true. So there are no counter-examples. This is a valid form.

This example illustrates another advantage of the truth-table test over simple imagination. The complexity of this argument form makes it difficult to test imaginatively. And as complexity increases, imagination is quickly overwhelmed. But complexity is no obstacle for the truth-table test. Since truth-table construction is a simple computational operation, so long as we avoid careless errors (or better, let a computer do the job for us), there is no limit to the complexity of forms we can test. We can even test forms so complex that we have no idea what they mean.

Again, however, it is important to understand the limitations of this technique, as well as its advantages. It does provide a reliable test for validity, but only for validity due to truth functional operators. Moreover, the arguments to be tested must consist of bivalent statements and must first be translated into unambiguous symbolic notation. If an argument's truth table contains no line on which the premises are true and the conclusion false, then all arguments of that form are valid. But if it does contain one or more such lines, then we cannot conclude that a particular argument of that form is invalid unless we first rule out the possibility of validity due to other sources. There is no simple way to do this, since the sources of validity are numerous and diverse. So truth tables are not a sure test of the invalidity of individual arguments (though they do, as we saw above, establish the invalidity of argument *forms*).

One of the goals of formal logic is to locate and thoroughly understand all the sources of validity, and of rationality in general. Our brief study of the truth-table test is only the merest hint of what formal logic can accomplish. Much more than this is known, but much more still remains to be discovered. The work of formal logic is far from completion.

Exercise 10.5(a)   Use the truth-table test to verify the validity or invalidity of each of the argument forms discussed in Section 5.1.

Exercise 10.5(b)   Use the truth-table test to decide which of the following argument forms are valid and which are invalid.

1      $p \supset q$
        $q \supset \sim r$
        p
   $\therefore$ $\sim r$

2      $p \supset q$
        $r \supset q$
  $\therefore$ $p \supset r$

3     $(p \lor q) \lor r$
       $\sim p' \ \& \sim q$
∴ r

4   p
∴ $p \lor q$

5     $p \lor q$
∴ p

6     $p \ \& \sim p$
∴ q

7   q
∴ $p \lor \sim p$

8     $p \supset q$
∴ $\sim p \lor q$

9     $\sim p \lor q$
∴ $p \supset q$

10    $p \supset q$
      $r \supset s$
       $p \lor r$
       $\sim s$
∴ q

11    $(p \ \& \ q) \supset r$
      $p \lor q$
∴ r

12    $p \equiv q$
      $q \equiv r$
∴ $p \equiv r$

13    $p \equiv (q \ \& \ r)$
      $\sim p$
∴ $\sim r$

14    $p \equiv (q \lor r)$
      $\sim r$
∴ $p \equiv q$

Exercise 10.5(c) Translate each of the following arguments into symbolic form, using the symbol scheme provided. Then test each for validity by constructing its truth table.

1   Either he knows the truth and he's hiding it, or he doesn't know it. But he's not hiding it. So he doesn't know it. (p = He knows the truth; q = He's hiding it.)

2   It is not true that if you don't put garlic on your doorstep you fall prey to vampires. For though you have not put garlic on your door-

step, you have not fallen prey to vampires. (p = You put garlic on your doorstep; q = You fall prey to vampires.)

3 Our problems can be solved only if we have faith and moral courage. But these we have. Therefore, our problems are solvable. (p = Our problems are solvable; q = We have faith; r = We have moral courage.)

4 If she sent this message, as she did, then she was safe. But if Rasputin had found her, she would not have been safe. Therefore, Rasputin did not find her. (p = She sent this message; q = She was safe; r = Rasputin found her.)

5 This creature is warm-blooded if and only if it is either a mammal or a bird. But it is clearly not a mammal. So it must be a warm-blooded bird. (p = This creature is warm-blooded; q = It is a mammal; r = It is a bird.)

6 If there is no record of the matter, then either the police were not called or someone tampered with the records. There is no record of the matter, and yet the police were called. Therefore, someone tampered with the records. (p = There is a record of the matter; q = The police were called; r = Someone tampered with the records.)

7 If the chicken is over 100 feet tall and it's alive, then it's dangerous. But if it's over 100 feet tall, it's not alive. Therefore, it's not dangerous. (p = The chicken is over 100 feet tall; q = It's alive; r = It's dangerous.)

8 If people have souls and the soul survives death, then the soul is not a physical thing. But we can have knowledge of the soul only if it is a physical thing. Hence, if people have souls, then either we have no knowledge of the soul or the soul does not survive death. (p = People have souls; q = The soul survives death; r = The soul is a physical thing; s = We can have knowledge of the soul.)

9 If we survive a nuclear war, then we will either kill or be killed in the ensuing struggle for food. If we kill in this struggle, then we will be murderers. Hence, if we survive a nuclear war, either we will be killed in the struggle for food anyway, or we will be murderers. (p = We survive a nuclear war; q = We will kill in the ensuing struggle for food; r = We will be killed in the ensuing struggle for food; s = We will be murderers.)

10 All elves drink stout. Olaf is an elf. Therefore, Olaf drinks stout. (p = All elves drink stout; q = Olaf is an elf; r = Olaf drinks stout.)

Exercise 10.5(d) Explain why problem 10 of Exercise 10.5(c) comes out the way it does.

348

10.6   A BRIEF HISTORY OF LOGIC

It is not possible to understand ideas thoroughly unless we also understand their historical roots. Logic is not, as some have thought, a crystalline structure fixed in the cosmic order of things. It is a human endeavor, with a rich and ancient history and a lively and controversial present. This book is a product of that controversial present, and it takes sides on a number of disputed issues. Therefore, it would be a serious omission if the ideas presented here were not, at least in a cursory way, set into context and contrasted with opposing views.

The first person to study logic systematically was the Greek philosopher Aristotle (384–322 B.C.). Aristotle was mainly concerned with arguments consisting of **categorical propositions**—that is, statements of the following four forms:

All S is P No S is P

Some S is P Some S is not P

The letters "S" and "P" stand for "subject term" and "predicate term," respectively. Subject terms are generally common nouns or noun phrases, like "person," "anemone," "toy," and "nasty sharp thing." Predicate terms are usually nouns, noun phrases, or adjectives, like "blue" and "ridiculous." Aristotle was especially concerned with a class of inferences called **categorical syllogisms.** These consist of three categorical propositions, two premises and a conclusion, where the premises share a term. Here's an example:

All people are ridiculous.

No anemones are ridiculous.

∴ No people are anemones.

Aristotle realized that the validity or invalidity of such inferences depends on their form. The form of the argument above, for example, is:

All F are G.

No H are G.

∴ No F are H.

This is valid, no matter what terms are substituted for the three variables. There are, of course, other categorical syllogistic forms which are invalid.

Categorical syllogisms differ from arguments using truth functional operators in several respects. First, the variables stand for nouns, adjectives, or phrases, not whole sentences. Second, they always consist of two premises and a conclusion. The most important difference, however, is that the non-variable terms their forms contain—words like "all," "no," and "some"—are not truth functional operators. They cannot be truth functional because the terms on which they operate—namely the nouns, adjectives, or phrases represented by the variables—have no truth value. "All," "no," and "some" are called **quantifiers,** and their role in modern formal logic is, if anything, even more central than it was in Aristotle's time. But we shall not discuss their semantics or logic here.

Aristotle's theory of categorical syllogisms, though limited in scope, was a groundbreaking achievement. It had one serious drawback, however; it did not apply to arguments containing empty terms—that is, terms which, like "unicorn" or "rattlesnake over a mile long," apply to nothing actual. All terms in Aristotelian logic are presumed to be nonempty. This limitation was not satisfactorily overcome until the nineteenth century.

Aristotle's work also included some early discoveries in modal logic, the study of inferences concerning possibility and necessity. It is in this field that the concept of a possible world has its most fruitful applications today, but Aristotle was unfamiliar with this concept. Aristotle also seems not to have been much concerned with inferences involving truth functional operators. Their study was left to certain of his successors among the Greeks and medievals.

It is a tribute to Aristotle's genius that his logical discoveries were not significantly superseded until modern times. The intervening period saw many stormy controversies in the philosophy of logic and scattered developments in the theories of conditionals, identity, tenses, modality, and belief. But the Aristotelian categorical syllogism remained the centerpiece of virtually all logical theory until the development of more efficient and comprehensive formalisms late in the nineteenth century.

This development was anticipated in the early eighteenth century by Gottfried Wilhelm Leibniz (1646–1717). Leibniz, who is perhaps best known for his discovery, along with Newton, of the infinitesimal calculus, envisioned a universal formal logic embracing all of mathematics and indeed all of human thought. But he was still too much in the grip of Aristotelian thinking to carry the project very far.

To Leibniz, however, belongs another distinction of interest. He invented the idea of a possible world. His motive, oddly enough, was less logical than theological. In attempting to solve the problem of evil (see Section 3.6) he hit upon the idea that before the creation God surveyed all possible worlds and chose just one, the best and most perfect of all, to be actual. This best of all possible worlds, said Leibniz, is the one we inhabit. Whatever its evils and imperfections, they must exist for the greater perfection and goodness of the whole. Leibniz took comfort in this idea, but others with less sanguine outlooks have been appalled by it.

Though possible worlds were central to Leibniz' thinking, they played virtually no role in the important developments which followed. In the middle of the nineteenth century George Boole (1815–1864) invented an algebraic form of truth functional and class logic which exhibited underlying unity among syllogistic and truth functional inferences. John Venn (1834–1923) modified Aristotelian logic to allow for empty terms and devised a convenient system of diagrams to test categorical syllogisms for validity.

But the first truly modern system of logic was developed by Gottlob Frege (1848–1925). Frege sought to fulfill Leibniz' dream of a universal formal logic which would characterize all rational thought. To this end he developed a formal system encompassing all valid inferences involving truth functional operators, quantifiers, and identity. This system is known today as the **predicate calculus.** Using the predicate calculus, together with some basic assumptions of what is now known as set theory, Frege set out to prove the power of his system by deducing all the known truths of mathematics. For a time this project seemed on the verge of success. But at the dawn of the twentieth century it was utterly demolished by a brilliant young Englishman named Bertrand Russell (1872–1970).

To understand the awful problem Russell posed to Frege, we must return once more to the time of the ancient Greeks. The Greeks had discovered a curious puzzle called the **paradox of the liar.** It concerned Epimenides, a Cretan, who said that all Cretans are liars. His statement was puzzling, because if he was telling the truth, then he was a liar. More vexing versions of this puzzle emerged later. Consider, for example, the statement "I am now lying." If true, it must be false. But what's worse, if it is false, then I'm not lying and so what I'm saying must be true! This is a paradox indeed, and the only possible solution is that the sentence is neither true nor false. You saw this with respect to the related sentence "This sentence is false" if you worked problems 7 and 8 of Exercise 5.5(b).

Russell was fascinated by this paradox and similar puzzles which had arisen in some of the obscure mathematics of his day, and he wondered how they affected Frege's system. One of Frege's assumptions implied that corresponding to every property, there exists a class consisting of just those things having that property. Corresponding to the property of squareness, for example, there is the class of all square things. Corresponding to the property of being a vile knave, there exists the class of all vile knaves. Now some classes are members of themselves and some are not. The class of all vile knaves is not itself a vile knave and therefore is not a member of itself. But the class of all classes is a member of itself, since it does have the property of being a class.

At this point Russell asked his fateful question: what about the class of all classes which are not members of themselves? Is it a member of itself or not? He then argued by reductio. Suppose it is a member of itself. Then since every one of its members has the property of not being a member of itself, it is not a member of itself. Therefore, it both is and is not a member of itself—a contradiction. Hence it is not a member of itself.

So far so good. We have what appears to be a sound argument showing that the class is not a member of itself. But now comes the other half of the vice. Suppose it is not a member of itself. Then since it contains every class which is not a member of itself, it must be a member of itself. Hence again it both is and is not a member of itself!

We have now derived contradictions both from the assertion that this class is a member of itself and from the assertion that it is not. (The similarity of our arguments to problems 7 and 8 of Exercise 5.5(b) should be obvious. They also bear an obvious resemblance to the argument in Section 5.4 showing that you can't like just the people who don't like themselves.) What these two contradictions show, as Russell well understood, is that the very idea of a class of all classes which are not members of themselves is incoherent. This class is a logically impossible object. It exists in no possible world. Since Frege's basic assumptions implied the existence of this class, they themselves were incoherent. Frege's project disintegrated, like a building hit by a bomb.

It should be noted that it was Frege's mathematical assumptions which were at fault, not his logic. The predicate calculus which he invented was perfectly consistent and remains the standard tool of formal logic today. But the foundations of mathematics were in serious trouble.

Russell spent the next decade working with his collaborator Alfred North Whitehead to reconstruct a coherent mathematics. He noticed that objects which engender logical paradox, like the liar sentence or the class of all classes which are not members of themselves, all possess a peculiar sort of self-reference. (The liar sentence talks about itself; the Russell class is defined by the property of non-*self*-membership.) And he sought to expunge self-reference from mathematics.

The result was a magnificent three-volume treatise called *Principia Mathematica*, in which Russell and Whitehead successfully deduced all known mathematics from a few basic assumptions. *Principia* is a monument to human ingenuity and effort. Its several thousand pages, written almost entirely in the symbolism of formal logic, are so dense that only a few people have ever read them all. But though it was a stunning achievement, it was not the last word. The paradoxes came back to haunt mathematical logic again in a totally new and unexpected guise.

Russell and Whitehead had deduced all *known* mathematics. But they had not shown that their assumptions were strong enough to prove all mathematical truths. In 1931 the logician Kurt Gödel showed that they were not. In fact, Gödel went much further. He proved that no assumptions we can ever formulate, even if they are infinite in number, can suffice to prove all the truths of mathematics. Mathematics as a whole must remain forever beyond our deductive grasp.

We cannot discuss the details of Gödel's argument here. But one aspect of it certainly deserves mention. What Gödel discovered was that Russell and Whitehead had not expunged self-reference from mathematics completely. Their failure was not due to any inadequacy in their thinking, but to the essence of mathematics. Gödel found that in any logical system strong enough to prove even the most basic mathematical truths it is possible to formulate a sentence which in effect says "I am not provable." While this sentence is self-referential and similar in form to the liar sentence, it is known to be either true or false. Now suppose it is false. Then it is not the case that it is unprovable, and so it must be provable. But no falsehoods are provable, and so we have a contradiction. It follows that this statement is true. This is not, however, paradoxical as in the previous cases. Since the sentence is true, what it says is correct; it *is* unprovable. Hence mathematics contains at least one unprovable truth. (There are, in fact, infinitely many, but I won't show that here.) This is the core of Gödel's argument, though I have omitted details and qualifications.

Gödel's proof shows that there will always be unsolved problems in mathematics, no matter how intelligent we become or how sophisticated we make our computers. Indeed, it even implies certain surprising limitations on computers themselves. Since Gödel first presented his result, an entire discipline (recursive function theory) has developed to explore these limitations.

Throughout the period from Leibniz to Gödel, logicians paid little attention to possible worlds. But in the 1940s and 1950s Rudolph Carnap made advances in modal and inductive logic by appealing to the concept of a state description, which is in many ways similar to the idea of a possible world. Carnap was among the first to investigate logical, or inherent, probability in a systematic way, and this book's discussion both of inherent and inductive probability is derived, though distantly, from his work. Because of certain difficulties which arose from Carnap's study of induction, many logicians still distrust the use of possible worlds or state descriptions in explaining probability and prefer a more intuitive or subjective approach. But there seems to be no consensus on this issue.

Possible worlds as such were introduced into contemporary logic in 1959 by Saul Kripke, who used them to solve some outstanding technical problems in modal logic. Since then, possible worlds have become increasingly prominent in logic and analytic philosophy, where they have been used to clarify and elaborate a wide variety of ideas (just as we used them to clarify and elaborate the concepts of validity, induction, probability, statement strength, the strict conditional, contingency, necessity, and so on). Many philosophers and logicians, however, continue to regard them as something of a gimmick.

Perhaps the foremost opponent of possible worlds is Willard Van Orman Quine. Quine prefers to define logical concepts, not in terms of possible worlds—indeed, not in terms of possibility at all—but rather on the basis of logical form. Since English grammar is an unreliable guide to logical form, Quine's concepts can be profitably applied only to symbolic formulas, not directly to arguments in English. Quine therefore holds that all serious logical work must be carried out in an unambiguous artificial symbolic language, the so-called "canonical idiom." Consequently, his approach is formal from the start.

There are many others who, though lacking Quine's passion for formal regimentation, still feel uneasy about possible worlds. Among the most common criticisms are that possible worlds are too vague and ill-defined, that it makes no sense to talk about individuals existing in more than one possible world, and that the notion of a majority of possible worlds, crucial for our discussion of induction, is terminally unclear. Those with a philosophical bent also question the intelligibility of talk about things which don't actually exist.

These are all troublesome problems, but the last word has yet to be said on any of them. My conviction in writing this book has been that none of them is serious enough to undermine the worlds concept and that satisfactory answers will eventually emerge. But many logicians—both those who, like Quine, advocate a consistently formal approach and those who indulge in informal logic—disagree.

Informal logic texts not based on possible worlds generally include a study of fallacies, rhetorical tricks, and uses of language, together with a smattering of inductive and deductive methods. All of these things are discussed separately, and relations among them are difficult to discern; for without something like possible worlds as a theoretical basis, informal logic lacks conceptual unity. Those who advocate this style of informal logic argue that the disunity is inherent in its subject matter and cannot be avoided. This book has taken the opposite view. Among the logical community as a whole, the issue remains unsettled.

Suggestions for Further Study

If you want to know more about formal deductive logic, there is no better place to start than E. J. Lemmon's *Beginning Logic* (Hackett, 1978). Lemmon does not discuss possible worlds, but his system of natural deduction is readily seen as a formal development of ideas discussed in this book. (One word of caution: Lemmon uses "sound" to mean "valid.") A broader but less detailed introduction to current work in the formalization of natural languages is *Logic in Linguistics* by Jens Allwood, Lars-Gunnar Andersson, and Östen Dahl (Cambridge, 1977).

Readers with an interest in mathematics may enjoy the very compact book *What is Mathematical Logic?* by J. N. Crossley, C. J. Ash, C. J. Brickhill, J. C. Stillwell, and N. H. Williams (Oxford, 1972). This book covers the predicate calculus, Gödel's theorem, and some logical results about computability. A very readable introduction to Gödel's theorem itself is *Gödel's Proof*, by Ernest Nagel and James R. Newman (New York University Press, 1958). For a spectacularly imaginative approach to formal logic, paradoxes, Gödel's theorem, and a host of other topics, see Douglas R. Hofstadter's

Pulitzer Prize winning book *Gödel, Escher, Bach: An Eternal Golden Braid* (Vintage, 1979).

Readers interested in inductive logic will find Brian Skyrms' *Choice and Chance: An Introduction to Inductive Logic*, 2d ed., (Dickenson, 1975) helpful. Skyrms' book contains extensive discussions of the various kinds of probability, and philosophical problems of induction, the formal probability calculus, and other topics. *Probabilities, Problems, and Paradoxes: Readings in Inductive Logic*, edited by Sidney A. Luckenbach (Dickenson, 1972), is a collection containing many seminal articles on philosophical problems. If you're interested in the more practical problems of sampling, experimentation, and statistical inference, a good source is David S. Moore's *Statistics: Concepts and Controversies* (W. H. Freeman and Company, 1979).

Those of you who are intrigued by the concept of possible worlds will find a thorough treatment in *Possible Worlds: An Introduction to Logic and Its Philosophy* by Raymond Bradley and Norman Swartz (Hackett, 1979). Some of the philosophical controversies surrounding the concept are surveyed in *The Possible and the Actual: Readings in the Metaphysics of Modality*, edited by Michael J. Loux (Cornell, 1979). For a more sustained theoretical treatment, which includes some fascinating material on philosophical theology, see Alvin Plantinga's *The Nature of Necessity* (Oxford, 1974).

If you want to know more about the rhetorical aspects of argument, see *Logic and Contemporary Rhetoric: The Use of Reason in Everyday Life*, 3d ed., by Howard Kahane (Wadsworth, 1980). This book contains many excellent examples, but watch Kahane's terminology; his notion of a fallacy is quite different from the one used here.

Finally, those who wish to compare this book with a more traditional approach to logic should see Irving Copi's *Introduction to Logic*, 6th ed., (Macmillan, 1982), which has been the standard introductory text for many years. Once again, watch out for terminological differences.

Appendix:
The Paradoxes of
Inductive Probability

As I noted at the end of Section 3.3 and again near the end of Section 6.3, the concept of inductive probability (i.e., the probability of a conclusion, given certain premises) is extremely controversial. The controversy arises from paradoxes which emerge when we try to evaluate certain types of nondeductive inferences. What happens in these cases is that we get two or more conflicting estimates of inductive probability by equally plausible and precise lines of reasoning.

   Perhaps the simplest example is Bertrand's paradox. One version of this paradox concerns the argument:

   The ratio of water to wine in a glass is somewhere between 1/1 and 2/1.
   ∴ The ratio of water to wine is less than 1.5/1.

The most obvious way to evaluate this argument is as follows. Since there are equally many possibilities for the proportion to fall between 1.5/1 and 2/1 as between 1/1 and 1.5/1, the conclusion, given the premise, is no more than 50 percent probable, and so the argument is fallacious.

But there are other ways of looking at it. If the ratio of water to wine is between 1/1 and 2/1, then the ratio of wine to water is between 1/2 and 1/1. Now the conclusion is equivalent to saying that the ratio of wine to water is *greater than* 1/1.5—that is, greater than 2/3. But there are twice as many possibilities between 2/3 and 1/1 as between 1/2 and 2/3 (since 2/3 − 1/2 = 1/6, while 1/1 − 2/3 = 1/3 = 2/6). Hence, given the premise, it is twice as probable that the ratio of wine to water will lie between 2/3 and 1/1 as between 1/2 and 2/3. Since, given the premise, it must lie in one of the two intervals (ignoring the infinitesimal possibility that it is exactly 2/3), the chance of its lying between 1/2 and 2/3 is 33$\frac{1}{3}$ percent, and the chance of its lying between 2/3 and 1/1 is 66$\frac{2}{3}$ percent. But the chance of its lying between 2/3 and 1/1 is just the probability of the argument's conclusion, given its premise. Hence the argument's inductive probability is 66$\frac{2}{3}$ percent. The argument is therefore inductive, not fallacious. The conflict of this result with the previous one constitutes the paradox.

I have not formulated this reasoning explicitly in terms of possible worlds, for two reasons: first, because it's simpler this way, and second, because I wanted to show that it is independent of the possible worlds analysis. Possible worlds are not the problem; the concept of inductive probability itself is. From the standpoint of possible worlds, the argument is the same, only the "possibilities" (i.e., values of the ratio) must be understood as classes of possible worlds. More specifically, each "possibility" is the class of possible worlds in which the ratio takes one of the specific values permitted by the premise. Since there is no reason to regard some of these classes as more numerous than others, we assume them all to be equal and then reason exactly as above. We still get two incompatible evaluations.

Which is correct? Most of those who have wrestled with this problem have ultimately concluded that there is no correct answer and that the argument lacks a specific inductive probability. Some have drawn the further conclusion that the very notion of inductive probability is incoherent.

Surely this further conclusion goes too far. Even if this argument and others like it have no precise inductive probability, this does not show that the idea of inductive probability is completely incoherent. It shows only that, strictly speaking, this idea is not applicable to certain arguments. There remain many nondeductive forms, such as statistical syllogism, which do have precise numerical inductive probabilities. And, of course, all deductive arguments do as well. These kinds of arguments are untainted by paradox. Hence at worst we must concede that the applicability of the concept of inductive probability is limited. It does not follow that the concept is incoherent.

My policy in this book has been to cite specific inductive probabilities where they are clearly calculable and to rely on nonnumerical qualitative estimates otherwise. While the paradoxes of inductive probability cast serious doubt on some of these qualitative estimates, I know of no better way to proceed if we wish to evaluate nondeductive arguments at all. This policy is totally unsatisfactory from a theoretical point of view, but something like it is unavoidable if we aim to answer the practical question "How good is the reasoning?" for arguments in natural language.

Answers to Selected Exercises

Since informal arguments are frequently ambiguous or indefinite in structure, there is often more than one way of interpreting them. The answers listed below are the ones I consider best, but in some cases other answers may be reasonable as well. When an answer is surprising, I explain it. You should do that, too.

Exercise 1.3

1   Hemlock is poison.   Basic premise
∴ You shouldn't drink it.   Conclusion

3   All even numbers are divisible by two.   Basic premise
All prime numbers are divisible only by themselves and one.   Basic premise
∴ Two is the only even prime.   Conclusion

5 Oil reserves are finite.   Basic premise
  Consumption is continuing at a rapid rate. Basic premise
  ∴ Eventually the world will run out of oil. Conclusion

7 This argument is a tough one. First of all, the author is reporting the argument, not giving it. The tone of the passage suggests that he or she doesn't endorse it. But let's consider the argument as reported. The "because" seems to link the two components of the first statement directly, which would mean that the "therefore" indicates the final conclusion, like this:

  Two people in communication must employ Basic premise
  a common language.

  ∴ All communication is based on selective in- Nonbasic premise
  formation.

  ∴ The art of communication consists merely Conclusion
  in passing to each other selected words out
  of the previously agreed dictionary.

But though this is the most obvious interpretation, I don't think it is the best. The third statement contains too much information to follow simply from the second. That makes me doubt that it is intended to. Moreover, the phrase "it is arguable that" suggests that the ultimate point of the whole passage is the general assertion that all communication is based on selective information. Therefore, I think that the author intended the reasoning to work this way:

  Two people in communication must employ Basic premise
  a common language.

  ∴ The art of communication consists merely Nonbasic premise
  in passing to each other selected words out
  of the previously agreed dictionary.

  ∴ All communication is based on selective in- Conclusion
  formation.

Notice that on this interpretation the "because" still serves its customary function of showing that the sentence which follows it is a premise supporting the one that precedes it. But now the support is by way of an intermediate conclusion. The second version makes more sense than the first, which further confirms my hunch that it is what the author really meant.

9 An oily face begins within your   Basic premise
 pores.

∴ That's where your cleanser should reach   Nonbasic premise
for your face to be really clean.
∴ You need pHisoDerm Skin Cleanser.   Conclusion

Exercise 1.5

1   It's raining.
∴ You'll get wet if you go out.

3   Every time I say something, you change the subject.
∴ You never pay any attention to me.

5 Not an argument. Neither statement is intended as evidence for the other, though taken together they might be regarded as evidence for the implicit conclusion: "When an engine is burning a lot of oil, repair is usually expensive." I'll discuss implicit conclusions in Chapter 4. Until then, you should simply note that the statements given here do not constitute an argument.

7   We've still got ten minutes of break time left.
∴ It's not time to go back to work yet.

9 Not an argument. This is a description of how the child arrives at a certain conclusion, but is not itself an argument. The author does not intend any statement given here as evidence for any other.

Exercise 1.6

1 This is a description of cause or an explanation, not an argument. There is no attempt to give evidence that he loves her.

3 Again, probably an explanation, not an argument. The fact that you two have a lot in common is not evidence for, but an explanation of, the fact that the author wants you to meet his or her sister.

5 Yet another explanation. "So" is not a conclusion indicator in this context. It introduces the author's explanation of why he or she wants to know the time.

7   If I am told a number and merely think about   Basic premise
it, I am likely to forget it or transpose some
of the digits.
If I repeat the numbers out loud or write   Basic premise
them down, then I can remember them quite
well.

∴ There is a part of our brain which remem-   Conclusion
bers sounds and images, but not thoughts.

9   From the moment of its birth, surrealism   Basic premise
was an international phenomenon—the
spontaneous generation of an international
and fraternal *organism* in total contrast to
the artificial manufacture of a collective *organization* such as the League of Nations.

∴ It would be contrary to the nature of the   Conclusion
movement to disengage, as some have sug-
gested, a specifically English version of 'surréalisme.'

11   The things confession is concerned with be-   Basic premise
long to the very heart of personality, to its
freedom and responsibility.

The danger of psycho-analysis is that it will   Basic premise
deal with these same things from the point
of view of natural occurrences and that it
will constantly direct the attention of the
patient to himself and his temporal existence.

∴ The soul's center of gravity may be trans-   Conclusion
ferred from the center—from the point of
personal responsibility in the presence of the
Unconditioned—to the impersonal, unconscious, purely natural sphere.

13   There is no greatest prime number.   Basic premise
Of all the prime numbers that we shall have   Basic premise
ever thought of, there certainly is a greatest.

∴ There are prime numbers greater than any   Conclusion
we shall have ever thought of.

Exercise 2(a)

1   Basic premises: ②, ③, ④, ⑤
Nonbasic premise: ①
Final conclusion: ⑥

Argument is normal.

3   Basic premises: ①, ⑤
Nonbasic premises: ②, ③
Final conclusion: ④

Argument is split support.

Exercise 2(c)

1 ①[Olaf is hairy and ugly as a wart hog.] And besides, ②[he never brushes his teeth.] ⑤ₒ ③[he wouldn't be very pleasant to live with.]

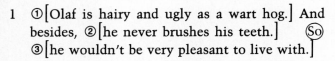

3 ⑤ᵢₙ𝒸ₑ ①[steak bones are high in iron] and ②[Olaf eats large quantities of steak bones,] (it follows that) ③[Olaf ingests an adequate supply of iron.] But ④[anyone whose iron intake is adequate has healthy, deep red blood.] ⑤ₒ ⑤[Olaf's blood must be healthy.]

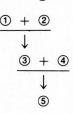

5 Not an argument. "Then" functions here, not as a conclusion indicator, but to indicate order in time.

7 ①[She left because the pay was too low.] ⑤ₒ ②[she obviously won't go back unless they offer her a raise.]

Note that "because" in the first sentence indicates an explanation, not an inference. Thus the first sentence must be treated as a single unit. The second sentence is a compound formed by "unless." This construction should not be split up either, as I explained at the end of Section 2.1.

9 ①[You can see that this argument is valid,] too. (For) ②[anyone who knows some logic, ③[as you do,] can see that it is.]

Note the nesting of statement ③ inside statement ② (see Section 2.4).

11 ①[My battery is dead, which is why my car won't start.] ⑤ₒ ②[I'll need to have it jumped before I can drive anywhere.]

The first sentence is an explanation.

13 ①[Solar power is better for the economy] (because) ②[it is labor intensive] and (therefore) ③[(it is) likely to stimulate employment.] And ④[solar power is much less likely to damage the environment or endanger human life than either nuclear power or coal.] Moreover, ⑤[the sun is a nearly inexhaustible energy

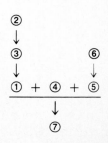

source;] ⑥[it will continue to supply light and heat for billions of years to come.] (Thus) ⑦[solar power is by far the best choice as the major energy source for our nation's future.]

15 ①[Large diamonds are becoming rarer every day.] (That's why) ②[choosing a larger diamond makes good sense.] (For) ③[size affects value.] (So) ④[you shouldn't be too shy about looking for diamonds that are a bit bigger.]

```
①  +  ③              ①        ③
   ↓                    ↘ ↙
   ②     or maybe        ②
   ↓                     ↓
   ④                     ④
```

17 ①[Gay people suffer a great deal of discrimination.] ②[In the past, gays were burned, hanged, or imprisoned for the crime of loving someone of the same sex.] ③[Even today, in what we call our permissive society, a gay person can be fired from a job or arrested for no greater crime than sexual preference.]

```
② + ③
  ↓
  ①
```

19 ①[What is dreamt within a dream after waking from the 'dream within a dream,' is what the dream-wish seeks to put in place of an obliterated reality.] (It is safe to suppose, therefore, that) ②[what has been 'dreamt' in the dream is a representation of the reality, the true recollection, while the continuation of the dream, on the contrary, merely represents what the dreamer wishes.] ③[To include something in a 'dream within a dream' is (thus) equivalent to wishing that the thing described as a dream had never happened.]

```
①
↓
②
↓
③
```

21 ①[So long as an opinion is strongly rooted in the feelings, it gains rather than loses in stability by having a preponderating weight of argument against it.] (For) ②[if it were accepted as a result of argument, the refutation of the argument might shake the solidity of the conviction;] but ③[when it rests

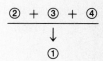

```
② + ③ + ④
    ↓
    ①
```

solely on feeling, the worse it fares in argumentative contest, the more persuaded
its adherents are that their feeling must have
some deeper ground, which the arguments
do not reach;] and ④[while the feeling remains, it is always throwing up fresh intrenchments of argument to repair any
breach made in the old.]

This argument is normal rather than split support. Statement ③
could perhaps stand alone in its support of ①, but ② and ④ could
not and therefore must be regarded as supplementing ③.

23 ①[Today, the male/female division of labor, with all its complicated psychological,
political, economic and cultural elaborations, is obsolete.] ②[It has lost whatever
correspondence with objective conditions it
may once have had.] ③[In America today
physical strength and speed of foot are of
negligible importance, especially in more
highly valued and rewarded work.]
④[Women spend only a small part of their
lives bearing children and even for the most
part of that period are not incapacitated from
tasks that men perform.]

25 ①[Self-expression is impossible in relation
with other men;] ②[their self-expression
interferes with it.] ③[The greatest heights
of self-expression—in poetry, music, painting—are achieved by men who are supremely alone.] And (it is for this reason
that) ④[the idea of the 'beatific vision' is
easier for the artist to grasp than for anyone
else.] ⑤[He has only to imagine his moment of 'greatest aloneness' intensified to
a point where it would fill up his life and
make all other relations impossible or unnecessary.]

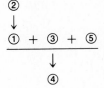

Inadequate use of indicators hinders our understanding of the structure of this passage. Other analyses are possible.

27 ①[To justify ethically any human activity, we must inquire—"Is this a means to good states of mind?"] ②[In the case of art, our answer will be prompt and emphatic.] ③[Art is not only a means to good states of mind, but, perhaps, the most direct and potent means that we possess.] ④[Nothing is more direct,] (because) ⑤[nothing affects the mind more immediately;] ⑥[nothing is more potent,] (because) ⑦[there is no state of mind more excellent or more intense than the state of aesthetic contemplation.] (This being so) , ⑧[to seek in art a means to anything less than good states of mind, is an act of wrong-headedness.]

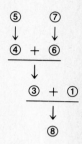

Note that statement ② should be omitted from the diagram.

Exercise 3.2(a)

1 Logically possible.
3 Logically possible.
5 Logically impossible.
7 Logically impossible.
9 Logically possible.

Exercise 3.2(b)

1 Valid.
3 Invalid. Counterexample: A world in which some elements (like zinc or copper) are metals, but no elements are alloys, yet in which there are alloys (like bronze or stainless steel). The actual world fits this description.
5 Valid.

7   Invalid. Counterexample: A world in which my car won't start, but in which I could walk or take a bus to work.

9   Invalid. Counterexample: A world in which weeks consist of seven days, just as in our world, and in which Olaf sings as he wakes up every day of the week, except Monday, on which he never sings, and in which it is now Monday morning and Olaf is waking up.

Exercise 3.3

1   Fallacious. Counterexample: A world in which the moon is made of green cheese, but in which green cheese explodes as soon as it comes in contact with a living organism.

3   Deductive.

5   Inductive. Counterexample: A world in which only a few old folks fly hang gliders, but Oscar is one of them.

7   Deductive.

9   Deductive.

11 Inductive. Counterexample: A world in which the die is as described in the premises, it it lands showing one anyway.

Exercise 3.4

1   ①[All pizza eaters are cowards,] and ②[some cowards drink beer.] (Therefore) , ③[all pizza eaters drink beer.]

$$\frac{① + ②}{③} \quad \downarrow F$$

3   ①[Grandma was either a mobster or a sweet old lady.] But ②[she was not a sweet old lady.] (Therefore), ③[she was a mobster.]

$$\frac{① + ②}{③} \quad \downarrow D$$

5   ①[If you eat an ox you will die.] ②[If you die you won't be able to disco anymore.] (Therefore), ③[if you eat an ox you won't be able to disco anymore.]

$$\frac{① + ②}{③} \quad \downarrow D$$

7   ①[If we had received messages from deep space, we could be confident that alien civilizations exist on other planets.] But ②[we have received no such messages.] (Hence) ③[we cannot be confident of the existence of alien civilizations.]

$$\frac{① + ②}{③} \quad \downarrow F$$

A number of counterexamples to this argument are mentioned in Section 10.5.

9   ①[Every being that is not God, is God's creature.] Now ②[every creature of God is good] and ③[God is the greatest Good.] (Therefore), ④[every being is good.]

$$\frac{① + ② + ③}{④} \quad \downarrow D$$

In this context, the term "creature" means "created thing." But you don't have to know that to see that the argument is valid.

Exercise 3.5

1 (Because) ①[Olaf is in such good shape,] ②[he must play either tennis or handball.] But ③[he doesn't play tennis,] (for) ④[he never gets any sun.] (So) ⑤[he must play handball.]

3 ①[The deliciously creamy taste of Sealtest cottage cheese stands out no matter what you make with it.] (Because) ②[we make Sealtest cottage cheese with pure Sealtest sweet cream dressing for an outstandingly fresh natural flavor.] (That's why) ③[Sealtest cottage cheese is so good just by itself, or as a delicious ingredient.]

or maybe

Some people might want to regard statement ③ as a mere repetition of statement ①, so that the argument becomes:

But I think this is a mistake. To say that the deliciously creamy taste *stands out* is not to say that it's *good* as an ingredient, which is what ③ says. It may stand out, for example, in combination with mustard and molasses, but I doubt that it's good that way. Conversely, to say that it is good as an ingredient does not necessarily imply that it stands out. Thus both the inference from ① to ③ and the inference from ③ to ① are invalid. Moreover, it seems to me that among the cases I can imagine, there are enough counterexamples to make each inference fallacious, though I'm less sure of this.

This argument nicely illustrates some common rhetorical aspects of advertisements. Notice in particular the ungrammatical use of "because" to introduce a single statement. This produces a clipped style which suggests forthright frankness. Note also the frequent repetition of the product name, which helps to etch the name into the reader's mind.

5 ①[The thief got away,] and ②[there are only two ways he could have gone—to the left, down the long hallway, or to the right, down the shorter one.] ③[If he had gone down the long hallway, he would have been seen by the guard stationed there.] But ④[the guard saw nothing.] ⑤o it is certain that ⑤[he did not go down the long hallway.] ⑥[he must have escaped by the shorter one.]

$$\frac{③ + ④}{\downarrow D}$$

$$\frac{① + ② + ⑤}{\downarrow D} \quad \boxed{D}$$
$$⑥$$

Therefore ,

7 ①[If you search in your heart, you will find a yearning there, a deep unsatisfied longing which you do not understand.] Thus ②[you can feel that Lord Krishna is calling you to Cosmic Consciousness.] ③[If Lord Krishna calls to you and you follow his path, you will have abundant life.] And surely ④[you desire abundant life.] Therefore , ⑤[you should heed Lord Krishna's call and seek his Consciousness.]

$$① \atop \downarrow F$$

$$\frac{② + ③ + ④}{\downarrow F} \quad \boxed{F}$$
$$⑤$$

The second inference is a fairly seductive fallacy. Even if ②, ③, and ④ were true, it needn't be true that you should follow Krishna. We can easily imagine circumstances under which you shouldn't fulfill your desire. And we can also imagine indefinitely many other ways to achieve abundant life, so that even if you should fulfill this desire, you needn't do it by following Krishna. These constitute a host of counterexamples.

9 ①[The butler must have stabbed Rumsford.] For ②[only three people could have done it—the butler, the cook, or the maid.] But ③[it wasn't the cook,] because ④[he was probably away in London shopping at the time of the stabbing— at least 20 miles from the scene of the crime.] And ⑤[the maid didn't do it,] because ⑥[she almost surely lacked the necessary physical strength.]

$$④ \qquad ⑥$$
$$\downarrow I \qquad \downarrow I$$
$$\frac{② + ③ + ⑤}{\downarrow D} \quad \boxed{I}$$
$$①$$

The words "almost surely" in ⑥ make the inference from ⑥ to ⑤ inductive, rather than deductive. "Probably" works similarly in ④. But I'm less sure about the inductiveness of the inference from ④ to ③. We can imagine very bizarre situations in which the cook stabs Rumsford even if he is 20 miles away. His arm might be 20 miles long. Or he might do it by telekinesis. So perhaps this inference is fallacious. If it is, then so is the argument as a whole.

Exercise 3.6(a)

1   "Exactly one elf drinks stout" is stronger.

3   "The President is a woman" is stronger.

5   "Most crows are black" is stronger.

Exercise 3.6(b)

1   ①[The population of the earth is over two billion,] and (since) ②[most people sleep about a third of the time] and ③[people on different parts of the earth sleep at different times,] ④[at any given moment someone is asleep.]

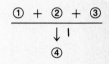

The reasoning here is weakly or moderately inductive. Because of the large number of people involved, it seems likely that in *most* possible worlds in which the premises are true, so is the conclusion. The premises are certainly true. Therefore, this is a reasonably strong argument.

3   ①[If the Loch Ness Monster exists, it is either a mammal, a reptile, or an amphibian;] (for) ②[no other sorts of animals could be responsible for the sightings reported at the Loch.] But ③[it is not a mammal or a reptile,] (since) ④[if it were, it would have to surface frequently for air,] and ⑤[it does not do so.] Moreover, ⑥[it is not an amphibian,] (for) ⑦[no amphibian is large enough to be the monster.] (Thus) ⑧[the monster does not exist.]

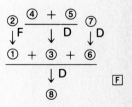

To see that the inference from ② to ① is invalid, consider the worlds in which the only sorts of *animals* that could be responsible for the sightings are mammals, reptiles, or amphibians, but in which the monster is not an animal. It could be a robot, a peculiar sort of wave, a submarine, a patch of seaweed, or any of countless other inanimate things. There are so many counterexamples of this sort that the inference is surely fallacious. Thus the entire argument is fallacious. If its basic premises are true, the monster may still exist, so long as it is inanimate. I don't know whether the basic premises are true. But even if they are, the argument is too weak to be convincing. Is there any way to strengthen it?

5 ①[A line segment is a subset of a line consisting of two distinct points and all points of the line between these two points.] (Since) ②[there are infinitely many points between every two distinct points of a line,] ③[every line segment is an infinite set of points.] And (since) ④[a polygon is the union of three or more line segments,] (it follows that) ⑤[a polygon, too, is an infinite set of points.] This argument is sound.

```
① + ②
  ↓D
③ + ④
  ↓D        D
  ⑤
```

7 ①[If the universe were to crush him, man would still be more noble than that which killed him,] (because) ②[he knows that he dies and the advantage which the universe has over him;] ③[the universe knows nothing of this.] ④[All our dignity consists, (then), in thought.]

```
② + ③
  ↓F
  ①         F
  ↓F
  ④
```

Though the basic premises both are true, the argument is hopelessly weak, because both inferences are fallacious. We can readily imagine worlds in which both ② and ③ are true, and yet man is a sniveling coward, a vicious criminal, or a lewd and soulless pleasure seeker, while the universe (the world itself) is stately and noble. Likewise, it is easy to imagine that ① is true and yet that not all of man's dignity consists in thought. (Some of it, for example, might consist in work, in love, in free will, in being created in God's image, etc.) Each case of this sort is a counterexample to the second inference.

9 ①[Creating is obviously present in the universe.] ②[Life is more than bare matter, yet emerged from it in the temporal process;] ③[mind is more than life, yet appeared in the evolutionary scale.] ④[Time must (therefore) be conceived of not merely as change, but as *creative* change; not merely as replacement of specific qualities by other specific qualities, but as the origination of new genera.] (Hence) ⑤[something comes from nothing.]

```
② + ③
  ↓D
  ①
  ↓F        F
  ④
  ↓F
  ⑤
```

The structure of this argument is not fully clear. Statements ② and ③ could be regarded as compound sentences and split up. But this would not affect the overall evaluation, and I've avoided it for simplicity's sake. Statement ④ might also be regarded as two statements, but since it all follows from ① and goes on as a unit to support ⑤, the best thing is to leave it whole. Otherwise, we would have to split the argument into two separate pieces (see Section 2.7). Basic premises ② and ③ seem true. The inference from them to ① is valid if we regard "creation" as meaning "the production of new phenomena," which seems to have been the author's intention. (If "creation" is interpreted to mean something else, the inference could be weaker.) The inference from ① to ④ is, taken literally, obviously fallacious. From the fact that creating is present, nothing follows about how we *must* conceive things. Nothing prevents us from conceiving them wrongly. But it is unfair to the author to insist strictly on this literal reading. What the author means by ④ is something more like this: "*In order to conceive time correctly*, we must conceive it not merely as change, but as creative change. . . . " However, this still seems fallacious, because even if creating is present in the universe, it doesn't follow that time itself is creative change. We can imagine, for example, worlds in which time continues to pass between sporadic periods of creation. During such intervals, time would not be creative change.

The final inference is also fallacious. We can imagine all sorts of worlds in which time is creative change and new genera are created, but in which it never happens that something comes from nothing. Rather, the creative change could be the transformation of one thing into another. Thus the whole argument is fallacious and hence very weak.

Exercise 3.7

1. ①[Olaf is a sparkling conversationalist,] (be-cause) ②[he is a logician] and (because) ③[he has nice eyes.]

   ②   ③
   F ↘ ↙ F   F
       ①

3. (Since) ①[too much sun dries your skin] and ②[(too much sun) can even cause skin cancer,] ③[to maintain healthy skin you should avoid the sun.]

   ①   ②
   F ↘ ↙ F   F
       ③

The argument's structure is unclear. Statements ① and ② could also be regarded as a single statement or as separate but linked reasons. I've split them, because neither really depends on the other and because the author's use of the term "even" suggests that ② is intended as a further, separate reason for the conclusion. In any case, the argument is fallacious. If the premises show anything, it's only that to stay healthy you should avoid getting *too much* sun, not that you should avoid the sun altogether.

5   ①[In order to evaluate arguments well, you need a vivid imagination.] ②[Some people don't have vivid imaginations.] (Therefore), ③[some people can't evaluate arguments well.] Now clearly ④[no drunkard can evaluate arguments well.] (Therefore), ⑤[some people are drunkards.]

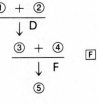

Any world in which some people can't evaluate arguments well and in which there are no drunkards (or no drunkards who are people) is a counterexample to the second inference.

7   (Since)   ①[it was cold,] ②[if any of the party survived the avalanche, they would have built a fire.] ③[If there were any survivors, (then), they should have been easy to spot.] (Another reason for thinking this is that) ④[they were all wearing orange coats.] But ⑤[the searchers saw nothing.] (So) probably ⑥[no one survived.]

①
↓F
②   ④   [F]
F ↘ ↙ F
③ + ⑤
↓I
⑥

There may have been survivors who were too injured to start a fire, or perhaps they could find no fuel. Such situations, among others, are counterexamples to the inference from ① to ②. We can imagine many conditions under which fires are not easy to spot. These are counterexamples to the inference from ② to ③. We can also imagine many conditions under which orange coats can't be seen (fog, darkness, etc.). These are counterexamples to the inference from ④ to ③. If we regard statement ③ as meaning that survivors *probably* would have been easy to spot, then it is apparent that the last inference is inductive. Under most conditions in which ③ and ⑤ are true, ⑥ would be true as well. Note that I left the word "probably" out of ⑥. I took it to be the author's way of hinting that the final inference is supposed to be inductive. This is the simplest way to handle things when "probably" prefixes a conclusion. If we include it in ⑥, then ⑥ becomes a weaker statement, but the inference from ③ and ⑤ to ⑥ becomes stronger—perhaps even deductive. There's a tradeoff here between strength of inference and strength of conclusion, and this tradeoff obeys the principle discussed near the end of Section 3.6. In any case, the argument as a whole is completely fallacious. If I were one of the victims' relatives, I'd be pretty unhappy with it.

Exercise 3.8

1   ①[Olaf and Ophelia really are elves.]
(Thus)   ②[there are some intelligent
creatures less than 2 feet tall,] (from
which it follows that)   ③[elvish folk
really do exist.]

This argument is fortuitously strong, because ① deductively implies
③.

3   ①[Without natural selection, evolution would
cease.] But ②[natural selection no longer operates in human beings,] (for)   ③[it requires
that a greater proportion of weak individuals
than strong ones perish before reproducing.]
④[Modern medicine, however, permits the
weak to survive and reproduce as readily as the strong.] ⑤[Human
evolution has (therefore) come to a standstill.]

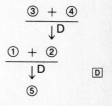

This is neither self-weakening nor fortuitously strong.

5   (Since)   ①[Olaf delivers letters] and
②[at least 90 percent of letter deliverers are postal employees,] it seems
likely that ③[Olaf is a postal employee.] It is nearly certain that ①[he
delivers letters,] (since)   ④[he is a
mailman] and ⑤[almost all mailmen
deliver letters.] And certainly ②[at least
90 percent of letter deliverers are postal
employees,] (because)   ⑥[all mailmen are postal employees] and ⑦[90
percent of letter deliverers are mailmen.]

$$\frac{④ \;+\; ⑤}{\underset{\downarrow I}{①}} \quad \frac{⑥ \;+\; ⑦}{\underset{\downarrow D}{}}$$

$$\frac{① \quad + \quad ②}{\underset{\downarrow I}{③}} \quad \boxed{D}$$

The argument is fortuitously strong, for premises ④ and ⑥ alone
deductively imply the final conclusion, ③. Note that despite the
statistical nature of premise ⑦, the inference from ⑥ and ⑦ to ②
is deductive, not inductive. I have not included the phrases "it seems
likely that," "it is nearly certain that," and "certainly" in the statements they introduce, because I'm regarding them as the author's
comments on the strengths of the inferences to those statements.
(This is the same policy I followed with "probably" in the answer
to problem (7) of Exercise 3.7.)

Exercise 4.1

1 ①[She's human,] ⑤ⓞ ②[she's
bound to make a mistake sooner
or later.] Ⓐ[Any human being is
bound to make a mistake sooner
or later.]

$$\frac{① + Ⓐ}{\downarrow D}$$
②

3 ①[Wisdom is a product of good judgment.]
②[Good judgment is a product of experience.]
And ③[experience is a product of bad judgment.] Ⓐ[Wisdom is a product of bad judgment.]

$$\frac{① + ② + ③}{\downarrow D}$$
Ⓐ

There's a subtlety here. If by "product" we mean something produced directly (without any intermediate steps), then this argument
is not deductive. But I don't think this is what the author intended.
As the author seems to be using the term, it means anything that
results either directly or indirectly from a thing. On this meaning,
the argument is certainly deductive.

5 ①[When guns are outlawed, only
outlaws will have guns.] Ⓐ[It
shouldn't be that only outlaws
have guns.] Ⓑ[Guns should not
be outlawed.]

$$\frac{① + Ⓐ}{\downarrow D}$$
Ⓑ

The structure of this argument, based on a slogan popular among
opponents of gun control, is fairly clear. The strength of the reasoning, however, is not. It is peculiarly sensitive to the meaning
of the moral principle expressed in Ⓐ. If this is taken to be an
absolute, exceptionless moral rule, then the argument is valid. But
if it is understood as a general principle which could conceivably
be overruled by higher moral principles, then the argument is invalid. I have interpreted it as an absolute moral rule, but that makes
its truth questionable.

7 ①[I said I'd do the job.] ⑤ⓞ
②[if I didn't do it I'd be a liar.]
Don't you worry; ③[it'll get done.]
Ⓐ[I'm not a liar.]

①
↓ F
$$\frac{② + Ⓐ}{\downarrow D}$$ Ⓕ
③

The inference from ① to ② is fallacious, because a liar is a person
who knowingly says something false. The author of this argument
might have been sincere in saying that he or she would do the job,
but then be prevented from doing it by unforeseeable circumstances. In all such cases ① would be true and ② false, so that all
such cases are counterexamples. Notice that I didn't bracket or

number the phrase "Don't you worry." This is a command, not a statement, and it is not essential to the argument.

9 ①[Ophelia must be a Scorpio.] ②[She's so clever and strong willed.] Ⓐ[Scorpios are clever and strong willed.]

$$\frac{② + Ⓐ}{\downarrow F}$$
$$①$$

Counterexamples are to be found among worlds in which ② and Ⓐ are both true, but some people who are not Scorpios are also clever and strong willed, and Ophelia is one of them. The argument would be deductive if we changed Ⓐ to "Only Scorpios are clever and strong willed." But this is so obviously false that the author could hardly have intended it, and so adding it would violate criterion (1). Another possibility is to add "Most clever and strong-willed people are Scorpios." Perhaps the author believed this; if so, the intended argument is inductive. But I really doubt it. Most probably the author simply reasoned fallaciously.

11 ①[The film must have been exposed either to excessive light or to radiation,] (for) ②[the negatives are all completely dark.] But ③[it wasn't exposed to light,] (for) ④[it remained sealed in my camera from the time I opened the package until the time I developed it.] (Therefore), ⑤[it must have been exposed to some sort of radiation.] Ⓐ[Only by exposure to light or radiation could the negatives be dark.]

$$\frac{② + Ⓐ}{\downarrow D} \quad ④ \downarrow F$$
$$\frac{① + ③}{\downarrow D} \quad \boxed{F}$$
$$⑤$$

The author's wording makes it clear that he or she is assuming Ⓐ. The inference from ④ to ③ is fallacious because the film could have been exposed to light before it was packaged, while being loaded into the camera, while in the camera (as a result of light leaks or an interior light source), or during (or even after) the time of development. All such possibilities constitute counterexamples. There is no clear indication that the author has considered any of these possibilities; thus, by criterion (1), we would not add premises to rule them out. The author's reasoning, or at least what we know of it, is faulty.

13 ①[There can be no voice where there is no motion or percussion of the air;] ②[there can be no mo-

$$\frac{① + ② + ③ + Ⓐ + Ⓑ}{\downarrow D}$$
$$④$$

tion or percussion of the air where there is no instrument;] ③[there can be no instrument without a body;] and (this being so) , ④[a spirit can have neither voice, nor form, nor strength.] Ⓐ[A spirit has no body.] Ⓑ[Without a body there can be no form or strength.]

15 ①[Atheists ought to say what is perfectly evident;] now ②[it is not perfectly evident that the soul is material.] Ⓐ[Atheists ought not to say that the soul is material.]

① + ②
―――――
↓ F
Ⓐ

This is a peculiar case. It's fallacious because we can readily imagine that atheists ought to say what is perfectly evident and *also* say some things that are not perfectly evident. But Pascal has not really said what he intended to say. What he intended to say (as is obvious from the context) was, "Atheists ought to say *only* what is perfectly evident." Using this statement instead of ①, the argument becomes deductive. What should we say about this example? Our four criteria don't cover cases in which the author misstates his or her own ideas. Obviously, we should say that the argument as stated (with the implicit conclusion added) is fallacious; the argument as intended is deductive. I've evaluated it as stated.

Exercise 4.2

1 ①[You'd better not ask for a raise today.] ②[The boss is still beet-faced crazy mad about what Olaf did this morning.] Ⓐ[You'd better not ask for a raise when the boss is mad.] Ⓑ[The boss is likely to remain mad all day.]

② + Ⓐ + Ⓑ
―――――
↓ I
①

The author is clearly assuming Ⓐ. I'm less sure about Ⓑ. Perhaps the author hasn't really considered the possibility that the boss might calm down later in the day. If so, then Ⓑ should be omitted and the argument should be judged fallacious.

3 ①[It is preposterous to speak of poverty in America.] After all, ②[we are the richest nation in the world.]

②
↓ F
①

I haven't added anything here, because the extra premises needed— "There can be no poverty in the richest nation in the world," and "It is preposterous to speak of poverty where none exists"—are so absurdly false (especially the first) that it seems unlikely that the author seriously intended them. This sounds to me like a foolishly offhand fallacious inference. If the extra premises are added, the argument becomes deductive but unsound. Either way you look at it, it's a lousy argument.

5   ①[If thine enemy hunger, you should feed him;   ② + Ⓐ
    if he thirst, you should give him drink:] (for)   ────────
    ②[in so doing thou shalt heap coals of fire on   ↓ F
    his head.] Ⓐ[You should "heap coals of fire" on   ①
    the head of your enemy.]

Notice that I have reworded this passage slightly (thereby doing violence, I'm afraid, to its poetry) in order to change ① from a command into a statement (see Section 1.3). I have also kept ① as a single statement to avoid having to split this into two arguments (see Section 2.7). The talk about "coals of fire" is not to be taken literally, of course. It's a metaphor for infliction of guilt and shame. The inference is fallacious, because there might be many other ways to "heap coals of fire" besides those stated in ①. In situations where there are, ② and Ⓐ could be true and ① false; perhaps you should do it some other way. To make the inference deductive, Ⓐ would have to be, "You should do whatever will 'heap coals of fire' on the head of your enemy." But this is a most unbiblical sentiment, and is certainly not intended.

7   ①[If you make Right your master and   ② + Ⓐ
    do away with Wrong, or make Order your   ────────
    master and do away with Disorder, you   ↓F
    have not understood the principle of   ③ + Ⓑ   F
    heaven and earth or the nature of the   ────────
    ten thousand things.] ②[This is like   ↓D
    saying that you are going to make Heaven   ①
    your master and do away with Earth, or
    make Yin your master and do away with Yang.] Obviously ③[it
    (making Right your master, etc.) is impossible.] Ⓐ[It is impossible
    to make Heaven your master and do away with Earth or to make
    Yin your master and do away with Yang.] Ⓑ[Whoever attempts
    the impossible has not understood the principle of heaven and earth
    or the nature of the ten thousand things.]

As you can see, I've reworded slightly. The structure of this argument is difficult to discern, since there are no indicators. But I think this construal captures the author's thought pretty well. The inference from ② and Ⓐ to ③ is an instance of argument by analogy (see Section 6.6). Its strength depends on the nature and respect of the likeness mentioned in ②. Because ② is quite vague about the nature of this likeness, I've judged the inference fallacious.

9 ①[The practicality of a
space-based laser weapon
as an antisatellite system
is highly questionable.] In
the first place, ②[satellites
in orbit are already vulnerable to explosive weapons,
which can be placed accu-
rately in space or even made
to home in on a warm object in orbit.] ③[A space-based antisatellite laser would itself be vulnerable to the same weapons.] ④[The
laser system would also be complex and fragile] and (therefore)
⑤[(it would be) expensive and difficult to maintain.] ⑥[Antisa-
tellite lasers will never become more cost-effective than mechanical satellite killers launched from the earth.] Ⓐ[A space-based
antisatellite laser is itself a satellite, no less vulnerable than others.]
Ⓑ[What is complex is expensive.] Ⓒ[What is fragile is difficult to
maintain.] Ⓓ[The practicality of a weapon is highly questionable
when there are more cost-effective weapons.]

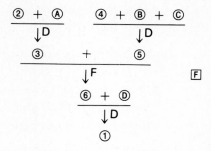

Again, I've done some rewording. The inference from ③ and ⑤ to
⑥ is fallacious because the author does not give us enough information about either system—especially not about mechanical satellite killers—to assure us that laser weapons will *always* be less
cost-effective. We can easily imagine situations in which ③ and
⑤ are true but further technological developments render lasers
more cost-effective. (Perhaps, too, mechanical satellite killers will
become more vulnerable.)

11 ①[The people considered that the Congress of 1774 was composed
of many wise and experienced men.] ②[(The people considered)
that being convened from different parts of the country, they brought
with them and communicated to each other a variety of useful
information.] ③[(The people considered) that in the course of the
time they passed together in inquiring into and discussing the true
interests of their country, they must have acquired some very accurate knowledge on that head.] ④[(The people considered) that
they were individually interested in the public liberty and prosperity, and therefore that it was not less their inclination than their
duty, to recommend only such measures as after the most mature
deliberation they really thought prudent and advisable.]

⑤[These
and similar con-
siderations then
induced the
people to rely
greatly on the
judgment and

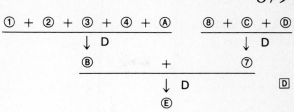

integrity of the Congress;] and ⑥[they took their advice, notwithstanding the various arts and endeavors used to deter and dissuade
them from it.] But ⑦[if the people at large had reason to confide
in the men of that Congress, few of whom had been fully tried or
generally known, still greater reason have they now to respect the
judgment and advice of the Convention,] (for) it is well known
that ⑧[some of the most distinguished members of that Congress,
who have since been tried and justly approved for patriotism and
abilities, and who have grown old in acquiring political information,
were also members of this Convention, and carried into it their
accumulated knowledge and experience.] Ⓐ[These are all reasons
for confiding in the Congress.] Ⓑ[The people had reason to confide
in the Congress of 1774.] Ⓒ[This is an additional reason to confide
in the new Congress.] Ⓓ[There is no reason to confide less in the
new Congress than in the old.] Ⓔ[The people had reason to confide
in the Congress of 1774, but they have still more reason to confide
in the new Congress.]

Note the omission of ⑤ and ⑥, which make no essential contribution to the argument. The "therefore" in ④ indicates, not the
author's inference, but the people's inference, which he is reporting.
It is therefore as if it appeared in a quotation (see Section 2.8). It
is not an inference indicator of the author's argument. The weakest
point in this argument is premise Ⓓ. It's not obviously true, and
I'm not even entirely sure that the author intended it; but it is
necessary to make the argument deductive. If the author didn't
intend it, then it should not be included here, and the inference
from ⑧ and Ⓒ to ⑦ would be fallacious. But it seems to me likely
that it was in the back of the author's mind, so I included it. Again,
however, note that this choice does not affect our overall evaluation. The argument is either fallacious or deductive, but with a
dubious premise. Either way the weakness of the argument is apparent.

Exercise 4.3 Answers to these problems should be expected to vary even more than in previous exercises, because they are more complex and require more interpretation. I have only done one of the more difficult examples, in order to indicate roughly what a good answer looks like. Numbered premises are taken from the text. Premises labeled with letters have been added.

8 ① Species present individual differences.

② No one has drawn any clear distinction between individual differences and slight varieties; or between more plainly marked varieties and subspecies and species.

Ⓐ Many people have tried to draw such distinctions.

Ⓑ We would probably have been able to draw such distinctions if animals and plants did not vary naturally.

∴Ⓒ Animals and plants vary naturally.   ①,②,Ⓐ, Ⓑ

③ If animals and plants do vary, let it be ever so slightly or slowly, (it is highly probable that) variations or individual differences which are in any way beneficial would be preserved and accumulated through natural selection, or the survival of the fittest.

Ⓓ The theory of natural selection is the idea that natural selection (survival of the fittest) occurs.

∴④ The theory of natural selection is highly probable.   Ⓒ,③,Ⓓ

There is also a separate argument for Ⓒ, which runs like this:

⑤ Man, though acting on external characters alone and often capriciously, can produce within a short period considerable variation by adding up mere individual differences in his domestic productions (i.e., by selective breeding).

⑥ If man can by patience select variations useful to him, then under the changing and complex conditions of life (it is probable that) variations will also arise among nature's living products.

∴Ⓒ Animals and plants vary naturally.   ⑤,⑥

Putting these two lines of reasoning together, we get a split-support diagram, as follows:

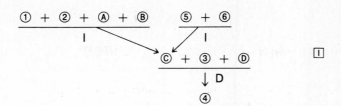

There are also interspersed with this reasoning some comments on the limitlessness of natural selection. But these seem insufficient to constitute an argument.

Exercise 5.1

1 ①[If he kidnapped the maiden, then he's the vilest of villains.] But ②[he did not kidnap the maiden.] (Therefore), ③[he is not the vilest of villains.]

$$\frac{① + ②}{↓ \quad \text{I}}$$
$$③$$

Denying the antecedent

This inference is clearly invalid. We can imagine a world in which the person in question is the vilest of villains and only the vilest of villains would kidnap the maiden, but in which the maiden was not kidnapped at all. Such a world is a counterexample. But I have judged the reasoning "inductive," rather than "fallacious," because in most of the possible worlds in which the premises are true (and indeed in most possible worlds in general) people who are the vilest of villains are rare. Thus in most of the worlds in which the premises are true, the "he" referred to in the argument is not the vilest of villains. In fact "he" may not be a villain at all. If this evaluation baffles you, see the remarks on negative conclusions near the end of Section 6.3.

3 ①[If he moves, I'll see him,] and ②[if I see him I'll squash him like a bug;] (so) ③[if he moves, I'll squash him like a bug.]

$$\frac{① + ②}{↓ \quad \text{D}}$$
$$③$$

Hypothetical syllogism

5 ①[If she had talked to him, she would have told him the news.] But it's clear that ②[she didn't tell him the news,] (because) ③[he didn't know it.] (Therefore), ④[she didn't talk to him.]

$$③$$
$$↓ \quad \text{I or F}$$
$$\frac{① + ②}{}$$
Modus $↓$ D $\boxed{\text{I or F}}$
tollens ④

The inference from ③ to ② is difficult to evaluate. It's clearly invalid; she might have told him the news and he forgot. But it's not clear whether ② is true in most of the worlds in which ③ is true. Either "fallacious" or "inductive" is a reasonable guess here.

7   ①[Ron loves either you or Samantha.] Now ②[if he loved Samantha, he would help her with her homework.] But I know ③[he doesn't (help her with her homework),] (because) ④[her sister says so] and ⑤[she's telling the truth.] (So) ⑥[it's not Samantha that he loves.] (Therefore) , ⑦[it must be you.]

$$\frac{④ + ⑤}{↓ \; D}$$

$$\frac{② + ③}{↓ \; D} \quad \text{Modus} \atop \text{tollens}$$

$$\frac{① + ⑥}{↓ \; D} \quad \text{Disjunctive} \atop \text{syllogism}$$

⑦

[D]

9   ①[If you wait for me in the rain, you'll get soaked;] and ②[if you get soaked, you'll get sick.] (So) ③[if you wait for me in the rain, you'll get sick.] Now ④[I don't want you getting sick.] (Therefore), ⑤[you shouldn't wait for me in the rain.]

$$\frac{① + ②}{↓ \; D} \quad \text{Hypothetical} \atop \text{syllogism}$$

$$\frac{③ + ④}{↓ \; F}$$

⑤

[F]

The inference from ③ and ④ to ⑤ is fallacious, because of the preponderance of possible circumstances under which the speaker's desires have little or nothing to do with how you ought to behave.

Exercise 5.2(a)   Statements 1, 4, 7, 8, 9, and 10 are ways of saying "If he's full, then he's contented." The others are all ways of saying "If he's contented, then he's full."

Exercise 5.2(b)

1   ①[Truth would matter to poetry if poetry described the world.] But (since) ②[the function of poetry is to express emotion,] ③[it does not describe the world.] (Therefore) , ④[truth does not matter to poetry.]

②

I or F ↓   I or F

$$\frac{① + ③}{I \; or \; F \; ↓} \quad \text{Denying the} \atop \text{antecedent}$$

④

Both inferences are certainly invalid, but proportions of worlds are very difficult to estimate here. If the argument is inductive (which I doubt), it is only weakly so.

3 ①[If there were gods, I could not endure not to be a god.] (Hence)
②[there are no gods.] Ⓐ[I can endure
not being a god.]

$$\frac{① + Ⓐ}{↓ \; D}$$
②

Modus
tollens

Note the change in wording to convert ① from a question into a
statement. (An irrelevant aside: one might argue that Nietzsche's
ultimate insanity was evidence that he could not endure not being
a god and hence that the implicit premise is false!)

5 ①[Only if the burglars were sophisticated professionals could they have
successfully dismantled the alarm system.] (Hence) ②[they were not sophisticated professionals,]   (for)
③[they were unable to dismantle it.]

$$\frac{① + ③}{↓ \quad \text{I or F}}$$
②

Denying the
antecedent

Again, though the inference is certainly invalid, it is difficult to tell
whether or not the conclusion is true in *most* of the worlds in which
the premises are true.

7 ①[An eruption would have occurred
if and only if the pressure of the lava
exceeded the strength of the overlying
rock.] (Therefore) , (since) ②[there
was no eruption,] (we may infer that)
③[the pressure of the lava did not exceed the strength of the rock mantle
above it.]

$$\frac{① + ②}{↓ \; D}$$
③

The inference here is similar to modus tollens, but since statement
① says "if and only if" instead of just "if," technically speaking it
is not modus tollens.

9 ①[If the future (after death) holds travail and
anguish in store, the self must be in existence,
when that time comes, in order to experience
it.] But ②[from this fate (travail and anguish
after death) we are redeemed by death.] ③[Death
denies existence to the self that might have
suffered these tribulations.] Rest assured,
(therefore) , that
④[we have nothing to fear in death.]

$$\frac{① + ③}{↓ \; D}$$
②
↓ F
④

Modus
tollens

F

I've reworded slightly to make things clearer. The final inference is
fallacious, because we can imagine a great variety of worlds in which

there is no travail and anguish after death and yet there is something to fear—pain to others, boredom, endless pleasure (that could conceivably be undesirable!), even nonexistence itself.

Exercise 5.3

1 ①[If you get flattened by a steam roller, you will die.] (For) suppose ②[a steam roller flattens you.] ③[What flattens you must crush your internal organs,] and (so) ④[your internal organs would be crushed.] Now ⑤[crushed organs do not function,] and ⑥[if your internal organs are not functioning you will die.] (Thus) it is clear that ⑦[you would die.]

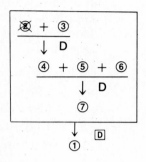

3 ①[If we continue to consume oil at the present rate, world supplies will be exhausted within 200 years.] (For) suppose ②[the current consumption rate continues.] ③[The world now consumes five billion barrels of oil a year.] (This means that) ④[in 200 years we will have burned or otherwise eliminated an additional trillion barrels of oil.] But ⑤[world oil reserves today do not exceed a trillion barrels.] (Hence) ⑥[in another 200 years, not a drop of oil will remain.]

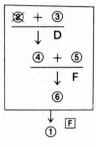

The step from ④ and ⑤ to ⑥ is invalid and probably fallacious, because of the situations we can imagine in which world oil supplies increase over the next 200 years (due, say, to natural processes or production of synthetic oil). The fallacy could be blocked by adding the premise that no new oil will be added to world resources. But we have no evidence that the author intended this premise, and so I've left it out. In actual practice, of course, we'd want to consider whether this premise (or something like it) were true, because if so and if the other basic premises, ③ and ⑤, were true, then we'd have a sound argument.

5   ①[If you are repeatedly unfaithful, you will not have a lasting, satisfying relationship with your mate.] That's simply a matter of logic. (For) suppose ②[you are unfaithful, not just once, but again and again.] (Then) ③[there are three possibilities: either your mate never finds out, or your mate finds out and puts up with your misbehavior, or your mate finds out and leaves you.] ④[If your mate never finds out, then he or she must be gullible, stupid, or easily manipulable.] ⑤[You can't have a satisfying relationship with a person like that.] ⑥[If he or she finds out and puts up with your cheating, then still there will be resentment boiling inside—the kind of resentment that prevents satisfying relationships.] And finally, of course, ⑦[if your mate finds out and leaves, then your relationship will not have been lasting.] Ⓐ[Your relationship with your mate will not be both lasting and satisfying.]

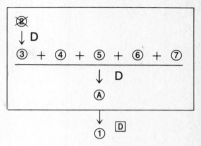

The inference from ② to ③ is deductive, provided that "putting up with your misbehavior" is taken to mean simply that your mate does not leave you. The other inference is complex, but deductive as well, provided that ⑥ means that such resentment *always* prevents satisfying relationships. The reasoning is unimpeachable. To avoid the conclusion, you'd have to find fault with one or more of the premises.

7   Let's say ①[you do make a million dollars.] ②[You still won't be happy.] ③[You're not happy now,] and ④[the more money you make, the more your troubles will multiply.] Ⓐ[The more your troubles multiply, the less happy you'll be.] Ⓑ[If you make a million dollars, you still won't be happy.]

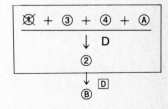

Exercise 5.4

1 ①[Abortion is undeniably wrong.] (For)
suppose ②[it weren't (wrong).] (Then) ,
(since) ③[murder is wrong,] ④[abor-
tion is not murder.] But clearly ⑤[abor-
tion is murder,] (for) ⑥[abortion is the
killing of a human being] and ⑦[killing
a human being is murder.] (Therefore) ,
⑧[abortion is both murder and not murder,] which of course is absurd.

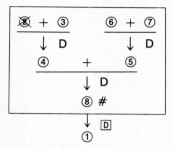

Though this argument is deductive, it wouldn't be an effective tool
of persuasion, since a person who rejects the final conclusion ① will
undoubtedly reject assumption ⑥ or assumption ⑦. In this sense
it is much like begging the question (see Section 5.6).

3 ①[There can't be anything so small it
can't be seen.] Suppose ②[there were
(something so small it couldn't be seen).]
Now ③[what can never be seen does not
exist.] (Therefore) , ④[it would both
exist and not exist,] which is silly. Ⓐ[It
would exist.] Ⓑ[It would not exist.]

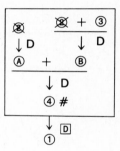

This argument is silly. It's deductive, but because ③ is false, unsound. It would also be reasonable to leave Ⓐ and Ⓑ out and have
④ deduced directly from ② and ③.

5 Suppose ①[there were no absolute truth.]
(Then) ②[the statement "There is no
absolute truth" would be absolutely true.]
(Hence) ③[there would be an absolute
truth.] (Thus) ④[there would both be
and not be an absolute truth,] which is
impossible. (Therefore) , ⑤[there must
be some absolute truth.]

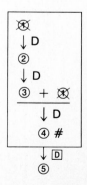

7 ①[There will always be wars.] Just think what would happen if ②[they stopped.] ③[The generals would have no place to play with their guns,] and ④[they'd get bored.] And ⑤[the young men would have no outlet for their thoughtless aggressions.] ⑥[They'd all be nervous wrecks.] (So) ⑦[they'd start a war again just to relieve the tension.] ⓐ[War would have both stopped and not stopped.]

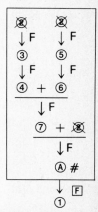

This is a sloppy argument, both structurally and logically. There are few indicators, and the contradiction is unstated, so there is room for disagreement about structure. As I've interpreted the argument, all the inferences are fallacious. Perhaps this could be remedied by the addition of implicit premises. But there are few clues to what the author had in mind, so I haven't made the attempt. The fallaciousness of all the inferences, except the one from ⑦ and ② to ⓐ, should be obvious to you. But the inference from ⑦ and ② to ⓐ might at first seem deductive. The reason it isn't is that statement ⑦, "They'd start a war again just to relieve the tension," does not imply that war did not at one time stop. All it implies is that it would start again. So from ⑦ and ② it follows only that war would stop and then start again—not that it would both stop and not stop.

9 Suppose ①[Muldoon did not have an accomplice in his prison escape.] Now ②[he knew exactly when the guards were changing,] and ③[he could not have known this unless he or an accomplice in communication with him was in the main compound at the changing of the guard.] But (we're assuming) ①[he had no accomplice.] (So on our hypothesis it follows that) ④[he was in the main compound as the guard changed.] But ⑤[he wasn't.] ⑥[He couldn't have gotten there until after his cell was unlocked,] and ⑦[his cell was unlocked only several minutes after the changing of the guard.] (Therefore), ⑧[he must have had an accomplice.] ⓐ[He both was and was not in the main compound as the guard changed.]

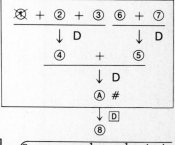

Exercise 5.5(a)

1 Contingent.

3 Logically necessary.

5 Inconsistent.

7 Contingent—it could be frozen!

9 Contingent.

11 Logically necessary.

13 Contingent.

Exercise 5.5(b)

1 ①[Olaf is both real and not real.] (Therefore),
②[he is immensely puzzling to his cat, Fuzzball.]
Inference is deductive because ① is inconsistent.

> ①
> ↓ D
> ②

3 ①[This argument is illogical.] ②[I dislike everything that is illogical.] (Therefore), ③[I dislike
this argument.]

> ① + ②
> ↓ D
> ③

5 ①[If Ophelia is either a man or a woman, and she's
not a man, then she's female.] (For) suppose that
②[she is either a man or a woman, but not a man.]
(Then) ③[she's a woman.] (Hence) ④[she's
female.]

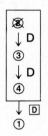

The trick in understanding this conditional proof is to see that ①
is a complex conditional whose antecedent is ② and whose consequent is ④. Since the argument is valid and has no basic premises,
① is logically necessary.

7 ①[The sentence "This sentence is false" is not true.]
(For) suppose ②[it were (true).] (Then) ③[it
would have to be false,] and (so) ①[it would not
be true.] (Hence) ④[it would be both true and
not true]—a contradiction.

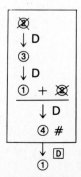

Since the argument is valid and has no basic premises, the conclusion is logically necessary. Note the double use of ① in the argument. This is perfectly legitimate.

Exercise 5.6

1 ①[Pornography is im-
moral,] (for) ①[the
use of explicitly sexual
material for erotic pur-
poses transgresses eth-
ical precepts.]

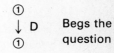

Begs the
question

The second statement is just a fancier version of the first.

3 It is clear that ①[the
moon is the size of a
nickel,] (because)
②[it looks like it is the
size of a nickel.] And
③[it *must* look like it
is the size of a nickel,]
(because) ①[that is
just how big it is.]

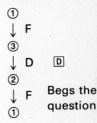

Begs the
question

If we don't take the "must" in ③ too seriously, then we could count ② and ③ as the same statement. This argument is fortuitously strong (see Section 3.8).

5 Suppose that ①[1 + 1 = 3.] (Then) ②[anything
would be true.] (Therefore), ③[if 1 + 1 = 3, anything is true.]

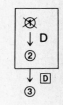

This is a valid conditional proof with no basic premises. Therefore the conclusion, ③, is logically necessary and hence indisputably true! The inference from ① to ② is deductive because ① is inconsistent. The peculiarity of the conclusion results from the fact that any world in which 1 + 1 = 3 is an incoherent world—a world in which logic breaks down altogether.

7 ①[Majority rule, without safeguards, could lead to some rather absurd situations.] For example, ②[if 51 per cent rather mildly favor the confiscation of property of the other 49 per cent of the society, the logic of unrestrained majoritarianism would so dictate.]

The occurrence of the term "absurd" suggests that this argument is a reductio. Perhaps it is, but to complete it we'd need to read a great deal into the author's thinking on the basis of very few clues. Therefore, I think it's best to stick with the simple analysis given here. The term "absurd" is so vague in this context that I judged the argument fallacious (see Section 7.7), but this evaluation could be disputed.

9 ①[If you capture my knight, you'll lose more than you gain.] (For) suppose ②[you do (capture my knight).] ③[That will leave your king open to check on the next move,] and ④[I would certainly take that op-

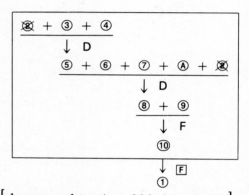

portunity.] Okay, (so) ⑤[then your king (would be) in check.] ⑥[Your only move at that point is to pull your king back.] But ⑦[doing so exposes your rook, which I can then capture at no immediate cost to me.] (Therefore), ⑧[you would have lost a rook and I a knight.] And (since) ⑨[a rook is more valuable than a knight,] ⑩[you would have lost more than you gained,] just as I said. Ⓐ[If I can capture your rook at no immediate cost to me, I will.]

This is a conditional proof. Note that ② must be added to the second inference, for ⑧ does not follow simply from ⑤, ⑥, ⑦, and Ⓐ. The inference from ⑧ and ⑨ to ⑩ is invalid and probably fallacious, because there is nothing to guarantee that the rook and the knight are the only factors to be considered. Perhaps this exchange is part of a broader strategy in which the player who loses the rook ultimately makes other gains. Any such situation would be counterexample.

11 ①[If God cre-
ated the uni-
verse, there was
a time when he
commenced to
create.] ②[(If so,
then) back of that
commencement
there must have
been an etern-
ity.] ③[(In that
eternity) he cer-
tainly did not
think.]   ④[(If
there was an
eternity before creation, then in it) there was nothing to think
about.] ⑤[(In that eternity) he did not remember.] ⑥[(If there was
an eternity before creation, then in it) nothing had ever happened.]
⑦[(There could not be) an infinite intelligence in infinite nothing
wasting an eternity.] Ⓐ[God created the universe.] Ⓑ[There was
a time when he commenced to create.] Ⓒ[God is by definition an
infinite intelligence.] Ⓓ[God was an infinite intelligence in infinite nothing wasting an eternity.] Ⓔ[There both was and was not
an infinite intelligence in infinite nothing wasting an eternity.]
Ⓕ[God did not create the universe.]

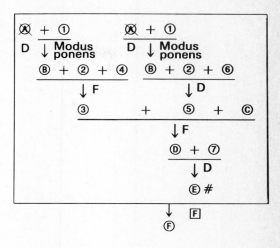

This is a sketchy, complicated, and poorly stated argument. I've
had to read a lot between the lines—perhaps too much—in order
to make sense of it. I'm fairly certain that the point of this passage
is that God did not create the universe (Ingersoll was a noted religious sceptic), and so I've made that the ultimate conclusion.
Apart from that, there's plenty of room for disagreement about the
argument's structure. But I suspect that anyway you look at it, the
argument is quite weak. Incidentally, the reason why the inference
from Ⓑ, ②, and ④ to ③ is fallacious is that God could exist in a
world in which there is nothing at all to think about and yet still
be thinking—about things in other possible worlds! Thought, in
other words, does not require the presence of its objects, as your
experience in constructing imaginative counterexamples should by
now abundantly confirm. By contrast, the inference from Ⓑ, ②,
and ⑥ to ⑤ is deductive, because since memory is an event, if

nothing at all happened, then it follows that no memories occurred. (Probably the author did not realize this and was thinking in parallel with the fallacious inference from ⑧, ②, and ④ to ③, but the inference is deductive in spite of itself!)

Exercise 6.2

1   (Since)   ①[most people never experience a major earthquake,] the chances are that ②[you won't.] ⓐ[You are a person.]

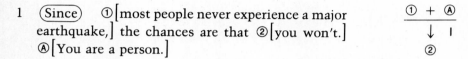

Both premises are true. Whether or not there is any suppressed evidence depends on certain facts about you. If you already have experienced a major earthquake, then of course that's suppressed evidence; for the conclusion, though it contains the term "won't," seems to be talking about your entire life. Also, if you live in an earthquake-prone region, or plan to, that's suppressed evidence. If not, and if there's no other special reason to think you'll experience a major earthquake, then no relevant evidence is suppressed, and this is a good inductive argument. The chances are that its conclusion is correct.

3   ①[Most movie stars never become President.] ②[Ronald Reagan was a movie star.]   (Therefore), ③[Ronald Reagan never became President.]

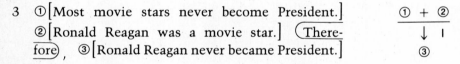

Both premises are true. But this is a very bad argument, because the well-known fact that Reagan did become President is suppressed.

5   ①[Less than 50 percent of the population has type O positive blood.] (Therefore), ②[you do not have type O positive blood.] ⓐ[You are a member of the population.]

Both premises are true. But if you know what your blood type is, then from your standpoint as this argument's evaluator, the argument violates the requirement of total evidence. If your blood type is O positive and you know it, then you already have more evidence than this argument provides. If your blood type is not O positive and you know it, then you already have more evidence than the argument contains. But if you know nothing about your blood type, then for you this is a good argument; given the information it provides you, it is indeed improbable that you have type O positive blood.

7   In spite of the myth that divorce is a psychological cop out, ①[in reality it is considerably easier, legally and emotionally, to get married and stay married than it is to divorce.] ②[Marriage is (therefore) much more likely to be a cop out for young people who substitute artificial supports for genuine emotional maturity.] Ⓐ[Copping out involves doing what is easy.]

$$\frac{① + Ⓐ}{↓ \quad |}$$
$$②$$

I'm a bit hesitant to call this inductive, because of its vagueness. It may well be fallacious. But let's suppose it's inductive. Still, it's a bad argument. Premise ① is false if it is meant to apply to every case. Certainly there are actual situations in which divorce is easier than continued marriage. Even if ① is meant to be a general but not universal assertion, it's not obviously true. Moreover, the argument ignores relevant evidence contrary to the conclusion. It ignores, for example, the fact that marriage begins with a vow of permanence. That is surely evidence against calling its continuation a cop out (which implies abandonment of responsibilities). It also ignores the fact that there are often selfish motives for divorce. And it ignores the fact that marriage—especially marriage with children—carries many more responsibilities than single life. All these things and more are relevant. Divorce is a complex problem, and this argument treats it too simply to be effective.

Exercise 6.3

1   Epistemic probability: It depends on what you know about tomorrow's weather.

Inherent probability: Very low. Many possible worlds contain no earthlike planets and hence have no weather as we know it. Even among those that do, the worlds in which it will rain tomorrow (on earth where you now are) are a minority.

3   Epistemic probability: Very high. There's a lot of evidence in favor of this statement (e.g., the testimony of reliable history books), which I am sure you are aware of, and none against it.

Inherent probability: Very low. In most possible worlds Columbus never existed, and in most of the ones in which he did exist, he didn't come to America in 1492.

5   Epistemic probability: Zero.

Inherent probability: Zero. This statement is inconsistent.

7 Epistemic probability: Zero. You know you exist.

Inherent probability: Very high. You don't exist in most possible worlds.

9 Epistemic probability: 100 percent. You know that $1 + 1 = 2$.

Inherent probability: 100 percent. This statement is logically necessary.

Exercise 6.4

1 ①[I talked at random to three of the students in Miss Thistlebottom's English class yesterday,] and ②[all of them said they didn't like her.] (Therefore) , ③[Miss Thistlebottom is a very unpopular teacher.]

Fallacy of small sample. Since this example is fictional, the premises are literally false, and there is no genuine contrary evidence to be suppressed. But if the case were real, there could be suppressed evidence. Suppose, for example, that Miss Thistlebottom had just given a very difficult assignment, which her class resented. That might cause them to respond in an uncharacteristically negative way to the interviewer. If not reported in the argument, this source of bias would constitute suppressed evidence.

3 Contrary to what they always tell you, ①[tossed coins do come up heads more often than tails.] ②[I was tossing coins last night and got five heads in a row!]

Fallacy of possible bias. It sounds as though the author made a good many more than five tosses but chose to report only the five consecutive ones that came up heads. This sample is obviously not random, since it was chosen precisely because it was unusual. But if the author really made only five tosses and they all came up heads (which is possible, but unlikely), there are still two grounds for objection: (1) the sample is very small, and (2) evidence of the fact that coin tossings usually do produce about 50 percent heads and 50 percent tails is suppressed. Since the example is fictional, there's no point in considering the truth or falsity of the premises.

5 ①[Voters are angry about the economy.] ②[A
recent randomly conducted CBS/*New York Times*
survey of 1572 registered voters revealed that 73
percent believe their economic circumstances to
be worse now than five years ago.]

②
↓ F
①

The reasoning is fallacious, because even if the voters believe they're
worse off, it doesn't follow that they're angry about it. They could
be resigned, depressed, or discouraged. They might not care. They
might (if they were especially spiritual in temperament) even welcome economic recession as a liberation from the materialistic temp-
tations of prosperity. All these situations constitute counterexamples. Moreover, although this example is fictional, if it were real
there would be good reason to doubt the truth of the premise. As I
noted in this section, polls don't measure what people believe—only
what they say they believe.

7 ①[The orchard is badly infested.] ②[We picked
a bushel of apples from there this morning,] and
③[over half of them had worms.]

② + ③
↓ F
①

If the picking was random—not just, say, from one side of the orchard—then the reasoning would be inductive. A bushel is a fairly
large sample of apples, and the conclusion is not too specific. But
since we are told nothing about how the apples were picked, we
should not assume that the picking was random. That's why I've
called the inference fallacious. It's a fallacy of possible bias. The
example is fictional, so I won't consider truth or suppressed evidence.

9 ①[Americans came to believe the national fortunes were in decline.] ②[That was the famous
"malaise" Jimmy Carter cited on July 15 of last
year when he addressed the nation after weeks
of musing at Camp David.] ③[The gloomy feeling persisted,] however. ④[A Gallup poll at the
beginning of this year (1980) found Americans
less optimistic about the future than the people
of any other major country excepting Great Britain and India.] ⑤[Fifty-six percent of those surveyed in the United States believed this year
would be worse than last year.]

① + ④ + ⑤
↓ F
③

I've left statement ② out of the diagram, because though it might be construed as evidence for ①, it is surely not the author's only reason for believing ①. To diagram it as such would be misleading. Therefore ② is best regarded simply as a comment on ①. Statement ① itself is, however, necessary to establish ③, since to conclude that a feeling has *persisted*, we must know that it was there before. I've judged the inference fallacious, because there are many ways we can imagine the gloomy feeling being interrupted (i.e., not persisting), despite the fact that it was there on July 15, 1979, and again six months later at the beginning of 1980. But I'm not sure I'm right. Because polls measure what people say, not what they believe, the truth of statements ④ and ⑤ may be doubted. But in this case I suspect that people were generally responding truthfully. Moreover, I know of no suppressed evidence. So I'd regard this argument as weak, but not completely negligible.

Exercise 6.5

1 ①[Most of the Hispanics in my neighborhood are rowdy.] ⟨Therefore⟩, ②[most Hispanics are rowdy.] Ⓐ[Most regularities present in observed regions of space and time extend as well to unobserved regions.]

Without knowing how many Hispanics in the neighborhood in question, we can't tell if much of a regularity is asserted here. If, for example, there are only three, then that hardly constitutes a regularity. That's why I've labeled the inference fallacious. If it were asserted that there were many Hispanics in this neighborhood, then the reasoning would clearly be inductive. But the argument suppresses evidence of the wide variation in customs, culture, and behavior among Hispanic people around the world, and hence it would still be too weak to merit serious consideration.

3 Though ①[many people have passed the threshold of death,] ②[none has ever returned to tell about it.] ③[No one ever will return to tell about it.] Ⓐ[Most regularities present in observed regions of space and time extend as well to unobserved regions.]

$$\frac{① + ② + Ⓐ}{↓ \text{ I}}$$
$$③$$

I've done some rewriting in order to treat the phrase "It is unlikely . . . that" in the original as a comment on the strength of the inference, rather than as a part of the conclusion. If it is a part of ③, then ③ is weaker, but the inference is stronger. On my interpretation, the inference is inductive. A purportedly well established regularity is reasonably extrapolated into the future. The real controversy will arise over the truth of premise ②. One often hears dramatic stories about people who have "died" and returned to life a short while later. If these stories are accurate, then ② is false. Moreover, they would also constitute suppressed evidence. Obviously, their accuracy is too complex a question to take up here.

5 ①[Cave paintings made by primitive people today all seem to have some religious or ritual significance.] (Therefore), it seems likely that ②[the cave paintings of our remote ancestors served similar purposes.] Ⓐ[Most regularities present in observed regions of space and time extend as well to unobserved regions.]

$$\frac{① + Ⓐ}{↓ \text{ F}}$$
$$②$$

Again, as in problem 1, there is a question about whether a real regularity is asserted here. We're not told how many cave paintings are made today. Given the assumption that many are, we'd have a definite regularity, and the reasoning would be inductive. But since this is not asserted, I've conservatively judged the inference to be fallacious. (But I have the feeling that I'm being too picky.) I know of no suppressed evidence. If ① is true and if a good many cave paintings are made by primitive people today, then there is good evidence for the conclusion.

7 ①[It's not a good idea to take your cat camping.] ②[In my long association with cats, they have not been good travelers and have done much better left in familiar surroundings or even in a good boarding kennel.] ③[The stories of cats lost en route are legion.] ④[They have shown an uncanny ability to escape almost any kind of restraint.] Ⓐ[Many of these stories are true.] Ⓑ[It's not a good idea to risk allowing cats to escape.] Ⓒ[Most regularities present in observed regions of space and time extend as well to unobserved regions.]

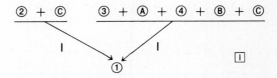

I've reworded to emphasize the fact that the conclusion is extrapolated from past experience. Since there seem to be two independent lines of reasoning, I've diagrammed the argument as split support. But it could also be treated as normal, with all the premises supporting ①. The premises seem true enough, except that ④ is an exaggeration. Moreover, I know of no suppressed evidence—though perhaps you do. My one experience in traveling with cats strongly supports the author's view.

9 ①[In all the great ages of the past, people have believed themselves very close to possession of the ultimate truth about the universe.] ②[In each age, they have pointed to their technological and intellectual achievements as evidence of this.] But ③[the thought of each past age, as we now know, was riddled with falsehood, superstition, and half-truths.] Likewise, ④[today we see our technological wizardry as evidence of a thorough comprehension of reality.] Is it not likely, however, that ⑤[much of what seems so certain now will later prove to be mistaken]? ⓐ[Most regularities present in observed regions of space and time extend as well to unobserved regions.]

$$① + ② + ③ + ④ + ⓐ$$
$$\downarrow \quad |$$
$$⑤$$

The reasoning here is fairly good, and the premises seem true. But the unparalleled growth of knowledge in modern times provides some contrary evidence. We are much more skillful at ascertaining scientific truth than ever before. On the whole, I'd say that this argument, though not strong, lends some credence to its conclusion.

Exercise 6.6

1 ①[Katherine's car gets excellent mileage, needs few repairs, and handles well on the road.] ②[The one I'm about to buy is the same make, model, and year.] (Therefore), ③[I can expect the same from it.] ⓐ[Objects or events closely similar in observed respects are usually similar in most unobserved respects.]

$$① + ② + ⓐ$$
$$\downarrow \quad |$$
$$③$$

This is a good induction by analogy. Since it's fictional, there is no real suppressed evidence. But we can imagine situations under which there would be. Perhaps, for example, the car the author is about to buy was previously owned by a teenager who neglected even the most basic maintenance operations and constantly drove it at speeds around a hundred miles an hour on back country roads. If known, that would reduce the epistemic probability of the conclusion considerably.

3 ①[I should have a good crop of spinach this spring.] ②[I planted, fertilized, watered, and hoed it just as I did
last year,] and ③[the weather this
spring has been similar.] Ⓐ[I had a
good spinach crop last spring.] Ⓑ[Objects or events closely similar
in observed respects are usually similar in most unobserved respects.]

$$\frac{② + ③ + Ⓐ + Ⓑ}{\underset{①}{\downarrow \ \text{I}}}$$

Another analogical argument. In terms of the schema discussed in
this section, *x* is last spring's spinach crop, *y* is this spring's, and *F*
is the property of being good. The respects of the comparison between *x* and *y* are laid out in premises ② and ③. Again the reasoning
is pretty good. Possible kinds of contrary evidence might include
the planting of a different variety of spinach, an attack of insects or
disease, or even the sickly appearance of the plants themselves. But
if we have no evidence of any such thing and if the premises are
true, then the argument provides good evidence for the conclusion.

5 You agree that ①[it's wrong to shoplift.] Ⓢ̶ⓞ̶
②[stealing from your employer is wrong, too.]
③[One is just like the other.] Ⓐ[Objects or
events closely similar in observed respects are
usually similar in most unobserved respects.]

$$\frac{① + ③ + Ⓐ}{\underset{②}{\downarrow \ \text{I}}}$$

By asserting a very close similarity, premise ③ makes the argument
strongly inductive, but is itself so strong a statement that it is probably false. Here the word "observed" in premise Ⓐ, the principle of
analogy, may not be quite appropriate, since the respects of the
similarity (which include morally relevant characteristics of the action) may not be observable. Perhaps Ⓐ should be replaced in this
instance by a similar but more judiciously worded principle. Can
you suggest one?

7 Obviously ①[there is no way that the
Air Force or anyone else can prove that
alien spacecraft are not visiting us.]
②[No amount of cases in which a
grownup is caught pushing a quarter
under a child's pillow will add up to
irrefutable negative evidence.] ③[Always there is a small residue
of cases in which grownups are not caught, and the morning appearance of money remains mysterious.] ④[No matter how many

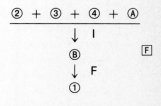

sightings of UFOs are shown to have natural explanations, there is always a residue of cases for which information is insufficient for judgment.] Ⓐ[Objects or events closely similar in observed respects are usually similar in most unobserved respects.] Ⓑ[No amount of cases in which UFOs are explained will add up to irrefutable evidence that alien spacecraft are not visiting us.]

This is a difficult argument to analyze. As I've construed it, there are two inferences: an induction by analogy to the implicit conclusion, Ⓑ, and an inference to the final conclusion, ①. Applying our schema for analogical arguments to the first inference, we see that *x* is the assertion that there is not a tooth fairy, *y* is the assertion that alien spacecraft are not visiting us, and *F* is the property of not being irrefutably demonstrable by explaining away contrary claims. Premises ③ and ④ lay out the observed similarity between *x* and *y*—namely, that for each there is a residue of unexplained contrary cases. The analogical inference is quite good; it establishes Ⓑ with a high degree of probability. But the further inference to ① is fallacious, because there are many conceivable modes of proof besides explaining away contrary cases. (One, for example, might involve setting up a sophisticated radar network capable of detecting all objects entering the earth's atmosphere.)

9 ①[The first of these suppositions about the effects of mass media violence is that to see vicarious violence on film or television will 'discharge' the aggressive energy of the individual.] ②[This is called *catharsis*.] ③[To ar-

$$\frac{③ \; + \; ④ \; + \; Ⓐ}{\underset{Ⓑ}{\downarrow F}}$$

gue that media violence is cathartic is tantamount to suggesting that witnessing people eating when one is hungry will make one feel less hungry.] ④[Vicarious eating does not reduce hunger.] Ⓐ[Objects or events closely similar in observed respects are usually similar in most unobserved respects.] Ⓑ[Media violence is not cathartic.]

The first two statements introduce the issue, but are not essential to the argument, so I have omitted them from the diagram. This is an argument by analogy, where *x* is the claim that vicarious eating reduces hunger, *y* is the claim that vicarious violence produces catharsis, and *F* is the property of being false. Premise ③ is terribly unspecific about the nature and degree of the similarity between *x* and *y*, and so I have judged the inference fallacious. (However, if we interpret the phrase "tantamount to" as implying a very strong similarity—as I did with the phrase "just like" in problem ⑤—then we'd judge the inference to be pretty strong, but we should have serious doubts about the truth of premise ③.)

Exercise 6.7

Being a plant is logically necessary for being a tree.

Being a tree is both logically necessary and logically sufficient for being a tree.

There is a contingent statistical correlation between crowds and noise.

There is a contingent statistical correlation between rain and heavy overcast.

Being an even number is logically sufficient for being a whole number.

Electrochemical or electrical stimulation of muscles is a contingently necessary condition of human walking.

Exercise 6.8(a)

Joke-telling is a partial cause of laughter.

Heating ice above 0°C is both causally necessary and causally sufficient for melting it.

Obtaining nourishment is causally necessary for living more than a year.

Irritation of a cat is a partial cause of the cat's hissing.

Today's being Tuesday is a necessary and sufficient condition of tomorrow's being Wednesday. It is not logically necessary and sufficient, since we can imagine worlds in which the days of the week are arranged differently. It is not causally necessary and sufficient either.

Oxygen is a causally necessary condition of fire. (Technically, this is not quite correct, since fires can occur in an atmosphere of pure fluorine. Thus to be absolutely faithful to the facts of chemistry, we must say that oxygen is only a partial cause of fire.)

Smoke is sufficient, but not causally sufficient for fire. (Here again, I fear contradiction from the chemists. Well, chemists, is there ever smoke without fire? If so, then I have to take this back. Smoke would not be sufficient for fire, and since it certainly is not necessary, it would be correlated only statistically.)

Exercise 6.8(b)

1 ①[Prior to every great war there has been an increase in defense spending among the participants.] (Therefore), ②[increased defense spending is a cause of major wars.] Ⓐ[Most regularities present in observed regions of space and time extend as well to unobserved regions.]

$$\frac{① + Ⓐ}{\downarrow \;\; F}$$
$$②$$

This appears to be an attempt to establish defense spending as a causally necessary condition of major wars (so that, presumably, wars could be prevented by keeping defense budgets down). It requires the principle of the uniformity of nature even to establish from past cases that increased defense spending is a necessary condition of major wars. But in going beyond this to the conclusion that it is a causally necessary condition, the argument commits a false cause fallacy. Chief among counterexamples to this argument would be situations in which the same international tension that gives rise to war also generates higher defense spending.

3 A marine biologist investigating a skin disease in fish discovers that ①⌈all fish afflicted with the disease have a certain crustacean parasite beneath their scales,⌋ whereas ②⌈most healthy fish do not.⌋ (She concludes that) ③⌈the parasite causes the disease.⌋

① + ②
↓ F
③

False cause fallacy. Given the assumption that the parasite is a necessary condition of the disease, the author draws the conclusion that it is causally necessary. But this does not follow. Perhaps the disease weakens the fish, making it susceptible to the parasite. Or perhaps the presence of both parasite and disease are produced by a third factor—water pollution, for example, which might be causally sufficient for the disease, while lowering the fish's resistance to the parasite. Or maybe the correlation is coincidental. These cases are all counterexamples. The principle of the uniformity of nature is not needed here, because premise ① already concerns all fish; there is no need to extrapolate further. However, for this very reason, we might have some doubts about the truth of premise ① itself.

5 ①⌈The ancient Chinese, who believed that solar eclipses were caused by a dragon devouring the sun, used to beat gongs and set off fireworks during an eclipse to frighten the dragon away.⌋ Remarkably, ②⌈each time they did this, the eclipse came to an end.⌋ (This incredible correlation shows that) ③⌈their technique actually produced the desired result.⌋

① + ②
↓ F
③

False cause fallacy. The conclusion is that the beating of gongs and shooting of fireworks was causally sufficient for terminating solar eclipses. Even if the argument were inductive, suppressed evidence would undermine it. We know that gongs and fireworks do not influence eclipses. Rather, the moon's passage across the face of the sun was both causally sufficient for the eclipse and a partial cause of the noisy behavior of the ancient Chinese. The completion of its passage, not the frightening of a dragon, was causally sufficient to bring the eclipse to an end.

7　①[Studies have shown that abused children are much more likely to become abusive parents than are children who have not been subjected to violence.]
(Thus)　②[abusive parents are a cause of child abuse in the succeeding generation.]

$$\frac{①}{↓ \; F}$$
$$②$$

Another false cause fallacy. The reasoning is from a statistical correlation to a partial cause. But there are many kinds of counterexamples. Perhaps, for example, child abuse is due largely, not to abuse by parents, but to a genetic predisposition to violence passed on from parents to children. The premise is true, and the conclusion may be as well, but only controlled experiments, not inference from a mere correlation, could establish it.

9　①[Sales of all-savers certificates are helping to reduce deficits at savings and loan institutions.] ②[For October 1981, the first month all-savers were offered for sale, the U.S. League of Savings Associations reported S&Ls experienced a net savings gain of $4.3 billion.] ③[This compares to a $2.0 billion net savings gain for September and a $1.3 billion net savings gain for August.]

$$\frac{② + ③}{↓ \; F}$$
$$①$$

False cause fallacy. The sales of all-savers certificates is asserted to have been a partial cause of deficit reductions at savings and loan institutions on the basis of a "regularity" observed over three months. There are innumerable possible alternative explanations for this "regularity."

11　①[The researchers had given bacteria a "whopping" dose of phenol, an antiseptic.] ②[Olga briefly held her hands near micro-

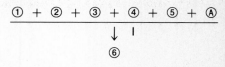

scope slides on which the bacteria had been placed.] ③[In over 30 previous experiments Rubik had found that the phenol would paralyze all the bacteria within two minutes.] ④[In the control sample, which Olga did not treat, all the bacteria were again paralyzed,] but ⑤[on Olga's slides 7 percent of the bacteria were still swim-

ming around 12 minutes after the phenol had been administered.]
Concluded Rauscher: "I'd say it appeared that ⑥[Olga was able
to overcome the effects of the chemicals."] Ⓐ[The control sample
was subjected to the same conditions as the sample Olga treated,
except that she did not treat it.]

This argument would be much stronger if it were asserted that the
experiment was repeated many times, but it is probably inductive
as it stands. Note, however, that the conclusion is rather weak. It
is not that Olga was able to overcome the effects of the chemicals
by some mysterious power—only that she was able to overcome
them. Perhaps this had something to do with the heat of her hand
or the shadow it cast on the slides. Or perhaps she tampered chem-
ically with the solution. (Fraud of this sort should not be ruled out
lightly; many people with allegedly occult powers have been caught
at it.) In this case I'd also want to verify the premises—especially
the implicit premise, Ⓐ—very carefully before accepting the argument. Some investigators of paranormal phenomena have been
notoriously sloppy in their laboratory technique. (For a good account of the sloppiness and fraud in these areas, see Martin Gardner's *Science: Good, Bad and Bogus*, Prometheus Books, Buffalo,
1981.)

Exercise 7

1 ①[There's nothing wrong with
cheating on your taxes.]
②[Everyone does it.]

②
↓ F
①

Appeal to
popularity

This inference is so thoughtless that probably no implicit premise
is intended.

4 ①[There is too a Santa Claus!]
②[My mom says so.]

②
↓ F
①

Appeal to
authority

7 ①[The defendant was in the alley behind the liquor store.]
②[The witness saw him there.]

②
↓ D
①

I've judged this inference deductive, because "see" is probably used
as a success verb here. If not, then it's a kind of aesthetic fallacy.

10 ①[Even some scientists and engineers reject the theory of evolution.] (So) ②[I should reject it too.]

①
↓ F   Appeal to authority
②

13 ①[Nothing is better than sex.] ②[Logic is better than nothing.] (Therefore), ③[logic is better than sex.]

$$\frac{① + ②}{↓ \; F}$$
③   Equivocation

Statement ① is amphibolous. It could mean either that the state of doing or having nothing is better than sex or that there is nothing at all that is better than sex. These meanings are almost opposites. The conclusion follows deductively if the first meaning is intended, but the author seems to have intended the second.

16 ①[This car gets excellent mileage.] ②[They say it goes 25 percent farther on a tank of gas.]

②
↓ F   Vagueness and appeal to
①   authority

19 ①[Historically, it has been the Soviets' explicit intention to impose their iron dictatorship over the entire world.] ②[There is no evidence that this intention has changed.] Ⓐ[The Soviets still intend to impose their dictatorship over the entire world.]

$$\frac{① + ②}{↓ \; F}$$
Ⓐ   Ignorance

From the fact that we have no evidence that something has changed, it does not follow that it hasn't. If the Soviets' intention were a well-established regularity, then it would be rational to extrapolate it to the present using the principle of the uniformity of nature. But there is no indication that this author intended to reason that way.

22 ①[Nobody can't walk much faster than you do, or else he'd have been here first.] Ⓐ[He was not here first.] Ⓑ[He can't walk much faster than you do.]

$$\frac{① + Ⓐ}{↓ \; D}$$
Ⓑ

The king's argument is deductive. In fact, it's disjunctive syllogism (see Section 5.1). But it is based on a misunderstanding of what Alice, the speaker of the first sentence, said. When Alice says "Nobody walks much faster than I do," she means that there is no one at all who walks much faster than she does. But the king consistently interprets "nobody" as the name of a person, thus construing her statement equivocally and responding to the unintended meaning. However, because the king does not shift meanings within his argument, he is guilty only of misinterpretation, not of equivocal reasoning.

25 ①[It has never been shown that   ①
    increasing levels of atmos-   ↓ I
    pheric carbon dioxide produced   ②
    by the burning of fossil fuels
    have caused any alteration in the world's climate.] (Therefore),
    contrary to the claims of many environmentalists, ②[such fears
    are illusory.]

This argument from ignorance is inductive because of the inherent probability of the negative conclusion, which says in effect that increasing carbon dioxide levels are not altering world climate (see Section 7.4). However, it suppresses a great deal of known evidence about the dependence of climate on the composition of the atmosphere, and is therefore far too simple to be credible.

28 ①[It would not be impossible   ② + ③ Equivocation
    to prove with sufficient repe-   ↓ F
    tition and psychological under-   ①
    standing of the people con-
    cerned that a square is a circle.]
    ②[A square and a circle are mere words] and ③[words can be
    moulded until they clothe ideas in disguise.]

Statement ② contains a use-mention ambiguity. It is true if Hitler is talking about the words "square" and "circle," but false if he is talking about squares and circles. I've taken him to be talking about the words. Hitler's equivocations notwithstanding, it is not possible to prove that a square is a circle. People can be deluded into believing it, but that's a different matter.

31   In fact, recently we have come
to the realization that ①[there
is no such thing as insanity.] It
is true that ②[the "mentally ill"
exhibit bizarre behaviors and
beliefs.] But ③[these are hardly
different from the behaviors and
beliefs of normal members of
less advanced cultures.] ④[It is
only a matter of time and tech-
nical sophistication which separates us from these so-called "primitives."]   In this way the insight has dawned that   ⑤[the so-
called "mentally ill" are essentially as sane as the rest of us.]

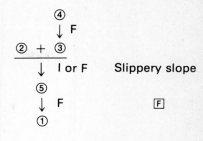

The slippery-slope inference from ② and ③ to ⑤ may be inductive,
because the "slope" is not very long. But the other two inferences
are surely fallacious. Counterexamples to the last inference occur
in part among worlds in which no one is especially sane.

34   ①[Nature is governed by fixed
and immutable laws,] and
②[there is no law that is not
the work of a legislator.]
(Therefore) ,   ③[nature itself
is governed by a sublime and
powerful legislator,] and ④[it is he whom we know by the name
of "God."] Ⓐ[God exists.]

$$\frac{① + ②}{↓ \; F} \qquad \text{Equivocation}$$

$$\frac{③ + ④}{↓ \; D} \qquad \boxed{F}$$

Ⓐ

"Law" is ambiguous, meaning "principle of nature" in ① and "rule
of conduct" in ②. Any consistent interpretation of "law" renders
either ① or ② false.

37   This reply to Jesus is an abusive ad hominem (argument against
the person). Instead of weighing the evidence for or against his
claims, his attackers charge that he is possessed and that he thinks
he is greater than Abraham and the prophets (and is therefore guilty
of the sin of pride). From there they jump fallaciously to the implicit
conclusion that his claims are wrong.

40   Technically, this is not an argument at all, but a complex conditional statement. If regarded as an argument, however, it commits the fallacies of appeal to popularity, appeal to authority, and two wrongs make a right.

Exercise 8

1   ①[You never leave me alone.]
②[You're always telling me that
I need to lose weight.]

The premise would undoubtedly be false.

4   ①[Cruelty is undeserved suffering.] But ②[the violent criminal
deserves to suffer.]   (Therefore)
③[to cause him suffering is not
cruel.]

The vagueness of the conclusion makes this inference fallacious. It's too open-ended. We can think of many instances in which the premises would be true and yet causing the criminal certain kinds or degrees of suffering would still be cruel. More to the point as far as this chapter is concerned is the fact that ① is a potentially confusing persuasive definition. That's not what most people mean by "cruelty"; as we normally use the term, one can be cruel even in inflicting deserved suffering.

7   This ad plays on romantic emotions. It's not an argument. It stimulates readers to want, not to think.

10   ①[Either we disarm or we destroy
ourselves.] It's that simple. Ⓐ[We
should not destroy ourselves.]
Ⓑ[We should disarm.]

This may be a false dilemma, for there seem to be alternatives other than the two mentioned in ①. I say "may be," because I'm not sure that in our world there are any such alternatives; that is, I'm not sure that ① is false. (My remarks here conceal some knotty practical and philosophical problems about actual alternative futures, which are too complicated to discuss in this context.)

13 (Because) ①[patriotism means doing the will of one's country as expressed in the decisions of its leaders,] ②[when a nation's leaders call citizens to their country's defense, all those motivated by patriotism will heed the call.] ③[The rest, (then), are unpatriotic] and (hence) ④[(they are) unworthy of citizenship.] Ⓐ[Only patriots are worthy of citizenship.]

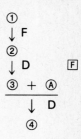

Statement ① is a potentially troublesome persuasive definition because of its identification of patriotism with obedience to the will of leaders. That's a very narrow definition, one which certainly is not shared by everyone, and so it is likely to generate confusion. The inference from ① to ② is fallacious, because one might be motivated by patriotism, but also by a conflicting motive which overrides it; or one might be motivated by patriotism but be unable to heed the call. The inference from ② to ③ is deductive, provided that "unpatriotic" is interpreted to mean "not patriotic" (which includes being neutral), rather than "opposed to patriotism." On the latter interpretation, it is fallacious.

16 ①[The basic state of sight shows itself in a peculiar tendency-of-Being which belongs to everydayness—the tendency towards 'seeing'.] ②[We designate this tendency by the term "curiosity."] ③[In this kind of seeing, that which is an issue for care does not lie in grasping something and being knowingly in its truth;] ④[it lies rather in its possibilities of abandoning itself to the world.] (Therefore) ⑤[curiosity is characterized by a specific way of *not tarrying* alongside what is closest.]

① + ② + ③ + ④
↓ F
⑤

The salient point of this argument is its definition of "curiosity." This definition conflicts with common usage and is therefore quite likely to cause misunderstanding. Such misunderstanding is rife in interpretations of Heidegger, a twentieth-century German philosopher, partly because he gives ordinary terms such peculiar meanings. Heidegger is also frequently charged with perpetrating philosophical gobbledygook, though his defenders claim that his strange locutions are legitimate technical terms. To decide who is right, we'd need to know much more about his system of thought than we can learn from this brief argument. The argument is fallacious as it stands; there is no clear connection between premises and conclusion. I suspect that Heidegger had some hidden premises in mind, but to discover them we'd again need to know more than is given in this passage.

19 ①[For the average teacher, diagnostic validity is related to an instrument's ability to be translated into practical classroom realities.] ②[In effect, valid diagnostic instruments describe aspects of children's behavior which can be directly observed and quantified.] ③[They further provide information which is useful to the teacher; that is, information which suggests constructive courses of action for behavior modification, instruction, and parent involvement.] (For this reason) , ④[individual instruments are more likely to be valid than those involving mass test administrations.] ⑤[The former allows the test examiner to observe the behavior of the child during test administration;] ⑥[the latter does not.]

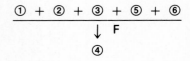

This argument commits the fallacy of vagueness (see Section 7.7). Premise ①, for example, is so diffuse that it says practically nothing. The structure of the reasoning, too, is uncertain. It might be seen as split support, with ⑤ and ⑥ constituting a separate line of reasoning for ④. Moreover, the argument is a frightful example of gobbledygook. "Diagnostic instruments" is an imposing way of saying "tests," "diagnostic validity" means merely "accuracy," "mass test administrations" means "tests given to a group," and so on. The gobbledygook is so thick that it even seems to entrap the author, who erroneously makes the verbs in ⑤ and ⑥ singular rather than plural.

22 ①[I shall use 'alienation' in this study in the special sense of powerless/meaninglessness, a subjective feeling of helplessness in the face of an all-pervasive social control, and an apparently endless social complexity.] ②[From this viewpoint, it is precisely the radical activist who is *not* alienated,] (since) ③[he has grasped (rightly or wrongly) at least part of his situation, and is trying to take control of his own destiny.] In other words, ④[we can view radical ideologies as avenues of *escape* from alienation.] Ⓐ[One who is trying to take control of his destiny does not feel helpless.]

$$\frac{① \;+\; ③ \;+\; Ⓐ}{\downarrow \text{D}}$$

②   Ⓕ

↓ F

④

Premise ① is a technical definition of alienation—one which might be useful for sociological purposes. It does not conflict markedly with our rather vague ordinary conception of alienation, and might therefore be viewed as an attempt to make this ordinary concept more precise. If so, and if it were useful and generated no special confusions, then there could be no objection against it. In order to evaluate its usefulness, we'd have to see what sort of work it does in the context of the author's study. Obviously, we can't do that here. I have judged the final inference fallacious, largely because of the vagueness of the term "avenues of escape."

Exercise 10.1(b)

1	p	q	r	$(p$	&	$q)$	&	r
	T	T	T	T	T	T	(T)	T
	T	T	F	T	T	T	F	F
	T	F	T	T	F	F	F	T
	T	F	F	T	F	F	F	F
	F	T	T	F	F	T	F	T
	F	T	F	F	F	T	F	F
	F	F	T	F	F	F	F	T
	F	F	F	F	F	F	(F)	F

3

p	q	r	(~p & ~q) & r				
T	T	T	F	F	F	(F)	T
T	T	F	F	F	F	(F)	F
T	F	T	F	F	T	(F)	T
T	F	F	F	F	T	(F)	F
F	T	T	T	F	F	(F)	T
F	T	F	T	F	F	(F)	F
F	F	T	T	T	T	(T)	T
F	F	F	T	T	T	(F)	F

This statement could also be translated as ~(p ∨ q) & r. The resulting truth table is the same.

5

p	p & ~p		
T	T	(F)	F
F	F	(F)	T

7

r	~ ~ ~r		
T	(F)	T	F
F	(T)	F	T

9

p	r	~p ∨ r		
T	T	F	(T)	T
T	F	F	(F)	F
F	T	T	(T)	T
F	F	T	(T)	F

Exercise 10.2(b)

1

p	q	q ⊃ p		
T	T	T	(T)	T
T	F	F	(T)	T
F	T	T	(F)	F
F	F	F	(T)	F

3

p	q	r	p ⊃ (q ⊃ ~r)				
T	T	T	T	(F)	T	F	F
T	T	F	T	(T)	T	T	T
T	F	T	T	(T)	F	T	F
T	F	F	T	(T)	F	T	T
F	T	T	F	(T)	T	F	F
F	T	F	F	(T)	T	T	T
F	F	T	F	(T)	F	T	F
F	F	F	F	(T)	F	T	T

5	p	q	r	q	⊃	(~r	&	~p)
	T	T	T	T	(F)	F	F	F
	T	T	F	T	F	T	F	F
	T	F	T	F	T	F	F	F
	T	F	F	F	T	T	F	F
	F	T	T	T	F	F	F	T
	F	T	F	T	T	T	T	T
	F	F	T	F	T	F	F	T
	F	F	F	F	(T)	T	T	T

This statement could also be translated as $q \supset \sim(r \lor p)$.

7	p	q	r	(p	∨	q)	⊃	~r
	T	T	T	T	T	T	(F)	F
	T	T	F	T	T	T	T	T
	T	F	T	T	T	F	F	F
	T	F	F	T	T	F	T	T
	F	T	T	F	T	T	F	F
	F	T	F	F	T	T	T	T
	F	F	T	F	F	F	T	F
	F	F	F	F	F	F	(T)	T

9	q	~	(q	⊃	q)
	T	(F)	T	T	T
	F	(F)	F	T	F

Exercise 10.3(b)

1	p	q	~q	⊃	p
	T	T	F	(T)	T
	T	F	T	(T)	T
	F	T	F	(T)	F
	F	F	T	(F)	F

The other half of the biconditional, $p \supset \sim q$, is probably not intended.

3	q	r	(q	&	r)	≡	(~q	&	~r)
	T	T	T	T	T	(F)	F	F	F
	T	F	T	F	F	T	F	F	T
	F	T	F	F	T	T	T	F	F
	F	F	F	F	F	(F)	T	T	T

This could also be translated as $(q \& r) \equiv \sim(q \lor r)$. The two middle cases in which the formula is true are a bit surprising. They result from the peculiar properties of the material biconditional.

5	p	q	r		$\sim p$	$\equiv$	(q	&	r)
	T	T	T		F	F	T	T	T
	T	T	F		F	T	T	F	F
	T	F	T		F	T	F	F	T
	T	F	F		F	T	F	F	F
	F	T	T		T	T	T	T	T
	F	T	F		T	F	T	F	F
	F	F	T		T	F	F	F	T
	F	F	F		T	F	F	F	F

Exercise 10.4(b)

1	p		p	$\lor$	$\sim p$
	T		T	T	F
	F		F	T	T

Logically necessary

2	p		p	$\supset$	$\sim p$
	T		T	F	F
	F		F	T	T

5	p	q		$\sim$	(p	$\lor$	q)	&	p
	T	T		F	T	T	T	F	T
	T	F		F	T	T	F	F	T
	F	T		F	F	T	T	F	F
	F	F		T	F	F	F	F	F

Inconsistent

7	p		p	&	p
	T		T	T	T
	F		F	F	F

9	p		p	$\lor$	p
	T		T	T	T
	F		F	F	F

Exercise 10.5(b)

1	p	q	r		p	$\supset$	q		q	$\supset$	$\sim r$		p	$\therefore$	$\sim r$
	T	T	T		T	T	T		T	F	F		T		F
	T	T	F		T	T	T		T	T	T		T		T
	T	F	T		T	F	F		F	T	F		T		F
	T	F	F		T	F	F		F	T	T		T		T
	F	T	T		F	T	T		T	F	F		F		F
	F	T	F		F	T	T		T	T	T		F		T
	F	F	T		F	T	F		F	T	F		F		F
	F	F	F		F	T	F		F	T	T		F		T

The only class of worlds in which all the premises are true is that represented by the second line. But in these worlds the conclusion is true as well. So the argument is valid.

5	p	q		$p \vee q$		∴	p
	T	T	T	(T)	T		T
	T	F	T	T	F		T
	F	T	F	T	T		F
	F	F	F	(F)	F		F

The third line shows that the premise is true and the conclusion false in all worlds in which p is false and q is true. So the form is invalid.

10	p	q	r	s		$p \supset q$			$r \supset s$			$p \vee r$		$\sim s$	∴	q
	T	T	T	T	T	(T)	T	T	(T)	T	T	(T)	T	F		T
	T	T	T	F	T	T	T	T	F	F	T	T	T	T		T
	T	T	F	T	T	T	T	F	T	T	T	T	F	F		T
	T	T	F	F	T	T	T	F	T	F	T	T	F	T		T
	T	F	T	T	T	F	F	T	T	T	T	T	T	F		F
	T	F	T	F	T	F	F	T	F	F	T	T	T	T		F
	T	F	F	T	T	F	F	F	T	T	T	T	F	F		F
	T	F	F	F	T	F	F	F	T	F	T	T	F	T		F
	F	T	T	T	F	T	T	T	T	T	F	T	T	F		T
	F	T	T	F	F	T	T	T	F	F	F	T	T	T		T
	F	T	F	T	F	T	T	F	T	T	F	F	F	F		T
	F	T	F	F	F	T	T	F	T	F	F	F	F	T		T
	F	F	T	T	F	T	F	T	T	T	F	T	T	F		F
	F	F	T	F	F	T	F	T	F	F	F	T	T	T		F
	F	F	F	T	F	T	F	F	T	T	F	F	F	F		F
	F	F	F	F	F	(T)	F	F	(T)	F	F	(F)	F	T		F

The premises all are true only in the class of worlds represented by line four. But in these worlds the conclusion is true. Therefore the form is valid.

Exercise 10.5(c)

1	p	q		$(p$ & $q) \vee \sim p$					$\sim q$	∴	$\sim p$
	T	T	T	T	T	(T)	F		F		F
	T	F	T	F	F	F	F		T		F
	F	T	F	F	T	T	T		F		T
	F	F	F	F	T	(T)	T		T		T

This table shows that the premises are both true only if p and q are both false. But under these conditions the conclusion must be true, so that the form is valid. It follows that the argument is valid as well.

5	p	q	r		$p \equiv (q \vee r)$					$\sim q$	∴	p & r	
	T	T	T	T	(T)	T	T	T		F		T	(T)	T
	T	T	F	T	T	T	T	F		F		T	F	F
	T	F	T	T	T	F	T	T		T		T	T	T
	T	F	F	T	F	F	F	F		T		T	F	F
	F	T	T	F	F	T	T	T		F		F	F	T
	F	T	F	F	F	T	T	F		F		F	F	F
	F	F	T	F	F	F	T	T		T		F	F	T
	F	F	F	F	(T)	F	F	F		T		F	(F)	F

The last line of the truth table shows that the form is invalid. This does not prove, however, that argument 5 is invalid, since it could be valid as a result of factors other than the truth functional operators. To prove the *argument* invalid we need a counterexample. The truth table shows us that counterexamples, if they exist, must occur among worlds in which p, q, and r are all false—that is, worlds in which the creature is not warm-blooded and is neither a mammal nor a bird. Can we imagine such situations? Yes! We can coherently imagine many warm-blooded forms which fit none of our classifications. Possible worlds in which they exist constitute counterexamples. So the argument is invalid.

Acknowledgments

Index

Index